The Baader–Meinhof Complex

Stefan Aust

Translated from the German

THE BODLEY HEAD
LONDON

Published by The Bodley Head 2008

2 4 6 8 10 9 7 5 3 1

First published in Great Britain as
The Baader–Meinhof Group: The Inside Story of a Phenomenon by
The Bodley Head in 1987
Fully revised edition first published in Great Britain in 2008
as *The Baader–Meinhof Complex*
by The Bodley Head
Random House, 20 Vauxhall Bridge Road,
London SW1V 2SA

www.rbooks.co.uk

Addresses for companies within The Random House Group Limited can be found at: www.randomhouse.co.uk/offices.htm

The Random House Group Limited Reg. No. 954009

A CIP catalogue record for this book
is available from the British Library

ISBN 9781847921178

The Random House Group Limited supports The Forest Stewardship Council (FSC), the leading international forest certification organisation. All our titles that are printed on Greenpeace approved FSC certified paper carry the FSC logo. Our paper procurement policy can be found at www.rbooks.co.uk/environment

FSC
Mixed Sources
Product group from well-managed
forests and other controlled sources
www.fsc.org Cert no. TT-COC-2139
© 1996 Forest Stewardship Council

Typeset in Dante by Palimpsest Book Production Limited,
Grangemouth, Stirlingshire
Printed in the UK by CPI Bookmarque, Croydon, CR0 4TD

Contents

PART TWO
'The Wild Glory of Terror'

PART FIVE
Forty-Four Days in Autumn

Preface

It was one of those moments that make you feel you are getting a little closer to the truth when, twenty years or so ago, I came upon a document in one of the files on the Baader–Meinhof group that cover sixty metres of shelf-space in my apartment; it was a secret letter in which Gudrun Ensslin gave her fellow prisoners cover names out of *Moby Dick*. Only then did I read that novel in the original – and I gleaned some idea of the exaggerated importance imputed by the prisoners to their struggle against reality. They compared their fight against the 'system' to Captain Ahab's insane pursuit of the Great White Whale, the leviathan that, in Herman Melville's classic novel, also stands for the system of the state. They constructed an image of themselves as icons, and they did indeed became icons in all the severity and brutality with which they turned on those whom they considered their adversaries, those who were not involved, their own comrades, and in the end themselves.

Besides *Moby Dick*, another work was also required reading for the prisoners in Stammheim and other jails. This was Bertolt Brecht's drama of revolution, *The Measures Taken (Die Massnahne)*. I came upon that too in looking through the circulars that passed between the cells. Ulrike Meinhof had quoted a passage from the play:

It is a terrible thing to kill.
But we will kill not only others, we will kill ourselves too if necessary,
For this murdering world can be changed by force alone, as
Every living person knows.

This slogan determined the actions of the Baader–Meinhof Group – or, as they called themselves, the Red Army Faction (RAF) – as with almost all the terrorists in the world, whether their motivation is predominantly political or religious. They share a form of violence that is both murderous and suicidal.

Terrorists regard themselves as martyrs. They hope that with the example they set, their experimenting on a living subject, they will go down in history, or at least enter Paradise with its seventy virgins.

To that extent the Attas and the Baaders of this world have much in common – each in his own time, but always embedded in a revolutionary mainstream whether of a socialist or, as at present, an Islamist nature. Both Mohammed Atta and Andreas Baader came very close to their aim of gaining immortality through their deaths.

The history of the RAF is part of the history of the Federal Republic of Germany. Above all, the 'German Autumn' of 1977, which saw the abduction and later the murder of Hanns Martin Schleyer, president of the German Employers' Association, and the hijacking of the Lufthansa aircraft Landshut, ending in Mogadishu, was the greatest challenge yet to post-war German society. At least so far as their effects on internal German politics were concerned, these dramatic events are comparable with the significance for the USA of 11 September 2001.

And of course both also have something to do with conditions in their respective countries. That is clearer in the case of the RAF than in the attacks on the World Trade Center in New York. The latter, to touch on the subject only briefly, certainly relate to the role of the United States in the Middle East, the unresolved conflict in Palestine, the power of oil, the re-Islamization of large parts of the world – in fact to global conflict, not that that is to be taken as any excuse for the murderous pilots. But every act of terror always has its background in a wider conflict, from which – and from which alone – it derives its power and the support of its clandestine and murderous groups.

If we look, then, at the history of the RAF, it relates to German history both before and after the Second World War. The RAF is like a small boat navigating the seas of its times – a gunboat, if you like. That does not diminish the responsibility of those involved, but perhaps it explains what they were doing.

For this book, I have reconstructed the stories of Andreas Baader, Ulrike Meinhof, Gudrun Ensslin, Jan-Carl Raspe and many other members of the group as closely as I could. I was able to do it only because my own life history sometimes ran parallel to theirs, so that I was able to follow many of the events when they were of topical interest, from my own personal point of view and from that of a professional journalist.

I was still a schoolboy in the north German town of Stade when I met Klaus Rainer Röhl, editor of the left-wing journal *konkret*. At the time I was working with his much younger brother on our school magazine. Röhl was married to Ulrike Meinhof, who was first editor-in-chief and then a columnist on *konkret*. I met her too at that time, and I also watched her films on the *Panorama* TV programme. When I had finished school Röhl asked if I would like to work at *konkret* myself. I said I would.

These were the early days of the student movement, and my work for *konkret* brought me very close to the events of the time. I met not just Ulrike Meinhof but also the student leader Rudi Dutschke, the left-wing lawyer Horst Mahler and the student Jan-Carl Raspe, as well as the lawyer Otto Schily, who later defended Gudrun Ensslin in court and later still became interior minister of the Federal Republic of Germany. I was present at the demonstrations against the American war in Vietnam and in support of Ho Chi Minh, the North Vietnamese head of state and Communist party leader. I saw eggs thrown at the America House, then paint bombs instead of eggs, then stones instead of paint bombs. The journal *konkret* published articles by the German writer and dramatist Peter Weiss – my favourite writer when I was taking my final school examinations – in which he called for the creation of 'two, three, many Vietnams'. I was, so to speak, a participating observer of all these events, which brought a sense of adventure into the boring everyday life of the Federal German Republic. The façade of the main lecture hall of the Technical University of Berlin bore, in gigantic letters, Che Guevara's maxim: 'It is the duty of the revolutionary to foment revolution'. And it was only a matter of time before some members of the mass left-wing movement obeyed the many slogans urging them to fight imperialism, colonialism and capitalism, and put revolutionary theory into violent practice.

When Commune 1 produced a satirical pamphlet inciting readers to commit arson in department stores, it followed that sooner or later someone was going to throw a Molotov cocktail into the ladies' clothing department of a large store. At the time Ulrike Meinhof praised the progressive aspect of this illegal action. That was one more small step towards the abyss.

Indignation turned to protest, protest to resistance, resistance to violence and violence to outright terrorism. And from the first, parallels were drawn between the Federal Republic and the Third Reich. In 1967 Ulrike Meinhof said: 'At the moment when solidarity with the Vietnamese becomes a matter of serious concern, when people want to weaken the American position all over the world as far as possible in the interests of the Vietnamese, then I really see no difference left between the police terrorist methods that we have already seen in Berlin, and that threaten us now, and the terrorism of the SA in the 1930s.'

As the rebellious students and their advocates perceived it, the state was becoming a police state. The Commune 1 provocateurs, for instance, provided enjoyable titillation in depicting the police as the enemy. Theirs was a political culture of 'happenings' that a great many found attractive. And it became a game played with violence.

The wall of the SDS Centre on Kurfürstendamm bore the slogan, 'It's burning, it's burning, a store is burning . . .' In front of it, the student leader Rudi Dutschke sat at a table giving a TV interview on the subject of violence, lecturing his audience in his hoarse, sonorous voice: 'Here in the metropolis those of us who have developed a certain awareness have a duty: we must take action against this system, which is inevitably moving towards disaster, we must proceed against the system with all our might.' And as if it were the most natural thing in the world, he added: 'We therefore cannot rule out the use of violence on our own part from the outset, for that would only mean granting a licence to the organized violence of the system.'

'Violence on our own part' was not long in coming. Andreas Baader and Gudrun Ensslin started fires in two Frankfurt department stories.

When they were arrested for it, Gudrun Ensslin's father, a Protestant vicar, said: 'It has astonished me to find that Gudrun, who has always thought in a very rational, intelligent way, has experienced what is almost a condition of euphoric self-realization, a really holy self-realization such as we find mentioned in connection with saints. To me, that is more of a beacon light than the fire of the arson itself – seeing a human being make her way to self-realization through such acts.' Pastor Ensslin had recognized, at a very early stage, an important factor in the motivation of his daughter and her comrades: violence as a quasi-religious experience.

Then came the springing of Baader from jail. Guns were fired; Ulrike Meinhof jumped out of the window of the Institute for Social Issues in Berlin, where Baader had been brought, and went underground with the others.

With the help of the representative of the PLO in Berlin – even then, the Palestinian conflict was a red thread running through the continuity of terrorism – they went from the immediate east to the Middle East, from East Berlin to Beirut. The German Democratic Republic's Ministry of State Security was of course informed, but did nothing to interfere with the handiwork of the budding terrorists. Later a profitable camaraderie developed between 'Comrade Stasi' and 'Comrade RAF' – but at this point hardly anyone could yet imagine that connection.

From Lebanon they went on by car to Jordan where, in an Al Fatah training camp, the group who had freed Baader had to take a crash course in the military training deemed necessary for urban guerrillas.

I received a first-hand eyewitness report on life in the camp at the time. A friend who had worked at *konkret* with me had gone to Jordan with the group. It was known to the Berlin police that he had been living with Ulrike Meinhof before the springing of Baader from jail. Although in fact he had taken no part in the operation, he was suspected of having been the group's marksman, so he was at the top of the Wanted list. In his well-justified fear of ending up behind bars, despite his innocence, he did the most stupid thing he could have done: he went to the guerrilla training camp with the others. There he crawled through the desert sand with Baader, Mahler and Meinhof, but he was soon at odds with his old drinking companion Baader. Baader and the lawyer Horst Mahler were playing at being Che Guevara and Fidel Castro, which their travelling companion from Berlin thought rather ridiculous. But Baader and his future comrades of the Red Army Faction did not see anything funny about it, and were planning to shoot the reluctant terrorist during training, claiming it was an accident. The Palestinian leadership of the camp intervened to prevent it. The man from Berlin left the camp, returned to Germany and got in touch with me. So at a time when many still felt sympathetic towards the allegedly revolutionary Robin Hood band around Baader, I saw the case in a clear and unromantic light. All this could end only in murder, prison, or their own deaths – as well as the rearmament of the Federal Republic of Germany in terms of interior security.

A few weeks later the group returned to Germany, not without first peremptorily arranging for Ulrike Meinhof's twin daughters, then seven years old, to be cared for by the Palestinians. The girls were to be sent to an Al Fatah children's camp, where they would be trained as young guerrillas. We did not think that at all suitable for two little girls from Blankenese near Hamburg who were being sought, through Interpol, by their father Klaus Rainer Röhl.

We found out where the children were, made contact with the people looking after them, gave the password, and I then flew to Sicily to receive them there, claiming to be the group's accredited emissary. Our operation was successful, and when Baader's real envoy and his women companions turned up near Mount Etna to take the girls away to the Jordanian camp, the birds had flown.

There was an attempt after that to shoot us in Hamburg, but it failed.

However, my interest in the RAF, as Baader and his followers had now christened themselves, did not die down. After all, I had a certain amount of inside knowledge.

I began working as a journalist for public service television. Whenever something connected with terrorism happened I was able to report on it for TV – indeed, I had to. I thus came to know the bizarre world of the secret services, their contacts and informers, and the traps they set, sometimes getting entangled in those traps themselves; I saw lawcourts and the interior of prisons, I read files by the metre, and I acquired a more than amateurish knowledge of jurisprudence.

The RAF's active underground combat was now beginning. It consisted mainly of raiding banks to fill the revolutionary war chest. The rather prosaic practice of revolutionary conflict was embellished with theory through various writings, mainly from the pen of Ulrike Meinhof. The anti-imperialist struggle drew its theoretical principles above all from the ideas of the now waning students' movement. In a sense, it was part of the mainstream thinking of the left-wing opposition of the time – only the consequences were different and more radical. No one wanted to talk about the need for revolution in other parts of the world any more; they wanted to bring it about here and now.

The one obstacle in the way of this proposition was the reality of the Federal Republic of Germany at the end of the 1960s. There was no revolutionary proletariat, and it was quite difficult to regard the state as a fascist police state: there were no concentration camps, no torture, it was a reasonably well-functioning constitutional state. But the RAF wanted to provoke it into showing its cunningly hidden and well-camouflaged 'true fascist face'. That, in theory, would cause the masses to rise up in revolution. As we know now, and as should have been obvious at the time, it was a fatal mistake.

Bombs were thrown into US institutions, a German police station and the high-rise Axel Springer Verlag building in Hamburg. Several people were killed, many were injured. The game of revolution had become deadly serious.

Some of those who until now had sympathized with the RAF also saw that. It became harder and harder for the group to find places to stay as they travelled zigzag fashion around the Republic of Germany. And in the end they were all turned in.

Pictures of the gunfight in which Andreas Baader and Holger Meins were arrested went around the world. For many the skinny image of Holger Meins stripped to his underpants in particular became a symbol. At last, in the eyes of the RAF, the state was presenting itself as they wanted it to be seen, as a police state.

One by one, all the leading members of the group fell into the hands of the police. And then they were all in jail. Since the freeing of Baader, the underground battle had lasted just a little over two years.

But only once imprisoned did the RAF assume the importance that it had not previously achieved with its own operations. The Red Army Faction became its own subject. It had its own high-security wing in Stuttgart-Stammheim prison, and next to it a specially erected courthouse. Stammheim became, in a way, the capital city of the RAF. The group was born again, and acting as midwives were the Federal Prosecutor's Office, the lawcourts, the politicians and the public of the Federal Republic.

The perpetrators of terrorist acts now took on the role of victims. In a post-war German society stricken with guilt, that lent them a position which they and their helpers outside prison exploited to the full. At last they could play the part of martyrs. They put on a virtuoso performance allowing them to feature as victims persecuted and tortured by an unconstitutional state. And the machinery of state readily, and stupidly, went along with them.

Ultimately, only one thing still mattered to the RAF: the release of their imprisoned founders. To that end an attack was carried out on the German Embassy in Stockholm – an operation that ended in disaster. Then they tried to kidnap a banker; when he resisted, he was shot. The chief federal prosecutor was murdered in the open street. But Operation 'Big Get-Out', as the group called it, came to its climax with the abduction of the president of the Employers' Association, Hanns Martin Schleyer, in which all his bodyguards and his driver were brutally shot dead. When the German government would not give in, a Palestinian commando hijacked the Lufthansa aircraft Landshut on its way from Palma de Mallorca to Frankfurt. A German special task force, GSG 9, succeeded in freeing the eighty passengers and crew members grounded in Mogadishu.

When they heard the news, the founders of the RAF imprisoned in Stammheim, Andreas Baader. Gudrun Ensslin and Jan-Carl Raspe committed suicide. For many of their followers and sympathizers both at home and abroad, they had now fully achieved the status of martyrdom.

When their cells in Stammheim prison were being cleared, a copy of Bertolt Brecht's play *The Measures Taken*, from which they kept quoting in their letters, was found in almost all of them. The play contained the creed of the RAF, talking of the absolute will to change the 'murdering world' by murders of their own and, if need be, by suicide. 'We are the missile,' they had written.

At Stuttgart's Waldfriedhof cemetery, their supporters staged a scene of farewell to Andreas Baader, Gudrun Ensslin and Jan-Carl Raspe, the RAF members whom they saw above all as victims. They regarded their suicides as murder, whether or not they had killed themselves in their cells. As for the real victims of the RAF, the bodies blown apart in bomb attacks, the policemen who had been shot dead, the executed federal prosecutor general and his companions, the kidnapped and subsequently murdered president of the Employers' Association, RAF supporters merely shrugged off the thought of them, sometimes even with a sense of 'furtive delight'.

The founders of the RAF, Baader, Meinhof and Ensslin, became icons. Blurred images, black-and-white paintings taken from their photographs in death, have become works of art and even made their way into the Museum of Modern Art in New York. The quasi-religious character of their deranged crusade, lasting from 2 June 1967, when a student was shot during a demonstration against a visit by the Shah of Persia, to 18 October 1977, when the RAF founders committed suicide in their cells, had made them immortal in the minds of many on the German Left. 'I want to have done something,' Gudrun Ensslin had said after the arson attacks on the two Frankfurt department stores. Her father, the Protestant theologian, had spoken of a 'really holy self-realization', and her mother too had expressed admiration: 'I feel that by her act she has achieved a kind of freedom, even for our family.' She herself, she said, had been released from the 'constraint and fear that – rightly or wrongly – dominated my life'.

The over-stern conscience nurtured and cultivated in the Ensslins' household in the parsonage seems to have yearned for violent expression. So Gudrun's war against 'the pigs and their system' had religious aspects from the first. She and her comrades in arms had never seen themselves as terrorists, but as legitimate resistance and freedom fighters against an inhuman 'system', justified by a quasi-religious right to resist tyranny in any form of organization. They largely erased from their minds the bloodstained and inhuman reality of what they did. Only in references to Brecht's play *The Measures Taken* is there sometimes a faint suggestion that Ulrike Meinhof at least had some idea of the enormity of her own actions. 'How low would you not stoop to exterminate the low?' she wrote, quoting Brecht, and added, 'Clearly a repellent idea . . .'

Even in their lifetime, the Stammheim founders of the RAF had become icons to be projected on any area that you liked. The image of them as Public Enemy Number One found its counterpart in their devout transfiguration by the members of the second generation of the RAF. To get the Stammheim prisoners released had become the whole meaning of their lives. To murder and if need be die for their leaders in Stammheim became the categorical imperative of their own revolutionary self-realization. When the prisoners on the seventh floor of Stuttgart-Stammheim jail had released themselves from the high-security wing by their suicide, the RAF as it still existed outside had lost its aim in life.

Like many of their generation, they had lined up to oppose the old style and what they thought was the new style, of fascism. They had tried to change that 'murderous world' by force, making themselves lords over life and death, and had ended up as guilty as many of their parents' generation. A number of the RAF members came to realize that. Others do not to this day.

The bloody end of the 'German Autumn' was not the end of terrorism in Germany. The new RAF had in fact learnt from it: they left no trails to be followed now. When some members of the group wanted to opt out of armed conflict, they were secretly given asylum in the GDR. The others continued as before.

On 20 April 1998 an eight-page letter arrived at the Cologne office of the Reuters news agency declaring that 'the urban guerrilla in the form of the raf is now history, the end of this project shows that we cannot get anywhere along these lines.' No regret is expressed for the victims of 'urban guerrilla' warfare, no self-criticism, no sense of guilt. Only the laconic statement that armed conflict is now wrong because it has no prospect of succeeding.

After listing the names of all the members of the RAF who had died since it was founded in 1970, the document dissolving it quoted the words: 'The revolution says: I was, I am, I will be.' They were written by Rosa Luxemburg in January 1919, a day before she was assassinated.

The murderous and suicidal horrors that had begun on 14 May 1970, with the springing of Andreas Baader from jail, had come to an end twenty-eight years later.

This book is not an indictment, nor a plea for the defence. Nor is it a judgment, in either the legal or the historical sense. I have tried to reconstruct the story of the Baader–Meinhof group as accurately as possible, from conversations with those involved, from the files, from records hitherto kept secret and material both published and unpublished.

The Baader–Meinhof Complex was first published in 1985, eight years after the suicides in Stammheim prison. From my work first at *konkret* and later for television I had known some of the characters in the drama personally. Some of them I met again in the course of my research, others were in jail and or had been released after years of imprisonment. I conducted interviews, collected files and evaluated any available evidence in order to tell the story of the Red Army Faction.

After German reunification in 1990 a group of former RAF members, who had lived unrecognised in the German Democratic Republic, fell into the hands of the Federal police. A special unit within the Ministry of State Security had provided some of those wanted in the West for terrorist activities with forged identities and integrated them into 'real socialist' society. Even RAF members who were still active had at times been looked after by the Stasi in the GDR, before returning to their West German 'theatre of operations'. The whole extent of Stasi cooperation with former or still active terrorists was only revealed over the course of the next few years.

The Stasi files shed light on a number of unsolved mysteries, for the RAF members seem to have opened up to the comrades of the Ministry of State Security. In addition, in West German custody the rehabilitated new GDR citizens frequently gave their statements very quickly. Some of them belonged to the kidnappers of Hanns Martin Schleyer. Their confessions in turn moved one of the key perpetrators to make a new statement. Peter Jürgen Boock, already sentenced to life imprisonment for his participation in the Schleyer kidnapping, gave something like a 'life's confession' to the Federal Prosecutor's Office.

Utilising the Stasi material, and after extensive interviews with some of those involved, I revised the book in 1997 and included new sections and even whole chapters. Now, thirty years after the 'German Autumn', I have worked through the text again and incorporated the results of new research. What has emerged now are numerous indications that the secret services were active in the high-security section of Stammheim prison. The suspicion, which I had already expressed in the original edition of the book, that the conversations of the prisoners in their cells had been bugged, seems to have deepened.

My views on the history of the RAF and the reaction of the state to their activities have not fundamentally changed in light of new revelations over the years – except perhaps on two points: how the RAF knew exactly that the prisoners in Stammheim had committed suicide and how systematically they constructed the myth of their murder; and how a massive failure of the police operation meant that Hanns Martin Schleyer was not freed, despite the fact that less than forty-eight hours after the kidnapping there were concrete clues of his hiding-place.

Some questions remain unresolved to this day. For instance, the strong suspicion persists that the prisoners' conversations in their Stammheim cells were bugged during the Schleyer kidnapping – and that tapes may exist of their last night.

There are limits to the description of past events. For one thing, not everyone is willing to offer information. For another, eyewitness accounts are bound to have a subjective colouring. I have tried to filter out what actually occurred from the various reports of any incident. Where versions flatly contradicted each other, I have given them both. In every instance, I have indicated my sources as clearly as possible. However, quite a number of informants asked to remain anonymous.

I have avoided value judgements to the best of my ability. But the choice of material, the weight given to it, and the way I have put it together is my own subjective verdict.

Stefan Aust
Hamburg
August 2008

PART ONE

Ways Underground

1
Death in Stammheim

'Thirty-eight minutes past midnight. This is German Radio with an important news flash. The eighty-six hostages hijacked by terrorists in a Lufthansa Boeing jet have all been safely freed. This has just been confirmed in Bonn by a spokesman for the Federal Ministry of the Interior. A special commando squad of the Border Police went into action at Mogadishu airport at midnight. According to initial reports, three terrorists were killed.'

Two minutes later, all the West German radio stations were putting out the same news flash on their joint late-night programme. It was Tuesday, 18 October 1977.

On the seventh floor of Stammheim jail in Stuttgart, Prison Officer Hans Rudolf Springer was on duty by himself, guarding the prisoners Andreas Baader, Gudrun Ensslin, Jan-Carl Raspe and Irmgard Möller. He was sitting in the guard's cubicle, separated from the prisoners by walls, bars and doors. He could watch the wide corridor outside the cells on television monitors. Nothing was stirring.

The news flash, interrupting the night-time music programme, brought Springer to his feet. He went to the rear wing of the cells section and stood at the barred door which led into the corridor. All was quiet. Springer returned to his cubicle and went on watching the monitors.

At 6.30, the prison officer was relieved by a colleague. Stammheim jail was slowly coming to life.

At 7.15 a.m., Prison Officers Miesterfeld, Stapf, Stoll, Griesinger and Hermann came on duty. Sergeant Miesterfeld collected the keys of the cells from the prison's administrative offices and signed for them. Then he switched off the alarm system. He opened the barred door into the corridor outside the cells and pulled up the blinds over the window at the end of it. Light fell in through the glass. Between them, the officers moved the padded panels intended to keep the prisoners from communicating with each other at night away from the cell doors.

Miesterfeld opened the safety locks of all four cells. At 7.41 a.m., Sergeant Stoll opened the door of Cell 716. He was accompanied by Sergeant Stapf. The two warders had wheeled the breakfast trolley, laid with coffee, rye bread and boiled eggs, into the cells section. They felt that something was odd. The prisoner Raspe was not standing by the door, as usual. Their colleagues, including Woman Prison Officer Renate Frede, who had been standing by for emergency duty overnight on the seventh floor, were a few paces away from them.

Stoll looked into the cell, then turned abruptly. 'Come over here. Look, there's something up!'

The officers crowded into the doorway. Raspe's bed stood at right angles to the door as usual, reaching almost from wall to wall of the cell. Raspe was sitting on the bed, legs outstretched, leaning back against the wall of the stairwell. His head was turned slightly to the right, and hanging down. Blood ran from the left side of his skull. There was a bloodstain on the wall behind his head. Stoll noticed that Raspe was breathing, and heard him groan.

'Close the door again at once!' Sergeant Miesterfeld ordered. None of the prison officers had entered the cell. Stoll closed the door again and informed Inspector Horst Bubeck, the deputy chief prison officer. Miesterfeld rang the sick bay.

The officers kept their voices down, so that the prisoners in the other cells would not hear what was going on. Scarcely three minutes later, two medical orderlies entered the cells section with Inspector Götz and Sergeant Münzing. The door was opened again and the officers went into Raspe's cell. 'There's a pistol here!' cried one of them.

'He's still alive,' said Götz. 'Better remove the pistol, to be on the safe side.' With his handkerchief, he took hold of the gun barrel and drew it towards him. Miesterfeld fetched a tea towel and wrapped it around the gun. Götz put his handkerchief away again. There was no blood on it.

Raspe was bleeding from his mouth, ears and nose. He had effusions of blood the size of a child's fist round both eyes. At first glance, the medical orderlies could not see any gunshot wound. Without moving Raspe, they called an ambulance.

The Red Cross ambulance arrived at about 8.00 a.m. Two ambulance men connected Raspe to a drip and put him on a stretcher. A little later, the doctor on emergency call arrived too. Raspe was taken to St Catherine's Hospital, accompanied by two prison officers. Two police cars drove in front of the ambulance, clearing the road.

Everything was ready in the operating theatre. Raspe was X-rayed and given medical treatment, but it was no use. Jan-Carl Raspe died at 9.40 a.m.

At 8.07, when Raspe had been taken away, the door of Baader's cell was opened. There was a foam mattress propped inside the doorway.

Medical Orderly Soukop pushed the mattress aside and went into the cell. The curtains over the windows were drawn. It was so dark that he could hardly make anything out at first. Baader was lying on the floor of the cell, his head in a pool of blood. His mouth was open, his eyes fixed and staring upwards. The medical orderly tried to feel his pulse, but Baader was already dead. His hand was cold. A pistol lay to the left of his body. 'Look, there we are – another pistol,' said one of the prison officers.

The door of Baader's cell was closed again on the orders of one of the prison's administrative staff, who had now come on the scene.

Since there was nothing they could do for Baader in Cell 719, the officers hurried on to Cell 720, which was opposite. The medical orderly was first to enter the darkened room again. A kind of screen, behind which Gudrun Ensslin slept on a mattress, stood to the left of the doorway. In the dim light, Soukop groped his way past this screen and looked behind it. Unable to see the prisoner, he called to her. No answer. When he turned, he saw two feet hanging down under a blanket draped over the right-hand window of the cell. At this moment Dr Majerowicz, the prison doctor, entered the cell. He took the prisoner's hand. It was cold.

The prison officers quickly went on to Cell 725. Irmgard Möller was lying huddled on her mattress in jeans and T-shirt, with a blanket pulled up to her chin. The medical orderly took hold of her right shoulder, turned her over on her back and removed the blanket. Irmgard Möller groaned. The medical orderly felt blood on his hands. Suspecting she had cut her arteries, he examined her wrists. When he could not find any injuries there, he pushed up the prisoner's dark blue T-shirt and saw several stab wounds in the region of her heart. Soukop felt her pulse, and found that its rate was 80 beats a minute. He tried to look at her pupils, but Irmgard Möller squeezed her eyes shut. Meanwhile, Dr Majerowicz, the prison doctor, entered the cell and examined the injured woman. He came to the conclusion that her stab wounds were unlikely to be fatal. It was his impression that Irmgard Möller was fully conscious. He injected her with a cardiac and circulatory stimulant and covered up her wounds.

The second ambulance had now arrived. Irmgard Möller was taken to the Robert Bosch Hospital. There was a bloodstained prison knife on the floor of her cell, to the right of the mattress: an ordinary table knife with a round end and a serrated blade.

In the Department of Heart, Chest and Vascular Surgery at the Surgical University Hospital, the doctors found that Irmgard Möller had four wounds, one and a half to two centimetres long, in the lower quarter of her left breast. When they operated, it turned out that the tissue around her heart sac was saturated with blood, but the heart sac itself was not injured.

2
The Rescue

On 14 May 1970, Sergeant Günter Wetter was on duty in Block 1 of Tegel Prison, Berlin. At the 6.30 a.m. duty conference, his superior officer detailed him to escort the prisoner Andreas Baader to the German Central Institute for Social Issues in Miquelstrasse, in the Dahlem district. Baader was to meet the journalist Ulrike Marie Meinhof at the Institute and work on some papers with her. Baader and Meinhof were planning to write a book about the organization of 'young outsiders'.

Sergeant Karl-Heinz Wegener was to accompany Wetter. Before they set out, Wetter had to report to his superior officer for another short briefing. He still had time to spare, and fetched Baader's prison records. On a piece of paper, he noted down the prisoner's date of birth, 6 May 1943; his crime, 'arson endangering human life'; and his expected date of release, early in 1972. He also made a note of Baader's personal details: 'Height 176 centimetres, slim build, oval face, high forehead, prominent chin, hair brown, earlobes pendulous, gaps in teeth.'

He then took a passport photo of Baader from the file, as required when a prisoner was being taken out of the jail. He collected the exit permit listing detailed instructions from the prison governor, Wilhelm Glaubrecht. The prisoner was to wear civilian clothing, the police officers to be in uniform and carrying guns. They were also to take handcuffs, but to use them only when necessary.

Baader was told how he must conduct himself. 'Don't worry,' he assured them. 'I'm not planning to make a break for it. After all, I've got a contract with a publisher to write a book. That'll make me quite a pile, and I can certainly do with it.' Wetter knew about the contract for the book, but he warned Baader, as laid down in the regulations, that the police officers would shoot if he tried to escape.

Baader was locked in a cell near the entrance of the building until the car which was taking him out arrived. The police officers fetched their pistols and loaded them with full clips. Soon afterwards the drive to Dahlem began. The car drew up outside the Institute at 9.29 a.m. Wetter told the driver, 'Come back for us at 1.30 at the latest.' Sergeant Wegener handcuffed his left arm to Baader's right arm and got out of the car with the prisoner. Wetter rang the bell, and after a brief wait Georg Linke, one of the Institute staff, opened the door. The officers showed their identification and told Linke their business. Frau Lorenz, the librarian, came to the door and took the three of them to Room 9.

Ulrike Meinhof was there already, looking through some card indexes. Wetter tried a second door into the room to make sure it was locked. Then he closed the window. Now that the room was secure, he took Baader's handcuffs off so that he could write. Baader asked for a cup of coffee, and one of the Institute staff at once brought instant coffee and hot water. Ulrike Meinhof asked the police officers if they were married and had children. Yes, they said, they had wives and children. They were surprised by the journalist's question, and particularly by the fact that their answers seemed to displease her. Ulrike Meinhof left the room several times to fetch more material. Then she sat down beside Baader, talking to him quietly.

The front door bell rang. Georg Linke, the Institute employee, opened the door. He saw two young women who had called at the Institute before, on the previous day. They tried to walk straight past Linke and into the reading room, but he blocked their way and referred them to the librarian. 'But yesterday I asked you not to come until this afternoon,' she said. 'The reading room's occupied.' Thereupon the two women sat down at a round table in the hall. Linke went back to his own office.

The policemen in the reading room had the impression that Baader and Ulrike Meinhof were hard at work. They were both chain-smoking. One of the officers opened the window a crack, to air the smoke-filled room. They had now been there for just under an hour. Suddenly Georg Linke heard sounds in the entrance hall. Thinking someone had left the front door open, he left his office to see about it. The two women were standing by the front door, operating the buzzer of the outer gate.

Next moment the door was pushed open. A man wearing a coarsely knitted green balaclava, with only his eyes showing, burst into the hall. He was followed by a woman, also masked.

'Quick, get into the room,' the man called to the two young women.

Linke tried to stop the masked man, although he saw a pistol in each hand. A shot rang out. The masked man had meant to use the air pistol he held in one hand, but in fact he fired the other, loaded pistol, which had a silencer. He hit Georg Linke. Despite his injury, Linke managed to get back to his office and lock the door on the inside. Then he tried to lock the communicating door to Frau Lorenz's room. Finding no key, he dropped to the floor, holding the handle jammed upwards with his outstretched arm. 'Jump out of the window,' he told two women who were working in his office. They jumped. When they had both landed in the garden, Georg Linke jumped out of the window himself. The three Institute employees ran into the street and tried to attract people's attention to the raid. Only now did Linke notice that he had blood on him.

The two women, later identified by the police as Ingrid Schubert and Irene Goergens, ran into the reading room, shooting off tear-gas pistols. One of them shouted, 'This is a raid!' They were followed by the masked man and the masked woman, who was carrying a small-bore rifle. This was Gudrun Ensslin. The policeman Wegener, sitting close to the door, jumped up and tackled the woman. 'I'll shoot!' she shouted, forcing the police officer into a corner of the reading room. A brief scuffle ensued, during which Wegener snatched a red wig off the woman's head, revealing short fair hair.

Sergeant Wetter attacked the masked man, knocking one of the pistols, the Beretta with the silencer, out of his hand. Wetter snatched his own gun from its holster and tried to manipulate the slide. At this moment the man in the balaclava shot tear gas into the left of his face at close range. Momentarily blinded, Wetter fired two shots at random. The bullets struck the walls. Andreas Baader was the first to jump out of the window, followed by Ulrike Meinhof. The others fired a few more tear-gas cartridges and jumped after them. The engines of two cars roared, and then there was silence.

Andreas Baader had been successfully sprung from custody.

3
Andreas Baader

The young man who had jumped out of the window to freedom on 14 May 1970, leaving behind him the study of social issues and an elderly man with a bullet in his body, had reached his twenty-seventh birthday not long before.

Andreas Baader was born in Munich on 6 May 1943, the son of Dr Berndt Phillipp Baader, a historian and archivist, who had been taken prisoner by the Russians in 1945 while serving in the army, and was reported missing.

His mother had not re-married.

The child Andi, as he was affectionately known, was spoiled by his mother Anneliese Baader, his grandmother and an aunt.

In the opinion of his teachers and his family, he was intelligent but volatile: lazy when he was not interested in something, but conspicuously strong-willed.

As a child he would never do what anyone told him, still less obey orders, without asking why. At some time or other his mother gave up trying to control him. She found his behaviour and reactions hard to predict. Sometimes he would generously give away everything he had, taking off his own pullover if he saw someone freezing; at other times he could unscrupulously relieve someone else of his money.

He rebelled against many of the rituals of a household of women: by way of protest, he would not wash, and often had to be made to come in for meals. If he didn't like the food put before him, he didn't eat it. He refused to be confirmed because he hated religious instruction, would not celebrate his birthday, and tried to persuade his mother not to observe Christmas.

In argument, he always held strong opinions which he would defend violently. He often got into a fight, but not only in his own interests.

His classmates, neighbours and teachers did not agree with each other about young Andreas Baader. 'There were no two ways about it,' according to his mother, 'you either loved him or you loathed him.'

4
Going Outside the Law

On 14 May 1970, generally regarded as the birthday of the Red Army Faction, Andreas Baader's rescuers had agreed that if anything unexpected happened they would go to ground in an apartment occupied by a woman friend of Ulrike Meinhof's. This friend was an actress and lived a few streets away from the Central Institute. Nobody had actually asked her in advance.

Now that shots had been fired, leaving a man seriously injured and turning the planned surprise coup into attempted murder, the actors in the drama fled to this apartment.

Ulrike Meinhof rang the bell. Her friend opened the door.

'We need your solidarity,' Ulrike told the wholly unsuspecting woman.

While the police began one of the biggest manhunts of post-war times, almost all the people they were after were sitting in an apartment a few hundred metres from the Institute, which had been cordoned off.

That evening Baader's rescuers met in an apartment at the back of a block. Apart from Ulrike Meinhof, they were all present and in good spirits: the rescue, after all, had succeeded. They brushed aside the fact that a man had been injured in the process, perhaps fatally.

They discussed their next move. They all agreed that the group must leave Berlin as quickly as possible. It was also obvious where they should go: the Middle East. They had already had talks with a representative of the Palestinians, from whom they wanted to get arms. However, he had told them that the Fatah organization would insist on military training in Jordan before any could be supplied. That evening, then, they shared out the jobs to be done over the next few days and weeks. Some of them were to organize the journey, others to get hold of the necessary papers and doctor them.

By now the hunt for Baader and his rescuers was in full cry. Wanted posters for Ulrike Meinhof went up on outdoor advertising pillars: 'Attempted Murder. DM 10,000 Reward.'

The Palestinian Said Dudin had contacted Jordan, tickets were booked with the East German Interflug airline, and nine rooms at the Strand Hotel in Beirut were reserved by telegram.

The first group of travellers was to leave from East Berlin's Schönefeld airport at 9.20 a.m. on 8 June 1970. But first they wanted some publicity.

A phone call was made to Michèle Ray, a French journalist and former Chanel model, in Paris. She and Ulrike Meinhof knew each other slightly from the magazine *konkret*. She was told, in English, that if she came to Berlin she could get 'a big story about the left'. Michèle Ray, then aged thirty-one and six months pregnant, decided to go when her caller gave the names of some prominent German left-wing figures as references.

On 4 June Michèle Ray arrived in West Berlin. She met Andreas Baader,

Gudrun Ensslin and Ulrike Meinhof on the upper floor of an apartment building. They were all three disguised, and bore hardly any resemblance to the Wanted pictures of them now stuck up everywhere. Ulrike Meinhof was wearing a long blonde wig and a mini-dress. Horst Mahler the lawyer was also present. The Frenchwoman drank tea and ate fresh strawberries with the fugitives.

That evening, Horst Mahler turned up where Ray was staying to bring her a tape made by Ulrike Meinhof. Next morning, Friday, 5 June, there was another group meeting over breakfast, and Michèle Ray learned what they planned to do next: they were leaving Berlin to join the Palestinian *fedayeen*.

Michèle Ray passed the tape to the news magazine *Der Spiegel*, which printed extracts.

Asked why they had sprung Baader from custody, Ulrike Meinhof replied: 'You could say there were three reasons. First, of course, because Andreas Baader is a cadre.' (The group sometimes used this word as a singular noun denoting one of its leading figures.) 'And because among those who have now grasped what must be done, and what is right, we can't afford the luxury of assuming we can dispense with certain individuals.

'Second, we freed a prisoner as our first action because we believe that the people whom we want to show what politics is all about today are the kind who will have no difficulty in identifying with the freeing of a prisoner themselves . . .

'Third, another reason we began by freeing a prisoner was to make it quite clear that we mean business.'

Ulrike Meinhof went on to discuss the police. 'As for the cops in this context, it is argued that they are naturally brutal because of their job, beating and shooting people is their job, repression is their job, but then again that's only the uniform, only the job, and the man who wears the uniform and does the job may be a perfectly pleasant character at home . . .

'This is a problem, and of course we say the cops are swine, we say a man in uniform's a pig, not a human being, so we must tackle him. I mean we mustn't talk to him; it's wrong to talk to these people at all, and of course there may be shooting.'

5
Ulrike Meinhof

Ulrike Marie Meinhof was born on 7 October 1934 in Oldenburg. Her father came from an old Württemberg family, notable for producing Protestant theologians. Werner Meinhof dropped out of school to become a locksmith and metal-worker, but under pressure from his family he then took the school-leaving exams that qualified him for a vocational diploma, and went to study art history at Halle. He joined the German National People's Party, found a post as a drawing teacher in Halle, and gained his doctoral degree in art history. In March 1928, after many unsuccessful applications, he was appointed assistant lecturer at the Oldenburg Museum of Art and Art History.

In 1925, when he was twenty-four, Werner Meinhof had met sixteen-year-old Ingeborg Guthardt, who would have liked to marry him at once. However, her parents insisted that their daughter must take her school-leaving exams first. The couple became engaged in 1926 and married in Halle on 28 December 1928. A year later they were living in Oldenburg, a city which came under National Socialist influence at an early date. In July 1931 Ingeborg Meinhof had her first child, a girl, who was christened Wienke.

At the end of January 1936 Ulrike Meinhof's father became curator of the Jena Museum. His wife and their two daughters Wienke and Ulrike went with him. The family lived on the outskirts of the inner city, on the top floor of a former retirement home with a large garden. The city of Jena sold this building to the army administration department in the spring of 1938, and the Meinhofs moved to a four-storey villa with half-timbering, little turrets and bay windows.

When Ulrike Meinhof was just five and a half years old, her father died of pancreatic cancer. Her mother received no state pension. Werner Meinhof had not held an official post, but was only an employee of the city, which all the same offered to finance the young widow so that she could continue the studies she had dropped after her marriage. The city grant was not large, the rent of the villa was too high, and Ingeborg Meinhof, now studying art history, started looking for a lodger.

She had met a young fellow student at the university, a good-looking, intelligent, energetic woman called Renate Riemeck who was studying history, German and art history. The women moved in together and began a love affair with each other.

From now on Ulrike and her sister had two mothers.

Both women passed their first state examinations and took their degrees. When the war was over, Jena was occupied by the Americans at first, but in accordance with the Yalta agreement they withdrew, leaving Jena in the Soviet zone. The two women and the children loaded a few of their belongings on a truck and went west, to Oldenburg, where they had friends and acquaintances. They found an apartment in a house with an overgrown garden.

The town was full of refugees from the East, the schools were overflowing. The only place they could find for Ulrike was at the School of Our Lady, run by Roman Catholic nuns.

Renate Riemeck and Ingeborg Meinhof took their second state examinations in their new home town and qualified as teachers. Both had joined the SPD, the Social Democratic Party of Germany, in 1945.

In March 1949, Ulrike's mother died of an infection after an operation for cancer. From then on Renate Riemeck was foster mother to her friend's two daughters.

In 1952 Renate Riemeck became professor at Weilburg Institute of Education. Ulrike moved to Weilburg with her. She admired her foster mother so much that she sometimes copied Renate. Renate wore trousers; so did Ulrike. Renate had her hair cut short; Ulrike followed suit. Ulrike even tried to imitate her foster mother's handwriting.

At school she was on the pupils' administrative committee, became a member of the Europa movement, was co-editor of a school magazine. Directly after her final school exams, she left Weilburg and Renate Riemeck, moved into a tiny furnished room in Marburg, and began studying education and psychology. As an orphan and a talented student, she had a grant from the Study Foundation of the German People.

The same year, 1955, when the SPD voted in favour of conscription and abandoned its long opposition to the rearmament of West Germany, Renate Riemeck left the party. She saw rearmament as a fateful step in the escalation of the Cold War. As a supporter of reconciliation with Poland through recognition of the Oder–Neisse border, as an opponent of Chancellor Konrad Adenauer's plans to arm the German forces with nuclear weapons, she attracted much hostility – and celebrity. At the end of the fifties, this brought her into conflict with her employer, the *Land* of North Rhine–Westphalia. In 1960, when she was elected to the committee of the German Peace Union, Renate Riemeck resigned her professorship.

Ulrike Meinhof had moved from Marburg to Münster in the winter term of 1957. Here, as in other university cities, an 'anti-atomic death committee' had formed around the Socialist German Students' Union (SDS), the student organization of the SPD. Ulrike Meinhof was elected its spokeswoman.

In May 1958 Ulrike Meinhof joined the SDS.

She published articles on the nuclear issue in many student journals, helped to organize functions, petitions, a boycott of lectures, and got up demonstrations against nuclear arms.

Word of the self-assured young peace activist reached the Hamburg editorial offices of the left-wing student journal *konkret*, a paper which itself was committed to the anti-nuclear movement.

6
The Editor-in-Chief

The *Studentenkurier* ('Student Courier') journal was first published in Hamburg in the early fifties. Initial help came from donations apparently collected by Klaus Hübotter, a young official of the Communist FDJ (Free German Youth) movement, banned in 1951, from the 'Paulskirche Circle', from publishers and independent politicians. Hübotter, Klaus Rainer Röhl and Peter Rühmkorf had started the paper together. In the autumn of 1957, the *Studentenkurier* was re-christened *konkret*.

In 1958, Röhl, the editor of *konkret*, had met the student Ulrike Meinhof, well known for her activities in Münster, at a press conference given by the opponents of nuclear arms. A few weeks later, he went to East Berlin with her and some other contributors to *konkret*, to meet members of the banned Communist Party of Germany. Scheppel, alias Manfred Kapluck, later a prominent figure in the newly founded West German Communist Party, the DKP, was enthusiastic: 'She has a great political career ahead of her. A really great career.'

In January 1960, Ulrike Meinhof became editor-in-chief of *konkret*. She and Klaus Rainer Röhl married on 27 December 1961.

* * *

At this period the SPD, in opposition, was preparing to take over in the forthcoming general election of 1965 from the Christian Democrat and Free Democrat coalition government. Günter Grass started the 'Writers' Election Workshop' to drum up support for the Social Democrats and their candidate for chancellor, Willy Brandt. A young student of German was working for the SPD at the Writers' Election Workshop in Berlin. Gudrun Ensslin had come to the old capital city from the Swabian Mountains at the beginning of 1964.

7
Gudrun Ensslin

The village of Bartholomä lies on the eastern borders of the Swabian Mountains, between Heidenheim, Schwäbisch-Gmünd and Geislingen. A dilapidated two-hundred-year-old parsonage with a garden stands next to the church. From 1937 to 1948, the Protestant Pastor Ensslin lived here with his wife Ilse and their family. They had seven children: Gudrun, the fourth, was born in 1940.

Gudrun Ensslin went to grammar school in Tuttlingen and followed in the footsteps of her parents, who had belonged to the 'Wandervogel' movement in their young days. She went on expeditions with the Protestant Girls' Club, soon became group leader, and conducted Bible study classes.

When Pastor Ensslin moved to the Martin Luther Church in Bad Cannstatt, a suburb of Stuttgart, at the end of 1958, Gudrun was in the USA for a year on a school exchange. She stayed with a Methodist community in Pennsylvania. The Americans liked her and still spoke highly of her years later. They thought Gudrun clever, socially committed, good at languages, cosmopolitan and pretty. She herself saw the New World through critical, Puritan eyes. In her diary, she commented on her dislike of the Christianity of America, where elegantly dressed churchgoers festooned with diamonds turned Sunday service into a fashion show.

At home, she had learned that Christianity does not stop at the church door, but embraces political and social action. She was appalled by the political *naïveté* of the America she saw in the Eisenhower era.

Back from her exchange, Gudrun prepared for her school-leaving exams. The teachers at the girls' grammar school remembered her as a gifted and receptive pupil.

In 1960 she began studying educational theory and German and English language and literature at Tübingen University.

On a weekend visit home in 1962, she asked her father, 'Did you ever hear of a writer called Vesper?'

Pastor Ensslin had indeed heard of the poet Will Vesper, author of verses such as the following:

> August 1939
>
> Your German people know
> Führer, you bear your part.
> To fight our fateful fight you go,
> within your inmost heart.
>
> So feel our hands laid here,
> in yours laid still!
> And dare what you must dare
> to do God's will!

Gudrun had met a young man studying German at Tübingen: Bernward Vesper, son of the poet Will, who had been a member of the blood-and-soil school of literature favoured by the Nazis. Bernward hated his Nazi father, though at the same time he was ready to publish selections from his works. The two students went on a first trip together, to Spain.

On their return, Pastor Ensslin thought his daughter was 'in a very eroticized state', and when Gudrun introduced her new boyfriend to her family at the parsonage, and he turned up on several other occasions, her father showed him the door every time 'because of the immorality'.

Their engagement mollified the family. It was celebrated in the spa rooms of Bad Cannstatt.

The young couple were making plans for the future. They wanted to start a publishing firm together. Gudrun Ensslin applied to the Study Foundation of the German People for a grant to continue her studies.

When she was awarded the grant after a second application, Gudrun Ensslin and her fiancé went to West Berlin, where they enrolled at the Free University. Soon after arriving in the city, they were both working at the Writers' Election Workshop for an SPD victory in the forthcoming 1965 parliamentary election.

Less than a year later, disillusionment set in. Chancellor Erhard resigned, the Grand Coalition of the SPD and the Christian Democratic Union (CDU, West Germany's conservative party) was formed. There were the Social Democrats Willy Brandt and Karl Schiller, to whose cause they had committed themselves, sitting on the Government benches side by side with their political opponents of yesterday, Kurt Georg Kiesinger and Franz Josef Strauss. 'We saw,' said Gudrun later, 'that the SPD leaders themselves were prisoners of the system, and had to take account of the economic and extra-parliamentary forces in the background.'

Gudrun distanced herself from the close-knit, severe, conventional parsonage household of Bad Cannstatt, where the stress was on family togetherness, and children and parents met in the evening in 'a cheerful community sing-song atmosphere', as Gudrun's brother-in-law was to put it later.

Gudrun Ensslin and Bernward Vesper immersed themselves in the life of the rebel students, like many young people who saw the anti-authoritarian movement of the sixties as liberation – both political and personal.

8
Protest

At the end of the fifties, some curious figures were to be seen amidst the affluent society of West Germany: long-haired young men in worn clothes, hitch-hiking their way through Western Europe, foregathering with friends of the same persuasion in Paris, Amsterdam, Munich, Hamburg, Copenhagen or Stockholm, at spots avoided by ordinary citizens. The girls who went around with them rejected the offerings of the fashion and cosmetics industries. These young dropouts did no work, did not trouble themselves with official politics, slept by day and travelled by night. Their bags contained the first packets of hashish to pass through North Africa on their way to North-Western Europe.

In the early sixties, there was public indignation in West Germany over those successors of the American beatniks who were visibly and provocatively making their appearance in the big city centres: long-haired, in unwashed and ragged clothes. Chancellor Ludwig Erhard himself stated that, 'As long as I am in power I shall do all I can to put an end to this deplorable state of affairs.'

In the summer of 1962, two guitarists were arrested in Munich's Leopoldstrasse for making a noise and disturbing the peace. Some young people tried to intervene. A hundred policemen waded in. News of the police action spread through the city like wildfire. Thousands of young people made for the Schwabing district. More and more troops of police were dispatched from their stations to the battlefield. The battle with the police raged for four hot June nights; it went down in history as 'the Schwabing riots'.

Andreas Baader had taken part in the fighting in Munich.

9
Andreas Baader in Berlin

In 1963, aged barely twenty, Andreas Baader came to West Berlin. It is not clear whether he made the move to another city because of his motorbike thefts and accidents with stolen cars, or the constant trouble he was in with the Munich police, or the frequent fights in which he got involved in the Bavarian capital, a smaller city where one could be more easily identified. In any event, moving meant he avoided being called up for military service.

At this time, after the building of the Wall, many young West Germans were attracted to West Berlin, wanting to get away from their parental homes, lodgings, or cramped student digs, to avoid military service, or simply to live in a city which at the time was still far removed from the boring uniformity of the reconstructed cities of West Germany.

West Berlin had something to offer them: a lively Bohemian society, more flourishing than anything to be found in other cities, and a number of large, empty buildings. Many prosperous citizens had left Berlin after the Wall was built. That meant you could find an apartment which would have been beyond your means elsewhere. No curfew was imposed on the night life of Berlin, and thanks to tax concessions it was incredibly cheap, compared to the West at the time.

Baader met Ellinor M. and Manfred H. in Berlin in 1964. Ellinor painted naïve pictures which sold well. She was married to Manfred H., another painter, just making his name in the art world. The couple had a child and lived in a large eight-roomed apartment in Schöneberg.

Manfred, Ellinor (Ello) and Baader, who was three years younger than the other two, were soon inseparable. Baader moved in with his friends. To outward appearance, it was a *ménage à trois* complete with boozing and brawling, nothing unusual in the Bohemian life of Berlin in the early sixties. Less usual in that environment was Andreas Baader's habit of visiting bars clad in expensive jackets at variance with his surroundings. He plainly enjoyed combining his boorish behaviour with elegant clothing.

His mistress Ello had a baby in 1965; Andreas was the father. He and her husband spent hours outside the hospital waiting for the baby to be born. Both men lived with Ellinor and the two children for nearly two years, as the nascent protest movement affected the artistic world too.

10
Napalm and Pudding

The United States Air Force had begun surface bombing of the rural areas of South Vietnam in 1963. From August 1964 onwards, American B-52 bombers flew over the cities of North Vietnam. In the spring of 1965, they were bombing the embankments of the Red River.

The terror inflicted on the civil population of Vietnam aroused indignation and set off a wave of protest marches, in the USA itself and many other countries.

On 5 February 1965, 2,500 students marched through the streets of West Berlin. Five hundred of them swerved aside from the demonstration route approved by the police and went to America House. They lowered the US flag to half-mast, and somebody threw five eggs at the building.

The public, and more particularly the Berlin papers published by the Axel Springer group, were horrified. The governing mayor of West Berlin, Willy Brandt, apologized to the American city commandant.

Ever-present at the time was the lawyer Horst Mahler, first left-wing, later a right-wing figure. 'We were all very moralistic, so it didn't leave us cold. I still remember an occasion when Ulrike Meinhof, watching one of those TV reports with dreadful pictures from Vietnam, jumped up in tears and said no one was going to do this to her, it debased everyone. We must act, she said, we couldn't just sit around doing nothing.'

War in Vietnam: the most powerful war machine in the world against a guerrilla army. Bombs, napalm, defoliation of the jungle. Pictures went around the world making their painful mark, calling for some response. Vietnam as the touchstone for the morale of the free West. At the time many regarded it as a fall from grace, and suddenly a number of people found that once again they could understand the idea of a 'just war'.

Indignation turned to protest, protest to resistance, resistance to violence. And from the first, parallels with the Third Reich were drawn. Ulrike Meinhof said: 'At the moment when solidarity with the Vietnamese becomes a matter of serious concern, when people want to weaken the American position all over the world as far as possible in the interests of the Vietnamese, then I really see no difference between the police terrorist methods that we have already seen in Berlin, and that threaten us now, and the terrorism of the SA in the 1930s.'

As the rebellious students and their advocates perceived it, the state was becoming a police state. The Commune 1 provocateurs, for instance, provided enjoyable titillation in depicting the police as the enemy. Theirs was a political culture of 'happenings' that attracted a great many adherents. And it became a game played with violence.

In April 1967 the American vice-president, Hubert Humphrey, announced his forthcoming visit to Berlin. The General Students' Council of the Free University called for a protest demonstration. Others prepared to welcome the vice-president in their own way.

Early in 1967, some Berlin students had started a commune which they called Commune 1. Its purpose was to 'attempt to revolutionize the bourgeois individual'. In this commune, sexual needs were 'to develop with less inhibition, isolation is to be eliminated, and the struggle for liberation from the pressures of the capitalist society more effectively carried on'.

Dieter Kunzelmann, the brain behind Commune 1, appealed: 'You must uproot yourselves! Reject your grants! Reject security! Give up your studies! Risk your personality!'

Custard pudding to be thrown at Hubert Humphrey was concocted on the commune's kitchen table. The group tested the pudding operation on some large trees in the Grunewald park. However, the project came to grief before it could ever be put into practice. The Berlin papers, and not the Berlin papers alone, spluttered indignantly, and the custard pudding attack suddenly turned into a bomb outrage.

The springer tabloid, *Bild*, carried a headline running half across the front page: 'BOMB ATTACK ON US VICE-PRESIDENT PLANNED IN BERLIN.'

On the basis of this inflated piece of bogus reporting, the paper commented, on its inside pages, 'We shall know how to deal with the bombers! The majority of the German people feel understanding for the American struggle in Asia . . .'

The 'conspirators' were arrested – only briefly, since very soon there could be no denying that their explosives had consisted of nothing but custard pudding and curd cheese.

The fire in the Brussels department store À l'Innovation on 22 May 1967, in which over 300 people died, gave the communards an idea for the staging of another macabre event. They wrote a series of leaflets and distributed them at the Free University.

The first leaflet was headed: 'New kinds of demonstration tried out for the first time in Brussels.'

The second leaflet bore the title: 'Why do you burn, consumer?'

'For the first time in any big European city, a burning store full of burning people gives that crackling Vietnam feeling (of being there and burning too), something previously unavailable here in Berlin . . . Sympathetic as we feel towards the pain of the bereaved in Brussels, yet being receptive to new ideas, we cannot help admiring the bold and unconventional character of the Brussels department store fire, despite all the human tragedy involved . . .'

The communards went even further in their third leaflet:

'When will the department stores of Berlin burn?'

It went on: 'Hitherto, the Yankees have been dying for Berlin in Vietnam. We were sorry to see the poor souls obliged to shed their Coca-Cola blood in the Vietnamese jungle. So we started by marching through empty streets with placards, throwing the occasional egg at America House, and we would have liked to finish by seeing HHH (Hubert Horatio Humphrey) die smothered in pudding.

'Our Belgian friends have at last found the knack of really involving the population in all the fun of Vietnam: they set fire to a department store, three hundred complacent citizens end their exciting lives, and

Brussels becomes Hanoi. None of us need shed any more tears for the poor Vietnamese over our morning paper at breakfast. Now you can just go to the clothing department of KaDeWe, Hertie, Woolworth, Bilka or Neckermann and light a discreet cigarette in the changing room.

'If there is a fire somewhere in the near future, if a barracks happens to blow up, if a stand happens to collapse in some stadium, then please don't be surprised. Any more than you are surprised by the bombing of the city centre of Hanoi.

'Brussels has given us the only answer: burn, warehouse, burn!'

(The last three words are in English in the original; the German word *Warenhaus* meaning 'department store.')

The Berlin public prosecutor charged seven of the communards with jointly distributing leaflets inciting the commission of criminal acts, namely premeditated arson on premises where persons were at certain times to be found, at a time when such persons were accustomed to be on those premises. 'The incitement,' according to the Public Prosecutor's Office, 'has not so far been successful.'

11
The Columnist

In the early sixties Ulrike Meinhof's name had suddenly sprung to fame. In May 1961, in a leading article in *konkret* headed 'Hitler in You', she wrote:

'As we now ask our parents about Hitler, we shall be asked about Herr Strauss one day.'

Franz Josef Strauss, chairman of the Christian Social Union (CSU), the Bavarian sister party of the Christian Democrats, sued but the court rejected the application for the opening of a trial.

The case of Strauss against Meinhof was in all the papers. It made the columnist a household name throughout West Germany. The circulation of her journal went up.

When Ulrike Meinhof became pregnant in 1962 she began to suffer from severe headaches and impaired vision. Tests of her reflexes showed that the trouble was in her brain. She was given the choice of having an operation or bearing her child. Ulrike did not want an abortion. Her symptoms grew worse, her eyes moved uncontrollably, the headaches became more severe, she could hardly open her mouth.

She went into hospital when she was seven and a half months pregnant, and was delivered of twins by Caesarean section. When the two baby girls, Bettina and Regine, were old enough to come out of their incubator, Ulrike Meinhof underwent brain surgery. The operation lasted five hours. The suspected 'tumour' turned out to be an enlarged blood vessel which could not be removed, because of the risk of haemorrhaging, and had to be clamped off with a silver clip instead.

She stayed in hospital for almost three months, while Renate Riemeck looked after the twins. When she was discharged, Ulrike Meinhof plunged into her work again.

Early in 1964, when Ulrike had just started back at her editorial job, *konkret* fell out with the illegal KPD. Jürgen Holtkamp, who wrote for the journal, had published an article expressing sympathy with the writers of the Prague Spring. The Party demanded Holtkamp's dismissal. Röhl refused. The Party then demanded Röhl's sacking from the editorship as well, but Ulrike refused to carry on as sole editor.

Hereupon East Berlin stopped the cash flow. In June 1964, the monthly 'contribution' of 40,000 West German marks was not forthcoming. Röhl decided to continue the paper himself without financial help from the East. Girls with big breasts now decked the front page; Röhl mingled sex with politics and culture on the inside pages. Within a few months, circulation had risen from 20,000 to 100,000 copies.

Ulrike Meinhof went on writing her column, but had withdrawn from editorial work. She was making current affairs programmes for radio, and did some work for the North German TV magazine programme *Panorama*. Her subjects were mostly sociological: young offenders in youth custody, work on assembly lines, discrimination against women at work. This was a relatively new development in post-war German journalism. Ulrike Meinhof became well known and highly regarded as a writer outside the pages of *konkret*. She was invited to appear on TV discussion programmes, where she could present a case well and argue cogently.

Early in 1967, she and Klaus Rainer Röhl bought a *Jugendstil* period villa in Blankenese with the money from her radio work, and did it up with old German furniture and antiques. In summer she and her husband

and children went to the fashionable resort of Kampen on the island of Sylt.

Ulrike Meinhof enjoyed this new environment, but simultaneously she felt drawn to the left-wing student movement. She was going to Berlin more and more frequently.

One day Röhl found her diary, and read: 'My relationship with Klaus, my acceptance by the Establishment, my work with the students – three aspects of my life that seem irreconcilable are pulling and tearing at me.

'Our house, the parties, Kampen, all of that's only partly enjoyable, but among other things it's the basis from which I can be a subversive element. TV appearances, contacts, the attention I get, they're all part of my career as a journalist and a Socialist, they get me a hearing beyond *konkret*, by way of radio and television. I even find it pleasant, but it doesn't satisfy my need for warmth, solidarity, belonging to a group. The part I play, the part which got me entry to that society, corresponds only very partially to my real nature and needs, because it involves me in adopting the attitude of a puppet, forcing me to say things smilingly when to me, to all of us, they are deadly serious – so I say them with a grin, as if masked.'

12
The Shock of 2 June

In the early summer of 1967, the Federal Republic was to be visited by the Shah of Persia, Reza Pahlevi, and his wife the Shahbanou. The more colourful sections of the press indulged in fabulous tales of the brilliance of the Peacock Throne. Empress Farah Diba described her family life in a 'personal' contribution to the illustrated paper *Die Neue Revue*.

In Berlin, the students prepared to demonstrate against the Iranian potentate. Ulrike Meinhof wrote an 'Open Letter to Farah Diba' for *konkret*:

'You tell us: "The summer is very hot in Iran, and like most Persians, I went to the Persian Riviera on the Caspian Sea with my family."

'Like most Persians . . . aren't you exaggerating? Most Persians are peasants with an annual income of less than 100 dollars. Most Persian women see every other child – fifty out of a hundred – die of starvation, poverty and disease. And do most of those children who work fourteen hours a day making rugs go to the Persian Riviera on the Caspian Sea in summer too?

'We do not want to insult you, but nor do we want to see the German public insulted by articles such as yours in the *Neue Revue*.

'Yours sincerely, Ulrike Meinhof.'

The West German government's security precautions for the Shah's visit were reminiscent of the methods of a police state. Iranians opposed to the Shah had been taken into preventive custody on no legal grounds whatever. The roads along which the imperial motorcade made its way through the Federal Republic were closed to ordinary traffic. The Shah was able to enjoy driving down an entirely empty autobahn – while the traffic slowed to a halt on the opposite carriageway.

On the morning of 2 June, Reza Pahlevi flew to Berlin. The Shah's Iranian supporters had permission to greet their emperor at the airport with flags and shouts of jubilation.

Towards 2.30 p.m., their majesties arrived at the Schöneberg City Hall, where they were to smile on the population of Berlin. Hundreds of students had assembled to demonstrate in the square in front of the City Hall; they were held back by red-and-white-striped metal barriers. Police officers were patrolling behind these barriers, reinforced by adherents of the Shah, mostly agents of the Iranian Savak secret service. They were armed with long wooden staves. The crowd of demonstrators had scarcely begun to shout choruses of protest – 'Shah, murderer', 'Mo-Mo-Mossadegh', referring to the head of government toppled by the Shah – a few plastic bags of paint, not thrown far enough to hit the Shah, had hardly started to fly, before the 'jubilant Persians' waded in. They used their wooden cudgels indiscriminately and without restraint, hitting out at the demonstrators. Blood flowed; students fell to the ground. The German police watched impassively, making no move to halt the violence.

It was several minutes before the police took any action, and when they did it was on the side of the Persians. German rubber truncheons reinforced the Iranian cudgels and steel bars. The Persian thugs were not arrested, nor did the police take down their particulars.

That evening, they were allowed to drive in two special buses, as part of the convoy of guests of honour, to the Opera House, where the imperial couple were to hear a performance of *The Magic Flute*. Once again the 'jubilant Persians', some of them armed with secret service pistols and identity cards, were permitted to form up in front of the barriers, and later to join in when the police were hunting down demonstrators.

At 7.56 p.m. the moment came. The imperial couple rolled up to the front of the Opera House in a Mercedes 600. Again, voices were raised in chorus on the opposite side of the road, a good thirty metres away from the state guests: 'Shah, Shah, charlatan', 'Murderer, murderer'. Tomatoes, containers of paint and bags of flour burst on the roadway, nowhere near their imperial target. The Shah and Shahbanou reached the Opera House unscathed. Erich Duensing, the Berlin chief commissioner of police, and Hans-Ulrich Werner, his commander of the City Police, were able to go in and watch the performance themselves. They had done their job.

The demonstrators slowly retreated, planning to disperse to nearby bars and reassemble at 10 p.m. to see the Shah off after the end of the opera. Suddenly a number of ambulances drove up, fourteen in all. The police officers who had stationed themselves in a line in front of the demonstrators took out their truncheons. Some onlookers tried to get away over the barriers, but were driven back.

Then the police attacked, wielding their truncheons without giving the usual warning first.

Many demonstrators collapsed, covered with blood. A young housewife fell full length in the road under the blows, was carried out of the hurly-burly by policemen, and found her picture in the paper next day, with a caption to the effect that brave police officers had saved her from a shower of stones flung by inhuman demonstrators. Within a few minutes the ambulances were full. Demonstrators ran away in panic – if the police would let them.

In the darkness, the students could hardly make out which were uniformed police, which were plainclothes men and which were agents of the Shah.

One of the plainclothes men was Detective Sergeant Karl-Heinz Kurras, aged thirty-nine, from Department 1 of the Political Police. He and his colleagues formed a snatch squad. About 10.30 p.m. these officers were near Nos 66 and 67, Krumme Strasse.

There was a line of policemen on one side, and facing them a last band of demonstrators, shouting, 'Murderers!' and 'Emergency practice!' Stones flew at the police.

One of the officers thought he spotted a ringleader, a man with a moustache, a red shirt, and bare, sandalled feet. The officer made for him. Karl-Heinz Kurras followed his colleague. They seized their suspect and flung him to the ground. Uniformed men came to their aid. Demonstrators arrived too, surrounded the policemen, and there was hand-to-hand fighting. The student who had been thrown to the ground tore himself free and tried to get away. The police gave chase, reached him and showered blows on him. The student hung limp in their arms and slumped slowly to the ground.

Karl-Heinz Kurras was among those on the spot at this moment, holding his 7.65-mm pistol with the safety catch off. The muzzle was less than half a metre away from the demonstrator's head, or that was how it looked to eye-witnesses. Suddenly a shot rang out. The bullet hit the man above the right ear, entered his brain and smashed the cranium. One of the police officers heard the shot, turned and saw Kurras holding his gun. 'Are you crazy, shooting around here?' he shouted. 'It just went off,' Kurras replied.

The dead man was Benno Ohnesorg, twenty-six years old, studying Romance languages and literature, a pacifist and an active member of the Protestant student community. It was the first time he had ever taken part in a demonstration.

The second of June 1967 became a historical date, a turning point in the thinking and feeling of many, not all of them students.

Beaten, desperate and filled with hatred, many of the demonstrators met that same night at the Berlin SDS centre on the Kurfürstendamm. There was much agitated discussion of the form reaction to Benno Ohnesorg's death should take. A slim young woman with long blonde hair was weeping uncontrollably, crying, 'This fascist state means to kill us all. We must organize resistance. Violence is the only way to answer violence. This is the Auschwitz generation, and there's no arguing with them!' Gudrun Ensslin had said exactly what many of them were thinking and feeling.

Next day she was one of a group of eight students staging a protest on the Kurfürstendamm, although there was a ban on all demonstrations.

Peter Homann, who had studied art in Hamburg and gone to Berlin in 1962, had an idea for getting around the prohibition on displaying banners. Large capital letters were painted on white T-shirts. Each student had a letter on his shirt. When they stood side by side, they spelled out the name of Berlin's mayor: A-L-B-E-R-T-Z. On their backs the letters spelled out A-B-T-R-E-T-E-N – 'resign'. At a signal, they all turned around. That evening their protest, with its call for Albertz's resignation, was shown on television all over the Federal Republic. Photographs appeared in the newspapers. Gudrun Ensslin was on the far right of the row, in a mini-skirt and white boots.

In September 1966 Bernward Vesper, Gudrun Ensslin's fiancé, had been offered an editorial job with the publishing firm of Luchterhand. The couple were so delighted, Gudrun told her father, that they had started a baby on purpose.

Two months before its birth, Gudrun suddenly broke off her engagement to Bernward Vesper. 'He's crazy,' she told her father. Helmut Ensslin could understand Gudrun's attitude, having found her fiancé rather eccentric himself. 'Bernward was sometimes abrupt and cutting, sometimes charming; he blew hot and cold.'

Andreas Baader was not in Berlin during the politically torrid weeks and months before and after the Shah's visit. He was in youth custody in Traunstein, doing time for driving without a licence and the theft of a motorbike. He suddenly surfaced again in the summer of 1967.

The people who had staged the alphabetical 'Albertz Resign' show met at the apartment occupied by Bernward Vesper, who was still living with Gudrun Ensslin at this point.

Hashish was smoked. Andreas Baader was there that evening, and met Gudrun Ensslin.

13
The Agent

Some time earlier in the sixties a young man, a plumber and fitter by trade, had applied for a job with the GDR-run German State Railway, which ran the suburban trains of West Berlin. His name was Peter Urbach.

Most State Railwaymen working in the West were members of the West Berlin branch of the East German Socialist Unity Party, the SED. Newcomers to the railway also had to obtain the red Party membership card.

Peter Urbach got his job on the railway and was accepted into the workers' party. Like the rest of his colleagues and comrades, he took the Party journal *The Truth*, a paper which advertised itself on railway platforms and in train compartments with the slogan, 'Get your facts straight, read the Truth!' But there were certain other facts Peter Urbach was after too, and he was involved in a more extensive kind of working relationship. He reported regularly to the regional Berlin Office for the Protection of the Constitution on what he had been able to discover about the Communists of West Berlin. (Each West German *Land*'s *Landesamt für Verfassungsschutz* – there is also a Federal Office for the Protection of the Constitution – belongs to that part of the German Security Service designed to counter espionage, subversion, sabotage, and is particularly concerned with terrorist activities.)

Peter Urbach was a Counter-Intelligence agent.

He lived quietly with his wife and two children in a rented apartment in a lower-middle-class area. In the mid-sixties, his masters directed him to become involved in the student movement. Skills such as his were wanted everywhere: by the newly founded Republican Club (a meeting place for left-wing students), in student apartments needing renovation, and particularly by Commune 1 in the Stuttgarter Platz. Peter Urbach was a helpful soul and always on the spot. He repaired sanitary fittings and faulty electrical items, he could obtain stolen building materials 'at cost price', he did building work and handyman's jobs in many of the apartments.

His story was that he had been sacked from the railway and thrown out of the West Berlin Socialist Unity Party, the SEW, for theft and other crooked dealings. This went down well with the anti-authoritarian students, who at this time thought as little of the SEW as they did of the Establishment parties in the City Hall. Urbach was represented by the lawyer Horst Mahler in an industrial suit against the suburban railways. From 1967 on, he was working full time for Berlin Counter-Intelligence, ever diligent in the students' cause and its expression in political action.

He always had the right equipment for such action about him: hashish and hard drugs, detonators and bombs made of metal tubing, pistols with blank cartridges, and large-bore guns. He supplied drug users, and procured materials for Commune 1's operations and later for the emerging urban guerrilla movement.

Urbach had particularly close and friendly relations with Commune 1: with Rainer Langhans, Fritz Teufel and Dieter Kunzelmann. He was with the communards when they were preparing for their custard pudding attack. The project promptly came to grief.

It was in the summer of 1967 that 'Bommi' Baumann, who later planted bombs, met Andreas Baader and Gudrun Ensslin around Commune 1 and the Zum Schotten bar patronized by figures prominent in what was known in anti-Establishment circles as the Extra-Parliamentary Opposition (*Ausserparlamentarische Opposition*, or APO). Baader, Bommi remembered, 'was always going on about something in a weird kind of way'. He would deliver hour-long monologues on his past and future ventures, which were all to do with 'terror'. Late at night Baader would sometimes follow a drunk to the toilets and relieve him of his wallet. His other speciality was car theft. Students of the APO persuasion did not on the whole think very ill of this; it showed that here at last was a man of action.

14
Arson, or, There's No Turning Back

On 22 March 1968 Rainer Langhans and Fritz Teufel of Commune 1 were found not guilty of incitement to arson.

At the trial, the defendant Langhans had said to the judge, 'May I ask how you got this notion that we were inciting people to arson?'

'What do you mean?' asked the judge.

'I mean we can only assume that anyone who feels he's been incited to arson's a fool – and this court's certainly distinguished itself in that line.'

'We of the older generation have seen burning buildings in our time,' remarked the judge.

'But you've forgotten them,' replied the communard.

The judge's colleague on the bench intervened. 'You claim that the leaflets weren't meant seriously. Would you be kind enough to tell us where the joke begins?'

In the end, both defendants were cleared, and costs paid by the state. The court decided that from an objective viewpoint they had indeed been inciting others to criminal actions – unsuccessfully – but it could not be proved that such was their intention.

The leaflet in which the communards called for arson in department stores was judged to be satire, and it found literary imitators.

Thorwald Proll, a Berlin student and the son of an architect, wrote a poem in his diary. It was produced later in a Frankfurt court as evidence of 'the imaginary world of the accused's mind'.

When will the Brandenburg Gate burn?
When will the Berlin
stores burn
When will Hamburg
warehouses burn
When will the rider
of Bamberg fall
When will the sparrows of Ulm
twitter from
their last holes
When will the October
fairgrounds of Munich turn red . . .

Proll had become friendly with Gudrun Ensslin and Andreas Baader. They visited Commune 1 the week Teufel and Langhans were cleared, and announced that they would very soon be 'playing with fire' in West German department stores.

They asked if anyone wanted to join them. Nobody did except Bommi Baumann, and the date did not suit his own arrangements.

So Proll, Ensslin and Baader set off on their own. They went to Munich first, to see an old friend of Baader's, Horst Söhnlein, who was now running the Action Theatre. The four of them hired a Volkswagen and drove north. Their baggage contained several incendiary bombs, made of plastic bottles and petrol, alarm clocks, torch batteries and detonators, embedded in home-made explosive, the whole thing held together with sellotape and plastic film. They stopped briefly at Gudrun's family home in Bad Cannstatt, near Stuttgart, and then drove on again.

On Tuesday, 2 April 1968, about 5.30 a.m., they reached Frankfurt. They were tired, and set out to find a place to stay. That afternoon they strolled through the city centre taking a look at several department stores near the main shopping street, the Zeil. Andreas Baader and Gudrun Ensslin went into the Kaufhaus Schneider store, rode up to the furnishing department on the third floor on the escalator, tried out a couple of camp beds, wandered briefly around the other floors, and left the store again.

Shortly before closing time, about 6.30 p.m., they came back. The

Kaufhaus Schneider was almost empty. The escalators had already stopped running, and the two late customers rushed hand in hand up the stairs. Their worn student-style clothing attracted attention. Some of the sales assistants watched in surprise as they passed.

The couple had a holdall with them. When they felt they were unobserved, they took an incendiary bomb out of it and left it on a shelving unit on the first floor, in the ladies' clothing department.

The second device was planted in the furnishing department, in a reproduction old German cupboard. The time fuses were set for midnight. Just before the doors of the store were closed, the couple disappeared out into the street again.

A few minutes after the fire in the Kaufhaus Schneider began shortly before midnight, the Kaufhof store too was burning. A member of the store staff was on his way to a group of decorators working a night shift on the fourth floor when he heard an explosion behind him. Turning round, he saw a wall of flames reaching to the ceiling five to seven metres away. The smoke was drifting towards him. He coughed, his eyes streamed, and he ran from the burning bedding department. Meanwhile a fire had broken out in the toys department too. The sprinkler system was automatically switched on. The firemen soon arrived. Nobody was hurt. The insurance companies bore the cost: DM 282,339 in the Kaufhaus Schneider, DM 390,865 in the Kaufhof.

Shortly before 10.00 a.m., the Frankfurt police received a 'definite tip-off' leading them to the arsonists. A few minutes later Baader, Ensslin and the other two, Söhnlein and Proll, were arrested. They and the car were searched. The police officers found a screw in Gudrun Ensslin's handbag which was a duplicate of a screw on one of the incendiary bombs. In the car they found parts of clocks, the hot-bulb section of a battery-powered detonator, bits of the sticky tape which had been wrapped around the bombs, and other material suitable for the construction of an explosive device.

After the arrest, Andreas Baader denied having taken any part in the arson attacks, and the others refused to say anything.

15
An Attempted Assassination

On 11 April 1968, at 9.10 a.m., Josef Bachmann, aged twenty-four, a house-painter, arrived at the Zoo station in West Berlin on the interzone train from Munich. His face was pale, his hair short and carefully parted, and he had a pistol in a shoulder holster under his light brown suede jacket. He was carrying ammunition and a second gun in a blue-green holdall, together with a cutting from the radical right-wing *Deutsche Nationalzeitung* in a brown cardboard folder. This cutting, under the date 22 March 1968, read as follows:

'Stop Dutschke now!

'Otherwise there will be civil war.

'The order of the day is: stop the radical left revolution now! If we don't, Germany will become a place of pilgrimage for malcontents from all over the world.'

Underneath the headlines were five photographs of Rudi Dutschke, lined up like pictures on a wanted poster.

Josef Bachmann left the station, took the portable radio he had brought with him into a second-hand shop, got 32 marks for it, bought rolls and sausage and breakfasted sitting on a bench.

Then he went to the residents' registration office, where he found that Dutschke was down as living at 140 Kurfürstendamm, Berlin 31. Bachmann took the bus back to the Zoo station, where he ate a plate of lentil soup and two meatballs, and then set off on foot for the SDS Centre. It was 4.25 p.m.

Bachmann saw Rudi Dutschke come out of No 140 Kurfürstendamm on a bicycle. He approached Dutschke, who was on his way to the pharmacy to get some medicine for his three-month-old son. Bachmann stood in his way. 'Are you Rudi Dutschke?' he asked.

'Yes.'

'Filthy Communist swine,' said Bachmann. Then he drew his pistol. Dutschke took a couple of steps towards him.

The first shot hit Rudi Dutschke in the right cheek. He fell off his bicycle into the road, losing his shoes and wristwatch. Bachmann shot twice more, hitting Dutschke in the head and shoulder.

Then he ran away and took refuge in the cellar of a building just finishing construction, a few hundred metres farther off.

Rudi Dutschke struggled up again and staggered towards the SDS Centre, calling out for his father and mother and adding, 'I have to go to the barber, I have to go to the barber.' After a few metres he collapsed, saying, 'Soldiers, soldiers.'

A few minutes later the police arrested Josef Bachmann, who had taken twenty sleeping tablets in his cellar hideout. His life was saved in hospital.

They operated on Rudi Dutschke in the West End Hospital. The doctors fought for his life.

News of the attempted assassination had spread through Berlin like wildfire. Rudi Dutschke's shoes still lay inside a chalk circle in front of the SDS Centre, where students gathered. It was deathly still. No loud discussion, no inflammatory speeches, only the silence of rage and despair.

They sat huddled together. Someone said Free Berlin Radio had announced that Rudi was dead.

At 6.30 p.m. news came over the radio that Dutschke was alive. He had a fifty-fifty chance. Only now did low-voiced discussions begin at the SDS Centre. What should they do? Demonstrate? Obstruct the traffic in West Berlin? Occupy the City Hall? Call for active resistance?

Suddenly it was clear to them all what they ought to do: demonstrate against the Springer press and stop distribution of its papers.

Ulrike Meinhof, the *konkret* columnist, was among those who had assembled at the SDS Centre. She kept quiet. When they all set off for the main auditorium of the Technical University, where a meeting already planned was now to be a protest meeting, she joined them.

The hall was overflowing with 2,000 perplexed, despondent, despairing people. Some of them were weeping.

In Rudi Dutschke, a symbolic figure had been shot down, one they all loved and respected over and beyond their various factions. It was an attack on themselves, all of them, on the entire extra-parliamentary movement.

Someone said that at that very minute barbed wire was going up around the Springer building in the Kochstrasse by the Wall. There were gales of laughter.

Bernd Rabehl of the SDS went to the microphone. 'The Springer building is now surrounded by barbed wire. So Springer expects us to attack. What shall we find when we get there? We shall come up against police cordons. But the police will hold back today, because their conscience is very uneasy . . .'

The procession of demonstrators moved away from the Technical University towards Kochstrasse, shouting, 'Murderer! Springer – murderer! Springer out of West Berlin! *Bild* fired the gun too!'

The demonstrators had linked arms and were marching along side by side, several abreast, carrying red banners and torches.

Ulrike Meinhof was not with them. She and a *konkret* colleague from Hamburg drove to Kochstrasse. Forty or fifty demonstrators had already assembled there, waiting for the main procession to arrive. Some people parked their cars so as to stop the newspaper delivery trucks leaving.

The students had spread the word: no Springer paper was to leave the printing works that day. When Ulrike Meinhof and her companion stopped at one of the gates to the Springer premises, a student came over to them. 'We need more cars,' he said, pointing to the road outside the gates. 'If we have a row standing side by side, none of the Springer trucks can get through.' He turned and spoke to the drivers of other cars. Ulrike looked at her colleague in annoyance.

'My car?' she said. 'But I need it, and it'll be a write-off after this.'

'Listen, I know what,' said her companion. 'Park it back there on the pavement, right beside the wall of the building. Then it will be part of the barricade in a way, but not directly blocking the exit.'

Ulrike nodded. She got into her blue Renault 4, drove it up over the edge of the pavement, and parked the car beside the wall. She carefully locked the door and rejoined her colleague. Together, they watched the barricade slowly closing up. More and more vehicles were ranged side by side. The police officers who had stationed themselves by the gateway did not intervene.

Students stood around talking, surprised to see the officers calmly watching the construction of the barricade. Suddenly a delivery truck approached from the Springer printing works. The policemen instantly ran forward, seized the parked cars, ten of them to each vehicle, tipped them over, attacked them with kicks and blows, and pushed them aside. When the street was cleared, the Springer truck raced through the gap.

Ulrike Meinhof was later charged with intimidation. At the trial, she explained that her car was incorrectly parked, but had not been part of the barricade. The public prosecutor asked for an acquittal, and the court agreed to grant one.

* * *

Towards 10.30 p.m. the procession of demonstrators arrived in Kochstrasse. The Springer building was surrounded by a strong body of police. The demonstrators, who by now numbered well over a thousand, pressed on towards the entrance. Stones flew; panes of glass splintered. Ulrike Meinhof and her colleagues were well to the back of the crowd. Cobblestones were being passed forward. Ulrike Meinhof took them and passed them on.

That day, 11 April 1968, the Counter-Intelligence agent Peter Urbach had with him a large wicker basket crammed with primed Molotov cocktails. He found plenty of takers for his wares among the demonstrators.

A little later the Springer delivery trucks were burning, set alight by Peter Urbach's Molotov cocktails. Pictures of the blazing trucks appeared in the papers, evidence of the Berlin students' violence.

Next day, at a teach-in held in the main auditorium of the Technical University, Ulrike Meinhof said, 'If you throw a stone, it's a crime. If a thousand stones are thrown, that's political. If you set fire to a car it's a crime; if a hundred cars are set on fire that's political.'

Ulrike Meinhof headed her *konkret* column written after the attempt on Dutschke's life 'From Protest to Resistance'.

'It is protest if I say this or that does not suit me. It is resistance if I ensure that what does not suit me no longer occurs. Counter-violence, as practised this Easter, is not calculated to arouse sympathy or bring alarmed liberals over to the side of the APO. Counter-violence runs the risk of turning to violence where police brutality decides the rules of the game, where helpless rage takes over from cool rationality, where the paramilitary actions of the police encounter a paramilitary reply . . .'

16
The Arson Trial

Throughout the stirring events of the summer of 1968, the Frankfurt department store arsonists were in custody.

On 14 October 1968 their trial began. Gudrun Ensslin was wear ing a military-look claret-coloured imitation-leather jacket. The four defendants hugged each other, laughing, and threw sweet papers.

There were nine lawyers on the defence bench, including Otto Schily, Horst Mahler and Professor Ernst Heinitz.

At first the defendants would not say anything about what they had done. 'It's not worthwhile defending ourselves against a class-based legal system when the script has already been written,' they explained. For the time being, the fear of spending years in jail took precedence over political demonstration in the form of claiming responsibility for acts of arson.

It was not until the third day of the trial that the defendants said anything. Then Gudrun Ensslin spoke up. 'I want to make a statement, with Andreas Baader's approval. He and I started the fire in the Kaufhaus Schneider. Neither of the others was involved.' They had not intended to endanger human life, she said, just cause damage to property. 'We did it in protest against people's indifference to the murder of the Vietnamese.' However, it was no use anyone saying glibly that protest can be openly expressed in a democracy. 'We have found that words are useless without action.' At the same time, she conceded that the operation had been 'a mistake, an error . . . however, I will discuss that with others, not you'.

Gudrun Ensslin was the only one of the four defendants who had been willing to talk to a court-appointed consultant, the Frankfurt psychiatrist and medico-legal expert Reinhard Rethardt. He had three conversations with her, each lasting one to two hours. The psychiatrist's impression was that she was 'remarkably civil and friendly, but rigid and inflexible inside'.

She said once, 'We don't want to be just a page in the history of culture.' 'That,' replied Rethardt, 'has been mankind's eternal cry.'

The psychiatrist came to the conclusion that 'hers was a heroic impatience. She suffers from the inadequacy of our existence. She was unwilling to wait any longer; she wanted to translate what she had learnt in the parsonage into action, to act on behalf of her neighbour – wholesale and against his will. The fire was an attempt to jump a few steps along the way. She thinks things out to the end, until she comes up against a wall.'

Horst Mahler, defending Andreas Baader, tried to explain the motives for the arson to the court. The basic motive had not been primarily a protest against the Vietnam war, but rebellion against a generation that had tolerated millions of crimes in the Nazi era, thereby incurring a share of the blame. The defendants had concluded that they could not possibly continue to go along with a society founded on exploitation, injustice and oppression.

Mahler remarked, resignedly, that he supposed the judges were probably in no position to understand these thought processes, 'or you would have to take off your robes and set yourselves in the forefront of the protest movement'. Finally, the defending lawyer asked for a lenient sentence. 'Prison is not the place for these defendants. But if they are sent to prison none the less, we might conclude that in this society prison is the only place for a decent human being.'

As Andreas Baader's lawyer, Mahler had originally intended to present a rather literary case for the defence. A document of several pages, labelled 'Note for the plea in the arson trial', was found later in the files of the Berlin Socialist Legal Collective. According to this document, he had been going to have a passage of some length from Hermann Hesse's *Steppenwolf* read out in court, on the grounds that it contained 'a coded presentation of the social significance of the defendants' actions'.

In his 'note', Mahler referred to what was then the cult novel of the left-wing alternative scene, identifying Baader with the protagonist: 'The hero and first-person narrator, a man of uncertain social origins, a professor or a writer, lives a life alienated from his conventional bourgeois surroundings . . . He becomes progressively more lifeless, more numb and rigid, he does not relate to other people or things. He experiences his bourgeois environment . . . as the reality of death, the violation of the human dream. He roams his world alone, growing cold, despairing, a wolf of the steppes. Then he meets the bisexual Hermine, who introduces him to her friends. He experiences the counter-world, the anti-bourgeois sub-culture . . . Gradually his paroxysms wear off; he returns to life . . . now he has the strength to realize his dream of living in opposition to the environment from which he is alienated . . . To assert life against the destructive force of this world can mean only destroying the system of the machinery of destruction, and so he is as one with the theologian to whom the theology of this world consists in action . . .'

Mahler describes the climax of the novel, in which a car-hunt begins on the night of a surrealist ball. 'They are shot down like game animals, perishing with those inside them . . . In this struggle there is a certain enjoyment in killing, albeit killing out of despair . . . They know that their actions cannot succeed in real terms. The others are stronger . . . But they also know they have no choice . . . Above all, one must take action . . . And in the end, yes, there is guilt, but it is the world that is guilty. They have killed human beings for the sake of humanity.'

Hardly ever did a member of the RAF pin down the psychopathology of the group as precisely as Horst Mahler in the plea that he never delivered. At the end he comes to the conclusion, crossed out in the manuscript: 'From the bourgeois humanist position, the individual can preserve himself as a human being only in the abstract negation of the bourgeois world, that is by destroying himself . . . The defendants were like Hesse's wolf of the steppes . . .'

Mahler, not himself a terrorist at the time, had identified the fundamental motive in literary terms: the act of liberation in the act of destruction. Suicide as the final act of rebellion.

During the trial itself, Ulrike Meinhof, as columnist for *konkret*, visited the defendant Gudrun Ensslin in the remand prison. She wanted to write an article for *konkret* and was deeply impressed by the Swabian pastor's daughter, who had so much in common with herself, her ways of thought, her own commitment. But Gudrun Ensslin had not just talked about it, she had done something. Ulrike Meinhof's account of her conversation with Gudrun Ensslin was never written. 'If what she told me was published,' she told the editorial staff of *konkret*, 'they would never get out of prison at all.'

Later, Klaus Rainer Röhl said: 'When the defendants were asked, "Would you still have committed arson if the caretaker and his wife had been in the building?" the answer came plain and clear: "Yes." It was given by Ensslin.'

Instead, Ulrike Meinhof wrote an article entitled 'Arson in Department Stores'.

'The progressive momentum of an act of arson in a department store does not lie in the destruction of goods but in the criminality of the act, the breaking of the law . . .'

On 31 October 1968, sentence was passed on the department store arsonists: they were all sent to prison for three years, more than most observers at the trial had expected. The presiding judge decided that the defendants had not really acted out of conviction, or it would not have taken them seven months to confess to their crime.

17
A Really Holy Self-Realization

After sentence had been passed, a television reporter interviewed Gudrun Ensslin's father.

'Do you condemn your daughter?'

'We condemn the act of arson,' said Pastor Ensslin. 'We are thankful that during the trial Gudrun herself refrained from using it as a means of getting a hearing.' Since his daughter had been in prison, he said, he had begun to immerse himself in the world of her political ideas.

'From the first, Gudrun was a very independent girl who went her own way. As parents, we were glad of that. She was gifted and hard-working.'

'What kind of relationship did you have with her before this, and what is it like now?'

'In Berlin she developed a life-style which we of an older generation couldn't understand. She probably meant this act of arson to demonstrate the viewpoint of left-wing students in our society. They have been cast in the role of drop-outs, potential criminals and traitors. I expect they wanted to say: look, here we are, this is what you have brought us to, this is the place you have given us.'

'As Gudrun's father, you're one of that generation which she meant to admonish by her act. Can you see any good grounds for it?'

'Well, I – like the whole Federal Republic – would object to any admonishments made in that way. However, what she wanted to say is this: a generation that has seen the building of concentration camps, the encouragement of anti-Semitism and the committing of genocide among and in the name of its own people must not allow any revival of such things, must not admit that hope of a new beginning, of reformation and rebirth can come to nothing. These are young people who are not willing to go on swallowing frustration and be corrupted by it. It has astonished me to find that Gudrun, who has always thought in a very rational, intelligent way, has experienced what is almost a condition of euphoric self-realization, a really holy self-realization such as we find mentioned in connection with saints. To me, that is more of a beacon light than the fire of the arson itself – seeing a human being make her way to self-realization through such acts.'

The crime as a means to self-realization and self-liberation: Gudrun

Ensslin's mother was able to feel the same way when she talked about the arson to her daughter in the remand prison.

'I feel that by her act she has achieved a kind of freedom, even for our family,' Frau Ensslin told the reporter. 'Quite suddenly, since I saw her in prison two days ago, I myself have been freed from constraint and fear that – rightly or wrongly – dominated my life. Perhaps it was church convention too. Gudrun always wanted to do away with such things, and I tried to stop her. The fact that there are people who are driven beyond convention to do things which I cannot condone, but will perhaps have to recognize as justified in ten years' time – well, I could never have said that a year ago, or maybe even a week ago. But she has taken fear away from me, and she has not shattered my faith in her.'

The television reporter was allowed to interview Gudrun Ensslin herself too. No camera was allowed, but tape recordings were permitted. Having set up his equipment, the journalist said, 'One reason why people feel they can't understand you is that you did not confess to your crime.'

Gudrun Ensslin contradicted him. She said they had in fact confessed to the arson, although not until they felt the time was ripe. Such a confession was of minor importance anyway. 'It isn't a matter of providing society with heroes or martyrs. One must show that one can justify one's ideas briefly, in a perfectly normal way, without any heroic euphoria.'

This, she said, was what she and Baader had done at the trial.

'But even if we'd gone on talking for two hours, it would still have been said afterwards that it was doubtful whether we acted out of conviction. They're only pretending, people would have said. They just wanted their fun. They were ruthless and thought nothing of what they did. That's how the other side would have argued, anyway.'

'Was what you did right, then?'

'It was right for something to be done. We have said clearly enough that we did the wrong thing. But there's no reason for us to discuss it with the law or the state. We must discuss it with people who think as we do.'

It would have been just as pointless, she said, to spend more than fifteen minutes trying to explain the motives behind the arson to the judges. 'They are like everyone else who's part of this society. They can't do as they really want because they want only what they're supposed to want.'

'Would you quarrel with a description of your crime as a liberating action – given the hopelessness of the situation?'

'Yes, definitely. There are a great many people now who really act as they think and think as they act. The bourgeois schizophrenia of forever doing things you don't believe in has reached the point where people who really want a democratic society are simultaneously constructing a fascist one.

'Our action is to do with development. And there's nothing to be ashamed of in realizing that it was not the right thing to do – that's something we can shout out loud without blushing for it.'

After a short pause: 'Someone's said that we are not the kind of mad people who believe some glorious deed can change the course of history and force it into a different direction. Nobody knows that better than we do ourselves. But as for the nightmare that haunts the good citizen, the idea that we have some notion of a group of twenty or so terrorists being able to seize power in the state, through a coup of some kind – well, we have absolutely nothing to do with that . . .'

The subject of liberation was at the top of the revolutionary agenda at the time. A prison sentence was regarded as ratification of the revolutionaries' determined political stance. Ensslin's father guessed as much. Of the effect of her jail sentence on Gudrun, he said: 'I am sure she will not deviate from her consistent line of argument, and prison will not deter her either. She has survived this entire affair in remarkably good health and – in personal terms – free. I am certain that she will also survive imprisonment well.'

After sentence had been passed, the defence lawyers appealed and tried to get the defendants released pending the result of the appeal.

18
Horst Mahler and the Battle of the Tegeler Weg

At the same time, in Berlin, disciplinary proceedings were being taken against the lawyer Horst Mahler. An application had been made to prohibit him from practising, mainly because of the part he had played in the anti-Springer demonstrations after the attempt on Rudi Dutschke's life. While the case was heard in the regional court in the Tegeler Weg, the worst street fighting Berlin had yet seen was taking place in the road outside.

One hundred and thirty police officers and twenty-two demonstrators were injured, some of them seriously, in the 'Battle of the Tegeler Weg'. For the first time, rockers fought on the side of the students, who numbered about a thousand. The advancing policemen encountered a hail of stones and were forced to retreat. This was the first time demonstrators had got the upper hand in a fight with the police. The political leaders of the city immediately drew their own conclusions. After the 'Battle of the Tegeler Weg' the police were given new equipment. The traditional police shako had had its day. Instead, offcers were armed with special helmets, face-guards, plastic riot shields and extra-long truncheons.

Horst Mahler was born on 23 January 1936, in Silesia, the son of a dentist. In February 1945 the family fled from the Red Army to Naumburg an der Saale. Less than a year later they moved to Dessau, and then to West Berlin after Mahler's father's death in 1949. Mahler's father, a fanatical Nazi and anti-Semite, had shot himself.

Horst Mahler took his school-leaving exams in Wilmersdorf, Berlin, in 1955. He studied law at the Free University of Berlin, and joined the Thuringia Association, a right-wing student fraternity of the old style. Soon afterwards, however, he became a member of the Socialist student body, the SDS, and opposed atomic arms along with its left wing.

Mahler had also joined the SPD, which expelled him in 1960 when the party declared membership of the SDS and the SPD incompatible.

In 1963 he set up in legal practice in Berlin, specializing mainly in industrial law, and was legal adviser to the Hotel am Kaiserdamm company, a West German limited partner's depreciation firm. He was professionally successful.

In 1966, in the early days of the student movement, Horst Mahler was one of the founders of the Republican Club, a West Berlin liberal and leftist organization, and was later one of the best known defenders of left-wing students in the courts.

Mahler's career as a legal adviser to industry was over.

At least since the Battle of the Tegeler Weg, sections of the APO had been deliberately escalating confrontation with the police and the law. For various factions of the protest movement, which itself was split, the theoretical formula 'Destroy the class-based legal system' soon turned into a call for armed struggle against the representatives of the state system.

There were slogans such as 'Smash the thing that smashes you', or 'To be high, to be free, then terror has to be'. Operations were carried out under all sorts of different labels at this time. There were groups calling themselves, for instance, the West Berlin Tupamaros, or the Black Rats. The police assumed these were largely the same set of people, simply changing the names they gave their commando squads. Their main targets were the institutions of the police, the law and the penal system. Their weapons were Molotov cocktails and home-made incendiary and explosive devices. The 'ringleaders' chiefly suspected by the police were Ralf Reinders, Georg von Rauch, Thomas Weisbecker and 'Bommi' Baumann, with Dieter Kunzelmann at the very top of the list of wanted men.

19
Ulrike Meinhof Leaves *konkret*

Early in 1968, Ulrike Meinhof divorced Klaus Rainer Röhl and went to Berlin with her children. She continued writing her columns, earning DM 1,500 for each piece, which came to DM 3,000 a month, since the magazine was now appearing fortnightly.

In December, Röhl visited her and the twins in Berlin. Ulrike Meinhof put an article in front of him. 'Read that, Klaus. I'm interested to know if you'll print it.' Röhl was horrified, for she had taken the journal itself as her subject, criticizing her own role as columnist. 'What does the financial backer expect of his columnist? The creation, by the columnist's writing, of a public of his own, if possible one that would not buy the paper without that columnist. That is the profit factor. A columnist who fails to deliver the goods will sooner or later be fired. The reverse side of the columnist's freedom is the editor's lack of it.'

Naturally Röhl did not want to lose Ulrike Meinhof as a columnist, and he tried to make a virtue of necessity. He printed the column, drawing attention to it in large type on the title page: 'Ulrike Marie Meinhof: Can *konkret* yet be saved?'

konkret had not been spared the conflicts within the left-wing protest movement. The solidarity of the days after the attempted assassination of Rudi Dutschke, the time of the great demonstrations against the emergency powers acts in Bonn, was now over. All kinds of left-wing circles, new parties and discussion groups were formed, and were soon occupied exclusively with themselves, seeing yesterday's comrades as a greater enemy than Springer or Strauss, against whom they had previously been united.

konkret seemed like a classic example of the way a publisher, in this case Klaus Rainer Röhl, can market left-wing views for which others had felt the blows of police truncheons.

On 5 May 1969, Ulrike Meinhof issued an invitation to a discussion of *konkret* at the Republican Club in Berlin. The matter was not to stop at discussion this time. It was proposed that they should occupy the editorial offices and confront the journal's proprietor with the demands of uncompromisingly left-wing journalists. Ulrike Meinhof had phoned and talked to a number of people, making sure of support for her action.

The evening before it was to take place, small groups assembled in various Berlin squares, ready to set off for Hamburg in a convoy of cars and prevent publication of the next issue of *konkret*.

Two days earlier, Röhl had learned of the plan, and taken action. He had the offices cleared and drafted a leaflet: '*konkret* Goes Underground'.

Towards 10 a.m., the Berlin activists arrived at the editorial offices of *konkret* in Hamburg's Gänsemarkt. The press and the police were there already. The forces of the law – not called in by *konkret* – were blocking the stairway. The Berliners handed out a leaflet to the editorial staff of *konkret*:

> Over the desk Che Guevara
> under the desk McNamara.
> You travel by tram,
> the boss drives a Porsche.
> End the stink of *konkret* now
> set up an APO collective.

20
Baader, Ensslin and Social Work

The four arsonists were released from prison on 13 June 1969. They had served fourteen months of their sentences: rather more than one-third. A decision on their appeal against those sentences was to be made in November; until then they could remain at liberty.

In Frankfurt, students of the SDS had been concerning themselves with conditions in state-run young people's homes. They were trying to politicize the inmates of these institutions by distributing leaflets and talking to them.

They saw potential for social change in the fringe groups of society. The idea was that those who had no sheltered family home, who were in the care of state institutions, at the mercy of the actual or supposed despotism of the people who ran such places, must learn to defend themselves.

Just out of jail, Baader and Ensslin turned up at the 'apprentices' collectives', as they were called, with practical experience to offer as distinct from the theories of the university students. To the 'apprentices', Baader was one of themselves, if older, and he did not ask them to conform to bourgeois norms. He was bent neither on forcing them into regular work, nor on constantly discussing politics.

'The Baader group,' said one of them later, 'appeals to the apprentices because there's adventure, wild, exciting driving, you're going into action in a minor way against anything that comes along. Getting the better of a waiter in a café, getting the better of this or that liberal shit. There's always something going on with the Baader group. That's why all the young people are drawn to them.'

A rapidly growing number of runaways from young offenders' institutions had gathered around the released arsonists. These young people became the target group of the revolutionaries' ambitions. Fortuitously, the court had made doing social work a condition of the arsonists' provisional release; it now proved to be a recruiting ground for young revolutionaries.

The Franco-German student leader Daniel Cohn-Bendit recognized the planning that lay behind that social work: 'Baader had already seen himself as general of the Red Army. And here were his soldiers. I mean, eighteen-year-olds: that's the age at which the Bolsheviks started the Russian Revolution. He was playing about with fantasies like that. Ensslin made all the arrangements; Baader simply tried to convey the spirit of revolution. And he didn't just try, he really succeeded with these young macho characters.'

21
Peter Jürgen Boock

When Peter Jürgen Boock was born on 3 September 1951, his parents were running a bar somewhere near Deich in Schleswig-Holstein. His father had returned from POW camp exactly two years earlier. He tried to join the Federal Army, the newly founded Bundeswehr, but was not accepted, and instead went to work for the Federal Post Office in Hamburg. Peter spent two years living with his grandmother, and then his parents sent for him. He exchanged the small town that had seemed to him the 'biggest playground in the world', for a satellite town on the outskirts of Hamburg. The town planners had sited an estate of terraced houses for public employees among the tall tower blocks occupied by people living on benefits.

Peter grew up here quietly until the wild sixties.

Boock had begun an apprenticeship with a business that manufactured large lathes. But his life was increasingly dominated by the extra-parliamentary political movement. And he kept meeting people who would cross his path as a terrorist later. He also made another acquaintance, like so many young people at the time: increasingly their intoxicant of choice was not red wine but hashish.

Peter Jürgen Boock left home again, this time for the Netherlands, the progressive country so highly rated by the late hippies; nowhere but Nepal could equal it.

However, the sense in the late sixties that a new dawn was coming had turned to deep depression. Peter Jürgen Boock was one of those who joined the demonstrations after the attempted assassination of Rudi

Dutschke, shouting hoarsely, in never-ending chorus, 'Ho-Ho-Ho-Chi-Minh . . . Ho-Ho . . .' The zest had gone out of things. People reminisced like veterans of the battle of Stalingrad about the days of the revolution – which was only a few months in the past.

In the Netherlands, on the other hand, the Dutch were seriously devoting themselves to living life on their own terms and enjoying it. They founded communes, the trend towards communal living grew, they tore up paving stones in the streets and planted trees instead. Peter Jürgen Boock, always active, always full of ideas, went to stay with one communal group, a motley crew said to have been joined at one time by Jim Morrison of The Doors.

In the Netherlands, Peter Jürgen Boock had met a woman living on the borderline between the political scene and prostitution. She was a few years older than him. At some point he conceived the idea of going to Hamburg and introducing her to his parents. They were horrified to learn of the disreputable company their son was keeping, and informed the Youth Office of the social services department. As soon as he was back in the Netherlands the police picked Boock up. The members of the commune in The Hague were searched for drugs, and it was in Boock's pocket that dope was found. He was expelled from the country, and at the border he was taken into the custody of social workers from the Hamburg Youth Office.

Peter Jürgen Boock was seventeen when, at his parents' request, he was handed over to the care of the Voluntary Educational Aid organization and sent for detention in a young offenders' institution at Glückstadt.

But rebellion did not stop short at the barred windows of the institution. One day, when a young inmate was sent a parcel from outside and the group leader would not hand it over to him, there was first argument and then a riot.

After an angry exchange of words, the inmate hit the group leader on the head with a brick and grabbed his parcel. Minutes later all hell was let loose. Radiators were torn out, beds wrecked. Someone poured liquid floor polish down the wooden staircase and set it on fire.

The management of the institution called the police, but the police felt unable to deal with the riot and brought in the Marines. Tear-gas grenades were tossed into the fire. In danger of choking to death, Boock and a few other boys managed to make their way down through the floor to the storey below, using knives, forks and chisels. They had got away with their lives, but soon found themselves in the institution's own detention cells. Three metres by three metres, a sea-grass mattress covered with mould, a skylight thirty by thirty centimetres. No light. No cigarettes. No exercise in the yard.

After fourteen days, the maximum permitted, the rioters were released from their cells. The staff had lined up with truncheons, and once they had been soundly beaten the young people went back to the cells again.

Peter Jürgen Boock was moved to Hesse. In Social Democrat Hesse, the new atmosphere of the time had made its way to the gates of youth detention centres.

He had hardly been in Hesse two weeks when a group from the Education Department of Frankfurt University turned up. Some of the students seemed unconventional, even in their appearance; they wore leather jackets and jeans, and their manner was casual, politically committed and combative. Boock had heard their names before: Andreas Baader, Gudrun Ensslin, Astrid and Thorwald Proll.

It transpired that the arsonists, only just out of jail, were now concentrating their revolutionary enthusiasm on the liberation of young offenders in care. Boock told the visitors his tale of the Glückstadt riot, and they appreciated it.

'Who are you?' asked Boock.

'We're arsonists.'

Boock knew that Baader, Ensslin and Thorwald Proll were out at liberty until their sentences were reviewed.

'They made social work a condition for letting us out,' said one of the members of the group. 'That's what we're doing now. We'll get you out of this place and see where we go from there.'

The arsonist social workers had brought Coca-Cola, tobacco and copies of Mao's Little Red Book with them. But Boock had his eye on Baader's leather jacket.

'Great jacket,' he said.

Baader took it off. 'Here you are,' he said, handing it to Boock – who knew at once that these were his kind of people.

Boock felt drawn to Baader and Ensslin as if by an invisible bond. From the first, he was fascinated by the way they could communicate with each other in silence, simply exchanging glances, how they conveyed meaning by gestures, how they finished one another's sentences, throwing the ball back and forth between them. The two of them didn't have to agree on anything or discuss it first. They were like one person. It was not the couple as individuals who appealed to Boock, not slender Gudrun with her long blonde hair and Swabian accent, not dark Andreas Baader with the small dark lenses of his John Lennon glasses. It was the symbiosis of the two of them that cast its spell on Boock.

Andreas, Gudrun and the others seemed to be rather unwell and weak. In prison they had imagined, in their wild dreams, what they would do once they were free again. One of those things was to take opium. On the very day of their release they had done just that, all using the same needle, and the needle wasn't clean. They had all contracted jaundice.

Peter Jürgen Boock ran away from the institution and on the evening when he turned up at the villa, Gudrun was in the bathtub.

'Hi, it's you,' she said. 'So where's Astrid?'

'I don't know. We missed each other.' Boock asked if he could have a bath too.

'Come on in with me,' said Gudrun. 'It's nice and full. Mustn't waste water. And we can talk.'

Peter went red, but then he undressed and got into the tub with Gudrun.

Word of the free-and-easy life outside the institutions soon got around. Abscond and go to Frankfurt. When Boock joined Baader and Ensslin, the social work imposed by the courts had reaped a harvest of some thirty former inmates of homes. A week later it was eighty, another week after that a hundred and twenty. The students' resources were being whittled away, and those already living in the communal apartments where the runaways went to stay began to protest: record collections were disappearing, books suddenly went missing from bookshelves, entire stereo systems were dismantled.

Andreas offered moral support to his young offenders when they went out marauding. 'Don't let it bother you. These are your future doctors and lawyers. They'll be living off you anyway. So help yourselves. No moral scruples.'

Meanwhile more contacts were being made with Berlin. They were making considerable progress towards armed conflict there. Slowly, the first urban guerrilla group crystallized out of the 'Blues', the scene around the roaming 'hash rebels' from which the 2 June Movement later arose. It was something that the former youth offenders couldn't resist. Jan-Carl Raspe in particular liked to talk, in his quiet and thoughtful way, about the prospect of an underground struggle on the Tupamaro model. Ulrike Meinhof was shooting her film *Bambule*, about a riot in a girls' home. To Boock, Ulrike represented theory, Baader and Ensslin practice.

22
On the Run

In November 1969, the Federal High Court rejected the arsonists' appeal against sentence. The verdict of the Frankfurt court thus came into effect again. Baader and Ensslin had petitioned for clemency shortly before, had fulfilled their obligations to report to the police, if rather haphazardly – but any day now they must expect a summons back to jail. They decided to go underground, together with Thorwald Proll. They got into a friend's car in the underground car park of the Hertie department store, and he drove them to Hanau. Here they changed to another car and went on to Saarbrücken. A third getaway vehicle was waiting, and took them over the border into France. One of the friends helping them to make their escape drove on ahead and found accommodation in Forbach, in Lorraine. The group reached Paris without incident, which was not surprising, since none of the arsonists was even being sought at the time.

They spent some weeks in the Paris apartment of the French writer and revolutionary theoretician Regis Debray, Che Guevara's comrade in arms. Debray had been taken prisoner in Bolivia in 1967 and sentenced to thirty years' imprisonment. A member of an influential French family, he was freed in 1970.

The apartment, in the Latin Quarter, was considered a safe house. 'The cops don't come here,' Gudrun Ensslin told a visitor, 'because Regis's father is a politician.' The three fugitives kept in touch with their friends in Germany by telephone. One of the first phone calls was from Andreas Baader to Thorwald Proll's sister Astrid. She was to bring books, papers and a Mercedes left behind at a Frankfurt garage to Paris.

Her brother was waiting for her outside police headquarters, among parked patrol cars, and guided her to Debray's apartment. During the next few days the four of them wandered round the city. They took photographs of each other in a café, laughing at their new short hairstyles. Baader had the pictures developed while Gudrun put her files in order: these consisted of a case full of newspaper cuttings, particularly about the arson trial.

At one point a deputation of former inmates of the detention centres turned up, wanting them to come back. 'They refused to understand that we had made this act of illegality our purpose,' Thorwald Proll remembered later. 'They wanted us to come back, it would all be all right, they said, and they needed us. We were a kind of space station to them. They could imagine doing anything if we were with them. But when we left them they felt abandoned.'

The group discussed their next move. One of them thought they might go to the Middle East and visit the Fatah organization of the PLO. Gudrun Ensslin, however, was more inclined to lie low for a while. She planned to write a book about the Frankfurt youth project.

Later, Thorwald Proll turned himself in to serve the rest of his prison sentence, as did the fourth arsonist, Horst Söhnlein. Neither of them ever had any further connection with the Baader–Ensslin group.

Baader, Ensslin and Astrid Proll went on to Italy. Here they stayed with acquaintances from Berlin, and also visited the writer Luise Rinser, who wrote to the Ensslin family later, 'Gudrun has a friend for life in me.'

At the beginning of February 1970 Karl Hempfler, the Hessian Minister of Justice, turned down the petition for clemency. The fugitives heard the news in Italy. Gudrun called Frankfurt and asked for details. 'We picked up something about it on the radio down here, but we couldn't make it out exactly.' Her friend at the other end of the line confirmed that the petition had been rejected. 'Well, we must just carry on, then,' replied Gudrun.

Shortly before, a tourist from Berlin visiting Italy had been to see them and suggested a way in which they could 'carry on'. He thought they should come back to Germany in any case and join a militant group now being formed. The tourist's name was Horst Mahler.

Andreas Baader and Gudrun Ensslin left Italy. They reached the Stuttgart parsonage in the middle of the night. Gudrun's father, who was surprised to see them, urged them both to go back and finish their sentences. 'Give yourselves up and serve the ten months,' he said, but his words fell on deaf ears. 'We are not going back to jail,' said Gudrun, categorically. 'We're going to Berlin. We'll go underground there, and then we'll see.' They took a shower, ate a meal, and went on their way the same night.

23
Bambule

Early in 1970 Ulrike Meinhof had moved from Dahlem to an apartment nearer the centre of Berlin. She and the twins were now living at 12 Kufsteiner Strasse, Schöneberg. Peter Homann, the former Hamburg art student who had participated in the 'Albertz Resign' demonstration with Gudrun Ensslin and others, lived there for a while too. Ulrike Meinhof had not found a circle of friends in Berlin like her old one in Hamburg, nor did she want that any more.

In the Eichenhof Youth Custody Home in Berlin, she had met three girls, Jynette, Irene and Monika, whose stories became the basis of the script for her film *Bambule*. Work on the shooting of Ulrike Meinhof's first and only television film began at the end of 1969.

She had written, in a radio report in 1969, 'Bambule means rebellion, resistance, counter-violence – efforts toward liberation. Such things happen mostly in summer, when it is hot, and the food is even less appealing than usual, and anger festers in the corners with the heat. Such things are in the air then – it could be compared to the hot summers in the black ghettoes of the United States.'

Ulrike Meinhof did not want to be separated from the subjects of her report, young people who expected more of her than simply to be described.

And soon they were at her door. Young people from the Frankfurt project, young Berliners asking to be let in. She let some of them stay, who slept in her beds, helped themselves from her refrigerator, stole things from the apartment and brought stolen goods into it, made a lot of noise and pelted the neighbours with eggs from the balcony. Ulrike found it hard to turn these young people out again. She had problems enough of her own. She plunged into numerous projects and discussions, she stayed out at night until early in the morning. A few hours later the twins would appear in her bedroom calling, 'Get up!' They were often late for school. Ulrike Meinhof felt guiltily that she was not doing enough for her children.

Around the turn of the year from 1969 to 1970, Ulrike Meinhof was interviewed in her apartment by the film-maker Helma Sanders. She kept nervously rolling paper pellets in her fingers and was chain-smoking. There was desperation in her face. 'Private life is always political,' she said. 'Bringing up children is terribly political, the relationships between people are terribly political because they say something about whether human beings are oppressed or free. Whether they can think for themselves or not, whether they can do something or not. From the point of view of the children's needs, the family, yes, the family is necessary, indispensable as a stable place with stable human relationships.'

Ulrike Meinhof paused. In a quiet voice, she went on: 'It's difficult – difficult – terribly difficult – oh, it's difficult, terribly difficult. Of course many things are easier if you're a man, and you have a wife to look after the children, and it all works out. And children really do need stable relationships and someone who has plenty of time for them. If you're a woman, so that you don't have a wife to do all that for you, then you have to do everything yourself – it's terribly difficult.'

She interrupted her flow of talk, as if catching herself giving away too much that was private. Suddenly she was very objective and political again:

'You can't support anti-authoritarian policies and hit your children at home. But nor, in the long run, can you refrain from hitting your children at home without being political – I mean, you can't give up competing within a family without also having to fight to neutralize competitive relationships outside the family, the sort of thing we all get involved in, so that . . .'

She hesitated, and then added very quietly: '. . . you begin to leave your family.' A few months later, Ulrike Meinhof was indeed to leave her children.

Shooting of the television film *Bambule* had ended in early February 1970. Soon afterwards Ulrike Meinhof had a visitor from Italy. Andreas Baader turned up at her door in Kufsteiner Strasse, elegant as ever, this time in custom-made silk shirts taken from the well-stocked wardrobe of a composer in Rome. With him was the pastor's forceful daughter Gudrun Ensslin. They were looking for somewhere to stay. They both thought they could move about unrecognized in Berlin and be politically active at the same time. Obviously the apartment of a prominent left-wing journalist could serve them only as temporary accommodation.

Ulrike Meinhof agreed. She wanted to help the couple. There seemed to her much more consistency in the arsonists' lives than in her own. She hoped to learn from them. On their flight through Italy, Baader and Ensslin had sometimes whiled away lonely hours by taking drugs, and they now tried getting Ulrike Meinhof to join them. Since her brain operation, however, their hostess was terrified of experimenting with any chemical substances. But one night she gave in to their persuasions, and they each took one of the yellow pills easily available on the drug scene of Berlin under the name of Sunshine; it was LSD.

The mood that night kept changing abruptly. By turns, it was cheerful, ironic, aggressive, brutal and then full of dreamy togetherness again. Ulrike could concentrate only by making a supreme effort, and experienced moments of terror in which she feared the effects would never wear off. It was like the fear of going mad she had known since her operation.

She would probably not have gone on this LSD trip with Andreas Baader alone. But Gudrun Ensslin was there, Gudrun in whose life she had discovered similarities with her own, and who fascinated her. Ulrike felt that Gudrun had acted with uncompromising resolution. That night, they discussed the way Gudrun had abandoned her child so as to make a complete break with the past. Gudrun Ensslin was a missionary figure representing a new morality. The morality of a revolutionary who must sever all connection with her origins and burn all her bridges behind her, so that the only life still open to her is one untrammelled by possessions and lived outside the law.

In the course of that euphoric night, Ensslin developed a new credo, running counter to her own background. All the Ten Commandments must be broken. In this world of violence, the biblical 'Thou shalt not kill' must become 'Thou shalt kill'. When the effects of the LSD wore off in the morning, they had breakfast together at the Café Kranzler.

Ensslin and Baader stayed in Kufsteiner Strasse for about two weeks. The twins Bettina and Regine, then seven years old, were told who the two visitors were, and that they had started a fire in a department store, so the police were looking for them. Hence they were not to mention the couple at play group or in school, and must call them just Hans and Grete at home. Baader and Ensslin used Hans and Grete later as cover names.

Ulrike thought of her two guests as comrades, indeed as particularly good comrades. The twins, however, did not like Baader at all. He was clearly not very fond of children. When Bettina fell and cut her knee one day, he did not pick her up, but just laughed at her mishap. Later, when the children were reading Karl May's adventure stories, Bettina found a character in his *Winnetou* who reminded her of Baader: Rattler, one of a band of rough-mannered land surveyors, an unscrupulous figure, and cowardly too, so much so that the Indians break off his execution at the stake in contempt and drown him in the river instead.

At this time Baader and Ensslin had no concrete plans for building up a body of urban guerrillas. They entertained some very vague notions of strategic activities carried out by fringe groups, which would certainly be outside the law, and militant, but by no means paramilitary. Their priorities were just to find accommodation, get hold of money and make contacts.

24
Arms in the Cemetery

One night there was a meeting with Dieter Kunzelmann, also wanted by the police. A long, intense discussion centred on the question of whether Baader and Ensslin should ally themselves with Kunzelmann's group. It quickly turned out that this was hardly feasible, since the radical Maoist course pursued by Baader and Ensslin – vaguely formulated as it might be – was incompatible with the ideas of the Blues.

In the background of the discussion, however, there was Baader's claim to leadership. Kunzelmann was not happy to go along with that; he had, after all, gathered a group of his own around himself. Nothing came of the projected cooperation.

Arms, of course, were required for the projected illegal struggle. Someone had the idea of stealing pistols from the police patrolling the Berlin Wall. They sat down with some odds and ends of fabric and made little bags to hold lead balls, the kind commonly used to weight down curtain hems. Andreas Baader, who often made his own trousers, showed particular skill with needle and thread. The bags, resembling short, heavy sausages, were for slugging a solitary policeman on patrol from behind, so that they could then take the stunned officer's pistol. A bludgeon or iron bar was out of the question: after all, they were not barbarians. Having made their coshes, they stole a car and drove to Neukölln and a secluded area near the Wall. But instead of the solitary officer on the beat they had expected, they found all the policemen going their nightly rounds in twos or threes. The operation was abandoned.

The group went to a late-night café on the Kurfürstendamm. An American woman tourist of about thirty was sitting at the next table, her handbag on a chair beside her. She got up to go to the Ladies, leaving her handbag where it was. Andreas Baader looked at Mahler. 'Do it now, Horst,' he said. And the lawyer 'did it'. He surrepitiously appropriated the bag, removed money and papers from it, and put it back again. White in the face, he left the café. The others stayed a moment longer, laughing.

The group's first attempt to get hold of arms had come to nothing, but Horst Mahler disclosed a new source. The unsuspecting lawyer told them that his old acquaintance Peter Urbach could provide the weapons they needed. Urbach had buried a crate of Second World War pistols, well packed and rust-free, in a cemetery in Buckow. Baader jumped at this idea. The initial meeting with the government agent took place in Nollendorfplatz. Then Baader, Mahler and a couple of others drove to the cemetery with Urbach. The agent indicated the spot where he said the arms were buried. But though it was night, the coast was not clear; a few passers-by, out late, prevented them from digging.

Next afternoon Andreas Baader was driving through Kreuzberg, well over the speed limit. He suddenly noticed a police car following him, but managed to shake it off. However, his car number had been taken.

That evening, the group discussed the abortive digging operation and what to make of it. They wondered if Urbach had just been talking big; no one was yet seriously wondering whether he might be an informer. They thought he should have one more chance.

Some days later, they met the Counter-Intelligence man late at night for the second time. As with the first digging operation, Urbach had brought the tools, such as spades and picks, which would be needed.

He pointed to a small mound of earth. Then he and Baader began digging, while another man stood guard, holding an airgun. Within half an hour it was obvious that their efforts were useless. There were no buried arms, or anyway not here. Urbach could not explain it. He tried to talk his way out of trouble by saying someone else must have been there digging before them. The little party set off for home.

Mahler and Urbach got into a car together and led the way, with Baader and the others following in a second car. About 3.15 am a police patrol car stopped this second vehicle in the Waltersdorfer Chaussee. The police officers acted as if it were a normal traffic check. In fact, they had stopped the car as the result of an order from police radio control headquarters. Urbach had set a trap.

'Your papers, please,' one of the policemen said to Baader. 'Have you been drinking?' Baader said he had not. The officer looked through his papers. He was carrying a driving licence and an identity card in the name of Peter C., born in Berlin on 14 June 1934. 'Where do you live, then?'

'4 Via Addia, Rome,' said Baader.

'Married, are you?' asked the officer. Baader nodded.

'How many children have you got?'

Baader couldn't answer that one. The number of children he was supposed to have was down on his identity card all right, but obviously he had never looked at it.

The police officer told the occupants of the car they must accompany him to the police station to have their identities checked.

Baader was the only one detained in police custody; the others were allowed to leave again. Mahler and Urbach had been watching the arrest from a side street. The Counter-Intelligence agent took Mahler on into the city and dropped him there.

Baader was taken to Tegel prison, to serve the rest of his sentence. During the days following Baader's arrest, his friends intensively discussed ways to free him. Somebody had the idea of fixing things so that he had to be taken out of the prison building: the only question was, how? Somebody else suggested that Ulrike Meinhof could make out she and Baader were planning a book, one which made it essential for Baader to be taken outside the jail. They planned this expedition to be to the Institute of Social Studies in Dahlem, and spied out the land thoroughly.

25
Preparing for a Rescue

Baader was still suffering from the effects of jaundice. After his arrest, therefore, he was initially sent to the sick bay of the Moabit prison. He was in a cell next door to Bommi Baumann, who had jaundice too, and to a man called Eckehard L.

They immediately agreed to break out together. Bommi had already begun loosening the door frame of his cell, although he then decided there was no point in it, since the prison officers always left his door unlocked anyway. Bommi was an amiable soul who maintained a good relationship with the prison staff 'as one member of the proletariat to another'. Not so his next-door neighbour Andreas Baader. He constantly swore at the officers, in the filthiest language. Consequently his cell door was kept locked. The prison doctors visited Bommi now and then and expressed their surprise. 'Well now, Herr Baumann – you're a nice chap, but your friend Baader is a terror.'

Gudrun Ensslin, meanwhile, was going around drumming up the help of friends for a rescue operation. Nobody really wanted to join in. Theoretically, the freeing of prisoners was at the heart of current political arguments. But actually planning and organizing a rescue? As far as most of them were concerned, it just was not their kind of thing.

By now Andreas Baader had been moved from the remand section to a cell in Block I of Tegel jail. Over the next few days and weeks, he had regular visitors. His mother Anneliese Baader came to see him, so did Horst Mahler as his lawyer, and so did Ulrike Meinhof: she visited him five times.

And one day, 30 April, a woman turned up at the gates of the prison after twelve noon showing an identity card in the name of Dr Gretel Weitemeir. None of the prison officers realized that this was really Gudrun Ensslin, also wanted by the police, come to visit her lover Andreas. They were allowed an hour together, under a warder's eye. As all had gone well, Ensslin visited twice more, the last time being only a day before the rescue.

That same day, a letter from the publishing firm of Klaus Wagenbach arrived at the prison, informing the authorities that Andreas Baader and

Ulrike Meinhof were to collaborate on a book about young outsiders in society.

On one of her visits, Ulrike Meinhof asked if it would be possible for Andreas Baader to be allowed out of the prison to look at the literature on the subject. There were journals of the twenties at an academic institute in Berlin which he absolutely must read for the book they were planning.

Governor Glaubrecht refused. 'We just don't have the staff to escort him out several times.'

Baader's lawyer Horst Mahler happened to be in Tegel at the time; he was not standing for this, and insisted on speaking to the governor at once. He then pulled out all the stops. Nobody else, he said, could pick relevant material from the card index of authors on Baader's behalf.

Glaubrecht seemed to take this point, and agreed to a single outing lasting two to three hours. Mahler told Baader, who had just had a visit from Ulrike Meinhof, of the success of his efforts.

When the lawyer had left, Glaubrecht asked for Baader's file. That same day, one of the prison governor's staff called the Institute for Social Issues and made an appointment for the prisoner to go there in two days' time, on Thursday 14 May 1970, at 9 a.m.

The crack unit whose aim it was to spring Andreas Baader from jail consisted mainly of women. It was plain to all that Horst Mahler, a well-known lawyer, could not take part in the operation. However, women's lib or no women's lib, they thought at least one man should be involved.

Mahler was able to help here. A few days before the rescue, Gudrun Ensslin talked to the man he suggested, at the Republican Club. She knew this man had already done time and committed serious offences. In her view, that made him ideal for the job. The man agreed at once, though he could hardly have foreseen the consequences of his decision.

What they lacked were weapons, which could most easily be acquired from the criminal fraternity. Two of the women followed up an underworld tip, and late one night visited a bar frequented by right-wing radicals and known as the Wolf's Lair. They asked the manager if he could sell them a pistol or even a submachine gun. He said no. 'Well, think it over,' said one of the women, as they left. Two days later she was back in the Wolf's Lair. This time the manager told her, 'I'll see what can be done.'

On 12 May, around 11 p.m., two days before Baader was to be escorted out to the Institute for Social Issues, they got what they were after. Günther

V., who had previously offered the proprietor weapons, was standing at the bar in the Wolf's Lair. The two women making the inquiry were sitting at a table. 'Look, that's the bird, sitting over there,' said the proprietor. The arms dealer went and sat down with them. After a while all three left the bar. The man, who called himself Teddy, took the women to a girlfriend's apartment where he kept a small stock of weapons. Teddy sold them two pistols, a Beretta and a Reck, with silencers. He had smuggled the pistols in from Switzerland, and made silencers to fit them himself. The women paid DM 1,000 each for the guns. Preparations for the rescue operation entered their final phase.

On 14 May 1970, at 9 a.m., the time came. Andreas Baader was sprung from custody with armed violence at the Institute for Social Issues, in the West Berlin district of Dahlem.

Georg Linke, on the staff of the Institute, was severely wounded in the course of the operation.

Baader and his rescuers got away.

With that leap out of the window of the Institute for Social Issues, Ulrike Meinhof ended her career as a journalist and went underground.

Her film *Bambule*, which was to have been transmitted about this time, was struck from the TV schedules at short notice.

PART TWO

'The Wild Glory of Terror'

1
The Journey to Jordan

On 8 June 1970, a group of West Berlin travellers flew to Beirut from East Berlin's Schönefeld airport. Later, the police found the names of Bäcker, Grashof, Schelm, Mahler, Dudin and Ray, among others, on the passenger list of the Interflug plane.

The French journalist Michèle Ray had obviously left her passport in Berlin. Said Dudin, acting as intermediary between the group and the PLO's Al Fatah organization, had bought the air tickets at the Karim travel agency in West Berlin.

The first group landed in Beirut at 15.30 hours. From there they were supposed to continue to Amman, in Jordan. Their journey ended in a training camp a few kilometres outside Amman, on the road to Jerusalem. The camp lay on a plateau surrounded by karstified hills in the middle of the mountainous desert. It consisted of two stone buildings, an open space for military exercises, a concrete indoor shooting range, some tents. That was all. The group began their training. Horst Mahler let his beard grow.

Ten days or so after the first group had flown out, Said Dudin returned to Berlin, with a clutch of United Arab Republic passports bearing photographs of Baader's rescuers in his baggage.

On 21 June, at 6.30 a.m., the travellers in the second group, which included Andreas Baader, Gudrun Ensslin and Ulrike Meinhof, were driven to Neukölln by friends. They took the underground to Friedrichstrasse station and East Berlin. After a cursory passport inspection the Germans, transformed into Arabs by hair dye, were allowed to continue to Schönefeld airport. The East German police made no trouble at all.

The fully booked plane landed in Damascus next afternoon. There were problems on arrival, but the Palestinians intervened. The group was held at the airport for only a few hours. Said Dudin, who alone had been allowed to leave, came back with a piece of paper and four armed Palestinians. The travellers were now allowed to enter the country. They got into taxis, and were driven to the same secret quarters in which the first group had stayed. One of the Palestinians was bragging of sophisticated technological feats of arms and other impressive acts. They ate a scanty meal, and slept in large rooms on camp beds piled on top of each other.

Next morning they continued their journey. At the border between Syria and Jordan, Said Dudin only had to wave an Al Fatah pass. All the border posts were also occupied by armed Palestinians: a kind of double rule existed in both countries at this time.

Early in the afternoon they reached Amman, and were welcomed by military leaders of the Fatah organization. Its secret service photographed their guests. Palestinian secret service men noted down all their significant personal details on filing cards, and each of them then had to sign with his or her real name. Later, the Israelis captured the Beirut headquarters of the Fatah secret service and came into possession of these files.

After less than an hour's journey, the group of travellers came to the camp outside the city. It was early evening, and still light. They turned off the main road and on to a winding, sandy track leading to the camp. They reached the entrance after a few hundred metres. The advance party from Berlin was waiting for them, and welcomed the new arrivals with hugs and back-slapping.

2
In the Camp

With his beard and his green military cap, Horst Mahler looked like Fidel Castro in the Sierra Maestra. He was beaming, very much the leader of a guerrilla band, accepted by his followers and recognized by the Palestinians.

This was to change within a few hours of Baader's arrival. Horst Mahler, the brilliant lawyer who could argue so cleverly in court, was no match for the aggressive, contemptuous Andreas Baader. Baader was able to accuse others of incompetence in a way that utterly confused them. He spat venom until he was literally foaming at the mouth. He was deaf to rational argument, and once he was through, Gudrun Ensslin would step in to preach her new morality of the violation of all bourgeois laws and the 'heartfelt spontaneity' with which every revolutionary must subordinate himself, or to hold forth on the text that illegality could be learned only outside the law. Baader's tirades were followed by Gudrun Ensslin's Maoist Bible classes. This division of labour soon made the couple undisputed leaders of the nascent RAF, or Red Army Faction.

Originally, their hosts had merely prepared them a programme consisting of a kind of revolutionary tourism, such as they offered to many of the foreigners who visited the fighting Palestinians at this time. Guests were shown the huge tent townships where many people were still living two decades after their expulsion from Palestine. There were hospitals with wounded men, women and children; schools where education was combined with military training. The Germans too saw all this. Then, however, they insisted on being allowed to participate in real military training.

They were all issued with suitable clothing: green battledress and caps. Only Andreas Baader preferred to retain the skin-tight velvet trousers in which he was later, during training, to wriggle his way through the stony desert on his belly. The German group consisted of over twenty men and women, for whom the Algerian camp commandant Achmed envisaged providing segregated accommodation. Women had never been trained in the camp before. The first protest was raised. Baader and Ensslin demanded mixed-sex sleeping quarters. They regarded getting agreement to this as a great blow struck for emancipation, failing to notice that they had laid the foundations of further conflict.

The building where they were all put up had four rooms. Two were for use as bedrooms, a third as a kitchen, dining and living room, where the Germans gathered around a large table to eat and talk. The fourth room was the commandant's own office and bedroom.

They were served the scanty food on which the Palestinians had been living for years: canned meat donated by UNRRA, the United Nations refugee relief organization, generally mixed with rice. With it they got flat cakes of Arab bread, water, fruit only occasionally, fresh meat never.

The Germans did not like this diet, and complained from the start. One of the young girls, in all seriousness, demanded the installation of a Coca-Cola machine in the desert camp.

At six in the morning there was strong, sweet tea; then training began with endurance running. This was followed by shooting practice in the open, with rifles, submachine guns and sometimes with howitzers. Everyone was armed with a Russian Kalashnikov, which was hung on the bedpost at night. The camp might be attacked at any time.

They also practised throwing hand grenades. One day Ulrike Meinhof got a Russian-style grenade. The instructor showed her how to unscrew the cap so as to free and pull the ring. Ulrike pulled. The grenade began to hiss quietly; smoke rose from it. Instead of throwing the grenade she was holding, Ulrike looked at it and inquired, 'Now what do I do?'

'Fling it away!' someone yelled. Ulrike managed to throw the sinister thing a few metres from her just before it exploded. Everybody had ducked for cover behind heaps of stones.

Andreas Baader in particular made fun of the clumsy intellectuals. 'Ulrike was treated like garbage,' Peter Homann remembers. 'It was pitiful to see it.' Losing his self-control, Baader shouted at her, 'You're the ultimate bourgeois sow.' Ulrike Meinhof had no reply to that.

There was trouble between Baader and Homann in particular. On one occasion Baader began laying savagely into Homann. Homann swung his arm back and punched Baader, who fell on the Jordanian sand. Ensslin and the other women screeched, 'You bastard, you've knocked him out.'

Homann was already regarded as a traitor to the cause.

Now and then they practised the guerrilla tactics the group intended to employ in the big cities of Germany when they got back. 'How to rob a bank' was another item on the training programme. The Algerian camp commandant was familiar with this subject. He had taken part in such 'expropriation actions' himself during the Algerian war of independence.

Baader made sure that their training had a close practical connection with 'the job', as he called urban guerrilla manoeuvres.

One day, when they were practising advancing on their bellies through almost impassable terrain, and the Palestinians, as usual, were shooting off live ammunition now and then to give a realistic impression of battle conditions, Baader protested. 'This is fine for you here, I'm sure, but we don't have such situations in our cities at home.'

Later, the Palestinian leader Abu Hassan, responsible for the training camps, inspected this one. In honour of his visit the young *fedayeen* cooked him a freshly killed chicken. Baader complained. 'You're an authoritarian crowd here. When the commander-in-chief turns up there's meat for him, but we don't get any.'

3
The Red Prince

Abu Hassan's real name was Ali Hassan Salameh. He was the son of the legendary Sheikh Hassan Salameh, one of the five leaders of the Arab revolt of 1936–39 against British rule and the British policy of the settlement of Jews in Palestine. Yasser Arafat, the Fatah leader, was a great admirer of that national hero Sheikh Hassan, and introduced his son to his deputy, Abu Iyad, who took the young Salameh into the PLO secret service, Jihad el Razd, of which he was head.

Among Ali Hassan Salameh's first assignments was hunting down suspected Israeli agents in the Palestinian guerrilla training camps. His influence kept growing. He picked men for commando raids into Israel, and soon had extensive control over the training camps themselves.

His *nom de guerre* was now Abu Hassan. When Georges Habash's rival PFLP, the Popular Front for the Liberation of Palestine, extended guerrilla activities world-wide, attacking Israeli institutions and hijacking planes, a special unit for operations abroad was set up within Al Fatah too. It consisted of a small group of a few picked individuals, later operating under the name of 'Black September'. Abu Hassan became its chief planner. The Israeli secret service Mossad were after him for years; he was regarded as the most wanted terrorist in the world.

The Israelis called him the Red Prince. In 1979, Mossad blew him up in his car, nine years after the Baader–Meinhof group had met him in Jordan. But even then, in 1970, he was one of the most important figures of Al Fatah. The Germans knew nothing about that.

4
Trouble in the Camp

From time to time the lightly armed *fedayeen* and their German guests could see Israeli bombers circling in the sky. Jordanian troops were massed a few kilometres away from the camp. War was in the air.

At the beginning of their training the group were allowed all the ammunition they wanted. However, the instructors soon discovered that the pointless way the Germans kept firing off their guns made for trouble with their own people, who were obliged to use ammunition sparingly.

So the guests were allowed only ten cartridges each a day. Baader saw this as discrimination by the Palestinians against his own urban guerrillas, and quarrelled noisily with the camp commandant, threatening a training strike. This initially left the commandant speechless; then he showed himself determind to exercise his authority in the camp. Cartridges would still be limited to ten a day. Next morning the guests refused to turn up for training, and Baader demanded equal rights of negotiation with Abu Hassan, as one partisan leader to another.

However, the Berliners had underestimated the influence of the wiry little camp commandant. He had proved himself in almost all the armed confrontations of the Arab world, starting with the Algerian war, and despite his relatively low rank his reputation was high among the Palestinians. Most important of all, he was on excellent terms with Abu Hassan. He had made several concessions to the Germans: men and women were allowed to spend the night together, and had even moved into a house of their own.

The guests themselves had little understanding of foreign customs. During their 'strike', the female members of the group sunbathed on the roof of their house, where the *fedayeen* could see them, and sunbathed naked at that. Most of the young Palestinian guerrillas had never seen a naked woman in their lives before. It made them restless.

The Algerian commandant exploded. 'This is not the tourists' beach in Beirut.'

The naked sunbathing had to stop. Heated discussions took place in the evenings. 'The anti-imperialist struggle and sexual emancipation go hand in hand.' Or to put it in Baader's own words: 'Fucking and shooting are the same thing.' The Germans wondered how they could enlighten the young Palestinians on their sexual oppression by their military leader.

The alarm was often raised at night. Everyone in the camp, including the urban guerrillas from Berlin, had to spend the night dressed and ready for combat. There was much dispute in the group on the question of present practice and their future course of action. Their arguments with Peter Homann were the most violent. The police had been after him since the rescue of Baader, wrongly suspecting that he was the marksman involved. He did not agree with Andreas Baader's politics or his claim to leadership, and had gone to Jordan with the others to get out of the way of the police for a while. He was aware of the real marksman's identity, but was unwilling to name him just to clear himself. He knew Baader well from their days in the artistic world of Berlin – too well to see him as a future national hero. They had clashed fiercely on several occasions. Homann had kept apart from the others in the camp, visited the *fedayeen* in their tents, and under the suspicious eyes of Baader and Ensslin had established a personal relationship with the Algerian commandant. When all the rest moved into another house he stayed on his own. They avoided each other. But in the evening, when he was sitting on the terrace of his own house, the wind blew scraps of the others' conversation over to him. He caught something about a 'people's trial' and 'making short work of it', which Baader suggested could be glossed over as a shooting accident. Most of this conversation was drowned out by the yelping of the dogs that roamed around the camp.

But he had heard correctly. The conversation between Andreas Baader, Gudrun Ensslin, Horst Mahler, Ulrike Meinhof, Hans-Jürgen Bäcker and some others concerned his own life. Baader and Ensslin demanded his liquidation: Homann, they said, was a traitor. As a lawyer, Horst Mahler was in favour of a trial, and Bäcker and Ulrike Meinhof wanted him locked up by the Palestinians.

Horst Mahler said later, 'And arguments derived from Brecht were always being put forward. *Die Massnahme* [the play, *The Measures Taken*] was at the heart of them, I think.' Again in Mahler's words: 'This was the exact situation of Brecht's character: he hadn't done anything yet, but he was regarded as a risk. He was liquidated in the name of a higher necessity, so as not to endanger the revolutionary action.'

Late that evening one of the women passed Homann's house. 'So what's going to happen?' he asked. She took a cartridge out of her pocket, holding it between thumb and forefinger.

'This,' she said, and disappeared into the darkness.

* * *

The Germans had ended their 'strike' quite soon. One day Abu Hassan came to the camp to check up. He tried to take this opportunity of giving the malcontent guests some idea of the political and military position of the Palestinian liberation movement, so as to make them more familiar with present circumstances.

However, he could not finish his lecture. The Germans kept interrupting him. They would not listen, and instead made new demands.

From this point things changed. Hassan ordered the camp commandant not to let the Germans get away with such behaviour any more. When they expressed dissatisfaction with the training programme next day, their hosts acted. A group of Palestinians stormed the house, taking them by surprise, and disarmed them. They were not allowed to leave the building. Two armed men guarded the door. Their military training was called off.

5
Reconnaissance

The Palestinians were anxious to get rid of their German guests as quickly as possible.

Hans-Jürgen Bäcker, who was not yet wanted by the police in Berlin, had his passport returned and was to go ahead of the rest and reconnoitre. The other passports remained under lock and key.

Bäcker flew to Schönefeld airport in East Berlin by way of Cyprus. He showed his Arab identity papers at the passport inspection desk. The East German border officials asked him a question, to which he replied in English. They noticed his German accent, and sent the supposed Arab for questioning.

'Undress,' an East German policeman told him.

'Help yourselves, gentlemen,' replied Bäcker, opening his denim jacket to reveal a pistol. The officers took away his weapon and fetched their secret service colleagues. Three men put Bäcker into a Wartburg and drove him to Karlshorst. His escort rang the door bell of what looked like a private house. A uniformed man opened the door, and Bäcker was taken to an apartment with barred windows. He was allowed to sit in an easy chair, and offered Western cigarettes. Then the interrogation began. It lasted twenty-four hours. Hans-Jürgen Bäcker was surprised to find how well informed the secret service men were about the Baader–Meinhof group. They knew who had taken part in the rescue of Baader, and who had done the shooting. They knew the cover names of the group members and had details of their training in the Palestinian camp.

Fortified with roast chicken, Coca-Cola and cigarettes, Bäcker wrote down his life history. Then the Stasi officers asked him questions about the group. Bäcker admitted to taking part in the eight weeks of 'training for hand-to-hand combat' in the Palestinian camp, but not to having been involved in springing Baader from jail. 'I never knew anything about it in detail,' he claimed.

In the course of their training at the Al Fatah commando camp, said Bäcker, they had been taught how to manufacture their own explosive charges and incendiary devices. 'And there was a plan to sabotage specialist printing machinery in the Springer printing works. They were also thinking of abducting Senator Neubauer of West Berlin, the senator with responsibility for internal affairs, and holding him hostage in order to get political prisoners freed.'

Of the group's motivation, Bäcker said, 'The aim of these operations was to force the US occupying troops out of West Berlin because of their criminal war in Indochina, to destabilize the arbitrary apparatus of the West Berlin police and judiciary and to demoralize their staff, as well as to exchange Senator Neubauer for the prisoners.'

When Bäcker had answered all the questions in writing one of the secret service men took the paper, waved it in the air and said, 'We'll get this checked now. If the office of the GDR public prosecutor general confirms that it's all correct, you can go.'

The GDR secret service officers put what Bäcker had said into a report and sent it to the 'Comrade Minister' and the heads of Stasi Principal Departments IX, VI, II/8 and II/2. The Ministry of State Security was now well informed about the plans of the emergent RAF.

Next day, the secret service men took Hans-Jürgen Bäcker to the Friedrichstrasse frontier crossing point. Here the officers gave him back his pistol, and he was allowed to leave East Germany for the West.

6
'Shoot Him'

At the same time, Peter Homann was taken out of the camp by the Palestinians and driven to Amman in an old Mercedes. He was given a room, English newspapers, and a minder. Then the PLO asked him to write them a report on the group and its relation to the political situation in the Federal German Republic. He wrote about ten pages, not hiding his unfavourable opinion of the Baader–Mahler–Meinhof set-up. When he had handed in his report, Abu Hassan took him for a meal. He brought up the subject of Homann's disagreements with the group again. 'I'll give you a chance to listen to them, hear what they have to say, and what they say about you.'

The meeting took place next evening, on the terrace of the house where Homann was staying. He could hear Abu Hassan's conversation with Baader, Ensslin, Mahler and Ulrike Meinhof through the open window, at a distance of five metres. The room in which he was sitting was dark, the terrace lit only by the night sky over Amman. Now and then shots and distant machine-gun fire could be heard. The others could not see him. At first they discussed the group's return to Germany. Diplomatically, and in a reserved manner, Abu Hassan said that naturally Al Fatah would make sure the group could return to Berlin unscathed. Gudrun Ensslin was spokeswoman for the four of them, as the only one who had fluent English. Baader made his remarks in German, whispering impatiently to Gudrun, 'Translate that for him; go on, translate that.' Gudrun asked if Al Fatah would give the group weapons. Abu Hassan thought it possible, but would make no promises.

Then Gudrun Ensslin mentioned Ulrike Meinhof's children, two little girls of seven, now in hiding in Sicily. But they couldn't stay there much longer, she said: would it be possible for the twins to be taken to Jordan and brought up there in one of the training camps for orphaned Palestinian children? Abu Hassan could envisage the possibility, but commented, 'If you do that you'll never see the children again. They will be Palestinian orphans then.'

Finally the conversation came around to Peter Homann.

'Where is he, anyway?' asked Gudrun Ensslin.

'We've had to separate him from you.'

'Shoot him,' said Gudrun. 'He's an Israeli spy.'

'You should have told me that before,' replied Abu Hassan.

A few days after that nocturnal conversation on the terrace, Abu Hassan spoke briefly to Homann once more about the Berliners and their journey. 'You came as friends, and will certainly be conducted out again as friends, according to the laws of Arab hospitality.' He would, he said, arrange another meeting between Homann and the main group, so that they could discuss the procedure for travelling out together.

The discussions, in a small Amman hotel, were brief. Homann wanted to go his own way.

The group flew back to Schönefeld airport in East Berlin, and travelled over to West Berlin by underground train. The police never noticed anything. They had not even ferreted out the apartments used by the group as hideouts before they left for Jordan. Those apartments could be used again.

The Palestinians provided Homann with an Arab passport in the name of Omar Sharif, gave him his forged German passport back, 200 US dollars for the journey, and an air ticket from Beirut to Rome. A week after the others arrived in Berlin, he went through passport control at Rome airport. He bought a ticket and boarded the train for Hamburg that evening.

7
Children's Stories

Directly after the freeing of Baader, I had been asked by the North German Television magazine programme *Panorama* to do some research for a portrait of Ulrike Meinhof, whom I knew from my days on *konkret* (1966–69). At the time, I tried to get hold of Peter Homann, whom I had also met working on *konkret*, and who I knew was in contact with Ulrike Meinhof. I failed to find him.

About three months afterwards, in the late summer of 1970, I suddenly had a phone call in Hamburg. I was to go to an apartment in the Himmelstrasse at once. Peter Homann was in the bathroom of this apartment, dyeing his hair.

He told me that the group was planning to send Ulrike Meinhof's children, the twins Bettina and Regine, to a Palestinian orphanage camp in Jordan. Klaus Rainer Röhl, the twins' father, had had Interpol searching for them unsuccessfully for months.

On the morning of 14 May, when Baader was freed, the children were at school. When the police hunt began, a woman friend of their mother went to the police station near Kufsteiner Strasse, where Ulrike Meinhof lived, and picked up the children's identity papers, which had been applied for some time earlier. The officer on duty did not notice that the children whose passports she was fetching were the daughters of the woman being sought at that very moment by the entire Berlin police force.

The children were sent first to an old friend of Ulrike's in Bremen. A few days later, two women came from Berlin to take the twins away again, and drove south with them. After crossing the border illegally, they continued their journey on foot to France. Here another woman was waiting, with a car. They reached the Italian border next evening.

The pass itself was closed, and would not be opened until next day, so there was no one on duty yet at border control either.

Two of the women got out and walked in front of the car, guiding it over the border past mounds of snow on one side and an abyss on the other. The children were lying on the back seat, half asleep, hidden under blankets.

Journey's end was an encampment of huts near Mount Etna, on Sicily. Here they were expected by Italian comrades, who gave the children and one of the women a hut. The two other women drove straight back to Germany.

The woman, whose name was Hanna, stayed with the twins for several weeks. They went down to the beach, caught sea urchins, sunbathed, played games, and Hanna made sure they studied their school textbooks too. There was guitar-playing and singing in the evenings. When Hanna heard news from Berlin that the children's father, Klaus Rainer Röhl, had put the police on their track, they practised playing hide and seek. Later, the woman and the two children were put up in a large, plain stone house looking out on the volcano.

Then Hanna had to return to Berlin, and the two little girls were taken back to the huts, where four German hippies looked after them. Two of the hippies soon moved on again, and the twins were left in the care of the other couple until the beginning of September.

* * *

Early in September, 1970, Peter Homann had been in touch with Hanna, and asked her to come to Hamburg. We met one Saturday.

Hanna told us the group had now returned to Berlin, and they were going to send someone to Sicily to take the children to the Jordanian orphanage camp.

We made a swift decision. We would have to steal a march on the group's envoy. We called the Italian contact man in Sicily, gave the password 'Professor Schnase', and told him someone would arrive at Palermo airport at 14.14 hours next day to fetch the children.

I was on board the plane for Rome at seven next morning, and flew on from there to Sicily. At Palermo airport I met a man dressed like a hippy, who looked German, and an Italian.

'I am Professor Schnase,' I said.

The two of them looked at the baggage labels on my case. 'How come you're from Hamburg, not Berlin?'

'I used to work on *konkret* with Ulrike.'

The couple took a dim view of the group. 'Not a word out of them for months. We had no idea what we were going to do with the children. We're out of money too,' said the hippie.

We drove to the coast in a small Fiat with Italian licence plates. A dilapidated Volkswagen minibus was waiting on a deserted beach. Two little girls were sitting in it, tanned brown, their hair bleached blonde by the sun: Ulrike Meinhof's daughters.

Bettina and Regine had often seen me at the *konkret* offices, in the Röhls' villa in Blankenese, and later too, in Berlin, where I sometimes used to visit Ulrike.

'We'll catch the next plane back,' I said.

'No use,' said the hippie. 'They'll check your papers at the airport, and we don't have passes for the children. But we've found out the rail connections.'

We were in Rome at seven next morning, and went to stay with friends. It was five days before we could reach the children's father by phone; he happened to be on holiday in Italy. The twins were handed back to him in an apartment on the Piazza Navona.

Meanwhile, someone in Berlin had called Sicily. 'We'll be fetching the children within the next few days.'

'But you already did. The children have gone.'

The group wondered who could have known where the children were hidden. They thought of Hanna, and set off in search of her. 'Where's

Hanna?' asked Baader at the door of one commune, drawing his pistol. 'Not here,' they told him, but they tipped him off about a place where she might be found. When the group had tracked Hanna down, they showed her a pistol too. She told them who had taken the children.

Soon afterwards, Baader and Mahler travelled to Hamburg.

We spent the night in my apartment in Hamburg Altona; there were six of us there in all. At 3 a.m., the doorbell rang. I found an old acquaintance outside, a former SDS activist, normally a bear of a man, always confident, always with an air of assurance, but now he was frantic. 'You must get out of here at once. They're going to kill you.'

Baader and Mahler, he said, had come to his apartment. At pistol point, they asked him where I lived. He had pretended to be on their side, had driven to my apartment with them and persuaded them to wait out in the car while he made sure there were no policemen inside.

We left the building in the dark, through a side entrance, and spent the rest of the night in a hotel.

Later, when it was publicly made known that the police no longer suspected Peter Homann of complicity in the freeing of Baader, he turned himself in, and after a brief period remanded in custody, he was released.

8
The Triple Coup

In Berlin, they were preparing for the 'underground struggle'. Apartments were rented, cars acquired. Ulrike Meinhof got in touch with leftists and liberals she had known in her journalist days. Some of them were very prominent people. Only a few sympathized with the idea of an armed struggle, but you did not just slam the door in the face of someone like Ulrike Meinhof, particularly when she was wanted by the police.

Ulrike herself was going around with a pistol in her handbag now. One day she tried learning how to break into a car. Clumsy as she was in technical matters, she managed to break off the car steering wheel, and brought it home as a trophy.

Sometimes she hinted at guilt feelings over her children. Such 'fits of weakness' were vigorously attacked by Baader and Ensslin. Baader called her a 'bourgeois cunt', and Ulrike said no more.

Courageous as she had always seemed outwardly in her political and journalistic work, she was very much inclined to give way, submit and abase herself in private, in any personal conflict. Her influence within the group was slight, or at least very much less than the catchphrase 'Baader–Meinhof group' suggested to the outside world.

On 14 August 1970 Eric G., a car mechanic, had some visitors to his Berlin garage. Hans-Jürgen Bäcker, a friend of his from the Republican Club, had brought two men to see him. Eric's wife made coffee and fetched Karl-Heinz Ruhland, a mechanic working there on a casual basis, to come from the workshop and join them.

After discussion of the political situation, the visitors came to the point.

'We need cars. We can either steal them or hire them and not return them, but either way they need doing up. Could you take that sort of job on?'

The money would be good. The cars would need to be equipped with new engine and bodywork numbers, and partly resprayed. New door and ignition locks would need fitting too. Both mechanics agreed to do the work.

Karl-Heinz Ruhland was deep in debt. He had trouble repaying instalments on his debts, came before the courts several times for deception and fraud, and was sentenced to short terms of imprisonment. He was more interested in the prospect of cash than Baader and Mahler's political aims.

The talk in the garage went on until evening. Ruhland assumed there was a sizeable 'fighting force' behind Baader and Mahler, and was disappointed to discover that the group planning the revolutionary overthrow of the Federal Republic of Germany numbered just twenty-five people. The wordy political discussions of the visitors bored him. He went back to his work.

At intervals over the next few days, more people turned up at the workshop. There was Irene Goergens, known as 'Peggy', Astrid Proll, called 'Rosi', Gudrun Ensslin under the name of 'Grete'. Horst Mahler and Andreas Baader were calling themselves 'James' and 'Hans'. They were the only two whose real names Ruhland learned.

The first cars came into the garage. They were resprayed and provided with new engine and chassis numbers. Hans and James lent a hand.

Around 1 September, the owner of the garage told his assistant Ruhland, 'They've been telling me they're planning a bank raid. They asked if I'd help.'

'What did you say?'

'I said yes, and I thought you would too.'

Ruhland was surprised. 'I'll have to think that over.'

A week later James was back, explaining that they wanted to attack four Berlin banks simultaneously, which meant forming four groups.

He asked Ruhland if he was prepared to help.

Ruhland agreed.

Zero hour was the morning of 29 September. Three Berlin banks were raided between 9.48 a.m. and 9.58 a.m. This was one of the rare cases of cooperation between the RAF and the 2 June Movement.

A week after the 'triple coup', as the group called it, they all met in an apartment in the Kurfürstenstrasse for a post mortem on the operation.

Over coffee and beer, they discussed the course of the bank raids. Mahler and Baader thought they could improve on their techniques of entering and getting away from a bank. Mahler, wearing his toupee as usual, offered moral justification for such raids. 'It's the capitalists' money we take. It doesn't harm the little man.'

Baader thought the group should be enlarged. Then he said that Bäcker and Ali Jansen, a member of the group since its return from Jordan, had gone to Munsterlager to find out about the chances of breaking into an Army arsenal.

A day after this, Karl-Heinz Ruhland received 1,000 Deutschmarks from the loot. He was not satisfied; this was not enough for him.

Bäcker and Ali Jansen came back from Munsterlager. The raid was planned for mid-October. Ulrike Meinhof and Ali were to prepare the ground for the action. On 8 October, the two of them were driven to Tempelhof airport, where they boarded a plane, unrecognized.

9
'My Compliments, Gentlemen!'

At 1.38 p.m. the same day, the telephone rang in the office of Detective Chief Superintendent Kotsch, of the State Security department of the Berlin police.

'Is that Herr Kotsch?'

'Yes.'

'Müller speaking. I have some important information for you. At two-thirty Baader, Mahler and Ensslin will be meeting at an apartment in the name of Hübner at 89 Knesebeckstrasse, front of the building, one staircase up. Baader's hair is dyed sandy and he has a moustache. They're all heavily armed. Or at other times, you'll find them at 19 Haupstrasse, apartment in the name of Wendt on the second floor. Baader's driving a green Mercedes, number plate B-MA 118. So please will you finally get on with it and do something!'

Kotsch was astonished. 'Have you given this information to someone else before?'

'I have,' said his caller, 'but they obviously think I'm crazy; they don't take it seriously.'

'Herr Müller, I don't know you,' replied Kotsch.

'Just as well,' said his caller, and hung up.

Twenty minutes later, observers moved unobtrusively into position outside the building at 89 Knesebeckstrasse.

Nothing happened throughout the afternoon, so the officer leading the squad decided to search the apartment. Fourteen policemen entered the building and crept upstairs to the first floor. They rang the bell of the Hübner apartment. Nobody opened the door. Light could be seen round the edge of the frame, and news came over the radio from the observers posted outside that a woman had shown herself at the balcony window. The police officers forced the door. At 5.40 p.m. they were in the corridor of the apartment. A young woman came out of the room with the balcony, wasted few words, but showed them an identity card and driving licence in the name of Dorothea R.

'I don't live here,' she said. 'I'm expecting my girl friend, it's her apartment. I was having a bath while I waited.'

'Please stay here while we search the place,' said the leader of the squad, offering the woman a chair. A policeman sat down beside her.

Rummaging through a black chest of drawers, one of the officers found a Llama 9-mm pistol in a green plastic bag.

There were several car number plates, one from a vehicle reported stolen, lying about the next room. A Molotov cocktail, various chemicals and inflammable liquids stood around another room. The woman, who later turned out to be Ingrid Schubert, was taken to Police Station 131 and searched. She had a loaded pistol under her clothes.

The policemen in the Knesebeckstrasse apartment were joined by a photographer and an officer from the criminal records department. They put the record player on and waited. Towards 6 p.m. the doorbell rang. The officers drew their pistols and cautiously opened the door. Outside stood a man with dark, fairly long hair combed forward, and a full beard and moustache. He was wearing a steel-blue jacket, dark trousers, a white shirt and a tie with orange and dark stripes.

The officers recognized Horst Mahler at once. They took him into the apartment and asked to see his papers.

'We know you're Horst Mahler.'

The man denied this. Thereupon one of the policemen pulled his wig off.

'My compliments, gentlemen,' said Horst Mahler.

The former lawyer let them search him, putting up no resistance. There was a loaded Llama Especial 9-mm pistol with its safety catch off in his back right trouser pocket. His jacket pocket contained two full magazines and thirty-six cartridges in all, along with a wad of banknotes.

The police officers took off his tie, loosened the belt of his trousers and took him to police headquarters. Other policemen remained in position.

Half an hour later, one of them spotted a young woman on the staircase listening at the door of the occupied apartment. He pulled her inside. They found a Reck pistol in her brown leather bag, and an identity card in the name of Monika Berberich.

A few minutes later the bell rang again. The woman tried to shout to warn the newcomer. At this several policemen threw themselves on her and pressed a cloth down on her face. Their pistols drawn, the officers opened the door. They found themselves facing the tenant of the apartment next door, an elderly gentleman who had come to complain about the loud music.

Towards 7.40 p.m. the bell rang once more, and this time the officers arrested Brigitte Asdonk. Three-quarters of an hour later Irene Goergens turned up too, and also got a police reception.

Meanwhile, dozens of reporters and curious onlookers had gathered outside the building. The police officers could not hope for any more members of the group to fall into their trap. They began collecting evidence.

Along with recipes and ingredients for the making of explosives, equipment for forgery, pamphlets, and items for the group's everyday requirements, they also found the gang's 'accounts' in the apartment.

The urban guerrillas had noted down their personal expenses on nine small pieces of paper, with a statement of the total. 'H' and 'G', Hans and Grete, i.e. Baader and Ensslin, had incurred total expenditure of 2,484 Deutschmarks: two jackets DM 500, two pairs of trousers DM 180, socks DM 18, hairdresser DM 9, cigarettes DM 60, and so forth.

'Anna', Ulrike Meinhof, had spent 1,300 Deutschmarks: a suit DM 220, two blouses DM 120, shoes DM 100, a coat DM 330, cigarettes, food, taxi fares and telephone DM 100, and so on.

The group's total expenditure came to DM 58,230. Comparisons of handwriting told the police that Gudrun Ensslin was their treasurer.

Two days after the arrests, the remainder of the group met at the Kurfürstenstrasse apartment to discuss the situation.

Someone suggested getting hold of plans of the remand prison's sewer system, so as to bring Mahler out to freedom underground.

The inventive Eric, owner of the garage, had another idea. 'We could build a mini-helicopter. Then we land it in the prison yard at exercise time and fly our comrades out.'

The others laughed, but he meant his suggestion seriously.

'Look, I've got drawings. It really is possible. We take the engine and gearbox out of a Volkswagen 1500. We can get hold of the other parts and put them together bit by bit.'

And he actually set to work before the end of October. He had the engine and gearbox to hand. The framework was constructed by reference to a handbook of helicopter technology from East Berlin. He had got the idea from a similar mini-helicopter he had seen in an aviation museum on a trip to England.

The car mechanic drew up his diagrams and worked away at the structure.

* * *

When police officers were searching his workshop in the middle of February 1971, they came upon bits of the unfinished mini-helicopter. The puzzled policemen noted: 'The garage contained a structure consisting of an engine with its machine parts, from which we may conclude that it was an attempt to build a device whose drive was hinged at a right angle to the actual crankshaft. This room contained the half-completed skeleton of a construction similar to a wing. We also found a framework presumably meant to be the supporting structure of a cabin housing.'

The police officers photographed this unidentified flying object.

10
Hither and Thither Across West Germany

Ruhland set off from Berlin for West Germany in his Volkswagen minibus. He was to meet Ulrike Meinhof in Hanover on 1 November 1970. 'Anna', whom he had previously known only casually, was waiting for him on the first floor of the railway station restaurant, a cup of coffee in front of her. Her hair was cut short and dyed blonde. They set off together on a disorganized tour of the Federal Republic. In Cologne, Oldenburg and Hanover they visited old acquaintances of Ulrike's. Later, when Ruhland had made his statements to the police, these people were charged with aiding and abetting a criminal association.

Ulrike Meinhof and Karl-Heinz Ruhland continued their zigzag tour of the Republic. Ali Jansen was to provide them with identity papers in Oberhausen. They met Jansen at mid-day in the Rex 2 bar at the main railway station, among a crowd of cheerful drinkers. He was so drunk himself that he could hardly speak. Meinhof and Ruhland dragged him to their car and drove to Cologne. He had not got hold of any papers, and had squandered the money intended for the purpose.

The group had developed a complicated but very effective system of disguising stolen cars, known as the 'doubles method'. Later, the officers of the Federal Criminal Investigation Office reacted to it with surprise and professional appreciation.

It involved members of the group stationing themselves in car parks outside apartment blocks. As soon as a car of the desired type turned up, they followed the driver to his apartment. A few days later they rang his bell, equipped with identification from an opinion poll outfit, and asked for details of his vehicle. After that a new logbook was forged, containing all the relevant details: owner's name, date of first registration, licence number, make, colour. Then they went in search of another car which exactly fitted the same technical data. They stole this duplicate and gave it number plates identical with those of the first car they had picked out. Thus there were suddenly two cars of identical appearance and with identical number plates around. If the police stopped someone in one of these 'doubles' and checked up on him, inquiries put to the Federal Motor Licensing Bureau would elicit the information that such a car really was registered in the name of such and such a holder and had not been reported stolen.

Later, when the group found it too much effort to keep stealing cars, they generally hired vehicles and did them up.

By that time the group had simplified their system: they gave up the tedious practice of 'interviewing' a car owner to get hold of the data on his vehicle. Instead, they listened in to details reported on the police radio, and then forged papers for their 'doubles'.

On orders from Berlin, Meinhof, Ruhland and Jansen set out in the second week of November to investigate town halls in the foothills of the Harz mountains and in the Weser mountains. They wanted to find out which offices issuing passports and identity cards might be worth breaking into. The group was in urgent need of blank forms and official seals for the forging of passports and identification papers.

On the night of 15 November, Ruhland forced the back door of the town hall of Neustadt am Rübenberge with a screwdriver, and crept into the building with Ulrike and Ali. Suddenly he felt afraid. 'I left my gloves in the car,' he told the others in a whisper, and disappeared.

A few minutes later Ulrike Meinhof and Ali came out laden with blank passports and identity card forms, official seals and notepaper. They got safely back to their quarters at Polle. Ruhland did up a parcel of the forms stolen from Neustadt town hall and sent it to Berlin, to a Schöneberg address where Baader and Ensslin were living. However, Ulrike Meinhof had made a mistake in taking down the address – she had looked two lines too low in the postal code table – so the parcel ended up not in Berlin, but labelled 'Could Not Be Delivered' in the central parcels delivery office in Bamberg.

So the same operation was repeated a week later. This time the target was the town hall of Langgöns near Giessen. They found an unlocked steel cupboard in the mayor's office, crammed with blank identity card forms. By the light of a torch, they took the forms, along with official seals and a punch complete with its rivets for fixing passport photos in place.

Ruhland also discovered a bottle of brandy, which he instantly opened, and drank half of it.

A few days later, Jan-Carl Raspe arrived in Polle in a red Renault 16. He brought several radio transmitters to be fitted to the group's cars. From now on he joined the reconnaissance trips. The idea was for all the other members of the Berlin group to transfer by stages to West Germany.

11
Jan-Carl Raspe

Jan-Carl Raspe was born in 1944. His father, a businessman, died before his birth. He and his two elder sisters were brought up by their mother in an old house full of nooks and crannies in East Berlin. Two aunts completed the fatherless household. After going to primary school in East Berlin he was not accepted for secondary school there, since as a child of upper-middle-class origin he had not shown the requisite 'social commitment'. So the boy travelled daily by train over to West Berlin, where he attended the Bertha von Suttner High School. He sometimes stayed overnight with relations in West Berlin. When the Wall went up on 13 August 1961, Jan-Carl Raspe wrote to his mother on the other side of the city: 'I want to stay here anyway. I don't see any future in East Berlin.'

The seventeen-year-old stayed on with his uncle and aunt on the western side of the city, took his school-leaving examinations two years later, and then went to study at the Free University: chemistry first, changing to sociology after two terms.

Like many West Berlin students, he opposed the emergency powers acts and demonstrated against the Shah's visit. He was one of those whose lives were changed by 2 June 1967 and the death of Benno Ohnesorg, killed by a bullet from a policeman's service pistol. He became a member of the SDS.

In August 1967 he was among the founders of a commune known as Commune 2. Four men, three women and two children went to live in a large apartment in an old building, hoping to change themselves so that they could then change society. They recorded details of their way of life, their conversations and their thoughts, and published this account of their experience in book form.

Raspe left Commune 2, took his sociology diploma, achieving a grade of 'Very good', and later moved into a small apartment in the Kurfürstenstrasse with his girlfriend Marianne.

Marianne was friendly with Ulrike Meinhof. After the group's return from Jordan, the apartment became one of their safe houses, and in the autumn of 1970 Jan-Carl Raspe and Marianne were participating in the group's operations as well as providing shelter.

12
A Police Check

The Renault 16 which Raspe had brought from Berlin had been left in a car park in the village of Heinsen. Ruhland and Ulrike Meinhof drove there to pick the car up. Just as Ulrike was about to get into the red Renault a police patrol car appeared. The officer in charge of the patrol had had his eye on the car for a couple of days. He approached Ulrike Meinhof. She showed him a passport, a driving licence in the name of Sabine M., and the car logbook, which stated that the holder of the vehicle was one Wolfgang B. of Berlin.

'You borrowed the car from him, did you?' asked the police officer.

'No, I don't know him. I got the car from a man whose name I'd rather not mention, for private reasons. I left it here. I only wanted to get something out of it. The car's staying where it is. I've come from Hameln with my friend there, and we're going on to Holzminden.'

She indicated Ruhland. The policeman thought she seemed unsure of herself and looked unkempt.

'I'll have to check what you say,' he told her.

'You can take the car key and the papers. There's something I want to do in Holzminden, and then I'll be back.'

The officer leafed through the papers, undecided. 'You're a teacher in Suhlendorf?'

'Yes,' said Ulrike Meinhof, 'but I've not been there for some time, while I was ill.'

'I see you've been to the GDR quite often?'

'Yes, visiting friends.'

The police officer asked her to get into his car while he checked up. He called back to headquarters on his radio and gave the teacher's name. Meanwhile Ulrike Meinhof was trying to get out of the patrol car.

'I'm just going for a little walk,' she said.

'Stay here, please.' But Ulrike Meinhof got the door open and ran in the direction of the main road, where Ruhland was waiting for her.

The police officer and his colleagues gave chase and caught her. Between them, they got Ulrike Meinhof back to their car. Half an hour later a message came over the radio: nothing was known against Sabine M., and the car had not been reported stolen.

The policemen searched the red Renault, but could find nothing suspicious. So they let Ulrike Meinhof go. She got into the other car with Ruhland.

The police officers noted his appearance, and said later in evidence that 'the driver was a man around forty, about 170 cm tall, with thinning red hair combed back'.

Ruhland was not wanted by the police at the time. However, Ulrike Meinhof's picture and description were pinned up in every police station in the country. It had taken them an hour to check her personal details.

13
'A Certain Psychological Disposition'

Some new members had joined the group in Berlin: Holger Meins, a student at the Berlin Film Academy, and Beate Sturm and Ulrich Scholze, both studying physics.

Beate Sturm was nineteen years old. She came from Leverkusen, and her father was a physicist with Bayer.

After taking her school-leaving examinations she enrolled in the department of physics at the Free University of Berlin. She could not understand the lectures, wandered aimlessly around the university, and soon joined a group of other students struggling with freshmen's difficulties similar to her own. Berlin was a shock to her, with its old buildings, asphalt backyards, piles of coal and refuse, rats with children playing among them. 'It simply makes you feel furious,' she said later. 'You don't just feel sorry, no, you feel real blind rage. That was the feeling in Berlin then: smash the thing that's smashing you.' In the autumn of 1969, Beate Sturm met Holger Meins, studying at the Film Academy; he always carried books around with him. She once saw him with four volumes of the works of Chairman Mao. He had underlined the great man's pithy sayings on almost every page.

Holger Meins was born in 1941. When he had taken his school-leaving examinations in Hamburg he went to the College of Art, and changed to the Film Academy in Berlin in the mid-sixties. He was quiet, shy, and inclined to depression. He was active in the student movement with his film camera, and was co-director of a documentary film about the Shah's visit in June, 1967. Two years later he made a short film about the making and use of Molotov cocktails, which got an enthusiastic reception from the students in the main lecture hall of the Free University.

Shortly after the freeing of Baader, Meins's apartment was searched by the police. He reached for the phone to call a lawyer. A police officer put a pistol to his forehead.

The police were raiding apartments more and more frequently now, and they were armed more heavily, with submachine guns. 'Out of bed!

Hands up!' That was how it felt to Holger Meins. Before long he joined the Baader–Meinhof group.

At the end of October he invited Beate Sturm to a political discussion in Kulmbacher Strasse. 'I want you to meet two interesting people.'

Holger Meins took her to an apartment furnished only with mattresses. After some time Ulrich Scholze, introduced to her as 'Ulli', turned up, and so did a man called 'Hans'. Hans began a cautious conversation. He said this was a group in the mould of the urban guerrillas of Latin America. Beate Sturm felt that Hans was trying to recruit her. She was impressed by him.

'So what would you like to know exactly?' Baader asked her. 'Something about the background, or how to break into cars?'

'How exactly to break into cars,' replied Beate Sturm, and Baader explained how to short-circuit the ignition. Beate got the impression that he was glad not to have to talk about politics.

'So Baader managed it that our heroic political notions went right out of the window, and there we were, right in the middle of a thriller,' Beate Sturm recollected later. 'We didn't really ask ourselves what we were actually looking for any more. You just slip into that sort of thing. And as we thought we knew we'd got into all this for the correct political reasons, we liked the thrill of it too.'

By the middle of November Beate Sturm was ready to take the plunge and go underground. She had hardly thought of the consequences. She hoped she could take her studies up again some day. She certainly did not want to lose touch entirely with her parents and the rest of the family.

On 6 December, there was another meeting in the Kulmbacher Strasse apartment. Andreas Baader, Holger Meins, a girl called 'Prinz' (Petra Schelm) and Ulrich Scholze were already there, on the mattresses. Baader seemed to be in a hectic, nervous state. 'Things are too hot for us in Berlin,' he said. 'We'll carry on the work in the Federal Republic, build up an organization there.' They would need to get hold of cars and car logbooks and money, he said. And they must mount attacks to bring the group's political struggle to the notice of the public.

'You'll go to West Germany in two groups,' Baader said. 'Beate and Holger go to Frankfurt, separately, and Teeny and Ulli go to Nuremberg.' Ilse S., known as Teeny, was only sixteen, the youngest of the group.

Meins gave Beate Sturm an envelope containing money, about DM 3,000. 'You can buy your air ticket out of that,' he told her. 'This is a bit too sudden for me,' she said. 'I really wanted to go home and see my parents at Christmas.' Meins soothed her. 'You'll be back long before Christmas.' He paused, and then added, rather more sharply, 'It's either tomorrow or not at all.'

Next morning Beate Sturm flew to Frankfurt. She waited for Holger Meins in the Aschinger restaurant, opposite the main railway station. He arrived from Berlin by car two hours later. They drove to a West End park together.

Meins stuck a copy of *Time* magazine under his arm and went to a phone booth, where he was to meet 'Anna', whom he had never seen before. Beate Sturm was to wait for him in a café. After a while he came back with Ulrike Meinhof.

They drove to the B. family's apartment, where Beate met some new comrades: 'Fred', otherwise Jan-Carl Raspe, and 'Kalle', Karl-Heinz Ruhland.

'Did you bring me any money from Berlin?' asked Ulrike Meinhof.

Beate Sturm gave her the envelope.

Meanwhile Ulli and Teeny had been reconnoitring banks in Nuremberg.

Ulrich Scholze had joined the group the same day as Beate Sturm. He was twenty-three, and a tutor in the physics department at the Free University.

He knew from his own experience how easy it was for the group to recruit new members at that time. 'A certain psychological disposition is a pre-condition of joining,' he said after his arrest. 'You have to be emotionally convinced that all attempts at reform simply stabilize the present system of society and consolidate capitalism. And the harmony of reason and emotions which then exists is the pre-condition of resolute action. Then the prosecuting authorities put pressure on you, and that confirms all you thought. And the sensational press reports and descriptions such as "Public Enemy Number 1" from government sources create a feeling of success that gives you the strength to carry on.'

You slip outside the law very fast, he said. First an interested party is asked to find an apartment, then he may help with a car theft, and it's not far from that to a bank raid.

Scholze got to know Baader as an 'intelligent, quick-witted man' who 'could weigh up a situation realistically and had great mental reserves'. But he was inclined to keep yelling at other people. Gudrun Ensslin, his lover in their underground existence, was not as impatient as Baader in discussions. Scholze thought Ulrike had the worst nerves of any of them, and was easily upset. She was extremely nervous and kept rubbing her right thumb, forefinger and middle finger together. As she did this, she would often roll torn-off scraps of paper into balls which she left lying about everywhere.

Later on, when other witnesses too had mentioned this habit to the police, they systematically searched 'illegal' apartments for similar little paper balls.

Andreas Baader and Gudrun Ensslin were now on their way to West Germany too. Ruhland and Ulrike Meinhof met them at Frankfurt main railway station.

Baader's hair, originally long and dark, was now short and very fair, almost white. He wore rimless glasses. Gudrun Ensslin had dyed her short hair dark. On the station platform, they arranged to meet and discuss operations.

14
Strategic Discussion in the Sanatorium

The later political manifestos of the group harped on 'the primacy of praxis'. 'Whether it is right to organize armed resistance now depends on whether it is possible.' That could be ascertained only in practice.

In their life outside the law, the 'primacy of praxis' became a commonplace reality. Apartments were requisitioned, cars stolen, sources of money found – i.e. banks raided. The organization of daily life underground was increasingly replacing political discussion. They were on the run, a fact which determined the group's life more than any strategic notions of their aims.

Jan-Carl Raspe had been staying with an old friend of Ulrike's, the daughter of a well-known psychoanalyst. When he left she gave him a picture postcard showing a building that had once been a sanatorium in Bad Kissingen. She wrote on the back that the bearer of the card could use the building. It was empty and rather dilapidated, used only for a few weeks in summer as a holiday base for children from one of the left-wing children's groups known as 'Kinderläden' (children's shops, so called because the first of them were started in empty shops in Berlin).

On the afternoon of 14 December Ruhland and Astrid Proll drove to Bad Kissingen, where they bought oil stoves, lamps and electric cable. Next day Baader, Ensslin, Jansen, Raspe and his former girlfriend Marianne arrived at the sanatorium. Meinhof, Meins and Sturm joined them late that evening.

They discussed future operations. It all struck Beate Sturm as nonsense. She had never known the group except on the run; its members felt they were constantly under observation, being pursued, they had changed their quarters at frequent intervals and never met without taking great precautions. She thought it absurd to be talking, at this point, of such grandiose projects as kidnappings.

Baader demanded action. Perhaps they could kidnap the newspaper publisher Axel Springer and thus bring pressure to bear to get the prisoners in Berlin freed.

'How about Franz Josef Strauss?'

'Nobody would want to see him back.' Everyone laughed.

Someone mentioned Willy Brandt. 'He often goes for walks in the evening in Bonn on his own, or just with one guard.'

There was no support for this idea. Kidnapping the Social Democrat chancellor could only help the Christian Democrats.

Their debate on strategy was getting nowhere. The group set about making concrete plans for further bank raids. This was an aim within their grasp; also, funds were running short. As usual Gudrun Ensslin was treasurer. Each member of the group got what he needed; life outside the law was expensive.

The meetings in the old sanatorium were unplanned and disorganized. The building was neglected, furniture almost entirely lacking. Ruhland had installed oil stoves in three rooms; the rest remained uninhabitable.

After a few days they had all had enough of each other's close proximity in this inhospitable refuge, and set out again to prepare for bank raids in the Ruhr.

15
Homesickness and Arrests

Kalle Ruhland and Beate Sturm set off in a Mercedes. Kalle told Beate about his family. She already knew, from Ulrike Meinhof, that his wife had leukaemia. Her illness had landed him in grave financial difficulties, said Ruhland. He had a police record and he had lost custody of his children. Beate Sturm remembered Ulrike telling her Ruhland was 'a victim of the system'.

As they approached Leverkusen, Beate said, 'That's where my parents live.'

'We could just drive past,' suggested Ruhland.

They drove slowly past the plot with the Sturms' modern house on it, and Beate Sturm got a brief glimpse over the fence. Then Ruhland stepped on the gas again. They knew this little excursion was against conspiratorial rules, but Kalle calmed the girl's fears. 'This is just between ourselves.'

Towards 10 p.m. they reached Oberhausen, where they were to meet Ali in the Rex 2 bar. The place was closed, so they knocked at the door. After a while Ali Jansen, who was friendly with the proprietor, came out and sat in the car with them. He was drunk. Ruhland remonstrated with him.

They drove through Oberhausen looking at the vehicles Ali had picked out to steal. The cars suited Ruhland's notions too. The men wanted to set to work that night; all they needed was the necessary tools.

'I know someone who can get hold of them,' said Ali. They drove back to the Rex 2. There were four or five customers still sitting in the bar. Ali brought a young man out, and Ruhland drove at high speed to his apartment in a suburb of Oberhausen. Suddenly a police patrol car appeared and settled down on the trail of the Mercedes. Ruhland tried to shake the pursuer off, but the policemen kept close behind him, and eventually overtook and flagged down the car.

Ruhland had to show them his papers. They were in his own name, but forged. The officers told him to come over to the police car while they checked the papers. As he got out, Ruhland whispered to the others, 'Clear off!' No sooner were he and the policemen a little way away than Beate Sturm, Ali and Ali's friend disappeared into the darkness.

Ruhland got into the patrol car. The police officers had been quick to realize there was something wrong about his papers. 'You'll have to come with us.' Ruhland took his loaded pistol with its safety catch off out of his belt and gave it to the policemen. They arrested him.

It was not long before he began to talk.

Ali had watched the arrest from a distance. Beate and Ali's friend had taken a taxi back to the city centre. Beate Sturm rang the Frankfurt apartment from a telephone booth. Gudrun Ensslin answered. Breathlessly, Beate told her what had happened. 'And I've only got four marks on me. What shall I do?'

Gudrun fetched Baader to the phone. 'Borrow some money from Ali's friend and go to Gelsenkirchen.' The group had a hideout there.

Early next morning, Ulrike Meinhof and Jan-Carl Raspe turned up. They too had run into a police patrol the previous night. 'When the cops were checking our papers I suddenly had my doubts,' said Ulrike Meinhof. While the policemen were checking her personal details over the radio, she suddenly stepped on the gas and drove off, leaving her papers in police hands. Thus the authorities acquired a new photograph for a Wanted poster, showing Ulrike Meinhof with short blonde hair.

Beate Sturm was exhausted, overtired and desperate. The arrest of Karl-Heinz Ruhland had affected her a good deal. She liked Kalle and Ali; you could go around and have a laugh with them. She was unhappy to hear the two of them criticized by the group: 'One always drunk, and the other will never really be a cadre.'

She had noticed a similar attitude towards the people who gave them shelter. 'Either they were politically active anyway, in Baader's sense of the word, or they were regarded as stupid, so then you needn't consider their feelings.'

She was having more and more misgivings. She spent the night with a friend in Cologne, a man who had nothing to do with the group. Next day, 21 December, he took her to Frankfurt. She met Andreas, Gudrun, Holger, Marianne, Ulrike and Teeny in the writer Michael Schulte's apartment.

They had given up the idea of bank raids in the Ruhr. They were going to try Nuremberg instead. Uli Scholze and Astrid Proll had already gone on ahead.

Baader had a low opinion of Scholze. When he showed Scholze how to use a Kalashnikov submachine gun, Scholze had accused him of irresponsibly getting group members to break the law. Baader reacted furiously. 'You can't half-heartedly take part in the group's illegal life and then go back within the law again.'

The others thought Baader was quite right. 'It's no good raiding a bank one day and going back to studying for your diploma the next,' said Beate Sturm.

They all met again in Nuremberg. Late at night, Ulrich Scholze and Astrid Proll drove to Watzmannstrasse, where Ulrike Meinhof and Ali Jansen were waiting. They had picked out a Mercedes. They managed to break into it and short-circuit the ignition, but the car refused to start, backfiring. The sudden noise woke its owner. He called the police, opened his window and shouted for help.

Alarmed, Ali jumped out of the car and ran to their own light-coloured Ford. Ulrike Meinhof ran to their other car, a BMW, which Astrid Proll started immediately, and both cars raced away. The two women turned into the car park of the Esso Hotel, the men drove straight on. They stopped just before they reached the Meistersinger Hall and got out. Ulrich Scholze was about to lock the car door when a Volkswagen drew up beside them. Two police officers in plain clothes asked for their papers. Scholze gave them his genuine driving licence. 'Somebody's been breaking into a car in Watzmannstrasse,' said one of the officers. 'Come with us, please; we'll have to let the vehicle's owner take a look at you.' At that moment a patrol car, alerted by radio, came up. Ali and Ulli were told to get into the two police cars, one of them into each. Ulli got into the Volkswagen with the plainclothes men and was driven off.

The uniformed men took Ali Jansen, who had produced a forged identity card, to the patrol car standing a little way off. One of the officers frisked him for weapons. Ali opened his coat, flicked it backwards, and swiftly reached for a pistol. The officers grabbed his wrist and tried to get the gun away from him. Jansen struggled, shouting, 'Get away, let go of me or I'll shoot.' He had his index finger on the trigger and was swinging the barrel to point first at one policeman and then at the other. One of them called to his colleague, 'Run for it!' The officer ran, weaving back and forth, and flung himself to the ground ten or fifteen metres away. His colleague dived into a bush for cover. Ali Jansen fired wildly at random and then jumped into the police car. When he tried to start the engine the policemen began shooting too. 'Stop!' called Jansen.

He got himself across the passenger seat and out of the patrol car, putting his hands up. His pistol was in his right hand.

'Throw the gun away!'

Jansen flung the Firebird away, and the policemen tackled him. They slipped; the ground was slippery with snow. Jansen's nose began bleeding.

One of the officers knelt on him while the other got handcuffs from the patrol car. Ali was taken to the CID office, where he was stripped and his clothing searched.

Later, at his trial, the judge said, 'The possibility that the defendant was assaulted cannot be ruled out.' In 1973, Ali Jansen was sentenced to ten years' imprisonment for attempted murder.

The police had found a forged identity card on Ulrich Scholze. He was arrested, but freed again next day. He went home to his mother. He had had enough of his brief adventure with the Baader–Meinhof group, and made no further contact with the rest of them.

But the others went on. Life underground was a strain. 'It was always like this: you were somewhere or other, then something or other happened and you had to move everything, go to some totally different place,' Astrid Proll remembered. Once, when she had almost been arrested in Frankfurt, she lapsed into a deep psychological low: 'I'd done everything wrong again, or maybe we'd all done something wrong to get us into this situation in the first place.' As usual on the German Left, members of the RAF were always criticizing each other. 'Instead of supporting people when they need help, they slag you off worse than ever. That's how it was in the group.' As a good driver, Astrid Proll was frequently with the others when they went into action. 'I often sat in the car as they checked out banks and so forth.'

Once, just before Christmas, she was out with Ulrike Meinhof. It was night, and Ulrike suddenly said, 'I'm fed up with this. All this hanging around, acting as look-out, checking out cars. I don't want to end up in jail for that kind of thing, not any more, not for such petty details.' Astrid felt the same. But the group wouldn't tolerate any discussion. Now that they had gone underground, the authority of the two leaders, Baader and Ensslin, was even more powerful than before. Astrid was glad when she had 'a job to do, some kind of project that I could carry out myself'.

16
The Christmas Crisis

They met on Boxing Day 1970 in Stuttgart: Andreas Baader, Gudrun Ensslin, Ulrike Meinhof, Jan-Carl Raspe, Holger Meins, Marianne, Beate and Teeny. After little more than six months underground, more members of the group had been arrested than were now gathered here. Their mood was subdued. Ulrike Meinhof was critical. Recent events, various arrests and accidents, she said, could be put down to the incorrect conduct of the group as a whole and mistaken overall planning. Baader protested, 'No, it's individual failure.' He wanted them to carry on along the same lines as before. 'We must plan better, be more circumspect,' Ulrike Meinhof insisted. Baader felt she was attacking him. 'We ought to take more precautions,' Ulrike said. 'We can't just go into a strange town and start operating without getting to know our way around.' Baader lost his temper. 'When we act it has to be fast, very fast. The failures are due to individual bungling. It's nothing to do with overall planning.' The argument became more heated, went round in circles. 'Now that we're all together,' said Ulrike Meinhof, 'we might as well try discussing the whole thing. If we're not getting anywhere, then we must have made mistakes.'

'Well, of course there've been mistakes. But made by individuals, not the group. So it's individuals and not the group who have to change,' replied Baader, his voice rising. Ulrike Meinhof's own voice rose. 'All this disorganized running about, chasing hither and thither – if things don't work out here, let's move on to the next town. We never stopped to think why something went wrong.'

'You cunts!' yelled Baader. 'Shouting at your menfolk, that's all your liberation amounts to.' Suddenly there was silence. Quite calmly, Gudrun Ensslin said, 'Baby, you haven't got a clue.'

Words failed Baader. Astrid Proll tried to intervene, but by now she was as good as a red rag to Baader anyway. The rest sat there in silence, horrified. Marianne broke this painful silence. 'Listen,' she told Baader, 'I can stand a lot, oh yes, I can take a great deal, but I am not going along with that, I simply will not stand for that. Why can't you talk to Ulrike objectively?'

'Anyone who's in this group,' said Baader, 'just has to be tough. Has to be able to take things. If you're not tough enough then you've no business here. Our aggression gets bottled up, with the pressures of living outside the law – it has to come out, we can't take it out on the outside world just because we're living underground, so we have to take it out on the group, and then of course we fight; we have to be able to handle that, we have to be tough enough for that.'

They talked for several hours. Finally Andreas Baader carried the day. New jobs were allocated.

This was the training phase of urban guerrilla warfare. No one could guess that the RAF would keep the country on edge for decades. The underground battle was developing its own dynamic.

It was never the group as a whole that determined the course of events, it was Baader and Ensslin.

Astrid Proll remembers: 'Of course people were afraid – afraid of being arrested, or they didn't feel happy under group pressure – but that kind of thing was never discussed. We were afraid of discussion; it seemed like treachery. And we tried fending off danger by involving ourselves in it more and more.'

Illegality became an end in itself, the means of holding the group together.

Before they left Nuremberg, Beate Sturm had called Leverkusen to find out how her parents had spent Christmas. Her mother was worried. 'The police were here, asking about you. They found a letter from you on someone who shot at them.'

Beate went to Kassel with the others to look for suitable savings banks to raid. As she went around town she thought about her situation. She was not experienced enough as a driver to be at the wheel of a getaway car. On the other hand, the group thought her too feeble to grab the money from the bank counter. She saw herself landed with the job of standing in a bank, gun in hand. In her imagination, she went over what might happen.

It only needed one person to get nervous and there would be shooting. She could not, would not get accustomed to that idea. It wouldn't be the class enemy that got hurt, she thought, just ordinary people in the shape of bank employees. The various mistakes and gaps in the whole ideological, theoretical concept kept going through her head.

The episode in Stuttgart, Baader's quarrel with Ulrike, had been the last straw. She was sick of it all. She had been feeling really emancipated, because there were some things women could simply do better than men, on account of being stronger, braver, less quarrelsome. But the differences in status had bothered her. She thought of Stuttgart, where they had stayed in various apartments. But who stayed where? One apartment had a bathroom, and it was clear as day that Andreas and Gudrun would get that one. Someone asked why. That particular apartment didn't come up to Baader's security standards, did it? Because it had a bathroom, that was why. So how come, asked the questioner, how come Andreas gets a bathroom and we don't?

That was clear as day too: he had been in jail. He couldn't be expected to do without, was the general feeling, not when he'd suffered so much in jail: he must always have a bathroom.

Beate had been unable to understand Andreas. She could make nothing of his fits of rage; she thought them pointless. You could only yell back at him.

Then, in Kassel, it finally got too much for her. A car wouldn't start. She pushed it; the engine still refused to catch. Fed up, she went to bed. Ulrike woke her in the middle of the night. She talked to Beate for four hours, and concluded that she lacked political motivation. Beate Sturm felt that Ulrike was going to repeat that eighty times over. 'Now, tell me!' Ulrike demanded. 'Go on, say something! You must surely be able to tell me – is the political motivation there or isn't it?'

'I can't say; I don't know,' replied Beate, but Ulrike wanted a straight yes or no.

'Think about it,' she said. And then everything was clear to Beate.

A few days later, when the others had gone to Frankfurt to break into some cars and steal them for bank raids, Beate Sturm called her parents in Leverkusen.

'I'm coming home,' she said, and burst into tears.

'Do that,' said her mother.

On 15 January 1971 two banks in Kassel were raided, both branches of the local savings bank, one in the Akademiestrasse and one in the Kirchweg. At 9.30 a.m. five group members drove up to the Akademiestrasse branch in a Mercedes they had stolen in Göttingen. One man stayed in the car, the rest of them entered the bank. They were all dressed in identical dark clothing and had balaclavas showing only their eyes pulled down over their faces.

'This is a raid!' one of them shouted. 'Hands up and keep still, and you won't be harmed!' They fired two warning shots. The loot came to 54,185 Deutschmarks. At the same time, a BMW 2000 stolen in Frankfurt stopped outside the Kirchweg branch of the savings bank. The second team, also disguised by dark balaclavas, rushed into the bank. 'This is a raid! Don't move! Hands up!' they cried. One of them jumped over the counter and stuffed DM 60,530 into his pocket.

Gudrun Esslin sent two parcels of money to the group's Stuttgart apartments that same day, and a third parcel followed a week later.

17
The Family Cop

Alfred Klaus is a tall, slim man, who smiles a lot and is extremely courteous. He dresses with casual elegance and usually wears a thin silk cravat at his throat. Alfred Klaus is a friendly soul whose blue eyes beam at you as you talk to him. When he goes visiting, especially if he is calling on ladies, he frequently takes flowers.

At the end of the year 1970 Alfred Klaus had just been equipping new offices in an annexe of the Bonn Security Group of the Federal Criminal Investigation Office with new furniture, house plants, the works. He was departmental head, with twelve employees answerable to him. Alfred Klaus and his subordinates were working on the murder of an exiled Algerian politician when he had a phone call in his new offices.

'Come on down,' said his caller. 'We've got to set up a Special Commission.'

It was a matter of countering terrorism. Hitherto, the local police authorities and the regional Criminal Investigation Offices of the various *Länder* had been responsible for tracking down the Baader–Meinhof group. A dozen or so group members had been arrested since Baader was sprung from custody in May of 1970, but the leaders – Baader, Ensslin and Meinhof – were still at large. Now Federal Interior Minister Hans Dietrich Genscher had persuaded the *Land* interior ministers, insistent as they were on their autonomy, to agree to transferring the headquarters of the investigation to the Federal Criminal Investigation Office (the Bundeskriminalamt, BKA for short) in Wiesbaden.

Alfred Klaus, in the opinion of his superiors, was the man to play a decisive part in setting up a Special Commission on Terrorism. Even in the fifties, he had concerned himself with political crimes – or what were then taken for political crimes. He had investigated the banned KPD, the Communist Party of Germany, and had turned his professional attention to its ideological background and the theory and practice of Marxism.

Klaus and his colleagues moved into a suite of offices in the Bonn Security Group building, and took delivery of three large cartons full of files, mainly from Berlin – from the police Political Department, or State Security.

First of all Alfred Klaus wanted to discover, for himself and the BKA, just what kind of people had been making the headlines throughout 1970. He also wanted to know what political aims and intentions lay behind their actions. He began work on 1 February 1971, going through the Berlin files and filtering out what information he could find on the 'Baader–Meinhof complex', as it soon, with unintentional ambiguity, became known in the department.

His preliminary report was ready on 19 February. It ran to sixty-one pages, covering the history of the group from the trial of the department stores arsonists to the bank raids in Kassel.

In a separate section, he sketched in the 'Ideological Background':

'The motives for the crimes perpetrated by these people, and the revolutionary aims they pursue, have their origin in the social conflicts of recent years, set off by the anti-authoritarian student movement and other forces of the APO.'

Klaus had worked his way through stacks of books, periodicals, leaflets, pamphlets. It was his view that the police hunting the gang would succeed only if they had a real understanding of their quarry's mentality.

In April 1971 he toured the Federal Republic, visiting the gang's families. He talked to Andreas Baader's mother, Gudrun Ensslin's parents, Ulrike Meinhof's foster mother Renate Riemeck, the fathers of Astrid Proll and Holger Meins, and Manfred Grashof's parents. He wanted to know what kind of characters the police were dealing with, not because he thought the families would turn their children in, but in the vague hope that should there be any contact they might influence those children to 'desist from such dangerous mischief'.

Almost everywhere, Alfred Klaus met with a friendly reception. He drank red wine with Baader's mother and grandmother, and learned a great deal about the development of 'Andi'. He made notes about these conversations for the files. His reports later formed the basis of the BKA's personal files on the wanted men and women, known in official jargon as 'personagrams'.

Klaus was soon regarded within the department as a specialist on the group's personal and political backgrounds. He gave lectures and tried to explain the group's motives and the way its members' minds worked to police officers who regarded them simply as ordinary criminals. He himself became more and more fascinated by the subjects of his investigation. He was impressed by their absolute commitment, their fearlessness and their disregard for their own safety.

An entirely new picture of criminality presented itself to Alfred Klaus. These were 'criminal personalities' such as the police had never encountered before. They were intelligent and ready to do anything without thought for their own lives. This was something to which the police would have to adjust.

Klaus had the impression that in fact the police were better at adjusting than the judiciary; many a judge had declined promotion in order to avoid presiding over a criminal court that had to deal with terrorists.

The Special Section of the Bonn Security Group, to which Klaus belonged, now had prime responsibility for hunting down the terrorists. Officers from the Criminal Investigation Offices of the separate *Länder* were sent to Bad Godesberg for periods of some months to get on-the-spot training for the operation. This also helped the development of personal contacts, making quick communication possible between the Federal BKA and the Criminal Investigation Offices of the *Länder*. Federal Interior Minister Genscher put his faith in the Federal Criminal Investigation Office as a clearing house for the fight against crime. It had a budget of DM 24.8 million in 1969. This budget was increased by a third in 1970, to 36.8 million. It was to rise by another DM 20 million in each of the next two years. Over the same period, the Wiesbaden staff of 934 in early 1970 would almost double, rising to 1770 in 1972.

In addition, the *Länder* set up their own Special Commissions to fight terrorism.

Alfred Klaus remained responsible for information on the group's backgrounds, ideology and family relationships. Later, it was also his job to interview members of the group who were in custody. He tried to get them talking to him. Before long he was calling himself 'the family cop'.

The fight against terrorism became virtually the main business of life to him. He read and re-read the political manifestos of the group as they appeared, trying to impress upon his colleagues that they must not ignore political motivation. Many officers were not amenable to such ideas, and made comments along the lines of, 'You're the Red Army Faction's chief ideologist; you're the one who tells them what they're after.'

18
A Shoot-out in the West End and Its Consequences

On 10 February 1971, the Counter-Intelligence man Michael Grünhagen was sitting in the Schultheiss am West End restaurant in Frankfurt with a cup of soup in front of him. He had already paid for it.

When a young man and a girl from the next table left the restaurant, Grünhagen followed them. Thereupon Detective Chief Superintendent Heinz Simons of the Bonn Security Group got out of a car parked outside the Schultheiss and followed Grünhagen. Before reaching the nearby Staufenstrasse the quartet, its members still keeping their distance from each other, turned into the Unterlindau. The man and the woman hesitated outside Number 28 Unterlindau, looked back, and then hurried on.

Grünhagen and Simons closed in. A short time later they stopped the couple, saying they wanted to check their papers. It was then 10.15 p.m. Thereupon, as Simons remembered it later, the young man drew a pistol and shouted to his companion, 'Get out, run for it!' Simons fired his pistol after the fugitives. Nobody was injured. The couple escaped. They were Manfred Grashof and Astrid Proll.

Grashof had not fired his gun. Astrid Proll was unarmed.

Grashof ran away across a building site and mingled with passers-by. A little later he spoke to a young man, telling him what had happened. This man steered Grashof out of the danger zone and bought him an underground train ticket when they parted company.

The shooting in the Unterlindau was the main charge against Astrid Proll over two and a half years later. She was charged with attempted murder of the police officers by firing a gun at them. Even during her first trial there were some doubts of the two officers' credibility: their accounts of the incident differed too widely. But it was not until Proll's second trial – in the meantime she had been released from jail for health reasons, had absconded and got away to England, where, however, she was re-arrested – that the charge of attempted murder was dropped. For there had been other officers at the scene of the crime, Federal Counter-Intelligence men. They had filed a memo stating that Astrid Proll did not shoot. This memo, which cleared her, was not produced in court until eight years after the incident.

After the shoot-out in Frankfurt's West End, the first big nationwide hunt was on. The apartments Ruhland had named were searched, people who had sheltered the terrorists were arrested and questioned. The press got in on the act; details from the interrogation of Karl-Heinz Ruhland were going around torn out of context, distorted or exaggerated. The *Hamburger Morgenpost* wrote: 'By now the hunt for the members of the gang seems to be developing into a kind of hysteria. In the last few days the police have been alerted by a dozen or so erroneous reports, which have kept officers all over the Federal Republic busy.'

A landlord in the village of Wiershausen, near Münden in Hanover, thought he had seen Ulrike Meinhof and Manfred Grashof in his pub. A couple fitting their description had come into the pub and ordered something to drink. When they saw a newspaper with the Wanted pictures of the Baader–Meinhof group lying on the bar, said the landlord, they had paid at once and driven off at speed in their car, without switching the lights on first. The police were alerted at once, but their hunt for the couple was unsuccessful.

In Bremen, the staff of a hotel at the main station thought they had recognized one of their guests as Ulrike Meinhof. She was really a woman from Bonn who suffered from nervous illness. When she heard that she was suspected of being the Baader–Meinhof gang leader she tried to run for it. The police caught and arrested her. The woman vigorously denied that she was Ulrike Meinhof. She was taken away in handcuffs, and the mistake was not cleared up until two hours later, when she had been fingerprinted.

Ruhland's statements about those middle-class people who had sheltered the group provided the popular press with headlines day after day.

Bild: 'BAADER GANG BLACKMAILS THE PROMINENT'.

Die Welt: 'SYMPATHIZERS HAMPER HUNT FOR BAADER GROUP'.

Hamburger Abendblatt: 'CELEBRITIES PROTECT BAADER GANG'.

Bild: 'PASTOR HID BAADER GANG'S LOOT'.

The hunt for the terrorists became the dominant theme of domestic politics. The *Welt am Sonntag* reduced it to a formula: 'BONN SECRET POLICE HUNT PUBLIC ENEMY NUMBER 1: THE BAADER GANG'.

Journalists, politicians, police officers, psychologists and philosophers set to work to analyse the Baader–Meinhof phenomenon.

Günter Nollau, then in the Federal Interior Ministry and later President of the Federal Office for the Protection of the Constitution, saw 'something irrational about the whole thing'. He noticed the fact 'that so many girls are involved', and had an explanation ready to hand. 'This could be one of the excesses of Women's Lib.'

The Frankfurt philosopher Alfred Schmidt held the view that 'it is an historical relic of the subsiding protest movement. These people stand firm on principles of revolution, while others move on to the ordinary business of the day. It is like hearing 20,000 people shout "Goal!" when a goal is scored in a football match, and one man goes on shouting two minutes longer than the rest, whereupon they all turn round and think, "What a curious fellow!"'

19
A Christening Ceremony: The 'Red Army Faction'

The small company now travelling around the country was still known to the public as the Baader–Meinhof group or the Baader–Meinhof gang, according to one's political standpoint. Since the freeing of Baader, and the interview with Michèle Ray, the group had ceased to express itself theoretically and in writing.

Early in 1971 Horst Mahler wrote a 'Statement of Position' in his prison cell, trying to define the aims of the urban guerrilla. This paper was published, camouflaged under the title of *New Traffic Regulations*, and was later reissued by the Berlin publishing house of Klaus Wagenbach. Mahler had not checked out the contents of his paper with the comrades still operating at large. When the concept of their struggle as expounded by him came into the hands of Baader, Ensslin and

Meinhof, they were indignant. 'It has nothing whatever to do with us. As a concept of guerrilla action it's as inflated as a game of cowboys and Indians.'

Whenever they met helpers and sympathizers, they dissociated themselves from Mahler's reflections on strategy. Ulrike Meinhof was given the job of producing a manifesto of their own, with a view to the correct self-presentation of the group. It was called *The Urban Guerrilla Concept*, and contained the first use of the phrase 'Red Army Faction'.

The title page bore the emblem of a submachine gun, with the abbreviation RAF above it. The name and the emblem soon became the group's trademarks.

But it was not the Kalashnikov, the Russian submachine gun, the weapon of all the liberation movements in the world, that served as the RAF's emblem; it was a German Heckler & Koch. The revolutionaries had slipped up.

Page 1 of *The Urban Guerrilla Concept* quoted Mao: 'If the enemy fights us, that is good, not bad.' And further: 'If the enemy opposes us vigorously, paints us in the blackest colours, and will allow us no good points, that is even better; it shows that not only have we drawn a clear dividing line between ourselves and the enemy, our work has also proved brilliantly successful.'

'Many comrades,' wrote Ulrike Meinhof, 'are spreading lies about us. They make capital out of the fact that we stayed in their homes, they organized our journey to the Middle East, they knew about contacts and apartments, they say they did something for us, although they are doing nothing. Some of them just want to show that they are "in". Some are trying to prove that we are foolish, unreliable, incautious, burnt out. Thereby, they prejudice others against us. In reality, they are only judging us by themselves. They are consumers.

'We have nothing to do with these chatterers, for whom the anti-imperialist fight is conducted at coffee parties. There are plenty who do not gossip, who have some idea of resistance, who are sick enough of it all to wish us well, because they know that none of it's worth lifelong integration and adaptation . . .

'We do not "make reckless use of guns". The cop who finds himself in the contradictory situation of being a "little man" and a capitalist lackey, a low wage-earner and a police officer of monopoly capitalism, is not under absolute compulsion to act. We shoot when we are shot at. We spare the cop who spares us.

'People are right when they claim that all the resources expended on hunting us down are really intended for the whole socialist left in the Federal Republic and West Berlin. The small sums of money we are said to have stolen, the occasional thefts of cars and documents with which we are charged, the attempted murder they are trying to pin on us, are their justification for it all.

'Our rulers are afraid to the marrow of their bones . . .'

20
The First Trial

In the spring of 1971 Horst Mahler went on trial in Berlin, facing a charge of participating in the freeing of Baader. Irene Goergens and Ingrid Schubert, who had both been arrested with Mahler six months earlier, were tried with him.

The criminal court in the Moabit prison had been transformed into a fortress for the trial. There were policemen armed with submachine guns patrolling the corridors, the entrances and exits; outside the building stood vehicles with their engines running and carrying teams of men, there were officers carrying radio equipment, and more units waited in the inner courtyard to go into action if needed.

Leftist sympathizers who were prepared to use violence gathered in crowds outside the courthouse building. A young girl, speaking to a reporter with a TV camera, expressed the feelings of many of them: 'To some extent, I think the Baader–Meinhof group has been trying to put revolutionary ideas into practice, while the other groups just sit about nattering.'

Mahler and the two women were taken into the courtroom handcuffed. The lawyer had let his beard grow again in prison; he was obviously in a cheerful mood, and greeted the spectators in the public gallery by punching the air with his fist. When the trial had been in progress for some time, and it looked as if Mahler might be found not guilty, Kurt Neubauer, a member of the Berlin Senate, announced to the press that there would be a 'secret weapon' in the trial of Mahler: a Counter-Intelligence agent was to appear in court.

The agent, Peter Urbach, was able to give evidence only about events during the three days before Baader's arrest; he would not answer any questions from Mahler's defence counsel Otto Schily that went beyond that.

'Did you personally offer to supply weapons to the left-wing circles – pistols, submachine guns, even mortars and phosphorus shells?'

'I can't answer that question.'

'Did you plant a bomb in Commune 1?'

'I can't answer that question.'

'Were the bombs supplied by Counter-Intelligence?'

'I can't say anything about that.'

'Did you set fire to any vehicles on the occasion of the anti-Springer demonstration in 1968?'

'I can't tell you anything about that.'

'Were you responsible for a fire at a police stable in which the police horse Zerline was severely injured?'

'I can't answer that.'

The trial of Horst Mahler lasted twenty-two days. He was found not guilty. His co-defendants were found guilty of being accessories to the freeing of Baader. Irene Goergens was sentenced to four years' youth custody, Ingrid Schubert to six years.

The opinion of the court was that Mahler had known of the planned rescue, having been in close contact with the group around Baader and Ensslin just before, but his own complicity had not been proved – in spite of the evidence of the agent Peter Urbach.

However, Horst Mahler was not freed after being found not guilty. There were two other charges against him.

21
'Madmen to Arms!'

In February 1970, three months before the freeing of Baader, the 'Socialist Patients' Collective' had been founded in Heidelberg by Dr Wolfgang Huber. This thirty-five-year-old doctor, a scientific assistant at the Psychiatric and Neurological University Hospital of Heidelberg, was at odds with his superiors and colleagues, and got the sack. Thereupon he mobilized his patients, most of them students he had treated in group therapy. Together they occupied the offices of the hospital's administrative director and went on hunger strike. After that the university administration gave way, went on paying Huber his salary, and placed four rooms at the disposal of the group for the continuation of their social-cum-psychiatric project.

Early in the summer they had further problems with the university. Huber and his patients occupied the rector's office. The university yet again considered a compromise, but the Baden-Württemberg Ministry of Culture vetoed it, for by this time it was clear what Dr Huber and his Socialist Patients' Collective (SPK for short) meant by therapy.

A document entitled 'Patients' Info No 1' stated, 'Comrades! There can be no therapeutic act that is not previously shown clearly and unmistakably to be a revolutionary act . . . the system has made us sick, let us give the death blow to the sick system!'

The conflict between the SPK on the one hand and the university and the Ministry of Culture on the other became increasingly violent. Notice was given to the SPK to vacate its rooms, and its members expected police action any day. They felt rejected and despised, which boosted the aggressive mood of the group considerably. The SPK got a new structure: an 'inner circle' of about twelve people was created; they were to work as therapists and to constitute the political leadership. The existence of this inner circle was concealed from the remaining three hundred members and patients of the SPK. Furthermore, 'study groups' were set up, including a Radio Technology Study Group, an Explosives Technology Study Group, a Photographic Technology Study Group, and later a Karate Study Group.

The autonomous patients' organization of the original project was more and more developing into a 'revolutionary' combat group.

One day Andreas Baader and Gudrun Ensslin went to Heidelberg for talks, with a view to recruitment. Several SPK members were told the meeting place, and went there one by one, by tram, in a conspiratorial manner.

Among them was Gerhard Müller, then twenty-three years old. He had been born in a small village in Saxony, and moved to West Germany in 1955 with his parents. After a brief period at grammar school, Gerhard Müller went to a less academic school. He dropped out of an apprenticeship as a telecommunications engineer, ran off to France, came back and worked as a casual labourer in a brewery.

In his own mind, Gerhard Müller saw society in terms of circles, and came to the conclusion that he was moving in the wrong one. He began idealizing the underworld. Its people, he thought to himself, must relate to each other differently from people in bourgeois society. He had always felt that his previous attempts to get away from it all, with the ensuing sheepish return, were in the nature of defeats. This time he was going to burn his bridges. Burning bridges struck him as far from easy, so he decided to start by getting drunk. Once he had achieved this aim, he proceeded to Stage Two of his plan. He broke into a nearby laundry, stole thirty marks from the till, took some bottles of wine from the cellar of the building and cigarettes from the building next door.

There he was 'a hungry, homeless, stupid country boy,' as he put it himself, later. 'Before I went underground somebody'd once told me, jokingly, that there were men who walked the streets as well as women, and you could earn money that way. I was too proud to beg, so I soon became a casual male prostitute. After the first few times that way of earning money sickened me so much that I was very glad to be picked up by the police.' Gerhard Müller was given a year's suspended sentence of youth custody for various more or less minor offences.

He went to Heidelberg, lived by casual labouring jobs, and came into contact with the student movement. At this time Gerhard Müller suffered from allergies; the doctors at Heidelberg University Hospital could find nothing to account for them. In his hour of need, Müller turned to the founder and leader of the SPK, Wolfgang Huber. At this first 'consultation', Huber said, 'There is no cure to be found in capitalism. So we must first do away with capitalism.' Müller still had his allergies, but he joined the Socialist Patients' Collective, and from there, like many of its other members, found his way into the Red Army Faction.

Müller met Baader and Ensslin for the first time when they came to talk and make contacts in Heidelberg in the spring of 1971. Andreas Baader claimed that the RAF had now gone a step further than the SPK; they had begun logically putting theory into practice. Müller was impressed by Baader's manner. He seemed calm, resolute and self-confident. Gerhard Müller joined the RAF. From 1971 onwards, so did about a dozen people from within the sphere of the Socialist Patients' Collective, forming a large part of the so-called 'second generation' of the RAF: Elisabeth von Dyck, Knut Folkerts, Ralf Baptist Friedrich, Siegfried Hausner, Sieglinde Hofmann, Klaus Jünschke, Bernhard Rössner, Carmen Roll, Margrit Schiller, Lutz Taufer and some others.

While some of the SPK members were now in the RAF, others still thought of themselves as participating in a self-help project for the mentally unstable within the framework of society.

One of these was Klaus Jünschke, born in 1947, a psychology student from Mannheim and the son of a Federal Railways official. He had come into the SPK when it was already under considerable threat from the university administration and the Ministry of Culture. At a teach-in, he had heard Wolfgang Huber say, 'There are two alternatives: either you get kidney stones or you throw stones at the centres of capital. Mind you don't get kidney stones!' The audience in the lecture hall went wild with enthusiasm. The idea of self-defence, of refusing to let the system get you down any more, was a line many could see themselves adopting.

One night the SPK members were expecting a police raid, and barricaded themselves in their rooms. Some of them had bottles of petrol with them. They sat there waiting for the police. Anyone who liked could leave, Huber had said. He wanted to see how far each member was ready to defend himself. Some of the SPK members did get up and leave the place. Klaus Jünschke was one of them. When he was out in the street he felt more ashamed of himself than he had ever been in his life. 'Either what we've been doing so far was right,' he thought, 'in which case we must be ready to go on to the end, or else it was all wrong.' He had abruptly realized that those who stayed behind were the ones totally committed to the cause of the SPK, those who did not have their studies and a bourgeois way of life at the back of their minds.

When he got home to Mannheim, he was ready for anything. He picked up the phone and called the SPK. 'We don't need you now. You can come tomorrow morning,' was the cool reply. Next morning Klaus Jünschke flung himself back into working for the SPK again. Even though the police had not turned up that night, and no Molotov cocktails had been thrown at any officers, the frontier had been crossed.

At the end of June 1971, at about three in the morning, some SPK members were stopped by police at a traffic checkpoint. They showed forged papers and managed to get away. The police went after them, and shots were fired at the officers in the course of a wild chase. One of them had a bullet through his shoulder. 'BAADER–MEINHOF GANG IN HEIDELBERG?' asked the newspapers, in giant headlines. A little later a member of the SPK made a statement to the police, describing the structure and strategy of the collective, giving names and addresses. Thereupon the police turned up at their Heidelberg quarters. Klaus Jünschke was lying on a bed, fully clothed. The police officers, armed with submachine guns, stormed the building. Everyone there was arrested except for Jünschke; the law student who had given the police that statement about the SPK had not known his name. Apartments were searched, guns and ammunition found. The police came to the conclusion that, 'from the circumstances of the case as known to date, we may suppose that the persons named have been preparing a certain very treacherous project against the Federal Republic of Germany'.

Huber and his wife were arrested. They had had time to go underground, but had not gone. Other SPK comrades who managed to evade the police joined the RAF.

Huber had given the rallying cry: 'Madmen to arms!'

22
'If Women Rise Up and Fight, It Subverts the System'

Another who went over from the SPK to join the RAF was Margrit Schiller. Born in 1948, she was the daughter of a Bundeswehr major working in military counter-espionage in Bonn. At the age of eighteen, immediately after taking her school-leaving exams, she moved out of the family home, claiming that her father 'was stifling her'. Her mother was a school-teacher and a CDU deputy in Bonn.

She began studying. Later, in her memoirs, she gave serious thought to her time with the RAF: 'It was tough, remembering that.' And indeed, she was one of the few RAF members ever to appraise their life underground and in prison rigorously, not even sparing herself. Perhaps it was her time with the Socialist Patients' Collective that enabled her to investigate her own feelings on the way to the underground and through her time in it.

Once she was no longer living at home, and had control of her own life, she tried 'to shake off the grief that had accompanied me through the years'. She felt very lonely: 'That has been my fundamental awareness of life ever since I could think.' She experimented with drugs – hash, marijuana – listened to Deep Purple and Pink Floyd. 'It was beautiful and terribly sad.'

Then Margrit Schiller came upon a self-help group for drug addicts called Release. 'Breaking out, living in a different way, not alone any more but in a collective' became her guiding principle, as it was for many others of her generation. Overnight, she broke off her relationship with her boyfriend, had several other, brief relationships, 'some consecutively, some at the same time, went to bed with anyone I fancied and in any way I liked'.

Several of her friends from Release were also members of the SPK. Margrit Schiller joined its Individual Agitation study group. 'At the meetings,' she wrote later in her memoirs, 'I felt a great need to talk, first about myself, my life, my uncertainties and fears and my search for something else.' In the process she realized that 'my loneliness and sadness, the many problems I had with myself, were not my personal, inescapable fate'.

Early in February 1971, an acquaintance asked Margrit if she could make her passport available to help a couple of people 'in difficulty with the police'. She agreed, asking no further questions. Soon after that the same acquaintance asked if she could lend the same people her apartment for a few days. Yet again she asked no questions. 'But it wasn't very easy for me. This was going a step further, and it could put me in danger.' However, her anxiety was not as strong as her 'interest in getting to know people who lived their lives in a different way from any I had so far known, finding out about their struggle'.

On the first night after moving out, she felt so tense that she was physically sick.

After a few days of wandering around from place to place, she went back to her apartment. There sat Ulrike Meinhof, Andreas Baader, Gudrun Ensslin and Jan-Carl Raspe. None of them looked like their pictures on the Wanted posters that Margrit had seen.

'Gudrun had a lovely Afro hairstyle which suited her thin face and big eyes. Ulrike looked small and delicate, she was wearing a headscarf and chain-smoking, and she kept fidgeting with her fingers.'

All four were pale, as if they never saw the sun. One of the party asked, 'So what do you want to know?' Margrit felt uncomfortable. 'Well, the kind of thing you do. I just wanted to meet you.'

'Do you know who we are, then?'

Margrit shook her head.

'Can we go on using your apartment?'

She nodded. So these were the people wanted by the police everywhere. On the one hand she felt intimidated, on the other it was as if they made her 'important'. Baader, who had said nothing so far, added, 'For security reasons, it's better if you don't get to know us more closely anyway. And if the cops ever find out that we were here it's best for you to know as little as possible.'

Baader struck her as very decisive and full of energy. Then she was asked if she knew why they wanted to build up an urban guerrilla movement, and whether she knew what contact with them could mean for her.

Margrit Schiller felt both shy and defiant. 'If I'm lending you my apartment I want to know what I'm letting myself in for.'

Until June 1971 the four of them and Holger Meins regularly turned up at Margrit Schiller's small basement apartment, to read and to study technical drawings and town plans. Sometimes they just wanted to relax, listen to music, cook together. Now and then they smoked hashish; they seldom drank alcohol. Sometimes, as Margrit Schiller remembers it, there was a lot of joking and laughing. 'For instance, about the fact that Ulrike, who had spent most of her previous life sitting at a typewriter, was now the one who could break into a car faster and more skilfully than any of the others.'

They all read Donald Duck comic books, and could amuse themselves like kids with these comics. Their political discussions, their use of weapons, all this was new to Margrit Schiller, but it was 'the strong sense of belonging' that magically attracted her. 'They seemed to share a common feeling, they were all on the same wavelength, they almost shared the same thoughts.' Margrit Schiller never knew when one of the group would turn up at her place. They had not asked for a key, so that if anyone was arrested the apartment couldn't be identified as one of their hideouts. Meanwhile, Margrit had cut down on her contacts with her former friends. She found this particularly difficult where her friend Gabi was concerned. Gudrun Ensslin seemed to notice, and mentioned it to her one day. 'Are you fond of each other – I mean physically fond?' Confused and hesitant, Margrit Schiller nodded.

At this Gudrun told her that there were some lesbian love affairs among the women comrades of the RAF, and it was quite in order for everyone. 'The student riots and the first women's self-help groups were an attempt to find a different way of life, with new ideas and new values.' Margrit was astonished to hear her speak so frankly. She remembered how the press (especially in *Bild*) described the women members of the RAF: 'They are deranged Amazons, authoritarian, gun-toting, lesbian, tough, unfeeling, and enslaved to Andreas.' Margrit asked Ulrike and Gudrun why people hated the women in the RAF so much.

'If women rise up and fight persistently, it subverts the system,' was the reply. 'Women are at the heart of human reproduction. Women are supposed to be passive, obedient, available and conciliatory. Women who break away refuse to accept all this, may even take up arms: they're not supposed to do that. That's why people hate us.'

It was early May 1971 when Holger Meins met Margrit at the railway station. She got a room at a small hotel, and together they began studying ads for apartments. Holger told her what to look for: an apartment in a big high-rise building. 'Andreas and Ulrike could stand in the lift beside their own Wanted posters and still pass unrecognized there, even without make-up. People would just be thinking about their stress at work, or the old folk or the kids at home.'

They found a suitable place on the Mexikoring in the middle of a dreary new housing estate in the north of Hamburg, and Margrit Schiller, her hair decorously plaited into a braid, wearing a skirt and discreet make-up, visited the management office of the block. 'You want to look inconspicuous, something like a secretary,' said Holger Meins.

She rented the apartment and went back to Heidelberg. Holger Meins visited her there a couple of times, stayed the night, and they began a brief affair.

One day Ulrike came to Margrit Schiller's Heidelberg apartment on her own. She sat down at the typewriter, surrounded herself with papers and books, and wrote day and night, hardly stopping to sleep. At the same time she drank litres of coffee and chain-smoked. She handed Margrit a couple of pages and said, 'I'd like to know what you think of this.'

Margrit Schiller made her way laboriously through the text: 'The Urban Guerrilla Concept'. Although she had difficulty in understanding what it was about, she gave the sheets of paper back and said, 'I think it's really good.'

Ulrike told her, angrily, 'I don't want compliments. Shit, I want your opinion.'

Margrit Schiller listened as Ulrike and Andreas discussed the text for hours on end. She had the impression that they both enjoyed pitting themselves against each other. Once, when Baader criticized a passage too harshly, Ulrike snapped: 'You write it, then.' Baader laughed: 'You know I can't say these things as well as you can. I have an idea of what ought to go into it, but only you can write it.'

23
The First Deaths

On 6 May 1971, Astrid Proll was recognized by a petrol pump attendant in Hamburg and arrested by the police. The detective officers wanted to keep her arrest secret. They had found a keyring in her bag, and were looking for the apartment it belonged to, expecting to find more members of the group there. The police drew a circle with a radius of five hundred metres around the spot where she had been arrested. Then officers fanned out to find the lock which fitted the front door key. They spent three days putting three keys into 2,167 different locks, unbeknownst to the people living in the buildings. On the third day they found the right lock. It belonged to an apartment on the third floor of No 139 Lübecker Strasse.

However, all they found there were the fingerprints of Gudrun Ensslin and Andreas Baader – and papers showing that the group was planning to attack vans carrying money for the Hamburg Savings Bank and the Armoured Car Service.

The Federal Criminal Investigation Office worked out a new plan for the capture of the remaining nine members of the group. This operation, code-named 'Pike', was classified; only the heads of the various criminal investigation offices were informed about it.

On the morning of 15 July 1971, 3,000 police officers all over northern Germany cordoned off the main roads and carried out traffic checks. It was the 425th day of the hunt for the Baader–Meinhof gang.

At 2.15 p.m., on Stresemannstrasse in the Hamburg urban district of Bahrenfeld, a blue BMW 2002 approached one of the fifteen police roadblocks that had been set up in Hamburg that day. A blonde girl sat at the wheel, with a bearded young man beside her. The police showed their badges. They had been instructed to stop all BMWs. These fast, Bavarian-built cars were regarded at the time as the group's preferred vehicles; the

BMW was already popularly known as the Baader–Meinhof–Wagen (Baader–Meinhof car).

The girl at the wheel stepped on the accelerator, broke through the cordon and raced past eight policemen with submachine guns at the ready. A radio car took up the chase. A second police car, a Mercedes, overtook the BMW and swung in front of it, tyres squealing.

The girl and her companion jumped out of their car and ran away. As they ran, the police said later, the couple fired Belgian 9-mm FN army pistols.

The girl ducked into a gateway, the young man ran across a park towards a building site and hid under a crane. Police officers had been watching him as he ran, from the helicopter Dragonfly 1. They sent eighty of their colleagues in to arrest him. Surrounded by police, Werner Hoppe surrendered, and as the handcuffs snapped shut he swore at them: 'Fucking cops, kiss my arse.'

The girl thought she had shaken off her pursuers, and emerged from the gateway. A policeman saw her and shouted, 'Stop, girl – stay where you are!' She drew a pistol and fired. Another officer shouted, 'Don't be a fool, girl, give yourself up!' She turned and fired; the policeman fired back. His bullet hit the girl beneath her left eye.

At 4.23 p.m. the German Press Agency reported, 'Ulrike Meinhof Shot.' However, the dead woman was not Ulrike Meinhof, but Petra Schelm, aged twenty.

Three years earlier, Petra Schelm had been working as a hairdresser in Berlin. She wanted to become a make-up artist. After her apprenticeship, she worked for a short time in a handicrafts shop. She then, at just eighteen, got a job as a courier with an American tourist group. She sent picture postcards to her parents from Rome, Munich, Paris and Madrid. Then she came back to Berlin, lived in a commune, and was active in the APO. She met Manfred Grashof, the young student of cinema and Army deserter. Petra introduced him to her parents.

Later, after his daughter's death, Petra's father told a reporter, 'I may have made a big mistake then. She wanted to marry the man, and she wanted me to agree to the wedding. It was just beyond me to say I did. So there was a rift between me and my daughter for the first time. The lad didn't really behave at all badly. He sat at the table, in a quiet sort of way, and let my daughter do the talking. It wasn't till I said no and told them I didn't fancy having a weirdo for a son-in-law, I mean not till I was rather harsh, rather uncivil, that the young man tried to join in the conversation. I cut him short, which wasn't really right, and said there was nothing to argue about. And then the two of them got up and left.'

Petra Schelm's father next saw his daughter again in the Forensic Institute – dead.

She was the first casualty in the war of the 'six against sixty million', as Heinrich Böll later put it.

Ten days after the shoot-out in Hamburg, the Allensbacher Institute of Public Opinion published the results of a sample poll on the subject of 'The Baader–Meinhof group: criminals or heroes?' Out of a thousand people questioned, eighteen per cent thought that the underground group was 'still acting mainly from political conviction'. Thirty-one per cent expressed no opinion. Eighty-two per cent had heard of the Baader–Meinhof group. One in four West German citizens under thirty admitted feeling 'a certain sympathy' for the Red Army Faction. One in ten North Germans even said they would be ready to shelter wanted underground fighters overnight; the average for the whole Federal Republic was one in twenty.

The pollsters came to the conclusion that their survey had established the existence of 'an unfavourable social and political climate for the police hunt'. The *Frankfurter Allgemeine Zeitung* expressed concern at the readiness of West German citizens to help the outlaws: 'In this case, five per cent makes as much impression as a hundred per cent.'

In their writings, the RAF kept quoting the result of this poll, which must surely have been partly reaction to the death of young Petra Schelm at the time. Years later, at the Stammheim trial, Baader cited the survey as proof of the extent to which the RAF's ideas had spread among the population.

24
Late Vintage

When the Socialist Patients' Collective in Heidelberg heard the news of Petra Schelm's death, its members felt confirmed in their view that it was necessary to go underground.

Klaus Jünschke was going around in a Volkswagen jeep belonging to

Dr Huber, head of the SPK, practising cross-country driving. A police patrol, ever on the look-out for SPK members, stopped him and checked his papers. Jünschke took out his identity card and handed it to the officers. They looked first at the photograph, then at him.

He had exchanged his own photograph for a picture of Mao Tse Tung. He was arrested, spent a couple of days in custody, and was then released again.

Not long after this, some former SPK members who had now joined the RAF visited him with a view to recruiting him.

If he agreed, they said, he must be in a Frankfurt park at 10 p.m. on a certain evening. He was to carry a copy of the *Welt am Sonntag* under his arm, as a recognition sign. Klaus Jünschke decided to take this trip – a trip ending in life imprisonment.

Later, after serving thirteen years, he said during a conversation in prison, 'I must have thought about it a thousand times, like anyone who gets life. You have plenty of time to torment yourself, puzzling it all out. There was the kind of atmosphere that makes you very ready to sacrifice yourself. Rational thought, in the sense of a calculation, didn't enter into it at all. Life imprisonment? So what? That may seem very frivolous to an outsider, but the willingness people felt to give their own lives was serious enough. After the SPK broke up there was this sense of desperation – we had to do something. When the SPK people were arrested, I leaned out of the window upstairs holding a copy of the Basic Law and recited its articles. "The dignity of mankind is unassailable." A few months later I was with the RAF.'

Jünschke was in the park at the appointed time. Nobody turned up. Another meeting place had been fixed for any such contingency: he was to be at an ice cream parlour an hour later. He stuck the newspaper under his arm and went into the café. Two rather shabby-looking men were sitting at a table. When they spotted the man with the newspaper they almost choked over their ice cream. Jünschke sat down at another table and waited. After a while one of the two men left the café, but came back shortly afterwards.

'Come with me,' Jan-Carl Raspe told Jünschke. Holger Meins followed the couple a hundred metres behind them.

Raspe rang the bell of an apartment in a new building. A woman opened the door and let the two of them into the apartment, which was completely empty. She looked American to Jünschke. She was wearing a grey wig with its hair piled high, and a headscarf over it. Her sweater fitted tightly, and she wore trousers. Jünschke leaned against the wall and waited. He had smartened himself up to an unusual degree for his first meeting with the outlaws: he was wearing a blazer, white shirt, tie, and grey trousers.

'Well, tell us who you are and what you do,' said Ulrike Meinhof. Jünschke told his life story, about which, as he realized from their questions, his interlocutors were already well informed. When they came to the Socialist Patients' Collective, Ulrike Meinhof said abruptly, 'But we don't go in for group sex here.'

'What makes you think I'm interested in group sex?'

Towards the end of the conversation, the others indicated what Jünschke could do for the group. 'There are various things it's important for us to get done. We can't do them ourselves without running risks. Stuff that has to be bought. Are you prepared to do that sort of thing?' Jünschke said he was. The principal requirement was car number plates.

Klaus Jünschke was a conscientious objector, and had given as his reason, 'I couldn't kill another human being.' It was not just something he had said: he meant it in all seriousness. And suddenly here he was, one of a group of people who went about armed and let there be no doubt that they would use their weapons. One night he was walking through Frankfurt with Holger Meins. 'Are you actually armed?' Holger asked him.

'No, of course not.'

'Well, you ought to have something on you. At least a knife.'

A few months later, shortly before his arrest, Holger Meins got into a fight with three drunk rockers. They beat him up. Later, the group discussed what should be done in such a situation. Although his nose had been broken, they were all relieved he had not brought out his weapon.

Klaus Jünschke was painfully aware of the dilemma in which he now found himself. 'I got into a situation where I ended up doing things I couldn't justify to myself. It just about broke me up. I've been spending all my time in jail suffering horribly, trying not to go crazy. Because I couldn't make it all fit together – the RAF and my own life and the future.'

In August 1971, Jünschke was told to go to Hamburg, where the group's main base had been since spring. He met the others there, in an apartment in the Schanzenviertel. Andreas Baader, his hair bleached, was on good form. Klaus Jünschke had to tell his life history once again. It was rather like a job interview. Jünschke thought Baader's tone very autocratic. After all, *he* wanted to know what he was facing. 'So now you're here, tell us what you're after,' said Baader. Klaus Jünschke had the feeling Baader was provocative on purpose in such conversations, to test the self-assertiveness of new recruits. They gave Jünschke the cover name 'Spätlese' – 'Late vintage'.

He was supposed to spend the first week getting to know the city. He spent days travelling around Hamburg on the underground by himself, changing trains frequently and exploring the various parts of the city. He had bought a street map, on which he entered the positions of all police stations, marking them with little flags. Now and then Gudrun Ensslin visited him, appraised his topographical labours, and expressed herself satisfied. Jünschke was given a new identity card and allowed to move into one of the illegal apartments. This was where he met Teeny. They walked the streets of Hamburg together, scanning the areas around their bases for any cars with two radio aerials – observation vehicles which might be standing around. They were generally out and about at night and did not go home to sleep until four or five in the morning. Jünschke did not feel too good about these nocturnal expeditions, and thought, 'We're really the only ones out in the street at night.'

He spoke to Ulrike Meinhof about it. 'Winter's my favourite time,' she replied. 'People can't see me then, it's dark in the streets and dim even in the daytime.' She was afraid of being recognized – by her walk, her figure, her voice – especially in Hamburg, where she had lived for so many years and countless people knew her. For a while, Jünschke lived in a three-roomed apartment with Ulrike Meinhof and two others. He did the cooking for his flatmates, and Ulrike Meinhof rinsed his hair with hydrogen peroxide, so that though naturally dark, he was now ash blond.

Manfred Grashof taught him the art of forgery, and they saw to the rest of their logistical requirements together, papering apartments, buying furnishings of a decidedly lower-middle-class nature in second-hand furniture stores.

Jünschke said later, 'You join the urban guerrilla and then you find yourself spending a month fixing up an apartment, and there's always shopping to be done, things that are needed. That's ninety-nine per cent of what goes on.' Every few hundred metres, they would pass their own photographs on Wanted posters, up on every advertising pillar, in every post office, every bank. It was only too clear to most members of the group that there could be nothing but prison or death at the end of their road. Many of them had doubts, and thought of getting out, but they were all afraid of telling anyone else, even though that other person might be thinking just the same way.

Sometimes Jünschke wondered whether it wouldn't be better to give up living outside the law and go to the cinema, go on holiday, lie on a Spanish beach for four weeks, without a gun, and think about his own situation, shake it all off and relax – 'Which would naturally have led to my not going back again.'

Hunted by the state, not popular with the left, they were dependent on each other. The group was all they had. 'It was nothing like normal life, where you have ordinary friends of both sexes.'

If they approached former comrades from the student movement or the base groups, the door was more than once shut in their faces. Most such people said, 'Leave us alone.' Or, sadly, 'They'll get you all, you know.'

Jünschke commented, 'But nobody tackled me and said, "Look, come to your senses, look at the facts of the matter, what you're doing is shit, stay here for a few days and sleep it all off!" We were the ones in authority, we were with the front-line troops.'

They were more likely to get help and support from former friends who belonged to no political grouping. You might be able to stay the night with them. And if these friends hesitantly uttered a few critical remarks about the RAF's policy of violence, you adopted a stubborn stance: 'What do you know about it, arsehole? Stop? Out of the question. Knuckle under? Never. I'd rather die than be part of such a rotten society again.'

Then there was the sense of disappointment. You knew a songwriter who had once sung 'There are no shadows of grey in the class struggle'. And when you went to his door he would say you had three minutes to get out or he was going to call the police.

In the middle of October 1971, Andreas Baader and Gudrun Ensslin came back to Berlin, where initial preparations for a major RAF operation had now been made: the idea was to kidnap the American, British and French city commandants at one fell swoop.

The rest of the group stayed in Hamburg. One of their bases was an apartment on the Heegbarg in the Poppenbüttel area. It belonged to a well-known musician. Gudrun Ensslin had approached him after a concert and asked about the possibility of spending the night at his place. The singer gave her his door-key and went off on a concert tour.

25
The Death of a Policeman

Margrit Schiller had been in Hamburg for four weeks now. The city was a dangerous place for the RAF after the arrest of Astrid Proll and the shoot-out with the police during which Petra Schelm had been killed. Margrit Schiller had to leave her hiding-place for the first time to go to a meeting. She cut her red-brown hair short and dyed it black, made up her face, and put on a red mini-dress and knee-length black coat by way of disguise, since her Wanted descriptions said she always wore trousers.

In the rush-hour traffic she set off for the meeting place. She chose a long way round, changing underground and suburban trains several times until she reached the apartment near the Alstertal shopping centre. It was already dark. One by one the others turned up: Ulrike Meinhof, Jan-Carl Raspe, Irmgard Möller, Manfred Grashof, Holger Meins, Klaus Jünschke and three or four other members of the group. Afterwards, Margrit Schiller couldn't remember whether Gudrun Ensslin and Andreas Baader joined them later or had stayed in Berlin.

The windows of the apartment were covered, with small observation slits looking out on the street. On the floor lay the usual jumble of foam mattresses, a telephone, radio sets, cases, bags, tools, ammunition and explosives. The police radio was transmitting constantly over one of the radio sets. The group members put their weapons down and began their discussion.

Holger Meins asked about the shoot-out in Freiburg. Margrit Schiller began telling him.

Meins interrupted her. 'Why didn't you shoot too?'

Margrit went red in the face and couldn't say a word. The question was still going round and round in her head as Holger Meins began talking about plans for a bank raid.

The group members were going to stay overnight in the apartment, and leave the hideout separately in the morning.

Ulrike Meinhof came into the room. 'I have to make a phone call,' she said, and turned to Gerhard Müller. 'You come with me.' Then she turned again, this time to Margrit Schiller. 'Come on, you too.' She needed company on her way to the telephone kiosk. They didn't use the phone in the apartment on principle, for fear of blanket coverage by bugging devices.

The three of them left the apartment and separated at the front door of the building. Ulrike Meinhof went ahead, Margrit Schiller and Gerhard Müller followed her at a little distance. When Ulrike Meinhof crossed the Heegbarg, Müller spotted a suspect car. He whispered to Margrit, 'Watch out – see that Ford ahead of us with the dipped lights? Those two guys in it – I'm sure they're cops.'

It was about 1.30 a.m., and the police officers in the civilian Ford 17M were Norbert Schmid and Heinz Lemke. At the suburban railway station they had seen a young woman, dark-haired, tall, wearing a black coat and horn-rimmed glasses. Margrit Schiller. Norbert Schmid got out of the car and tried to follow her. After a while he lost sight of her and went back to the patrol car. The two officers searched the surrounding area. They spotted the woman again in Wentzelplatz. She was coming out of the underground car park of the Alstertal shopping centre, a huge concrete complex. Realizing that she was under observation, she disappeared into the garden of a prefab. The police officers scanned the area through night-vision glasses.

Ulrike Meinhof had also seen the car, and she disappeared behind some bushes. A few minutes later she came out again. Müller and Schiller went towards her. Suddenly the Ford drove up with its headlights on full beam. Ulrike Meinhof was crossing the street while Margrit Schiller and Gerhard Müller waited for green at the traffic lights. Then they too crossed. The Ford followed Ulrike Meinhof. Suddenly there was a lot of noise. Margrit Schiller heard footsteps and squealing tyres. She looked round. Ulrike Meinhof was running towards her, shouting, 'Shit, it's the cops.' The Ford turned the corner and tried to cut Ulrike Meinhof off.

Police Sergeant Schmid wound down his window, shouting, 'Stop! Police – stay where you are!' The passenger door of the car swung open. Schmid jumped out of the car and gave chase. Ulrike Meinhof doubled back around the vehicle, shouting, 'Come on, let's get out of here!' Then she ran down the Heegbarg. Müller followed her, and together they fled down an alley past a row of buildings. Sergeant Schmid ran after them, followed by his colleague Sergeant Lemke. Margrit Schiller, rooted to the spot, saw the first police officer reach Ulrike Meinhof, take her by the arm and make a grab for her bag. Ulrike struggled but couldn't break free. 'They're armed!' Lemke shouted. According to Margrit Schiller later: 'Gerhard, who was running ahead of Ulrike, stopped, turned with his gun in his hand and fired it. The policeman fell, and his colleague, who had been pursuing the three of them, flung himself down on the ground. I heard more shots, and then Ulrike and Gerhard had disappeared in the darkness. I saw what had happened and couldn't take it in; it was the same situation as four weeks before during the shoot-out in Freiburg.'

Wounded in the foot, Lemke limped over to his colleague, who was lying in a pool of blood whispering, 'Help, help.' Lemke asked, 'What is it, Norbert?' But there was no answer. Police Sergeant Norbert Schmid, aged thirty-two, was dead.

Lemke dragged himself over to Number 61, Heegbarg, and rang the front-door bell of the building. No one stirred. Then he shouted, 'Help! Police!' No reply.

Margrit Schiller ran to the police car, in which Lemke had left the key, and raced away. She abandoned the Ford after driving two kilometres.

Soon afterwards the manhunt began. At 2.30 a.m., a patrol in a radio car noticed a woman standing in a telephone booth not far from the scene of the shooting. The officers drew their pistols and asked to see her identity card. 'Oh, I thought you wanted to fuck me,' said the woman, reaching for her black handbag. The officers snatched the bag away from her. Inside it they found a 9-mm pistol and the key of the patrol car.

The woman would say nothing at the police station. When asked questions, she merely shook her head. Her identity card was in the name of Dörte G. However, the detective officers were well aware by now who it was they had captured. Towards 5 a.m. the woman signed a form – with her real name: Margrit Schiller. When she realized her mistake, she began to weep.

She was shown to the press at 11 a.m. A woman police officer kept a stranglehold on her while a male officer held her legs.

Her skirt had slipped up. The photographers took pictures, television cameramen filmed her. 'Get her hair off her face,' one reporter called, whereupon a policeman hauled her hair up. The scene was shown on television all over West Germany that evening.

Margrit Schiller was placed under arrest, and the hunt for the other two went on.

The Hamburg police tied black crape to the aerials of their patrol cars. Mayor Schulz said, 'If the Baader–Meinhof group turns out to be responsible for this murder, we should now at last stop regarding them as an association with political aims. They are wholly criminal in the truest sense of the word.'

A reward of 10,000 Deutschmarks was offered for information leading to the capture of the killer.

It quickly became clear that Margrit Schiller herself had not killed the policeman. Technical examinations showed that her pistol had not been fired recently. Police Sergeant Lemke also stated that a man had fired at his colleague. At first suspicion fell on Holger Meins, who was on the run. However, Lemke then identified Gerhard Müller as the marksman, from police photographs. The woman with him was thought to be Irmgard Möller. In fact it had been Ulrike Meinhof.

While the Hamburg police were combing the Poppenbüttel area, the wanted RAF members were sitting in the Heegbarg apartment. Directly after the shooting, so several of them said later, Gerhard Müller had rushed in 'with his revolver practically smoking', boasting of having 'done in a cop'.

In the panic terror of being discovered that they all felt, Manfred Grashof, 'as the senior person present', took over the organization of 'security measures'. They stayed in the apartment for three days and three nights, feeling they were in a trap.

26 The State Witness

Irmgard Möller and Gerhard Müller went on trial over three and a half years later. The headline in the *Morgenpost* ran: 'IN COURT IN HAMBURG TODAY – MEINHOF'S LOVER, KILLER OF A POLICEMAN'.

Things looked bad for the defendant Gerhard Müller, since Police Sergeant Lemke had witnessed the shooting of his colleague Schmid at very close quarters. Moreover, Müller's fingerprints had been found in the Heegbarg apartment, in the immediate vicinity of the scene of the crime. In the preliminary inquiries, Lemke had testified to recognizing Müller as the killer.

When it came to the actual trial of Müller, Lemke toned his evidence down considerably. The public prosecutor dropped the charge of murdering a policeman. Müller also got off lightly on the other charges of complicity in the bombing attacks of spring 1972, which could have meant life imprisonment. He was sentenced to ten years for attempted murder and other offences, and served not much more than half his sentence.

Gerhard Müller was one of the principal prosecution witnesses at the Stammheim trial. The defending lawyers tried to discredit him as a 'bought state witness'. They suspected that Gerhard Müller had been let off conviction for the murder of the Hamburg policeman to induce him to give evidence for the prosecution.

Margrit Schiller, called to testify at the Stammheim trial, said, 'I saw Gerhard Müller shoot the police officer Schmid on the night of 21 to 22 October 1971.'

She stated that she had seen Schmid chasing the couple and eventually catching up with them. The policeman had snatched the woman's handbag from her. 'Müller was standing beside her, holding his pistol, and he fired it at Schmid. Schmid let go of the handbag and fell to the ground. Müller and the woman ran on, and as they ran I heard more shots.'

In fact, all kinds of inconsistencies to do with the witness Müller turned up at the Stammheim trial. For instance, his statements to the Hamburg police were kept in Special File 3 ARP 74/75 I, but not handed over to the Stammheim court. The Federal Justice Ministry had classified them 'secret'. Defending counsel managed to get hold of the file only after a long tussle, and fifteen pages still remained classified.

Federal Prosecutor General Buback is said to have remarked à propos of this, during a conversation at the Federal Prosecutor's Office, that 'if the contents of that file become known, we can all wave our jobs goodbye'.

As a witness at the Stammheim trial, Buback repeatedly pleaded his restricted freedom to give evidence when defending counsel's questions touched upon the secret file.

'Does the file, which obviously includes the accounts of Herr Müller's interrogation, contain the findings of investigations which might, however remotely, bear upon these proceedings?' asked Otto Schily, defending.

'I cannot make any statement about that point because my permission to testify does not cover it,' replied Buback.

Dr Heldmann, another defending lawyer, asked, 'Do you know about File 3 ARP 74/75 I?'

'Well, we keep coming back to the issue of my restricted freedom to testify. Naturally I am aware of the existence of that file.'

'The question refers to its contents. Are you conversant with the contents of the file?'

'I would like that question withdrawn because of my restricted freedom to testify.'

'Sir, did you cause this file to be classified as secret?'

'I suggested it.'

'Did you instruct or recommend the Federal Justice Minister not to give you unrestricted freedom to testify as a witness in these proceedings?'

'I cannot answer that question because of my restricted freedom to testify.'

The defence lawyers at Stammheim also questioned Gerhard Müller himself about the killing of the policeman Norbert Schmid and Secret File 3 ARP 74/75 I.

'Herr Müller, where were you in October, 1971?' asked Otto Schily on the hundred and twenty-sixth day of the trial.

'In Kiel and in Hamburg.'

'Do you know the street called the Heegbarg and the Saseler Damm?'

'Yes.'

'Do you also know the big car park behind the shopping centre?'

'Sir, I think that is going rather too far,' said Müller, turning to the presiding judge of the court, Dr Prinzing, for aid.

The judge told him that according to Paragraph 55 of the Code he need not say anything to incriminate himself. Müller replied, 'Yes,' to Schily's question.

'Where were you on the night of 21 to 22 October 1971?'

Müller turned to his own lawyer.

'We've switched off the microphone, so you can speak freely,' Dr Prinzing told him.

After a short consultation with his legal adviser, Müller said, 'Herr Schily's questions obviously refer to the killing of the police officer, Schmid. That case is still open. I have not yet made any statements about it, contrary to what the defending lawyers here suggest. I would rather not do so now, either, because the case is not closed yet. However, the fact is that I did not shoot the policeman Schmid. And I decline to give any more evidence in reply to further questions on that matter.'

Schily was not giving in quite so easily. 'Well, let us first ask the question: did you shoot the policeman Schmid?'

'He's already denied it,' said the presiding judge.

Schily did not let go. 'Did any other persons blame you for that shooting? Did you reply you were proud to have shot a cop?'

'This is too much!' said Müller.

Dr Helmann, defending, put a last question to the witness Gerhard Müller. 'If, as you have said here, it was not you who shot Norbert Schmid, then who did?'

'I decline to say anything about that.'

'No more questions.'

27
The RAF and the 2 June Movement – an Abortive Cooperation

Andreas Baader and Gudrun Ensslin had gone to Berlin a week before the murder of the police officer Norbert Schmid, and turned up one night to visit the 2 June Movement.

After his release from prison in the summer of 1971, Bommi Baumann had joined his old friends, who had now set up a kind of anarchist organization in competition with the RAF, the '2 June Movement', so called after the day on which the student Benno Ohnesorg died. Bommi and Georg von Rauch were now planning to free some prisoners from jail.

'What do you think you're up to? Chasing round apartments, fucking little girls, smoking hashish! It's all fun to you. It shouldn't be. This job we're doing is serious. It oughtn't to be fun,' said Gudrun Ensslin.

'You must be off your head,' replied Bommi.

'And just look at you,' said Ensslin, alluding to Baumann's long hair, beard, and slovenly appearance. She herself wore long jersey trousers, full as a skirt, with an elegant leather jacket over them. The combination didn't quite go together, but had something of a bourgeois look about it. Gudrun came back to the subject of the 2 June Movement's promiscuity. 'We're in favour of one-to-one relationships,' she said censoriously.

Ensslin and Baader almost always went about together. Their manner to each other might be extremely brusque, but it was always obvious that they belonged together and no one could drive a wedge between them. They always spoke of women as 'cunts'; Andreas Baader addressed Gudrun herself thus. She called him 'Baby'.

Their intentionally vulgar language got on Baumann's nerves; it had an unnatural, exaggerated, artificial effect.

When Andreas Baader embarked on one of his endless monologues, Ensslin would look silently from one listener to another, turning her head from left to right and back again. 'The way a cobra sways in front of its prey,' thought Baumann. Then she would suddenly make a remark. 'She saw just when someone was showing weakness, and she'd say something at just that moment. She always got it right, too. She was an excellent psychologist.'

Sometimes, so Baumann remembered, she would put the brakes on Baader, soothing him. 'Leave off, Baby,' she would tell him, 'you can't say a thing like that.'

By now Andreas Baader in particular was a bundle of nerves. Sometimes he seemed completely under the influence of speed – pep pills – at the meetings arranged between the groups. He drank excessive amounts of coffee and chain-smoked, preferring strong Celtic brand cigarettes. Bommi Baumann said, 'He would sit like that for nights on end, talking non-stop, about anything from Adam and Eve to Josef Stalin. There was saliva at the corners of his mouth. He was almost always tugging at his hair as he talked, pulling the bleached strands to right and left of his temples, twisting and pulling, twisting and pulling, until he had little blond horns above his forehead. He was forever delivering lectures; she sometimes touched a lighter note.'

At one of these nocturnal meetings Gudrun Ensslin picked up a book Bommi had been reading and held it in the air. Its title was *Name, Viktor Serge, Profession, Revolutionary*.

'A book,' she said curtly, her voice full of contempt. Then she dropped it on the floor.

28
'A Bucket of Tar in the Kisser'

Baader and Ensslin stayed on in Berlin. Brigitte Mohnhaupt and her boyfriend were active for the Red Army Faction in Berlin too. A string of acquaintances from the days of the student movement helped to get them apartments, visit RAF members in custody, and generally make themselves useful. One of these was Edelgard G., aged twenty-seven, divorced and the mother of a five-year-old son.

After several meetings with Baader and Ensslin, she and her friend Katharina Hammerschmidt had rented apartments for the outlawed groups. However, she did not want to live outside the law herself, justifying her decision by her concern for her child.

'My own present activities have brought me to recognize my true identity for the first time,' said Ensslin, who had abandoned her own son. Edelgard could not make her out.

After quite a short time Edelgard and Katharine found the work they were doing for the RAF a nuisance. The apartments they found usually turned out not good enough for their clients. At one meeting, Katharina Hammerschmidt told Baader her misgivings about the illegal life.

Baader replied, 'This is a job you can do only out of a deep-seated voluntary impulse.' When she told her friend Edelgard about this episode, she added, 'I was looking for an apartment for myself a few months ago, I got footsore trudging about. The only difference between then and now is that now I'm doing it out of a deep-seated voluntary impulse.'

At the beginning of November 1971, the two women wanted to call a halt to their helpful activities. On 19 November, Edelgard fetched her son from his play group. As she was coming back to her apartment in Pariser Strasse, she saw a large detachment of police around the place. She parked her car and met a neighbour in the yard of the building. 'There's a big green police van come for you outside, Willi,' she said to him, jokingly. 'The cops are in your apartment,' he told her. 'They're looking for guns.' Edelgard handed the neighbour her son and ran towards the headquarters of the Socialist Lawyers' Collective. She met her own lawyer on the way there.

They went back to her apartment together. Edelgard was arrested. The police told her she would never see her child again unless she told them what she knew. Three weeks later she made a statement, and was allowed to go back to her child.

On 27 March 1972, towards 10.00 p.m., an anonymous express letter was handed in at the German Press Agency in Berlin. The envelope contained a typed note: 'This is Edelgard G., an informer who is hand in glove with the killer pigs. Long live the RAF!'

There was a photograph enclosed, showing a woman covered with some dark fluid. The German Press Agency editor on duty passed the note on to the police. Two detectives set off for Pariser Strasse. The policemen showed Edelgard G. the note and the photograph.

'I was expecting to see that picture published in the newspaper within the next few days,' she said.

'Can you tell us anything about where it comes from?' She shook her head.

'Could it be a photo-montage?'

She did not reply. When the detectives asked more questions, she began trembling all over.

Later, the police report said: 'From her subsequent reactions and vague hints, we could gather without any doubt that she actually was tarred, and this was not a faked or retouched picture. Even afterwards she was not prepared to give further information about the perpetrators, the time or the place. The matter of her personal safety was then mentioned to her. Frau G. said that at the moment she is not sure herself whether such an action may be repeated or whether she faces a yet worse threat, possibly even endangering her life.'

The police report closed with the words: 'Nor can we assess at the moment how far the treatment she has suffered will affect her willingness to give further evidence. However, it must be feared that she will refuse to make any more statements in the immediate future.'

Afterwards, at the Stammheim trial, Brigitte Mohnhaupt was questioned about the treatment of renegades. 'Do you know anything about people who broke away from the group, and what went on when that happened?' Gerd Temming, defending, asked the witness.

'There was never any talk of liquidation, not when anyone split off.

There's that story that's well known in Berlin. About Edelgard G. who gave half a dozen people away. I mean, she informed on people, informed on apartments. What happened, what was done – well, she got a bucket of tar in the kisser and a notice hung round her neck.

'What I mean to say is, if it's known that somebody's informed on people, practically put them in the firing line, if that person just gets a bucket of tar over their head then it's all the more ridiculous to suppose that someone who never gave anyone away could be just shot down. That's quite out of the question.'

Edelgard G.'s friend Katharina Hammerschmidt gave herself up to the police after they had been hunting for her for some time.

In prison, she developed a malignant tumour which went unrecognized by the prison doctors, although it was clearly visible in X-ray pictures. It was a long time before doctors from outside had access to her. She died.

29
'Give up, Ulrike!'

In the middle of November 1971, Ulrike Meinhof's foster mother Renate Riemeck wrote an open letter, published in *konkret*, under the title, 'Give up, Ulrike!'

'You are not like that, Ulrike. Not at all the way people think you are when they have seen your picture up on a Wanted poster and heard about you in the press, on radio and television. Those who know you better know that you do not shoot down anyone who stands in your way. You have your fears, like everyone else. But you are brave, braver than most. And you stand by your friends.

'You have an advantage over the younger of your comrades in that you were politically committed while they were still at school, taking no interest in such things. You were in the forefront of the anti-atom bomb movement of 1958/59. So you know that the political movements can suddenly arise and then subside again, and that one gains nothing by running amok. To know this is a good deal.

'You could not, therefore, make the mistake of confusing anti-authoritarian rebelliousness with the start of a great revolution.

'We were in full agreement on the justification for attacking institutions and structures – you were still sometimes speaking to me at that time. You had no illusions about the actual strength of the power machine. It all turned out just as might have been foreseen: when the protest movement failed to bring about solidarity between the masses who depend on a wage, when revolution conspicuously failed to materialize, disappointment was inevitable.

'The Federal Republic is not the place for an urban guerrilla movement in the Latin American style. This country offers, at most, suitable conditions for a gangster drama. Ulrike, you know that you and your friends can expect nothing but bitter enmity from the German public. You also know that you are condemned to play the part of a company of spectres serving the forces of reaction as an excuse for a massive revival of that anti-Communist witchhunt which was perceptibly discouraged by the student movement.

'Who – apart from a handful of sympathisers – still understands the political and moral impulse behind your actions? A spirit of sacrifice and the readiness to face death become ends in themselves if one cannot make them understood.

'The death of Petra Schelm and the fate of Margrit Schiller must surely shake you. You and your friends do not have the same justification as the Tupamaros of Uruguay for actions involving shooting and in which people lose their lives. You must correct yourselves.

'I do not know how far your own influence within the group extends, how far your friends are amenable to rational considerations. But you should try to measure up the chances of an urban guerrilla movement in the Federal Republic against the social reality of this country. You can do that, Ulrike.'

30
'A Slave Mother Entreats Her Child'

Three weeks after this issue of *konkret* went on sale, an employee of the Berlin Parks and Gardens Office found a plastic bag containing ammunition and some written papers in a waste bin in the Wittenbergplatz. Besides photocopies of a letter from the Red Army Faction to the Labour Party of the People's Republic of Korea, which judging by its style was composed by Ulrike Meinhof, and to which she had also made handwritten additions, the bag contained the carbon copy of a document entitled 'A Slave Mother Entreats Her Child'.

'Ulrike, you are not like your picture on the Wanted poster, but a slave child – you are a slave woman yourself.

'So how would you be capable of firing on your oppressors? Don't let those who refuse to be slaves any more lead you astray.

'You cannot protect them. I want you to remain a slave – like me. You and I – we have seen how our masters put down the slaves' revolt before it ever began.

'Many slaves died, but we survived. Those who speak bitterly of their masters today don't know what a wonderful feeling it is to have escaped so narrowly. Enjoy it – there is nothing else left for us to enjoy.

'Revolution is great – we are too small for it.

'Slave souls are quicksands upon which no victory can be built. When you awoke and demanded freedom, no one brought it to you. Why didn't you resign yourself, like other people?

'Look at me! I resisted when our masters struck me – I screamed.

'However, you enrage our masters, making them want to strike again. But who will want to go on screaming if we are to suffer further ill-treatment for that?

'You are a good child. It wasn't you who climbed over the masters' fence, it was the others. But they set the dogs on you.

'Oh, child, you deserved better. To think of what you might have been!

'I'm sure you would have risen to be an overseer.

'Don't you see how strong our masters are? All the slaves obey them. Even those who did protest, and won a victory, will lay that victory at their masters' feet, so that they may go on being slaves.

'Slaves hate those who want to be free. And they are not to help you, either; then you may learn at last how pointless your rebellion is.

'Your courage is heartless, for how can we conceal our cowardice from it? Even if you would rather be dead than a slave for ever, you have no right to make us feel uneasy.

'I know: you want us all to be free, but will we feel any better?

'May God forgive the slaves who were flogged in the plantations of Asia, Africa and South America and killed their overseers.

'We house slaves have no right to resist the masters who send out those overseers with their ox goads.

'It is our duty to keep their house in order.

'Do not transgress, my child. Do penance, even if our masters impose dreadful punishment on you. It is God's will.

'Be subject to the authorities who have power over you.

'Give up, Ulrike!

'Cursed be the God who made slaves for his entertainment.'

Ulrike Meinhof's reply to her foster mother Renate Riemeck lay there in the waste bin in the Wittenbergplatz.

31
The Chief Commissioner and His Computer World

That autumn of 1971, when the Red Army Faction was one and a half years old, when there had been two deaths, half of its first generation members were in custody, and new recruits were joining the underground struggle, the BKA got a new Chief Commissioner.

His name was Horst Herold, and he came to symbolize the hunt for the RAF terrorists, in the same way as the name of Baader symbolized the RAF itself. Horst Herold was head of the BKA for almost ten years, and built it up from an insignificant Federal office for the co-ordination of police work into a powerful man-hunting machine.

Something almost akin to a love-hate relationship unites him with Andreas Baader, who was his principal opponent in the years of the 'internal war'. Sometimes he lets slip such remarks as, 'Baader was the only man who ever really understood me, and I'm the only man who ever really understood him.' And he refers, with what is almost a trace of pride, to the fact that Baader made his, Horst Herold's, writings on methods of fighting terrorism required reading for the Red Army Faction.

In fact there were some remarkable areas of agreement between Herold and the RAF in their evaluation of the terrorist struggle against the state machine. Thus, Otto Schily, appearing for the defence at the Stammheim trial, quoted a speech by Horst Herold at the 'Hessian Forum', a conference held during the trial, as evidence supporting the RAF thesis that the court was not dealing with a normal criminal case, but a military and political conflict between the bourgeois capitalist state and its most radical opponents.

Herold had said: 'The first question is to decide whether terrorism, in its manifestations in Germany or indeed all over the world, is a product of the brains of its perpetrators, of the Baaders and the Meinhofs – of their sick brains, as many would say – or whether terrorism is a reflection of certain social situations in the Western and indeed in the Eastern world, so that its superstructure only mirrors problems which have an objective existence. In so doing, we would have to consider who, in that case, should be primarily engaged in the struggle against terrorism: the police or the politicians. In my opinion, it is the political powers who have to change those circumstances in which terrorism can arise . . . it is no use then knocking people over the head, or indeed taking their heads right off, as some demand; we are concerned with exerting influence on historical causes and effects.'

On the problem of that 'opposing power' which the terrorists were trying to set up, Herold said, further: 'Thus, in the struggle as a whole, we must think not solely in military terms, but increasingly – and I say so with reluctance, but the trend is clear – we must start thinking in terms of international law as well.'

After Otto Schily had finished his exposition of Herold's theses, Baader took issue with the Criminal Investigation Office chief's position. He remarked sarcastically that he supposed he had the right to cite Herold, since he 'has been making such excessive use of us for the last five years to inflate his own departmental machinery'.

'It is Herold, the policeman,' said Baader, 'who is fighting for legal, yes, internationally legal norms for the guerrilla movement, because they are of use in his claims to power. He says the trend is to take the war out of the domain of the police and shift military conflicts inwards. And I am the man who has to wage this war, so give me the machinery, give me the money, and above all give me the political power. Herold is at the peak of reaction.'

Horst Herold was born on 21 October 1923, in Thuringia. He went to a secondary school specializing in mathematics and science in Nuremberg, where he took his final school exams. He was in the army from 1941 to 1945, and was severely wounded by a shell splinter in 1942, when he was a tank commander outside Voronezh. He studied law and political science at the University of Erlangen, and took his doctorate in 1951 with a thesis on international law. A year later, he passed the state law examinations in Munich.

In 1953 he became public prosecutor in Nuremberg-Fürth; he was made judge of the Nuremberg district court in 1956, and associate judge of the *Land* regional court in 1957. In the early sixties, he had a complicated case involving fraudulent cheques and bills to deal with, and developed a new pattern of investigations whereby he was able to trace every detail of the perpetrators' proceedings and methods. As a result of this case, he went into the police service as Criminal Director in May 1964, became Deputy Chief Commissioner of Nuremberg, and was appointed to the post of Chief Commissioner of Nuremberg on 1 February 1967. It was not long before Herold was making a name for himself by introducing data processing as a means of fighting crime.

Herold's great moment came in July 1971. He was eating with the Mayor of Nuremberg when the latter was called to the telephone, and came back with the news, 'Horst, that was Genscher. He wants to make you head of the Federal Criminal Investigation Office.'

On 1 September 1971, Herold took up his new post in Wiesbaden. He was now chief terrorist hunter in the Federal Republic. He planned a complete restructuring of the BKA. Federal Interior Minister Genscher promised him all the support he needed, both politically and financially. The climate was favourable, with the Red Army Faction making life more and more difficult for the regional police authorities. The idea was to make the BKA a kind of German version of the American FBI which could come to their aid. The Interior Ministers of the various *Länder*, usually very insistent upon the autonomy of their police forces, were prepared to delegate a part of their powers to the BKA.

The BKA's anti-terrorism department was still operating from Bonn at this time. Fifty officers made up what was known as the Bonn Security Group. Herold flew from Wiesbaden to Bonn by helicopter every few days to confer with Genscher and the head of the Security Group, which had what was practically an independent existence, being a kind of self-styled elite troop of the BKA.

'What are we going to do about terrorism?' asked Genscher.

'We can't fight it from Bonn,' said Herold. 'We must decentralize to attack it at its roots.'

He then revealed his idea of a communications system between the Federal Criminal Investigation Office and the regional police authorities. Each of the *Länder* was to be required to set up a special anti-terrorist commission, to be controlled by the BKA. Genscher was on Herold's side. The Federal Criminal Investigation Office was authorized to control the regional special commissions: not by issuing directives, which as a Federal authority it was not empowered to do, but by the relaying of information. It was to act as the centre for gathering and evaluating information and the results of inquiries in terrorist cases, and – as a kind of super-brain – to convey information that could set off action to the associated regional police forces. Thus, in Herold's opinion, superiority in the field of information would achieve an effective result even without a clear command structure.

Herold used to work far into the night. The department had to be built up, a computer centre installed, new staff, computer operators and detective officers taken on.

During the installation of the hardware, Herold brooded over new models of application for his electronic brains. He worked out 'handicaps' and explained to his computer operators the broad lines along which he saw them as part of his programme. 'When you've done it, show me what the logical sequence will be, and then I'd like to see the way you planned your programme.' Herold checked every step in the calculations, thus gradually becoming a computer specialist himself. Once he had moved his own private living quarters to the office too, he left his personal 'Stammheim', as he sometimes called it later, only on business, and often played about with the computers even at night. He had them fed with data not only on people whom the police wanted to find and arrest, but on people against whom preliminary proceedings were being taken, or who 'represented a danger' – whatever that might mean.

Herold was creative, and he was a perfectionist. He made himself the kind of expert who would have everything there in his head and his electronic storehouse, down to the very smallest detail, down to the very last gun number. He slept less and less. He brought forth fantastic ideas for fighting all crime, not just terrorism, in its early stages. Vast quantities of data amassed by the police over decades were to act as the foundation for his plans.

It sometimes seemed as if Herold would keep alternating between over- and underestimating his office and himself, between fantasies of omnipotence and despondency, between self-adulation and self-pity. Sometimes he expressed the opinion that a Reich Criminal Investigation department, along the lines of his own Federal office, could have prevented the Nazis from coming to power.

He understood many of the political motives of 'the Baaders and the Meinhofs' very well, and this was not the least of the reasons why he was sometimes very successful in pursuing them.

At the peak of the terrorist hunt, Herold often felt as much a prisoner in his office as were the terrorists already arrested in their high-security wings. Unlike the terrorists, however, he complained, he got no sympathy from the public. Their close relationship bound him more to them than to the rest of society. If people attacked the conditions in which they lived so violently, then it must have something to do with those conditions themselves. It was his task, he said, to exert influence on politics within the framework available to him, unobtrusively but effectively.

Herold's data processing provided, for the first time, a system which simultaneously fulfilled two of a detective's dreams: the collection of as much information as possible, and the ability to fit the individual components together in the minimum time. In 1979, a review of the system by Gerhard Baum, later Federal Interior Minister, listed thirty-seven data files containing 4.7 million names and some 3,100 organizations. Many of these occurred several times. The fingerprints collection contained the prints of 2.1 million people. There was a photographic section with pictures of 1.9 million people. The 'personal identification centre' set up after the murder of Federal Prosecutor General Siegfried Buback in 1977 contained the names of over 3,500 people, with a short personal description of each and a list of material available for their identification such as photographs, fingerprints and handwriting tests. Many of these names were those of people who had been, for instance, suspected of terrorism in 1970, although nothing had been proved against them.

A computer printout of 15 January 1979 listed 6,047 persons with the note 'BEFA-7 contact' against their names. The initials were for *Beobachtende Fahndung*, which translates roughly as Investigation by Surveillance, and the names belonged to people who might, for instance, have been seen in the company of other people who were under surveillance and themselves had 'BEFA person' against their names.

Countless other data files on the criminal world in general existed side by side with these in the offices of the Federal Criminal Investigation Office.

It took many years to build up the entire body of equipment required by Big Brother BKA. A few of these data files were later destroyed on the orders of Federal Interior Minister Baum.

32
The Death of Georg von Rauch

When the the Red Army Faction shifted its field of operations back to Berlin, Hamburg sympathisers sent certain items of equipment after them by post. The parcels, at least fifteen of them, were so badly packed that some ammunition fell out. The Federal Mail officials alerted the police, and the entire consignment was confiscated.

Its contents comprised sixteen Firebird and Parabellum pistols, three automatic rifles, their silencers and telescopic sights, 3,280 cartridges of different calibres, two walkie-talkie radio sets, ten wigs, any amount of artificial beards, a plastic bag containing car number plates of various *Länder* of the Federal Republic, ampoules of assorted drugs and narcotics. Some items of uniform were also found, including a uniform jacket of the Bavarian Regional Police, a jacket of the Bavarian Border Police, and a First Lieutenant's uniform jacket. In addition, there were fifteen sticks of explosives and sixteen detonators.

A few days later the Berlin police began a large-scale round-up. Three thousand policemen were brought into the hunt. Security measures and identity checks were intensified at the border check-points. The police enlisted the aid of estate agents, property managers, filling stations, garages, key-cutting services and manufacturers of car number plates. The public was requested to keep a particularly sharp look-out for any suspect BMWs. The search was on for the 2 June Movement as well as members of the Red Army Faction.

The police operation began on 3 December 1971. A day later there was another death.

Two police officers in civilian cars, accompanied by Counter-Intelligence men, had been following a Ford Transit van reported stolen. They stopped the van, and a red Volkswagen Variant which had also been stolen, in Eisenacher Strasse. The police officers tried to arrest the four people in the two vehicles. One of them immediately ran away; the other three stood by the wall of a building with their hands up. One of the plainclothes police officers frisked them for weapons. A local resident observed this scene from his window and called the police, reporting excitedly, 'There's a man threatening three young people with a pistol in Eisenacher Strasse, on the corner by Fugger's. It could be to do with the hunt for the Baader gang, I don't know. Can you come at once, please?'

'Eisenacher Strasse . . . what corner did you say?' repeated the officer on duty at the other end of the line.

'The corner by Fugger's, the antique shop opposite the playground,' said the observer, who had taken his telephone to the window.

'And what did you say was going on?' asked the policemen.

'There's a man threatening three young people with a pistol. They're lined up against the wall now, hands up and so on.'

'Threatened with a pistol, right,' repeated the police officer.

'By a civilian, not the police.'

'We're on our way.' The officer had got the message. At that moment a shot was fired. 'He's firing, come quick!' shouted the caller.

'Yes, just stay right there, will you?'

The witness's voice was breaking in his excitement. 'There's a man down, there's a man down, shots are being fired. Listen, listen, listen! There's a man been shot . . .'

'Keep calm, sir, the radio car is on its way.'

'We're looking down from the balcony. Quick, quick . . . oh, my God, my nerves won't stand it!'

'Please keep quite calm,' said the policeman. 'The radio car is on its way. Can you give a description of the man with the gun?'

'No, no, I can't. We're too far off, we live on the third floor here.'

'Please stay on the line. I'm passing on your information to radio control.'

'There's somebody down there cleaning his car. One of them's lying there, lying there . . .'

'Are you still there?' asked the police officer.

'One of them's probably dead. He's lying there, he's not moving.'

'Somebody's lying there, right?' asked the police officer.

'Dead outside the shop opposite the playground.'

'Stay on the line, please,' said the officer.

'Right, yes.'

'We're on our way.'

'My God, what a thing, people still cleaning their cars as if nothing had happened, not taking a blind bit of notice. I don't understand it at all.'

'Hell, that's how it is these days,' said the policeman.

This conversation had been recorded on tape at police emergency call HQ. The dead man was Georg von Rauch, the professor's son from Kiel.

He had been Bommi Baumann's best friend. Now he lay there in the street, killed by a bullet through the eye. Baumann had seen that von Rauch was the first to draw his pistol and fire it, but what difference did that make now? Baumann made a break for it, his pistol still in his hand. He ran into a group of Hare Krishna disciples on the Kurfürstendamm. Brandishing the pistol, he made the orange-clad figures let him through. Then he fled to an apartment belonging to friends of his.

33
Revolutionary Fiction

Federal Interior Minister Genscher expressed cautious confidence. 'I don't say it will be soon, but within the foreseeable future.' The *Welt* made this into a headline: 'GENSCHER ANNOUNCES FINAL ATTACK ON ANARCHIST GANG'.

Some fringe members of the group had indeed been arrested shortly after the shooting incident in Berlin, but no decisive blow had been struck. The hard core of the RAF moved back to West Germany again.

Andreas Baader proposed laying false trails to lead the police astray. He issued directions for a Volkswagen and a Mercedes 280 SL, which had been stolen in Hamburg, to be abandoned in Munich. All the important members of the group had left their fingerprints in the Mercedes.

After more than a year and a half underground, a year and a half mainly spent constructing and reconstructing a logistical system of cars, apartments and forged papers, as well as the bank raids necessary to finance it all, the RAF now planned to draw attention to its political aims with bomb attacks.

But first the group needed money. Baader–Meinhof members had attacked and robbed banks now and then in the late autumn, but on the advice of the BKA, the ready cash kept at bank branches had been considerably reduced, so that raids brought in a good deal less than before.

It sometimes happened that the only takings were new notes, which it would have been too dangerous to exchange. So the group devised ways of transforming 'new' into 'used' money. The banknotes were rolled up, folded and re-folded with dirty hands. In one apartment, members of the group scattered notes on the floor and walked about on them for several days. Now and then they rather overdid it, and the notes were scarcely recognizable any more as valid currency.

Frankfurt became the group's new centre. Just before Christmas 1971, Dierk Hoff, a metal sculptor, had a visitor to his workshop, which was well equipped for artistic and craftsman's work. Three years earlier, in 1968, he had met Holger Meins, then studying at the Berlin Film Academy, in an acquaintance's junk shop. He had almost forgotten him. That December day, Holger Meins suddenly turned up in his workshop. He gave Hoff a friendly greeting, as if they were old acquaintances. At first Hoff could not remember him very well.

'Where was it we met?'

'Oh, everybody knows you, you're known all over town.'

Holger Meins said he was currently working on a film project, which needed some technical work done on it. If Hoff was interested, he could have the job. Dierk Hoff agreed.

Some time later Holger Meins came back to the workshop, this time with another young man: Jan-Carl Raspe, whom he introduced as 'Lester'. Holger Meins had not given his own name either, but from conversation between the pair of them Dierk Hoff gathered that he was called 'Erwin'. The three sat down on the upper floor of the two-storey workshop, talking about hippies and the subculture. They smoked a little hashish, and Hoff showed them the pattern book illustrating several examples of his work. Many of these items resembled weapons. His two visitors seemed to think it was all very remarkable, and offered Hoff the chance of making the props for their film. The project might be delayed a bit, but meanwhile perhaps he could construct a piece of equipment for the extraction of hollow metal pins. Holger Meins had brought an example with him, and Hoff agreed to make six of them. In fact, the item was a device for removing locks and thus breaking into cars.

A couple of days later Holger Meins came back, praised Hoff's good workmanship and paid him DM 200. 'We're getting on with the film now; we can think about the props,' said 'Erwin'. Hoff asked what the film was about. 'It's a kind of revolutionary fiction,' replied Holger Meins. You couldn't find anything but rather primitive stuff in the usual props catalogues, he said. He showed Hoff the upper part of a hand grenade with its metal frame sprayed sky-blue. The whole thing looked like a toy. Meins explained how it should function, and asked if he could make a version of the thing which would be rather more 'genuine' and pack more of a punch. Hoff made a round dozen duplicates, and was paid DM 500 in cash for them.

Within the group, the 'metal sculptor' was given the cover name of Peach.

34
'Six against Sixty Million'

On 22 December 1971, at least four people raided the Fackelstrasse branch of the Mortgage and Exchange Bank in Kaiserslautern. They got away with around DM 100,000, and foreign currency to the value of about DM 35,000. To ensure the smooth running of the operation, helpers had blocked the entrance of the police station near the bank with their cars shortly before the raid.

The raid began at 8 a.m. A red VW minibus stopped outside the bank. Except for the driver, everyone in it was wearing a balaclava pulled over the face, showing only the eyes, and they were all uniformly dressed in green parkas. They stormed into the bank, pistols drawn, shouting, 'This is a raid! Hands up! Over by the wall!' One of them vaulted the foreign currency counter and cleared it out, while another made for the main counter and stuffed money into his briefcase. Then the bank teller was ordered to open the safe.

Meanwhile, out in the street, a police officer who happened to be passing had noticed a red VW minibus parked outside the bank, contrary to traffic regulations. He went up to the passenger window. A shot was suddenly fired through the window from inside the vehicle. The policeman, Herbert Schoner, was injured by flying glass in the throat and face. The man in the driving seat fired a second shot which hit the policeman in the back. Severely wounded, the officer collapsed, but as he fell he raised his pistol and returned fire. He dragged himself into the bank. One of the bank robbers was crouching on the counter. He fired at the policeman. Later, forensic medical experts established that any of these shots on its own would have killed Schoner.

Without waiting for the safe to be opened, the bank robbers took flight, leaving behind them a lady's handbag and a cassette recorder which they had put on a table and switched on. They jumped into the VW minibus and raced away.

Next morning, 23 December 1971, the *Bild-Zeitung* came out with the headline: 'BAADER–MEINHOF GANG STRIKES AGAIN. BANK RAID: POLICEMAN SHOT'.

The precipitate haste with which the Baader–Meinhof group was increasingly being held responsible for anything and everything signalled a further intensification of the internal political climate. Two weeks later, *Der Spiegel* published an article by Heinrich Böll, under the heading, 'DOES ULRIKE WANT CLEMENCY OR A SAFE CONDUCT?' The text reflected the perplexity of many leftists and liberals in the face of the RAF's private war.

'It is a declaration of war made by desperate theoreticians,' wrote Böll, 'by people now being hunted and denounced, who have got themselves into a corner, have been driven into a corner, and whose theories sound far more violent than they are in practice . . . There can be no doubt about it: Ulrike Meinhof has declared war on this society, she knows what she is doing and what she has done, but who can tell her what she ought to do now? Is she really expected to turn herself in, with the prospect of ending up as the classic red witch in the cauldron of demagogy?'

The writer did a sum: six Red Army Faction members against sixty million West German citizens.

'That is indeed a most menacing situation for the Federal Republic of Germany. It is time to proclaim a state of national emergency. The emergency of the public consciousness, permanently heightened by such publications as *Bild* . . .

'Must it be like that? Does Ulrike Meinhof want it to be like that? Does she want clemency, or at least a safe conduct? Even if she wants neither, someone must offer them to her. That trial must take place, with Ulrike Meinhof alive, before the international public. Otherwise, not only will she and the rest of her group be lost, the German media and German legal history will continue to stink.'

From then on Heinrich Böll was regarded as a Baader–Meinhof sympathizer, like many others who tried to preserve a sense of proportion amidst the generally rising hysteria. Heinrich Böll's appeal aroused a storm of indignation, particularly in the more right-wing press. 'Armed Freedom of Thought' was the heading of a comment column in *Die Welt*.

In *Der Spiegel*, Diether Posser, Minister for Federal Affairs in North Rhine–Westphalia, replied to Böll's argument. 'Böll dangerously plays down the group's activities. Anger emotionalizes his criticism and deprives it of objectivity. His argument is not just exaggerated, but harmful. Intending to call for reason, he has written unreasonably himself.'

Heinrich Böll emended his remarks:

'The effect of my article does not correspond to what I had envisaged: I aimed for the introduction of a kind of relief from tension, with an appeal to the group, even in hiding, to give themselves up. I admit that I underestimated the extent of the demagogy I would be arousing . . .

'Possibly I assumed greater democratic self-understanding than I ought to have done.

'I am a writer, and to me the words "hunted", "clemency" and "criminality" do not necessarily have the same dimensions as they do to a civil servant, a lawyer, a minister, or to police officers.'

This was not the time for reason. The newspapers were stirring up more fear of the Baader–Meinhof group daily, whipping up emotions, and thus giving the members of the group, who regularly studied the reports of their activities in the press, a sense of their own importance. One police manhunt succeeded another, usually without any success. And success in the hunt for the fugitive RAF members became a question of political prestige to the Socialist–Liberal Bonn government under Chancellor Willy Brandt. Themselves suspected of being 'foster brothers of terrorism', the Social Democrats made haste to comply with the demands of the Conservative opposition.

It was no coincidence that it was at this point, on 28 January 1972, that the Prime Ministers of the West German *Länder*, under the chairmanship of Federal Chancellor Willy Brandt, unanimously adopted sanctions against the small handful of German Communist Party comrades, who were of negligible importance to internal security.

They did so in the so-called Radicals Edict which, at the height of the hunt for the Baader–Meinhof group, aimed to prevent political contamination of the healthy world of bureaucracy: 'If a candidate belongs to an organization which pursues aims inimical to the constitution, that membership is grounds for doubting whether he will always support the basic principles of the democracy. As a rule, these doubts will justify rejection of the application for a post.'

Supporting this argument, Chief Minister Heinz Kühn of North Rhine–Westphalia went so far as to remark, 'Ulrike Meinhof employed as a teacher, or Andreas Baader in the police force? That's out of the question.'

35
Andreas Baader's Thumb

In January 1972, there was another shooting incident in Cologne. A police sergeant discovered a BMW 2000 with Berlin plates in the Niehl dockland area. He immediately thought of the Baader–Meinhof group, and stationed his motorbike behind the car with its engine and headlights switched on. Then he took off his glove and loaded his service pistol. He knocked on the driver's window from behind. Baader wound the window down and looked at the policeman. 'Your vehicle's registration papers, please,' said the police officer, pointing the barrel of his pistol at Baader.

'Just a moment, please,' said Baader, leaning over to the glove compartment. He drew a long-barrelled pistol and fired it. The policeman had seen the gun and swerved quickly aside. The shot missed him. Baader raced away. The police officer shot after him, but failed to hit him.

At the end of January, *Bild* had another sensational news item to report. Apparently Andreas Baader had been in touch with a Hamburg lawyer. He wanted to give up the struggle and turn himself in. Andreas Baader read this report himself, and was indignant. He wrote to the Bavarian regional office of the German Press Agency, denying the *Bild* story. He signed the letter in his own hand, 'A. Baader', with his thumbprint beside it. The print turned out to be genuine.

Baader began his letter with a quotation from the South American guerrilla ideologist Marighella: 'The cops will go on groping in the dark until they find they are forced to turn the political into a military situation.'

Andreas Baader then went into detail:

'I have no intention of turning myself in. No RAF prisoner has made any statements as yet. Reports of success against us can say only arrested or dead. The strength of the guerrilla movement is the determination of every one of us. We are not in flight. We are here to organize armed resistance to the existing property-based order and the increasing exploitation of the people. The struggle has only just begun.'

This letter was circulated in millions of copies of newspapers.

•

On 21 February 1972, eight RAF members stormed the Ludwigshafen branch of the Mortgage Bank and got away with DM 285,000. They were disguised with carnival masks.

36 Peach

In the first few weeks of 1972, Dierk Hoff the Frankfurt metal sculptor was given more and more work to do. He still believed, or so he said later, anyway, that he was making props for a fictional story of revolution. On the occasion of one visit from his client Holger Meins, who called himself Erwin, Meins told him about the climax of the projected film. They had been thinking, said Meins, of making a bomb casing which could be fastened to a body belt resembling a woman's girdle. There was a scene in the film in which a woman was going to plant an explosive device in a lavatory, where she would unfasten it from the belt and replace it under her clothing with an inflatable balloon.

Hoff set to work. He bought a metal hemisphere and fixed it to a kind of canvas corset. Then he got an inflatable beach ball of the same size, which was not too easy in winter.

'Erwin' and 'Lester' were delighted. One of them put the bomb girdle on and mimed a pregnant woman, laughing. They gave Hoff DM 400. When 'Erwin' collected the 'baby bomb', he gave Dierk Hoff an empty shotgun cartridge and asked if he could make a device to fire it.

'A shotgun cartridge has too much of a kick. It's too dangerous,' said Dierk Hoff. 'I wouldn't know just how strong I'd need to make such a thing to keep it from coming apart.'

'That's not your problem. We have a specialist on the film set for that. He can alter cartridges to suit. It's just a matter of the gunflash coming out at the front.'

Dierk Hoff made three of the devices required, for DM 100 apiece. Next time, Holger Meins brought a shotgun with him. Its barrel and stock were sawn off. 'We were thinking a magazine could be fitted to this, and a metal butt, to make the thing look like a military weapon. It would come in useful for our film.'

Hoff had misgivings; fitting a magazine to reload the shotgun was rather a complicated piece of work from the mechanical point of view. He said he had no real idea how long it would take him.

'A few hundred Deutschmarks here and there don't matter. The whole film stands or falls by its props.' And Holger Meins made a few technical suggestions. To Hoff's own surprise, the newly constructed reloading device worked. He had turned the shotgun into a shot-loaded machine gun.

Dierk Hoff was getting a queasy feeling. He tried to back out. 'You're dragging me into some kind of business I don't altogether understand. Bring me back those bits and pieces I made you. I don't want any more to do with it. Or I'll have to go to the police.'

At the mention of the police, 'Erwin' drew a pistol, pointed it at Hoff, and spat, 'You did the job; you're up to your neck in it too. It's ridiculous to talk about the police.'

Hoff was afraid. 'Erwin' became a little less menacing. 'Going to the police just isn't on. And anyway, why would you do a thing like that? You'd only incriminate yourself.'

'Lester' intervened. 'Look, just don't panic, don't get scared. Don't you worry, there's no need at all to go to the police. The whole thing's harmless; don't take it so seriously.'

'Erwin' did not agree with his friend's approach. 'That shit! Talking about going to the police. Well, this is it. Only pressure helps now. The idiot, just look at him.'

A few days later Jan-Carl Raspe, alias Lester, turned up again. 'That was quite a scene last time,' he said, in his friendly manner. 'I didn't agree with that, pointing a gun at you.'

Hoff complained. 'Yes, well, that's what it boils down to, I make you guns, you wave them in my face. It's crazy, this thing you're doing with me.'

'I didn't think it was a good idea either. We'd better talk it over calmly. No point in fooling about.'

He put a leaflet down on the table, saying, 'That's ours.' The document was rather grubby and well thumbed. Hoff leafed through it, recognized the five-pointed star ornamented with a submachine gun and the letters RAF.

'Take a look at it at your leisure. I'm sure you'll find it useful,' said Raspe.

Hoff continued to cooperate.

One day Holger Meins pointedly kept his back turned to Hoff in the workshop. 'What's up?' asked Hoff.

Holger Meins whirled around, hands in his coat pockets. It was only at second glance that Hoff realized 'Erwin' had the barrel of a pistol trained on him, with the gun nestling in his pocket. He laughed, uneasily.

'Lester' sometimes played about with his pistol too. However, Hoff didn't take him so seriously. But Holger Meins made him feel that jest could easily become earnest. On his next visit, 'Erwin' brought along another young man, introduced to Hoff as 'Harry'. This was Gerhard Müller.

'He's one of us,' said 'Erwin'. 'One hundred per cent reliable. If there's a time I can't come, I'll send Harry.'

'Wow, what a great place, you could make anything here,' said 'Harry' enthusiastically, when 'Erwin' showed him the workshop. The pair of them had brought along a box of new detonators which Hoff was to screw to the casings of hand grenades. The threads did not fit, and would have to be recut on the lathe, then the detonators firmly screwed in place and tightened with pliers. Hoff was afraid the detonators might go off in his face with the rough handling they were given. 'No, wild horses wouldn't get me to do it. I'm not touching that shit, no way!'

'Erwin' calmed him down. 'Come on, don't be chicken, there's no problem. Go on, do it, I swear it isn't dangerous!'

'I said no, it's out of the question.'

Hoff held out obstinately, and went into the next room. Thereupon Holger Meins undertook the dangerous job himself. Hoff was surprised to see how well he could handle the tools. Not one of the detonators went off.

A little later Hoff had a fourth visitor. He was working, and heard men's voices in the backyard as they approached the workshop. He thought it could not be any of the RAF, who had hitherto acted in a quiet and conspiratorial manner. Hoff opened the door to admit 'Erwin', 'Lester' and their companion. This third man had hair dyed a pale blond and wore a red winter coat. He was not introduced to Dierk Hoff. Without saying a word, he went past him and into the workshop. He looked at the machinery, stopped, nodded, went into the next room, looked at the lathe. While the stranger inspected his workshop, Dierk Hoff stood there feeling rather awkward. It was as if this were his boss checking up on him. After twenty minutes and a few brief words, the trio left. The stranger was Andreas Baader.

After this they gave Dierk Hoff more and more jobs to do. When 'Erwin' turned up again one day, Hoff mentioned the fair man's visit. He did not like to think of a steadily growing number of people knowing what he was up to.

'Don't let that worry you,' said Holger Meins. 'The lads are all one hundred per cent. Totally reliable. You're the only uncertain factor. We started out with the wrong sort of assumptions. You're not our sort. We'll have to deal with you one way or another.'

Baader, Ensslin, Raspe and Meins had moved into a tower block apartment in Inheidener Strasse, Frankfurt. They took trips to other cities from this base. When the apartment was discovered later, detectives found the fingerprints of almost all members of the group in this hideout – but not Ulrike Meinhof's.

37
Baader and Ensslin Hunting for Ulrike Meinhof

In the middle of February Emiliane M., a qualified psychologist, was asked by an intermediary if she was willing to help a couple who were in difficulties. These people might approach her and ask if they could stay the night. The psychologist agreed. She soon realized who the couple with the difficulties were, namely Andreas Baader and Gudrun Ensslin. She had recognized Baader from a Wanted poster, and Gudrun Ensslin said her father was a Stuttgart pastor.

The psychologist had given the visitors keys to her apartment, and whenever they wanted to keep away from their other quarters, they turned up at her place. They generally came in late at night and very quietly. Once Gudrun Ensslin even took her shoes off so as not to disturb her. When the couple wanted to telephone, they left the apartment and went to a telephone booth. They had always parked their car some distance from the building, so that their hostess never saw it.

The psychologist thought they both looked very tired and harassed. Sometimes they jumped when Emiliane came into the apartment. At the same time, they seemed to be very busy. They explained their weapons by saying they could expect to encounter cops armed with submachine guns any time. In a way Emiliane felt sorry for them. The very fact that Baader and Ensslin had to fall back on people like herself seemed to show that the number of their helpers must have decreased a good deal recently. 'Otherwise,' she said later, 'they would have picked people who could take more of the weight and were ideologically more convinced.'

The psychologist felt increasingly worried. But her conscience would have pricked her if she had refused to help the wanted couple, and she did not want that. On one occasion she tried to break off the contact and wrote them a letter about her personal fears and weakness. Gudrun Ensslin gave her back the letter, smiling sympathetically and saying, 'Keep it and read it again in two years' time.' Emiliane M. felt ashamed, and never tried to get rid of her uninvited guests again.

* * *

Late in March 1972, she came home late one evening. Baader and Ensslin were in the apartment and seemed very agitated. They had had news by phone of a television report of the death of Ulrike Meinhof. They were thrown off balance, and thought for a moment the report might be true. There was no television set in the apartment, so they could not switch on for the next news bulletin. Without observing their usual precautions, they telephoned from the apartment to find out from other group members whether or not Ulrike Meinhof was still alive. After a while they got through to someone who had seen Ulrike Meinhof after the television report, and knew where she was.

There was indeed a rumour of Ulrike Meinhof's death rife in West Germany at the end of March. *Bild* printed a headline: 'HAS ULRIKE MEINHOF COMMITTED SUICIDE?' The *Frankfurter Allgemeine* too stated that according to reports from Bonn, Ulrike Meinhof had been dead since the end of February. There were several versions of the cause of death going about: death from a tumour, or suicide by poison because of depression over an incurable illness. *Bild* even referred to supposed tips given to the Hamburg police by left-wing radicals that Ulrike Meinhof had 'been burnt and buried in a Hamburg crematorium under a false name'.

When *Bild* published its headline claiming that Ulrike Meinhof had committed suicide because of far-reaching differences of opinion with the rest of the group, she was in fact in Margrit Schiller's apartment. Ulrike was extremely indignant: 'Those filthy bastards. These are *their* projections, that's the way *they* do things! They'll stoop to any of the dirty tricks the CIA use, hoping to leave us stranded. All over the world they work along the same lines to deprive revolutionaries of their credibility and brand them nut-cases.'

The Federal Criminal Investigation specialists had no information about Ulrike Meinhof's death. One thing, however, did make them think: they had picked up no trace at all of her since the end of 1971.

She did not turn up in Hamburg again until the middle of March 1972. Baader and Ensslin were keeping away from that city. Ulrike Meinhof and the others tried to recruit new members on their own initiative.

38
Statistical Life Expectation

Horst Mahler's second trial opened in Berlin at the beginning of 1972. He was accused of forming a criminal association and taking part in three bank raids.

As before, Mahler stood by the RAF, and gave *Der Spiegel* written answers to some questions about the strategy of the armed struggle. Asked whether he had failed politically, the former lawyer replied:

'Even a high probability of failure does not absolve one from the duty of doing what one can. The class war is not a civil service career entitling one to a pension. The Socialist revolution is making tremendous progress everywhere. I have a great desire to contribute all I still can to it. So I have not failed.'

Asked whether a call for armed struggle in West Germany did not in fact mean risking human life, and thus 'sending comrades to the slaughter', Mahler said:

'The concept of "sending comrades to the slaughter" betrays a positively ineradicable desire in the user of that term to preserve himself, come what may, for the day when all he has to do is applaud the revolutionary victory achieved by others. Humanly speaking, this desire may be comprehensible, but it is not one of the virtues of a revolutionary.'

Every comrade who was sick of 'bourgeois disorder' must ask himself, said Mahler, 'whether he would not make more of his life by breaking out of the ghetto at last and tearing down its walls, even if such an act were to decrease his statistical life expectation'.

In point of fact, the statistical expectation of life of the Red Army Faction comrades still underground was decreasing appreciably.

An estate agent in Augsburg reported to the police in February that a 'suspicious couple' had rented the apartment above his. He was sure the woman belonged to the Baader–Meinhof group. This tip set off a large-scale police operation. Thirteen men of the Bonn Security Group, Counter-Intelligence and the regional Criminal Investigation office checked into the Augsburger Hof hotel and kept watch on the suspect apartment. Bugs were installed. The best observation post, the officers discovered, was the vestry of St George's Church opposite. They took the pastor into their confidence. He willingly let the officers into the building, and went off on a trip to the Holy Land.

For the purposes of this operation, the Special Commission was equipped with seven cars, and radio transmitters employing a secret code: 201 for Baader, 202 for Meinhof and so on, in order of importance. The Commission had agreed with the Augsburg city police to radio 4444 as an emergency alert when the operation began.

Zero hour was Thursday, 2 March. The couple under surveillance drove into the city centre in a stolen car and parked quite correctly at a meter. They went into the Thalia hotel and came out again a few minutes later. As they reached their car, the woman turned round again. At this moment the police took action.

A shot was fired from a police pistol.

The bullet hit the young man in the heart. He was Thomas Weisbecker, aged twenty-three, the son of a professor from Kiel. The police said he had tried to draw his pistol. The woman, who was arrested shortly afterwards, was twenty-four years old, a member of the Socialist Patients' Collective, and was called Carmen Roll.

On the afternoon of that day Chief Superintendent Hans Eckhardt, leading the Baader–Meinhof Special Commission, with two colleagues, occupied an apartment in the Harvesterhude area of Hamburg where an RAF forgery workshop had been discovered. A fourth officer was posted on the stairs, and a fifth in the street outside the building.

After dark, Manfred Grashof and Wolfgang Grundmann, who had recently joined the RAF, drove to the apartment. No sooner had they opened the door than shots were fired.

Grundmann put his hands up. 'Don't shoot. I'm not armed.' Grashof fired.

The superintendent collapsed with two bullets in his body. His colleagues shot Grashof in the head and chest. At the Eppendorf University Hospital, doctors worked to save the lives of the police officer and the RAF man. The policeman died two weeks later. Grashof survived. He was identified from police records, and treated in the intensive care unit.

After a few days, the severely wounded man was whisked away from hospital by the security services and transferred to a prison cell, an ordinary unhygienic cell with an open lavatory in the corner, and sand blowing in through the window. There was a cardboard notice outside the door, indicating that the cell was to be considered a hospital room. The light was left on day and night, allegedly for Grashof's own safety.

He spent two months in this cell, unable either to leave it or to speak to anyone. Then he was transferred from the sick bay and moved five cells farther on, to the high-security section, which had double gratings on both sides of it. The cells above and below his were empty. He could stand and walk again, and had half an hour's exercise in the yard every day – with his wrists handcuffed behind his back. His wounds opened up again.

39
Cooking up Explosives

In Frankfurt at the beginning of April, the metal sculptor Dierk Hoff was increasingly pressed for time. His clients had brought him sections of metal pipe about eighty centimetres long and just under twenty centimetres in diameter, each of which they wanted cut in four and welded together at the ends. Gerhard Müller helped him carry the red-hot bomb casings into the bathroom, where they had to be cooled in the tub. A mighty cloud of steam arose.

In the preceding days and weeks, Müller had been to various cities buying several hundred kilograms of chemicals with which to fill the bombs: red lead, powdered aluminium, ammonium nitrate, potassium nitrate, potassium chlorate, sulphur, charcoal, wood meal, glycerine, iron oxide and assorted acids. Müller also laid in batteries, wires, cords, plugs, terminals, wire resistors and timers.

The group intended to make explosive devices of differing construction, so as to confuse the investigating authorities with more and more new types of bomb. Müller procured some steel balls four to nine millimetres thick to increase the fragmentation effect.

The raw materials needed for the making of these bombs were taken to the Inheidener Strasse apartment. Several of the chemicals had to be pulverized. Baader thought of using electric coffee mills for the purpose. He sent Müller off to buy some. As the capacity of the coffee mills was small and they wore out fast in the process of mass production, a larger mill was obtained, but this one wore out even faster. So they were stuck with grinding ammonium nitrate and charcoal in small quantities. Baader put the coffee mills in buckets, to reduce the nuisance of flying dust as much as possible. The police later discovered a whole battery of carefully packed coffee mills in the Inheidener Strasse apartment, ten of them in all. Kitchen appliances – hand mixers – were also used for mixing the explosives. However, these gadgets too stood up poorly to misuse in the long run. Baader screwed egg whisks into a drill and used them to beat the highly explosive mixtures. He tried making a device with several egg whisks on one threaded bar driven by a drill, to speed this laborious process up a bit and mix larger quantities all at once.

The recipe for a mixture of ammonium nitrate, red lead and powdered aluminium in the proportions of four to three or two did not have the desired result. Baader tried exploding it and found that there was too much red lead left over. So the amount of that substance in the red explosive they were making was reduced to two and a half parts. The grey explosive consisted of ammonium nitrate, potassium nitrate, sulphur, charcoal and wood meal. Both kinds of explosive, ten to twelve hundredweight in all, were poured into the bomb casings through funnels, and some of them were laced with the steel balls. Detonators and fuses were built in at the same time; only the electric ignition systems were left out for the time being, for safety's sake. They were not to be fitted until just before the bombs were used.

40
Bomb Attacks

In May 1972, the American Air Force mined harbours in North Vietnam.

Andreas Baader, Jan-Carl Raspe, Holger Meins, Gudrun Ensslin and Gerhard Müller were in Frankfurt, at the Inheidener Strasse apartment. They listened to the news. Gudrun Ensslin suggested a bomb attack on American installations in Germany as a counter-measure. 'Let's go, then!' said Baader, as Gerhard Müller remembered it. Raspe and Gudrun Ensslin set off in a red Volkswagen to look for a suitable target. When they came back to the apartment, a small gas cylinder was prepared for explosion. Raspe also assembled a pipe bomb and packed it in a leather bag. Gudrun Ensslin put another explosive device in a carton; she was going to camouflage it with a bunch of flowers on top, so that the parcel would look like a gift. Baader and Holger Meins took the gas cylinder, put it in a canvas bag, and covered it with a cloth.

On 11 May 1972, between 6.59 and 7.02 p.m., three pipe bombs wrecked the entrance and officers' mess of the Fifth US Army Corps stationed in the IG-Farben buildings in Frankfurt am Main.

A bus driver called Vömel saw the flash of the explosion at the entrance. Then there was smoke billowing everywhere. He thought it might be a gas explosion. 'We weren't used to having bombs go off, not since the war.' Two military policemen ran past him, their guns drawn. Shortly afterwards there was a second explosion. Vömel and the other people who had been standing near him ran away over rubble and broken glass.

A third bomb exploded in the mess. Somebody called, 'Put your jackets over your heads.' Four people had been hit by flying glass and were bleeding. They took refuge in the cellar, without knowing why. 'It could be an inherited German reaction,' said the bus driver, later. 'When there are bombs falling we run down to the cellar instead of straight out.' An American soldier shouted, 'Everybody out of the building!'

People wandered around the corridors looking for a way out. Suddenly they came to a door, and shook it, but it refused to open. Someone said, 'There aren't any panes left in that door.' They climbed through and came out into the open, bleeding.

When the bomb went off in the officers' mess, one of the waitresses thought at first that it was a thunderstorm. Then, however, there was a flash, a crash, and the main entrance and the ceiling of the mess caved in. The woman ran through the kitchen and out of doors, where she saw an American officer who had been paying his bill to her a few moments earlier. Lieutenant Colonel Paul A. Bloomquist, aged thirty-nine, was lying on the ground with a splinter of the glass pane from the mess door in his throat. No one went to help him; they were all afraid yet another bomb might explode. In any case, Bloomquist was past helping now.

Thirteen people were injured and one killed as a result of this attack.

The RAF's declaration of responsibility was signed 'Petra Schelm Commando', and said, 'West Germany and West Berlin will no longer be a safe hinterland for the strategists of extermination in Vietnam. They must know that their crimes against the Vietnamese people have made them new and bitter enemies, that there will be nowhere in the world left where they can be safe from the attacks of revolutionary guerrilla units.'

Next morning, Gerhard Müller was woken to be told that Andreas Baader, Holger Meins and Gudrun Ensslin were going to Munich, to plant a bomb there in revenge for the death of Thomas Weisbecker. Müller was to stay in Frankfurt, answer the phone, and stand by in reserve. As he was leaving, Baader dropped another hint. 'There'll be trouble in Augsburg too.' They collected a car from a garage in the Hofeckweg, loaded it up with explosive devices, and set off.

On 12 May 1972, soon after 12.15 p.m., two explosive devices made from steel piping went off in two office cabinets at Augsburg police headquarters. Five policemen were injured.

Two hours after the Augsburg explosion, a Ford 12 M loaded with explosives blew up in the car park of the Munich regional Criminal Investigation Office. Sixty cars were demolished. Windows shattered on six floors.

On 15 May 1972, at 12.40 p.m., a red Volkswagen exploded in Karlsruhe, in the Klosestrasse. It belonged to Federal Judge Buddenberg, but his wife was at the wheel.

Frau Buddenberg had been about to go shopping and then fetch her husband from the Federal Court. She got into the car, putting her bag on the back seat. When she turned the ignition key she noticed a smell of burning. Then there was an explosion. Frau Buddenberg was covered with bits of car, ash, dust and dirt. She managed to crawl out into the road, calling for help. 'It's a Baader–Meinhof attack. Please tell my husband Judge Buddenberg.' Neighbours looked out of their windows, but did nothing. 'Please get my things, get my things out of the car,' Frau Buddenberg kept crying. She was bleeding from several wounds: injuries to her lower left leg, splinters in her right leg and arm.

On 19 May 1972, about 3.30 p.m., a telephonist in the Springer building on Kaiser-Wilhelm-Strasse in Hamburg took a call. 'A bomb will go off in the building in five minutes' time.'

The woman did not take it seriously. Calls of this kind were quite common at the Springer headquarters. She engaged the caller in conversation. 'You swine never take anything seriously,' said the man, ringing off.

The telephonist took a few more calls at her leisure, and then told the administrative office of the Springer building about the bomb threat. Meanwhile, another call had come in, and was taken by one of her colleagues. Once again it was a man's voice, though rather a high one, saying, 'A bomb will go off in five minutes' time.' The caller added, furiously, 'Clear the building at once!'

'Is it that crazy man again?' asked her colleague, sitting beside her.

The second telephonist nodded. The caller said, 'You bloody swine!' and then rang off.

The telephonists had just got someone from administration on the line when there was an almighty crash. A bomb had indeed exploded. Directly afterwards the telephone rang again: a long-distance call this time. 'Did a bomb just go off in the building?' asked a woman. 'Yes,' said the telephonist. Then there was a click on the line.

The first device had gone off in the proofreading room of the Springer building. There were fifteen proofreaders working there. Most of them suffered injuries. Soon afterwards, two other bombs hidden in the toilets went off.

One of the injured proofreaders said later, at the Stammheim trial, 'Of course we knew the Springer building was often besieged by students, and we sometimes couldn't get in to work. But we really never reckoned on somebody attacking us directly, planting a bomb on us, none of us did.'

A Springer editor said, 'I was only surprised that if they wanted to hit the Springer building they'd go for the proofreaders, whose views are rather left of centre. I'd have thought there were more rewarding targets if they wanted to strike a real blow. If they'd picked the computer centre, that would have done the building much more damage.'

In all, seventeen people were injured, two of them seriously.

Next day another anonymous caller rang: 'There are more bombs in the building. The police are all fools, they're looking in the wrong place.' And the police did indeed find three more explosive devices in the building: one near the presses, one in the management offices, and one in a cupboard containing cleaning materials. The bombs were made safe.

Three days after this attack, letters claiming responsibility arrived at the German Press Agency, the UPI, the *Süddeutsche Zeitung* and *Bild*, signed

'2 June Commando'. They were typewritten on a machine found later by the police in a Hamburg apartment.

'Springer would rather risk seeing his workers and clerical staff injured by bombs than risk losing a few hours' working time, which means profit, over a false alarm. To capitalists, profit is everything and the people who create it are dirt. We are deeply upset to hear that workers and clerical staff were injured.'

On 24 May, at 6.10 p.m., two car bombs went off within fifteen seconds of each other outside Barracks Block 28 and the mess of the European headquarters of the US Army in Heidelberg. A German ambulance driver in the stand-by area of the American hospital had heard the explosion. Soon afterwards the telephone rang. He was summoned to the main gate, and sent straight on to the computer station at the end of the headquarters area.

The place was strewn with debris. The ambulance man and his colleagues asked some military policemen, 'What's up?' They shrugged their shoulders. 'What does it look like? An explosion.'

Ambulance men and soldiers searched for the injured under fallen brickwork, beams and broken glass. A body, still moving, was lying in front of a window that had been blown out. The man's clothes had been torn off by the shock wave. The ambulance driver supported his head.

When an ambulance reached the gate, an officer said, 'You can drive slowly, there's no hurry, the man's dead.' The ambulance men delivered the corpse to the hospital and then went back again.

Meanwhile, a second bomb victim had been found, lying beside a fallen wall. A heavy Coca-Cola machine had buried the soldier underneath it. Nothing was showing but one of his feet. The drinks machine was pushed aside, but it was too late to do anything for him.

The third victim had been blown apart. The upper part of his body still lay there. The ambulance man saw bits of corpse in the lime trees near the spot where the explosion had occurred, and the burned soles of the dead man's feet on the ground. They collected the remains in a pillow case.

Other injured people were being treated in the car park, where a second device had gone off. One officer looked as if he had been scalped, with his hair and the skin of his head torn away.

Three American soldiers in all had been killed in this attack: Clyde Bonner, Ronald Woodward and Charles Peck. Five more GIs were injured.

The letter claiming responsibility for this attack too was written on the typewriter found later in Hamburg:

'The people of the Federal Republic will not support the security forces in their hunt for the bombers, because they want nothing to do with the crimes of American imperialism and their condonation by the ruling class here; because they have not forgotten Auschwitz, Dresden and Hamburg; because they know that bomb attacks on the mass murderers of Vietnam are justified; because they have discovered that demonstrations and words are of no use against the imperialist criminals.'

To all appearances, this was written by Ulrike Meinhof.

41
'Operation Watersplash'

Five days after the Heidelberg attack, the Chief Commissioner of the Federal Criminal Investigation Office called the leaders of the regional Special Commissions and representatives of the Federal Border Police together and briefed them on a plan for a nationwide search operation in two days' time, on a scale hitherto unknown in the Federal Republic. To all intents and purposes, the entire police force was placed under the command of the Federal Criminal Investigation Office for a day. Genscher had given Herold the go-ahead. The Federal Interior Minister merely said, 'Do it that way if need be. If we're not getting anywhere, we might as well find out who's not on our side.'

Herold presented the regional police chiefs of the *Länder* with a *fait accompli*. 'Please inform your Ministers.' There were a few expressions of demurral, but in the end they cooperated.

On 31 May 1972 all available helicopters in public service in West Germany were in the air. Each had a group of police officers on board; they flew over the motorways, coming down briefly at junctions to set up road-blocks, stop all vehicles and check up on their drivers. Then the officers took to their helicopters again, flew a little farther on and set up another roadblock. Like this, said Herold, the Federal Republic would be 'well and truly flushed out'.

There was total traffic chaos, but the anxious citizens of West Germany were tolerant. It was not at all as the RAF had predicted when claiming responsibility for their bomb attack: 'The people of the Federal Republic will not support the security forces in their hunt for the bombers . . .'

'I have never seen such a high degree of identification between citizens and the police as I did that day,' Herold remembered later. 'I flew over some of the roads by helicopter myself, and we really met nothing but drivers waving to us everywhere. It's hard to imagine now just how deep the shock of those attacks went. The explicit aim of our operation was to make a big splash in the water and get the fish moving. It surprised the television people; they sent teams everywhere. It was the first and biggest public operation ever known, and has not been repeated.'

42
The Siege

Even before the big hunt, the police, tipped off by a local resident, had been watching a garage in the Hofeckweg in Frankfurt, very near Hessian Radio. BKA officers crept in and took a look at the place. There was about two hundredweight of grey powder which looked suspiciously like explosive there, in large buckets. The police officers took the containers away and had their contents analysed by the BKA. Their first impressions had been correct. They then made a bonemeal mixture which looked just like the grey explosive and took the buckets back next night.

A few hours after the end of Operation Watersplash, which had not really been very productive, things started moving in the Hofeckweg garage being kept under surveillance.

It was 5.50 a.m. on 1 June 1972. Three men in an aubergine Porsche Targa drove east along Kaiser-Sigmund-Strasse. They turned right into the Eckenheimer Landstrasse, and then right again into the Kühlhornshofweg. The policemen noticed that the Porsche was going the wrong way down a one-way street. The car turned just before it reached the

Hofeckweg. Three men got out. Two of them, Holger Meins and Andreas Baader, went straight into the garage. The third, Jan-Carl Raspe, stayed outside on guard.

Two police officers from the surveillance squad approached in their car. Through their side window, they told Raspe to stay where he was. Raspe put his hand in his right coat pocket and drew a pistol. At this moment two more policemen came running up from the Hofeckweg. Jan-Carl Raspe ran a few metres towards them, and fired from a distance of about twenty-eight metres. One of the officers threw himself down behind the parked car, the other dived into it for safety. Raspe ran on, past the buildings, making for a garden, where Chief Superintendent Irgel cornered him. Raspe put up no resistance on being arrested. A 9-mm Parabellum was found on him. Four months later, a schoolboy discovered a Smith & Wesson revolver in the garden earth; Jan-Carl Raspe had buried it just before he was arrested.

Meanwhile, Baader and Meins had gone into the garage and closed the door behind them. When they heard the shots, Holger Meins opened one side of the door to see what was going on outside. A police officer had come within fifteen metres of the garage. He pointed his submachine gun at Meins and told him to go back inside. When the door was closed again, the policemen pushed one of the cars they had been using for observation, an Audi, in front of the door to keep the couple inside from breaking out. One of the officers went cautiously up to it again to switch off the radio transmitter. Baader fired through the closed right-hand side of the garage door. No one was hit.

By now, police reinforcements had arrived. The garage was surrounded by officers. Some 150 guns were trained on the besieged men. Chief Criminal Director Scheicher of the BKA had taken over command of the operation on the spot.

Later, Chief Commissioner Herold expressed surprise that Baader and Meins had not surrendered at once. 'It still amazes me that they then ventured to fire. They must have been aware they were sitting on a powder keg.'

Meanwhile, the police officers had knocked holes in the thick glass at the back of the garage. Detective Sergeant Pfeiffer could make the two men out in the gloom. 'They were laughing at us some of the time,' he remembered, later. 'They were smoking cigarettes and pointing their pistols our way now and then.'

Containers of tear gas were thrown into the garage through the holes in the back wall. Scheicher spoke to the two men over a loudhailer.

'Throw your pistols or other weapons out into the yard, put your hands up and come out one by one. Then you won't be hurt. We have more patience than you do. Much more. And we're in a better situation. We have stronger forces at our disposal. They're on their way, and they're so strong that you have no chance left. So come on out. What do you think you're doing, skulking in there?'

Baader and Meins pushed one side of the door out against the Audi. The police, getting the impression they wanted to surrender, pulled the car away with a rope. Thereupon the garage door was opened a little wider from the inside so that the tear gas could drift out. Baader flung smoking tear gas grenades back. He was standing near the front of the garage, on the right, leaning against the metallic silver Iso Rivolta sports car parked there, a revolver in his left hand and a cigarette in his right. On the left, Holger Meins was lying in cover behind a gas cylinder, beside the car, pointing his pistol out of the garage.

Towards 7.45 a.m. an armoured car with four officers in it went in. The idea was to push back both sides of the garage door, closing them so that the tear gas could work better. However, they could only close the right side of the door.

'Surrender – resistance won't do you any good,' came the message over the police loudhailer. When the two men inside still did not leave the garage, more tear-gas grenades were fired into their lair from Very pistols. Police Officer Stumpf and his colleague Officer Brandau fired their tear-gas grenades alternately. They could make out the fair-haired man who raised his arm and took a bearing on the police officers over the top of his pistol. 'Watch out, he's going to shoot!' cried Brandau. A shot was fired, then another, and the two policemen ducked for cover. The wind blew tear gas into the officers' eyes, and they retreated further away. The armoured car had another go, drove at the garage and pushed the door shut.

Detective Sergeant Bernhard Honke had gone to the scene of the operation at about seven o'clock. The area around the Hofeckweg was already sealed off. He got his colleagues to give him a rundown on the situation. A woman living on the third floor of the apartment building opposite the garage called out to him, saying there was a good view of the yard and the garage entrance from her window. The officer went up to her apartment. From there he could see the fair-haired man, Baader.

Slowly, the police cordon was drawn more tightly around the garage. Detective Sergeant Honke left his observation post on the third floor and asked the leaders of the operation if they could get him a gun with a telescopic sight. A few minutes later the gun was handed to him, and he went back to the window on the third floor.

He aimed at Baader's thigh through his telescopic sight, and fired. Baader fell, screaming. Once again, the two men were told over the loud-speaker to surrender and throw their guns out. Holger Meins came out of the garage with his hands up. He was ordered to stay where he was, strip to his underpants, and come to the exit of the yard.

TV cameras were rolling. The pictures of the skinny, almost naked figure of Holger Meins went around the world.

And RAF sympathizers, or those close to them, were reminded of the pictures of concentration camp inmates.

The myth of the pitiless persecution of the RAF warriors had been born.

Police Officer Reinhold Stumpf took Holger Meins in a police grip and led him to the squad car.

'What about the other man?' he asked.

'Done for,' said Holger Meins.

Stumpf and two other policemen put their bullet-proof vests on again and went to the garage. They found Andreas Baader there, lying on his side, screaming. He was still clutching his pistol in his left hand. One of the policemen kicked the gun away from him. Then Baader was dragged out of the garage, put on a stretcher and carried to the ambulance standing by, crying, 'You swine, you fucking cops.'

43
Victor and Vanquished

Alfred Klaus of the BKA was with the Bonn Security Group when he got news of the Frankfurt arrest. He was told that Baader was injured and was to be taken to prison hospital in Düsseldorf. Klaus informed the air squad of the Federal Border Police, so as to get a helicopter laid on for transport. The Border Police colonel responsible was very keen to fly the gang leader to hospital in person. With some misgivings, Klaus agreed.

They took the helicopter to Frankfurt, where Baader had been given first aid in the University Hospital. The gunshot had smashed his thigh, but he refused to have an anaesthetic. 'You only want to pump me,' he said, when Alfred Klaus arrived and asked him why not. 'That's ridiculous,' said the BKA man. 'You try interrogating someone under anaesthetic!' He gave Andreas Baader a message from his grandmother, whom he had visited a little while before. 'Is there anything you'd like me to tell her?' Baader simply looked at Klaus uncomprehendingly.

After much persuasion by the doctors, Baader agreed to be anaesthetized. His leg was put in plaster, he was loaded on to a stretcher, and taken to the ambulance along an underground corridor. Outside, the place was swarming with press photographers, some of them disguised as doctors in order to get pictures of the captured terrorist leader.

It was the greatest success yet of the police operation: the RAF leader under arrest. But in fact the drama was only just beginning.

The Frankfurt lawyer Armin Golzem was the first at Baader's bedside. In his words: 'He wasn't a man whose bearing showed you, so to speak, that his political ambitions were over. Far from it. The RAF itself wasn't dead after this either. The RAF lived on in the figures now in jail. They might not be able to take any more immediate part in armed politics, but they were by no means to be underestimated as a factor on which those still outside could project their ideas.'

Peter Jürgen Boock was in the 'Kanne' (can), the communal apartment shared by a group from a drugs project, when news of the arrest of Andreas Baader, Jan-Carl Raspe and Holger Meins flashed up on the TV screen. Boock was frozen with horror. He stood up, switched off the set, and said, 'I'll have to go now.' Seeing Andreas lying there like that, he had realized that this was no longer the time for rendering small services. He himself must go underground now. He had to do something to get Baader out. '"It's our turn now. We must go into action," I thought. For me anyway. In fact for me it was even easier because I said to myself: "Right, they got me out of a hole. Now it's up to me to get them out of one." As simple as that.'

Over the next week he went the rounds of all those of his acquaintances who, he assumed, might be ready for illegality. Among them was one

Rolf Clemens Wagner. It was clear to Boock that, as he said, 'We are the next generation. The others have gone now; we must carry on.'

44
Arrest in a Boutique

After the arrest of the three men in Frankfurt, Gudrun Ensslin had gone to Hamburg, where she met Ulrike Meinhof, Klaus Jünschke and Gerhard Müller. They had seen the pictures of the arrest on television. Ulrike Meinhof had been deeply depressed since the bomb attack on the Springer building in Hamburg. Old friends who were still in touch with her had said, 'For heaven's sake, do give it up now!' She had replied, 'But it's only just beginning.' However, she did not really seem so convinced any more. 'It was like going downhill out of control,' Klaus Jünschke remembered. 'If you jump out you're done for, if you carry on you're done for just the same.'

The group's anxiety and nervousness increased. Gudrun Ensslin was now driving around not with Andreas Baader, as before, but with Klaus Jünschke. One day he couldn't get the right gears and started driving dangerously. Gudrun Ensslin panicked. They took a taxi, and its driver looked at her. She felt she had been recognized, and whispered, 'I must get myself something else to wear, now!' There was a boutique quite close.

It was 7 June 1972, exactly a week after the arrest of Andreas Baader. The manageress of the Linette boutique on Hamburg's Jungfernstieg was standing by the cash desk when a young woman came into the shop. She was wearing a red sweater, had curly, shoulder-length hair, and was very thin. The manageress looked hard at the woman, who replied with a smile. She did not seem at all well. She took off her jacket and asked to see several sweaters. Another customer had been trying on ten or fifteen pairs of trousers in the shop and left them scattered on a couch. The manageress went to put the trousers back where they had come from. In so doing she noticed a blue-grey leather jacket and was about to clear that away too. The jacket struck her as disproportionately heavy; she felt its patch pockets and turned to her colleagues on the staff of the shop.

'I think there's a pistol in here.' They thought she was joking. One of them felt the jacket too. 'You're right,' she said.

The manageress of the boutique rang the police.

Police Sergeant Reiner Freiberg was quite close to the spot in his radio patrol car. He received instructions to go there. His colleague, whose name was Millhahn, went into the boutique first. One of the shop's staff pointed out the woman with the curly hair. Gudrun Ensslin looked down at the ground and tried to walk calmly past the policeman. Millhahn took her arm, and at this point his colleague Freiberg came to his aid. Gudrun Ensslin fought desperately, flinging both police officers to the ground before they overpowered her. Freiberg took her handbag away from her, handed it to one of the saleswomen and said, 'Open that bag, please.' He searched Gudrun Ensslin's jacket himself, and took a shiny, silver-coloured revolver out of its pocket.

There was another gun in her handbag, a large-calibre pistol with a reserve magazine. A second radio patrol car arrived as he was going for handcuffs.

At the police station, women detective officers searched Gudrun Ensslin. Then she was asked if she would agree voluntarily to be fingerprinted and photographed.

'I'm saying nothing, and you won't get anything out of me,' she replied.

Thereupon she was fingerprinted by force. She clenched her hands into fists, but the police officers straightened each finger separately, pressed them first on an ink pad and then on a piece of paper. The next thing was for Gudrun Ensslin to be photographed; she hung her head and hid her face. There was a flower picture hanging on the wall of the interrogation room. Only if you got very close could you see that one of the painted flowers had a hole in it. There was a camera in the next room, behind it. One of the police officers gave Gudrun Ensslin a cigarette; she tore the filter off, smoked, but did not raise her head. Then another officer manipulated and tickled the back of her neck for several minutes. When Gudrun Ensslin looked up once, briefly, the photographs were taken.

In Essen jail, Gudrun Ensslin wrote a secret message for Ulrike Meinhof:

'CAUTION, keep your mouth shut and lie low. Liesel . . . two months that the rest of you must spend just repairing the structure . . .'

After a series of instructions as to which apartments were to be abandoned, where money should be deposited, what operations were to be planned, Gudrun Ensslin came to her arrest in Hamburg:

'Taxi, on the way to the bunker . . . driver saw me in the light from the Gitanes, recognized me. Felt like a beast in the jungle. But got the idea of different clothes. Then, in the shop, my mind was all mixed up, I was agitated, sweating. Or I'd surely have ticked over, but I was half asleep. It happened terribly fast, too, or there'd be a salesgirl dead now (a hostage), and me too and perhaps a couple of cops. Well, I'm not at all sure if I'd have got away, and it all happened so fast my hand was half broken by the cops' great paws before I could get it out of the pocket with the gun in it . . .'

At the time of her arrest, Gudrun Ensslin had a key in her bag which fitted the lock of one of the conspirators' apartments, in the Seidenstrasse in Stuttgart.

On 7 August 1972, police officers searched this hideout. A detective superintendent of the Stuttgart regional Criminal Investigation Office wrote a report:

'Re: hunt for violent anarchist criminals. Subject: conspirators' apartment at 71 Seidenstrasse.

'Attached: 22 Mickey Mouse comic books.

'The attached Mickey Mouse comic books were found in the above-mentioned apartment. There are good grounds for suspecting that these Mickey Mouse books were read by the gang member Andreas Baader.'

45
Arrested and Forcibly Anaesthetized

After Gudrun Ensslin had been arrested in Hamburg, Klaus Jünschke suggested taking cover. 'This is the end,' he told Ulrike Meinhof and Gerhard Müller. 'We don't move for six weeks, we just stay here. Anything else is stupid.'

Müller did not agree. 'There's a Volkswagen minibus needs some work done on it.'

'Not by me, I'm not doing any more,' Jünschke insisted.

At this Müller rose to his feet, drew his revolver and pointed it at Jünschke. He was quivering with rage. 'You'd better stop and think what's happening to us, if this is the way we act,' said Jünschke. Ulrike Meinhof rose too, and she and Gerhard Müller left the apartment.

Two days after Gudrun Ensslin's arrest, Brigitte Mohnhaupt and her boyfriend were arrested in Berlin. The Hamburg police had found a clue in one of the Berlin apartments used by the conspirators. Although the couple were armed, they put up no resistance. A police officer took the man's trousers down to prevent any attempt at flight.

On Thursday 15 June, half an hour after midnight, someone rang the doorbell of an apartment occupied by a teacher in Walsroder Strasse, in Langenhagen, Hanover. He opened the door in his dressing gown, and saw a young girl with long brown hair standing outside. The teacher told the police, later, that he did not know her. 'May I have a word with you?'

He let the woman, who looked distressed, into his living-room. 'Could two people spend tomorrow night with you?' she asked.

He agreed.

Next morning at breakfast, the teacher told his girlfriend about this nocturnal visit. She said there was only one 'very specific conclusion' to be drawn. 'You must go to the police.'

The teacher thought her suspicions excessive. He decided to go to work and think it over.

He did not feel happy at the idea of turning in people wanted by the police. At the same time he wondered what the consequences might be to himself, as a left-wing teacher and trade union member, if people from the Baader–Meinhof group actually did spend the night with him. At the end of the school day he discussed it with a friend.

'We came to this conclusion: if these people aren't from the RAF they have no reason to fear the police. If they *are* RAF members, we have every reason to fear for our own lives. So then I went to the police.'

At the police station, he was immediately referred to the Baader–Meinhof Special Commission.

Police Officer Robert Severin was approaching retirement. He and two younger colleagues were detailed to go and find out the best way of keeping watch on the Walsroder Strasse apartment. In plain clothes, they assessed the possibilities of the stairwell. As they were about to leave the building, at nearly 6.00 p.m., a woman and a young man came towards them.

The caretaker of the building was standing at the doorway, and asked the couple where they were going. They told him.

'Well, the teacher lives up there, second floor, but he probably won't be in.' The man and the woman went upstairs. The police officers asked for reinforcements. They were still discussing whether or not they ought to enter the apartment without a search warrant when the young man came out of the building. The officers picked him up in a telephone booth. He had just put a coin in the slot. The officers flung the door open and took his pistol from him. Severin, who had come out on the operation unarmed, pocketed it.

By now the reinforcements had arrived. Severin and three other officers went up to the second floor and rang the bell. The woman opened the door. She was dressed in black and had short, dishevelled hair. As the policemen seized her, she swore at them. 'Swine!' Not knowing if there were any more people in the apartment, the policemen called out, 'Everyone stay in there, nobody else come out or we'll fire.' They made their way cautiously into the apartment. There were guns, ammunition and hand grenades lying about everywhere.

'My God, look at that, this is no little fish we've caught,' said Severin. But none of them realized they had arrested Ulrike Meinhof. She had changed, was thinner, looked ill and not in the least like her photographs on the Wanted posters.

The policemen searched the apartment and found a bag containing an open copy of the illustrated magazine *Stern* showing X-ray pictures of Ulrike Meinhof's skull. Only then did they realize that they had apprehended the most wanted woman in West Germany.

The officers showed her the photograph from *Stern*. 'Is that you?'

Ulrike Meinhof said nothing.

Severin searched a black velvet jacket lying about the apartment, and fished a piece of paper out of its pocket.

It was Gudrun Ensslin's secret letter.

Ulrike Meinhof was taken straight to prison. Severin drove to the police station and discussed means of identifying the prisoner with his colleagues. The police had no fingerprints of Ulrike Meinhof. Severin thought of the X-ray photographs from the magazine, and suggested X-raying the prisoner's head. The silver clamp put in ten years before to stop the swollen vessel in her brain growing any larger would be visible in an X-ray picture.

The police consulted the Public Prosecutor's Office and a judge. No objections were made to having Ulrike Meinhof taken to a hospital and medically examined for purposes of police identification. Late that evening Severin drove to the hospital. Ulrike Meinhof had already been taken there. Severin gave the doctor on duty the copy of *Stern* with the story about Ulrike Meinhof's tumour operation. 'Well, if the woman you've arrested is the same person, she ought to have a scar somewhere on her head,' said the doctor. The policeman, the doctor and the nurses tried persuading her to let them examine her head voluntarily. After much argument, she agreed, but the doctor could find no scar. Finally, and against her will, Ulrike Meinhof was X-rayed. She was compulsorily anaesthetized for the purpose.

46
A Trap at the Kiosk

Klaus Jünschke left Hamburg and met Irmgard Möller, who took him to Offenbach with her for a meeting with Hans-Peter Konieczny. Nineteen-year-old 'Conny' had joined the RAF in February 1972 and as a printer's compositor, he had produced fake car registration certificates and letter-head paper for the group. They went for a walk in a park and discussed their situation. Those people on the fringe of the Red Army Faction who had not yet been arrested were dispersed all over the place. 'They've gone into their holes and they're keeping quiet,' said Jünschke. They had no money left either, and so the three of them made plans for another bank raid.

On 7 July 1972, the police suddenly turned up at the Tübingen printers where Konieczny worked. One of the officers ostentatiously opened his jacket to show the pistol he was carrying. Conny let them arrest him and put up no resistance. The investigating officers suggested that certain prospects were open to him if he helped get the rest of the group in prison. Conny agreed. He said he could fix a meeting in Offenbach that very day.

They discussed details in a bar. Günter Textor, heading the Stuttgart

Special Commission, wanted to give him a bullet-proof vest. Conny refused.

He left the bar about one-thirty and went the last 300 metres to the pre-arranged meeting place on foot. Some thirty police officers sealed off the area. They sat on park benches, at a bus stop, played with children, or pretended to be drunks at a park kiosk.

Klaus Jünschke got off a bus. He was carrying a black college briefcase under his arm; he looked around suspiciously, and realized at once that something was wrong. 'What's going on?' he asked.

'There are two people over there in a car,' replied Conny. He was frightened. The policemen did not seem to be taking much notice. 'Let's go over and take a look at them,' he suggested. Less than a minute later, policemen suddenly converged on them from all directions. They seized Jünschke from behind, pulled his legs from under him, and two of them knocked the briefcase out of his hand. Then Textor of the Special Commission joined them and put a pistol to Jünschke's throat. For the sake of appearance, Conny was also seized, threatened with a gun and led away in handcuffs.

At the police station, the cuffs were taken off him again, and they went back to the kiosk. No one turned up at two-thirty, or an hour later. Textor had already given the signal for the cancellation of the operation when Irmgard Möller suddenly arrived. Conny would hardly have recognized her, for 'Gabi' had changed her appearance completely. She had cut her hair short and looked like a well-groomed secretary. She was carrying her purse and fishing around in it. Conny pretended not to know her. When she was about to address him, he said, 'Watch out, the place is swarming with cops.' Then he made as if to walk on. She walked a few steps beside him.

However, Textor had realized that his decoy had met another member of the group. He and five other police officers ran towards the women. Irmgard Möller kicked the knee of the first man who tried to seize her. Then the other officers flung themselves on her. Irmgard Möller fought desperately, shouted, 'You swine!', and bit and scratched. Meanwhile, again for the sake of appearances, Conny had been pushed up against the wall of the kiosk by two policemen with pistols threateningly raised.

Hans-Peter Konieczny was released from jail two months later. After that he had to keep himself 'available', since there were members of other police forces who wanted to talk to him.

PART THREE

'The Costumes of Weariness'

1
'A Clear Awareness That Your Chance of Survival Is Nil'

The Red Army Faction prisoners spent their first year in custody separated from each other and isolated from the normal life of the prison: Andreas Baader was in jail in Schwalmstadt, Gudrun Ensslin in Essen, Holger Meins in Wittlich, Irmgard Möller in Rastatt, Gerhard Müller in Hamburg and Jan-Carl Raspe in Cologne.

Ulrike Meinhof was in Cologne's Ossendorf jail, in a cell previously occupied by Astrid Proll. The rest of the building was completely empty. The room was painted white and had a pale green door. The neon lighting was left on day and night; only after much argument did Ulrike Meinhof manage to get the tube changed for a weaker one in the evenings.

Astrid Proll had been moved to the neighbouring building, in the men's wing. She knew that Ulrike Meinhof was in her former cell. The prison officers did their utmost to keep the pair from seeing or hearing each other. When Astrid Proll was taken out for her daily exercise in the yard, which would normally have meant she had to pass Ulrike Meinhof's cell, the officers took a long way round through the prison grounds.

Through their lawyers, Astrid Proll let Ulrike Meinhof know the times at which she was taken to the bathroom, which was near Ulrike's cell. Once Ulrike called out, 'Astrid!' After this the warders always switched on a vacuum cleaner or ran a tap on bath days, to prevent even such contact as this.

Ulrike Meinhof stayed here in the 'dead section' of Ossendorf jail from 16 June 1972 to 9 February 1973. When it became publicly known that she was being kept in almost complete acoustic isolation, the authorities gave assurances that there was no 'dead section' in the prison. Governor Bücker described her conditions of imprisonment in a letter to the chairman of the Cologne Prisons Department:

'As is generally known, the remand prisoner Meinhof is accommodated in the women's wing of the psychiatric department. While the remand prisoner Proll, in the men's wing of the same department, can at least take part acoustically in the life of the institution, the prisoner Meinhof is acoustically as well as physically isolated in her cell.'

During her eight months in the 'quiet section', Ulrike Meinhof was allowed visits only from family, and then only for half an hour once a fortnight, under supervision.

Sitting alone in her cell, she recorded her feelings in writing:

'The feeling that your head is exploding.

'The feeling that the top of your skull must be going to split and come off.

'The feeling of your spinal cord being pressed into your brain . . .

'The feeling that the cell is moving. You wake up and open your eyes: the cell is moving; in the afternoon, when the sun shines in, it suddenly stops. You can't shake off that sense of movement . . .

'Furious aggression for which there's no outlet. That's the worst thing. A clear awareness that your chance of survival is nil. Utter failure to communicate that. Visits leave no trace behind them. Half an hour later, you can tell if the visit was today or last week only by mechanically reconstructing it.

'On the other hand, a bath once a week means a moment's thawing out, recovery – and that feeling persists for a few hours.

'The feeling that time and space interlock . . .'

Sometimes Ulrike Meinhof could no longer bear the silence, and she talked to the prison officers. She typed on a piece of paper:

'It isn't true that I have never spoken to the "crows". When I could get no further with my thoughts on the problem of anti-Semitism, having no books and a thousand questions, I began asking the warders. They knew quite a lot of what I wanted to know, and they got thinking too, and one of the cops promised to look up what I was after in his encyclopaedia at home. When I asked him next day, of course he'd forgotten. But the idea they could chat to me lingered on. So then I stopped doing it. Either you treat them like dogs, or they'll treat you like a dog.'

The RAF had drawn up a code of conduct in jail:

'Not a word to the pigs, in whatever guise they may appear, particularly as doctors. Not a single word.

'And naturally we give them no assistance, never lift a finger to help them, nothing but hostility and contempt . . .

'No provocation – that's important. But we will defend ourselves implacably, relentlessly, with what human methods we have.'

* * *

In his cell, Jan-Carl Raspe wrote down, 'When I came here I had just one thought in my head: to resist where possible so that they couldn't destroy me . . . That one idea quite soon turned into a question: for heaven's sake, *how*? And I went out of my mind over it, over not being able to answer that question.'

Horst Mahler made some suggestions. 'We can shout, sing, kick the door, throw cups and plates, overturn the police inspector's desk, a lot of other things. We do risk getting beaten up. We'll accept that risk . . . I've no taste at all for a passively masochistic form of resistance . . .'

Andreas Baader rejected individual forms of resistance. 'The machine is geared to just that, and it's exactly what gives them the chance of smashing us individually,' he replied to Horst Mahler's suggestions. 'Do that kind of thing only if you need to.'

2
Black September

They were to have been 'cheerful Games'. On 5 September 1972, at 4.30 a.m. a commando unit of the Palestinian terrorist organization Black September climbed the fence of the Olympic village in Munich, forced its way into the Israeli team's quarters, and shot two Israeli athletes. Nine others were taken hostage. The commando was demanding the release of Palestinian prisoners in Israel.

As the Games went on, police surrounded the Olympic village. The rest of the drama unfolded before the eyes of millions of television spectators all over the world. That evening, the hostages and their captors were taken to Fürstenfeldbruck airport, ostensibly to be flown to Cairo. As the first two Palestinians were about to enter the aircraft, two German sharp-shooters opened fire. The hostage-takers mowed down the Israelis with machine-gun fire from their Kalashnikovs. Then they fired on the police.

At the end of the day, eleven Israeli athletes, one German policeman and five terrorists were dead. Three Palestinians were arrested.

The organizer of the attack, according to investigations made by the Israeli secret service, was Hassan Salameh, that same Abu Hassan who had had the Baader–Meinhof group trained two years before in the Palestinian camp in Jordan.

After the Olympics massacre, Ulrike Meinhof, in her cell at Ossendorf prison, wrote a manifesto entitled, *The Action of Black September at Munich – Towards the Strategy of the Anti-imperialist Struggle.*

Although its title page showed the Red Army Faction emblem with the picture of the submachine gun, the other leading members of the RAF had not seen it before publication. Many copies circulated in the universities. The pamphlet paid tribute to the action of Black September in setting an example for the revolutionary strategy of the anti-imperialist struggle 'in which the West German Left could find its own identity again'.

'The comrades of the Black September movement,' wrote Ulrike Meinhof, 'have brought their own Black September of 1970 – when the Jordanian army slaughtered more than 20,000 Palestinians – home to the place whence that massacre sprang: West Germany, formerly Nazi Germany, now the centre of imperialism. The place from which Jews of Western and Eastern Europe were forced to emigrate to Israel, the place from which Israel derived its capital by way of restitution, and officially got its weapons until 1965. The place celebrated by the Springer press when they hailed Israel's blitzkrieg of June '67 as an anti-communist orgy . . .'

Gudrun Ensslin assumed that Horst Mahler was the author of this third RAF manifesto. She wrote to him:

'All crap . . . it would have been better if someone else had read it first . . . we wondered briefly why you didn't send it around in advance, but now of course the matter's important, because you're crazy to go letting out what our two years of practice have taught us . . .'

Ulrike Meinhof received a copy of this letter and reacted with a defence of the pamphlet mistakenly attributed to Horst Mahler. It had, she wrote, expressed the common aims of the RAF and Black September: 'Material annihilation of imperialist rule. Destruction of the myth of the all-powerful system. The propaganda operation expressed in material attack: the act of liberation in the act of annihilation.'

She added, 'Obviously – a repulsive idea – but "how low would you not stoop to exterminate the low . . .?"'

Not until she had Ulrike Meinhof's defence did Gudrun Ensslin realize who the real author of the pamphlet was, and then she performed a *volte-face*. 'I could still blush for the wording of my criticism . . . you sound somehow bitter, which I just don't understand, or how many more times must I say that if so, I'm the only one who'd have reasons (but I don't) to be upset not to have seen at once it was your head and hand at work in Black September . . . And in spite of all I know about that scrapheap, I was still idiot enough to think all that could be his [Horst Mahler's] work – but that just means I was or am or can be crazy . . .'

Ulrike Meinhof replied, in handwriting, 'Well, really, I do find my own stuff bleak – but one starts bottling it all up, and that's even bleaker.'

By now Horst Mahler himself had written another pamphlet on strategy. It did not meet with Gudrun Ensslin's approval. She wrote to him. 'And – wait for it! – I actually do think there's someone who believes you're a "ringleader": yourself.'

Quarrels were in the air.

In her letter to Gudrun Ensslin, Ulrike Meinhof had written, 'How low would you not stoop to exterminate the low . . . ?' She was quoting this line from Bertolt Brecht's didactic play *The Measures Taken*, which takes treachery as its subject. Brecht had stipulated that his play was not to be performed. Perhaps he guessed that there were many who might take its message only too literally.

> With whom would the just not sit
> To help the cause of justice?
> What medicine would taste too bitter
> To the dying?
> How low would you not stoop
> To exterminate the low?
> If you could change the world at last,
> What would be beneath you?
> Who are you?
> Sink in the dirt,
> Embrace the slaughterer,
> But change the world: the world needs it!

3
Letters from the Dead Section

Ulrike Meinhof's first letter to her children, who were now ten years old, was kept back by the remand judge.

When she had been remanded in custody for three months, on 12 August 1972, she wrote:

Dear Regina and Bettina,

It is all very difficult. It is all very simple.

You are thinking: Mummy might write at last. I was thinking: the children have got my letter now. You haven't got it – I know. There was something in it that the judge who checks my mail thought was offensive, and he didn't send the letter on to you . . . So now I'll begin again from the beginning. I have had two letters from you now. Of course I was very, very pleased. I've read them seven times over. And today I heard that you are going to visit me, and there needn't be any police officer there, just two of the prison wardresses.

Hallo there, mice! Grit your teeth! And don't think you have to be sad because you have a Mummy in prison. It's much better to be angry than sad. Oh, I'll be so glad to see you, so very glad . . .

15 September 1972

Hallo there, mice!

. . . I'm sitting in my cell, taking my thoughts for a walk, and my legs for a walk too once a day, in a yard where I go around in circles a hundred times or so. So you can't expect anything much from me, let alone me coming to see you, that's not on.

There's nothing else to tell you about me. I hear and see nobody and nothing, except the warders when they bring my meals – you learn not to be choosy about food if you don't want to starve, not that I think that's any reason you two should learn not to be choosy, prison's soon enough for that. And now and then a lawyer comes, and is surprised to find how many things are forbidden here. And then I read some of the books I was always meaning to read – there's nothing else to do in prison. Mind you grow cleverer as well as older, so that you'll know how to manage. And don't tell me you need to be pretty too – you are, anyway, but all the same that's totally unimportant . . .

I'm wearing a blue dress and a knitted cardigan. That's the prison clothing. A cell is a room with a lavatory in it. And the door opens only from the outside, and has no handle or keyhole on the inside. The door is much bigger than an ordinary door, too. It also has a peephole in it. Now and then a policeman looks through the keyhole to see if I'm still here. So far I always have been. Because the window is closed too, and it has concrete bars outside it, and wire mesh in front of the bars.

From the outside the prison looks quite pretty – I'm told. There's a huge white wall around it. The prison staff are nice to visitors, too, one can't deny it. They sometimes get stroppy with the prisoners – like that teacher in Berlin who called such names in the hall. Either you call names back or you just don't listen . . .

On 22 September 1972, she wrote: '. . . and then all of a sudden I was taken somewhere else, by helicopter, and of course that bit was fun – the rest of it wasn't such fun.'

4
'I Am Ulrike Meinhof'

In September 1972, Ulrike Meinhof was flown to Zweibrücken prison. Detective Chief Superintendent Ruckmich came to her cell on the afternoon of 20 September and handed her the warrant for an identity parade. 'I'm not taking part in any identity parade,' Ulrike Meinhof told the BKA man.

Ruckmich pointed out that the identity parade was going to take place anyway, whether she agreed to it or not.

A lecture hall in the prison had been chosen. Ulrike Meinhof and five other women were to be led separately through the hall and shown to the witnesses.

The five others were women detectives and secretaries from police headquarters, dressed in prison clothing. A make-up artist did their faces. Then they were given their instructions. 'The person to be identified will probably resist, so please act the same way. Object to being paraded, behave differently so the witnesses can have as wide as possible a choice.'

Then they had a drink to relax them.

Meanwhile the witnesses were shown to seats in the middle of the hall. Months before, in Hamburg, they had seen a woman who might possibly have been Ulrike Meinhof. The purpose of the identity parade was to verify their observations.

Thirteen terrorist-hunters joined the three witnesses: two public prosecutors, three BKA officers, two regional Criminal Investigation officers, four police detectives from Kaiserslautern, a woman detective officer, and the governor of Zweibrücken prison.

Ulrike Meinhof was brought from her cell 'with the use of slight force', as stated later in the official account. The parade began at 2.20 p.m. The first woman was led in. She was resisting and moaning out loud. Next came Number 2, Ulrike Meinhof. 'I'm Ulrike Meinhof! Is this supposed to be an identity parade?' she cried, and tried to turn her face away from the witnesses. Just before they got out of the room one of the officers leading her stumbled over the struggling Ulrike Meinhof, and the group of three almost fell to the ground. Number 3 was already shouting 'No!' at the top of her voice before she entered the hall, and was forcibly brought in. She too tried to hide her face, shouting, 'It's me you're supposed to look at, you people!'

Woman Number 4 turned her face away too, and the two officers accompanying her straightened her head.

Woman Number 6 had to have her head held when she reached the middle of the room, but otherwise acted quietly.

On their second progress through the hall, they had all got into their stride. Number 1 screeched, 'Can't you see it's all a show?' muttered something indistinct and then cried, 'I'm Ulrike Meinhof.' She was dragged through the hall, putting up little resistance.

Number 2 shouted, 'Swine!' and tried to shake her two officers off.

This time Ulrike Meinhof was Number 3. As she was being dragged into the hall she cried, 'And here's Ulrike Meinhof again.' Then she folded her legs so that she had to be carried. 'Do you recognize her?' Woman Number 4 said nothing and was carried across the hall with her legs drawn up too. Woman Number 5 had to be dragged and was groaning. Woman Number 6 was already shouting out in the corridor, and putting up such violent resistance that the sound could be heard in the hall. In front of the witnesses, she cried, 'Let me go, you swine! It's me again!' and struck out at the officers. Kess, a BKA man from the Bonn Security

Group, noted, 'The undersigned is convinced that it was impossible for the witnesses and the officers present in the hall to deduce the prisoner's identity from the behaviour of the women paraded.'

The witness Bernd M., who had seen a woman he suspected of being Meinhof in Poppenbüttel, told the investigating judge of the Federal High Court, 'I did not recognize the woman I saw on that occasion in the apartment already mentioned. I did recognize the accused, Ulrike Meinhof, who was among the six women in the identity parade, because I have seen her photograph on Wanted posters and elsewhere many times.'

However, he said, he did not know if she was the same as the woman in Hamburg.

5
Visit from the Children

Early in October 1972, Ulrike Meinhof's children visited their mother in prison for the first time. The girls were now ten, and living with their father. Klaus Rainer Röhl accompanied the twins as far as the waiting room just inside the prison gates. The children were met by two prison officers, a man and a woman, and taken to the visiting room. The two officers sat down, and a few moments later Ulrike Meinhof was brought into the room. She was thinner, but did not look as exhausted as the children remembered her from the pictures of her arrest. The officers locked the door and stepped aside. Ulrike Meinhof stood there for a moment, looking at the girls. The children thought she seemed as shy as they felt themselves. Then she hugged her daughters, asking if that was all right. 'Children don't always like to be hugged.' Then she laughed quietly. She looked the twins over. 'Hey, you two have grown.'

Sometimes Ulrike Meinhof looked around at the prison officers, almost proudly, yet at the same time concerned in case they got a glimpse of her own emotional world. It was almost three years since the children had seen their mother, but in a few minutes they were chattering away, telling her about school and their friends, their piano lessons, their life at home with their father. Ulrike Meinhof never asked directly after her ex-husband, but she wanted to know if the children were happy with him.

The twins asked about prison life, and what the food was like.

'Lousy,' said Ulrike Meinhof. One of the prison officers rose abruptly, came over to her and said, 'Frau Meinhof, you may only say you think the food is lousy, not that it *is* lousy.' Then he sat down again.

Ulrike Meinhof laughed ironically. 'Right, I think the food is lousy.'

Bettina and Regina were allowed to stay with their mother for two hours. After this, the children came to see her every month or so all the time she was in Ossendorf prison.

After their first visit, she wrote:

You were here! I think the whole prison was glad. That's how it seemed to me. Will you visit me again?

Not long ago, in October, there were brightly-coloured kites flying above the prison. So there must have been children around somewhere, flying them. They were very high up, green and red. It was really lovely. And then there were gulls – gulls from the Rhine. Do you know those birds that are mimics? They belong to the thrush and blackbird family, but they don't just sing like blackbirds, they can sing like other birds too, redstarts and wrens. Are there any birds like that in your garden? I once wanted to be a bird watcher. But bird watchers are a bit crazy too. All the same, they have good ears.

Write some time. Both of you.

Your Mummy.

The relationship between mother and daughters became increasingly intimate. Ulrike Meinhof gave the twins advice on how to get on with their friends, how much pocket money they ought to ask for, how to behave to the weaker pupils in their class. And now and then she tried telling the ten-year-old girls about the position of the working class in West Germany, explaining that Willy Brandt and the SPD were only the lesser evil.

6
'The Concept of Hatred'

At the end of the sixties, groups calling themselves Red Aid formed in support of 'political prisoners', especially in Berlin and Frankfurt. Their aim was to organize actions showing solidarity 'against the measures being taken by the law and the police'.

Late in 1972, the Berlin Red Aid group published a collection of documents about the 'preparation for the RAF trials by the press, the police and the law'. These documents were intended to show up the 'brutality with which the prisoners are to be broken, the audacity with which the rights of their defence are being set aside, the slanders, defamation and threats that are being employed'.

The actions undertaken by Red Aid did not on the whole go far enough for the prisoners. Gudrun Ensslin, to her comrades: 'I looked in vain in these documents for a comic-strip type speech bubble saying something like 'better kill a judge than be a judge', but there was no such thing.

'You can take it from us that the members of the RAF are all there, very much all there. A partial account of what we shit and spit on can be found in some of the RAF writings. We have nothing to prove, but something to say: we have to bring the people of the twenty-four-hour day round to the concept of hatred . . .

'The struggle begun by the RAF is attractive . . . you have no right to take the wind out of our sails to inflate your own flat tyre . . .'

Andreas Baader gave his own opinion of Red Aid's documentary offerings. 'Fucking themselves into the ground with those documents of theirs . . .

'What's to be done? Well, obvious: blather away about the fucking twenty-four-hour stuff so hard, nobody can make an academic paper out of it . . . Tear the whole rotten thing apart, so more people will see it the way we do: I-DEN-TI-FI-CA-TION. Because our comrades are half dead, they can't think we're anything else ourselves. They're twisting the thing the same way the pigs twist it worldwide: violence is taboo, they dig themselves in behind death like a lot of parsons . . .

'The gun livens things up. The colonialized European comes alive, not to the subject and problem of the violence of our circumstances, but because all armed action subjects the force of circumstances to the force of events . . .'

Baader concluded with a slogan for the group's projected book on the basic tenets of the Red Army Faction:

'I say our book should be entitled *The Gun Speaks*.'

7
The Body a Weapon

At the end of 1972, Andreas Baader was called to give evidence at the trial of Horst Mahler in Berlin. He, Ulrike Meinhof and Astrid Proll were called by the defence to supply information about conditions in jail. 'And from today,' said Baader, 'I won't eat until those conditions have changed.'

Baader's words were in every newspaper next day. They started all the RAF prisoners on a hunger strike, their first, which lasted for almost two months.

Hans Christian Ströbele, who was defending Andreas Baader at this point, telephoned Federal Prosecutor Dr Wunder in Karlsruhe and described the situation. Wunder agreed to an easing of prison conditions. Independent doctors were to examine the prisoners, and the investigating authorities would then proceed according to the suggestions they made. Ströbele trusted the Federal Prosecutor's promises, for as an advance concession Ulrike Meinhof had in fact been moved from the dead section of Ossendorf to another department while the hunger strike was still going on. The defending lawyer asked the federal prosecutor to allow him a telephone call to Andreas Baader. Ströbele told Baader about his conversation with Dr Wunder. Baader was sceptical. 'They won't stick to it. It's another dirty deal. They just want us to stop the strike . . .'

'If they don't keep their promises, you can always begin again if need be. But call it off for now, at least.'

Baader agreed, and Ströbele telephoned other prisoners to tell them Baader's views.

The hunger strike was called off. Hardly a week later, Ulrike Meinhof was back in the 'dead section' again. The other prisoners were still kept in isolation too. Ströbele felt he had been taken in by the Federal Prosecutor's Office. He had seen himself as a negotiator, and he had failed. Subsequently his word did not carry much weight with the prisoners.

When, in February 1973, a group of RAF defence lawyers demonstrated outside the Federal Supreme Court against the conditions of isolation in which their clients were being kept, and settled down in their legal gowns to a short hunger strike of their own, this action was not enough to satisfy the prisoners.

Manfred Grashof wrote to his lawyers, 'If you can't prove at once that you haven't been doing us down, as we suspect, then prospects for our future cooperation look to me gloomy . . .

'Our last and strongest weapon is the body; collectively, we have brought ours into the fight . . .

'I demand, at least, that you exercise thorough self-criticism . . .'

This was more than many of the lawyers could take. 'We're not standing for that sort of thing,' replied Ströbele. 'Perhaps by my next visit some time next week you'll do some thorough thinking about the function of lawyers yourselves . . . and realistically, please. Lawyers as the spearhead of the revolution, or of the RAF, or an extension of the RAF comrades in custody? Hardly! Or if that's the idea, there'll be no more legal help forthcoming!'

'No doubt every brief resigned or withdrawn is bloody awful,' wrote Gudrun Ensslin, 'it helps the cops . . . but naturally it doesn't mean we can be blackmailed.'

The first message that Peter Jürgen Boock sent to Andreas Baader in his cell was written on a tiny piece of paper, five by five centimetres in size. In minute letters Boock wrote that he was still around, that he hadn't disappeared into the hash scene. He wanted to carry on where they had stopped, and in the end there would be an operation to free them.

Baader replied rudely that this would have to happen much more quickly. Boock stood his ground in his next message. It wouldn't work like that; after all, they didn't want to make the same mistakes again. The situation had changed and the police resources had become much larger. It wouldn't make sense to go outside the law straight away; it would be better to prepare the fight within the bounds of legality.

'Do you belong to the property damage faction?' was the prisoners' spiteful response, referring to the 'Revolutionary Cells', who conducted their operations without going underground. They quoted Antonio Gramsci: 'The legal land isn't the real land.' Boock first had to look up Gramsci to understand what they meant. There he read that there always exists a legal surface, where everybody lives according to the law, where people marry each other, go to work and live their lives. One could maintain that this was reality – but it wouldn't be true. In reality the fathers steal from their employers, together they defraud the taxman, and now and again the children don't go to school. The legal land isn't the real land. The surface is not the reality.

In concrete terms this meant: 'You can only define, perceive and change reality if you live below the surface, if you don't live on the surface – or at least only use it for cover, deceit, camouflage.'

Ideologically instructed in that way, the 'Second Generation' gradually went underground. Different groups were formed that hardly knew of each other and whose only common denominator was their relationship with the prisoners. Like the secret services, they operated strictly on a need-to-know basis.

In Hamburg the so-called 'Hamburg aunties' – Silke Maier-Witt, Susanne Albrecht, Sigrid Sternebeck – congregated around the squads of Eckhoffstrasse, and were joined by Karl-Heinz Dellwo and Stefan Wisniewski. In Karlsruhe, Adelheid Schulz, Monika Helbing, Christian Klar and Knut Folkerts formed the southern-German wing of the RAF. Contact was facilitated through 'travel cadres'. They were held together mostly by the messages from the prisoners, which were kept strictly apart from each other. Everything had a certain conspiratorial logic, but it made communication extremely difficult and time-consuming.

8
Hunting Leviathan

In December 1972, while she was still on hunger strike, Ulrike Meinhof wrote to her children:

'When you were here I was rather cross about the Advent wreath. I thought it was only meant to take you in, and prison is really far from pleasant. But the wardress who put it up really meant well – I think – I see that now. She really did want to do something nice for you two. Nobody could mind that.

'If you visit Uncle Ebi again, take him Joseph Conrad's book *Lord Jim*. It's a good book to read in hospital, if he hasn't read it already.

'It's nice and long, and exciting as well. A seaman's yarn.

'*Moby Dick* is good too, if you have plenty of time. I haven't read it yet myself, though – I'm still waiting to get hold of it here . . .'

Gudrun Ensslin had been devising cover names for the members of the group, so as to confuse the censors of their mail. She took almost all these names from Herman Melville's novel *Moby Dick*.

Baader was 'Ahab', Holger Meins 'Starbuck'. Jan-Carl Raspe was 'Carpenter', Gerhard Müller 'Queequeg', Horst Mahler 'Bildad', and she herself 'Smutje'.

Ulrike Meinhof was the only one not made to figure in the story of the hunting of the white whale. Gudrun Ensslin gave her the name of 'Teresa'. *Meyer's Universal Encyclopaedia* of 1897 has the following entry under 'Teresa':

'Teresa of Jesus, saint, b. 1515 at Avila in Old Castile, where she entered a Carmelite convent in 1535. She restored the order of barefoot Carmelite nuns to its original purity in the convents she reformed, and had to withstand much opposition from Carmelites whose observance of the rule was less strict, opposition which even led to an attempt to get her tried for heresy. She died in 1582 in the convent of Alba de Liste in Old Castile, and was canonized in 1622.'

Along with the cover names she had borrowed from the crew of the whaler *Pequod*, Gudrun Ensslin handed out some interpretations.

Smutje the cook, she wrote to Ulrike Meinhof, was herself. (In fact the name is Fleece in Melville's original.) 'You'll remember that the cook keeps the pans well scoured and preaches to the sharks.' The cook of the whaler's crew, in the novel, is an old negro who delivers a sermon to the sharks from the deck, urging them to leave the dead sperm whale alone. He is not particularly successful, even when adjured by the second mate, 'Well done, old Fleece! . . . that's Christianity; go on.' But on board ship, added Ensslin, the cook is a kind of officer . . . such was the case on the *Pequod*, and in the Red Army Faction too.

Ahab, the ship's captain, destroying himself in the hunt for Moby Dick, the great White Whale, lent his name to Baader. Again, Gudrun Ensslin gave her fellow prisoners some helpful hints to understanding. She wrote to 'Teresa': 'Ahab makes a great impression on his first appearance in *Moby Dick*; it is very effective.' She quoted Melville: 'Nor will it at all detract from him, dramatically regarded, if either by birth or other circumstances, he have what seems a half wilful over-ruling morbidness at the bottom of his nature. For all men tragically great are made so through a certain morbidness.'

Captain Bildad, whose name Gudrun Ensslin had 'generously', she wrote, given Horst Mahler, is a prosperous retired whaler, whose 'ocean life . . . had not moved this native born Quaker a single jot, had not so much as altered one angle of his vest.'

Melville writes: 'Still, for all this immutableness, was there some lack of common consistency about worthy Captain Bildad. Though a sworn foe to human bloodshed, yet had he in his straight-bodied coat, spilled tuns upon tuns of leviathan gore. How now in the contemplative evening of his days, the pious Bildad reconciled these things in the reminiscence, I do not know; but it did not seem to concern him much, and very probably he had long since come to the sage and sensible conclusion that a man's religion is one thing, and this practical world quite another. This world pays dividends.'

Bildad alias Horst Mahler: the hypocrite of the group.

Holger Meins acquired the name of the chief mate, Starbuck. He is described in *Moby Dick* as, '. . . a long, earnest man, and though born on an icy coast, seemed well adapted to endure hot latitudes . . . Starbuck's body and Starbuck's coerced will were Ahab's, so long as Ahab kept his magnet at Starbuck's brain; still he knew that for all this the chief mate, in his soul, abhorred his captain's quest.'

Starbuck alias Holger Meins: the man subject to Baader?

Jan-Carl Raspe was given the cover name of 'Carpenter'. A maker of coffins for the victims of the hunt for the white whale, the ship's carpenter also carves Captain Ahab a new whalebone leg, and makes himself generally useful:

'He was like one of those unreasoning but still highly useful, *multum in parvo*, Sheffield contrivances, assuming the exterior – though a little swelled – of a common pocket knife; but containing, not only blades of various sizes, but also screw-drivers, cork-screws, tweezers, awls, pens, rulers, nail-filers, countersinkers. So, if his superiors wanted to sue the carpenter for a screw-driver, all they had to do was to open that part of him, and the screw was fast: or if for tweezers, take him up by the legs, and there they were.'

The Carpenter alias Jan-Carl Raspe: a tool without any will of his own?

Gerhard Müller was Queequeg, the harpooneer, a 'noble savage' from the South Seas, who takes his harpoon to bed with him. From the novel: 'And thus an old idolater at heart, he yet lived among these Christians, wore their clothes, and tried to talk their gibberish.'

Queequeg alias Gerhard Müller: the traitor?

As a group, isolated from the world like the crew of a death ship, the RAF leadership led a kind of mystical life of its own in the high-security wing of Stammheim. It was not by chance that Gudrun Ensslin and her comrades read Herman Melville's classic novel in the isolation of their cells. The story of Captain Ahab's fanatical pursuit of the white whale has all the characteristics of a revolutionary, anti-capitalist parable. Even in the opening of his book the American author, a contemporary of Karl Marx, sets out the entire spectrum of the sea monster's mythical transfiguration. He quotes the first sentence of Thomas Hobbes's *Leviathan*: 'By art is created that great Leviathan, called a Commonwealth or State – (in Latin, *civitas*) which is but an artificial man.'

To the group calling itself the Red Army Faction, the idea of the revolution for which they did not spare their own lives or those of others was something like the hunting of the great white whale, the Leviathan, the state that they frequently described as 'the machine'.

The murderous rage of Baader and his crew against the Leviathan of the state had features of a metaphysical final battle, similar to the war waged by the monomaniac madman Captain Ahab against the whale. 'I'd strike the sun if it insulted me,' says Ahab of himself in Melville's novel. And further: 'How can the prisoner reach outside except by thrusting through the wall? To me, the white whale is that wall, shoved near to me. Sometimes I think there's naught beyond.'

9
The 'Info-System'

Rechristened with their cover names from *Moby Dick*, the prisoners communicated with each other in the spring of 1973 by means of an information system they had recently constructed. Their aim was to preserve the coherence of the group, thus retaining their 'political identity' and 'revolutionary consciousness'.

News was sent to individual prisoners by way of mail to and from their lawyers, which was still uncensored at this time. According to Gudrun Ensslin, 'The Red lawyers are indispensable for this; it can't be done if they don't collect and sort the information.'

Initially, the offices of the Hamburg lawyer Kurt Groenewold were to serve as the 'contact and switchboard centre for information for all prisoners and between lawyers' offices, as well as for the committees'.

'If we don't make it systematic,' said Gudrun Ensslin, 'sooner or later there'll be a balls-up, and then there'll be people out of action, in jail, pious, stupid . . .'

Andreas Baader's cell was known in the 'Info-system' as the 'cabin'. Gudrun Ensslin called her own the 'secretariat'. From it, she directed operations. Together with Baader, also called 'the general manager' by the RAF prisoners, she formed the 'staff'. They made decisions on the distribution of 'Info' material, 'so that everyone who should be getting it does get it, and those who shouldn't be getting it don't. That can't be left to the lawyers.'

The idea was that if anyone offended against 'revolutionary discipline', information should be withheld from these 'deviationists', a plan which was in fact carried out. Gudrun Ensslin made a note to that effect on the back of a lawyer's letter:

'Sanction: no communication.'

She defined the RAF's idea of an order thus:

'What is an order?

'An order results from the construction of the collective and the breaking down of every kind of hierarchy.

'An order is something you're convinced of, or something you come to be convinced of. If that's not possible, then you're out . . .'

The meaning of 'revolutionary discipline' in practice was clearly shown in the case of Astrid Proll. Physically and mentally worn out by months spent in the 'quiet section' of Ossendorf jail, she had not participated whole-heartedly in the first hunger strike. Hereupon a request came from Andreas Baader: 'We want Astrid to let us know if it's true that she was on hunger strike only until she felt hungry. If she can't come up with any self-criticism over that, then we feel she ought to be excluded from the info-system . . .'

And Ulrike Meinhof wrote: 'Astrid. She's dithering. I told her she'll be thrown out of the RAF if . . . I didn't mean it as a threat, just as a fact.'

With their mail from their defending lawyers, the members of the group in custody regularly received copies of all the letters they wrote one another. These letters included private correspondence and sometimes exercises in what they called 'criticism and self-criticism'.

Klaus Jünschke wrote, in August 1974:

'I had been acting like a counter-revolutionary shit. Instead of exposing my deficiencies and consistently extending my training by means of info, etc, I just absorbed the info rather than using it as a tool, as equipment for the struggle.'

Equipment for the struggle was delivered directly and perfectly legally to the prisoners in their cells. Obviously none of the remand judges responsible for censoring mail and checking on books sent to the prisoners had any objection to their getting people to send them such literature as they needed for further training as urban guerrillas.

The RAF prisoners thus managed to accumulate an extensive library of handbooks on the detonation of explosive devices, means of preventing such devices from being de-activated, on recent police methods of hunting suspects, on new weapons, alarm systems, industrial security forces, miniaturized spying devices, the construction of police roadblocks, and similar subjects.

A small selection of these titles:

The German Journal of Weaponry, Defensive Technology, Military Technology, General Swiss Military Journal, Radio Technology, The Radio Ham, military publications from East Germany, *What We can Learn from the Tupamaros, Small-Scale Warfare Instructor, The Urban Guerrilla, Armed Rebellion, Urban Guerrilla Warfare* (an English-language title), *The Guerrilla in the Industrial State, The Partisans' Handbook, The Hidden Struggle, Theories of War, German*

Military Dictionary and the Nato ABC, The Special Forces Handbook (another English-language title), *The Coup d'Etat, Self-Defence, Policy of the Federal Republic of Germany, Basics of Command Technique, Assassins and Saboteurs: Modern Terrorism, The Explosives Expert: Modern Explosives Technology, Handbook of Small Offset Printing and Repro-photography* . . .

'These manuals of instruction,' commented the Federal Criminal Investigation officer Alfred Klaus, in a report, 'were exactly the thing to extend their readers' political, logistical and operational knowledge and put all the prisoners in a position to set up and lead their own guerrilla groups after their discharge or release from prison.'

While the contents of books which ordinary prisoners got sent in were carefully, often minutely checked, the Baader–Meinhof judges allowed instructional material such as this through.

10
'Damn It, That's an Order'

They had begun their underground struggle as a kind of experiment, staking life and freedom to show that the state was what they imagined it to be: a fascist one.

Now, in prison, they regarded themselves as victims and compared themselves with the inmates of Nazi concentration camps.

'The political concept behind the dead section at Cologne, I will say it straight out, is the gas chamber,' wrote Ulrike Meinhof. 'My ideas of Auschwitz became very realistic in there . . .'

And Gudrun Ensslin noted: 'The difference between the dead section and isolation is the difference between Auschwitz and Buchenwald. It's a simple distinction: more people survived Buchenwald than Auschwitz. Those of us in there, to put it bluntly, can only be surprised they don't spray the gas in. Nothing else surprises us . . .'

Communication between prisoners in the various jails had improved considerably with the introduction of the 'Info-system'. Some forty prisoners took part in the next hunger strike, including some who were not members of the RAF.

This second hunger strike lasted six weeks, from 8 May to 29 June 1973.

The prison authorities employed forcible feeding for the first time. After a slight easing of the conditions of imprisonment, probably partly due to the wide publicity given to the strike, the prisoners began taking nourishment again.

Even before the official end of their action, Gudrun Ensslin had written in a cell circular: 'The steam's gone out of the hunger strike . . . but the hell with that . . . We won't get an end to solitary confinement with the strike, or even, it seems, to the concentration camp approach.'

One reason for calling off the strike may have been that the health of some of the strikers was deteriorating rapidly. Consequently, directions went out over the 'Info-system':

'Everyone who doesn't mind or can stand the forcible feeding . . . go on refusing food. Everyone else – for instance, Andreas – stop at once. And damn it, that's an order!'

Ulrike Meinhof was still in touch with her children. On one occasion the twins were taken to see their mother while she was on hunger strike. She sat facing the girls in the visiting room, pale, thin and weak, her hands blue.

In May 1973, she wrote to her daughters:

'Cross your fingers and hope we get somewhere with our hunger strike. There's nothing else you can do yet, just cross your fingers.

Write again.

See you! Mummy.

Like to play football some time? I'd love to, naturally.'

At the same time, the Federal Constitutional Court turned down an appeal by the Baader–Meinhof defence lawyers against their clients' harsh conditions of imprisonment.

Late in the autumn of 1973, Ulrike Meinhof wrote to her children:

'I'm thinking about you a lot at the moment. I wish Granny would write and let me know how things are. Tell her that.

And come and see me!

And write to me – do! Or paint me a picture, will you? I think I could really do with a new picture. I know the ones I have inside out.

I don't think my idea of getting you to say what you call me now was a good one.

I'm just Mummy, your Mummy, and that's it.'

Shortly before Christmas 1973, Ulrike Meinhof suddenly broke off contact with her children. An Advent calendar they had made her was returned; she refused to accept it. She stopped answering their letters. The girls never saw their mother again.

On 5 February 1974, Gudrun Ensslin was transferred to Ossendorf jail, where she was put in a cell next to Ulrike Meinhof. The strict solitary confinement in which the women had been kept up to this point was relaxed. They were allowed to exercise in the yard together, and could spend up to two hours a day locked in the same cell.

Sometimes they played the board game of Nine Men's Morris together.

11
'Some People Will Die . . .'

The high-security wing of Stammheim had been prepared, at great expense, for the RAF prisoners; the prison officers had not. 'We had a premonition that Baader, Meinhof and the others were a different kind of prisoner,' Horst Bubeck told his biographer Kurt Oesterle later. 'First of all we were told by the state to accommodate them there until the end of the main trial – guarding them carefully and keeping them safe, as expected in a penal institution.' The prison officers guessed: 'This isn't going to be nice work.'

On 28 April 1974 the moment came. It was a Sunday. Bubeck was on the seventh floor of the building, waiting for the arrival of the helicopter that was bringing the prisoners Ulrike Meinhof and Gudrun Ensslin. He looked at the photographs he had taken of Cells 718 and 719, evidence that they were clean, bright and pleasant. Two colleagues accompanied him to the yard where a minibus was to drive the two women over from the helicopter pad. A large police contingent was present to ensure security, with a camera team ready to film the historic moment. Ulrike

Meinhof was the first to get out of the vehicle. Bubeck said, 'Good morning, Frau Meinhof.' The prisoner looked at him and went towards him without a word, swaying slightly. She was thin. When she saw that she was being filmed she tried to strike out at the cameraman with her cuffed hands. He avoided the blow and went on filming. Ulrike Meinhof moved unsteadily back on the path, kicked out with one leg and struck Horst Bubeck in the lower body. Gudrun Ensslin got out of the minibus and walked to the prison building with her head bent, not looking at the officers. Bubeck asked the man in charge of the camera team what the idea of filming them was. He said the police wanted to have it all on film in case their lawyers or the press made any complaints. 'We've delivered them safe and sound. Now they're all yours.'

A 'house order' set out their conditions of imprisonment. According to this order, their cells, Numbers 718 and 719 on the seventh floor of the building, were to be 'double-locked day and night'. Two men and one woman officer were to be present whenever the cells were opened. The prisoners were allowed to wear their own clothes and underwear. Food was handed out in the kitchen to the officers on duty in the wing, who signed for it.

Gudrun Ensslin and Ulrike Meinhof could take their hour and a half of 'yard exercise' together every day on the roofed terrace above the seventh floor of the building. During the day they could be locked in the same cell for four hours.

Their cells were to be 'particularly thoroughly' searched daily. They were to have body searches at irregular intervals. A woman prison officer had to look in on the prisoners at least once an hour until 8 p.m. They could have a bath twice a week 'though not on Saturdays, Sundays and holidays'. The prisoners were barred from all community activities 'including church-going'. Only visits from family and lawyers were allowed.

For the time being Baader stayed in Schwalmstadt, Holger Meins in Wittlich and Jan-Carl Raspe in Cologne.

Over a period of several months, the prisoners prepared for a new hunger strike, the third. It was to be the longest and the toughest, and it ended in two deaths.

'I don't think we shall call the hunger strike off this time. That means some people will die . . .' wrote Andreas Baader.

The aim was to have the prisoners brought together in large groups.

However, there was more involved than simply the ending of solitary confinement. Trials were in the offing.

Baader wrote: 'We shall certainly plan the hunger strike so that the prisoners won't be fit for trial as a result.'

In another document, Baader wrote, 'We envisage disruption of the prison system.'

A communication via the 'Info-system', probably by Gudrun Ensslin, ran: 'Hunger strikes are a weapon only when it is clear they will go on until the collective demand has been met – even if it means illness and death.'

Their aims – again according to Baader – must be so formulated that 'any rocker, anyone who has done in his old lady, will see himself in them'.

On 27 August 1974, Ulrike Meinhof was temporarily transferred from Stammheim to be tried in Berlin for her part in the freeing of Andreas Baader in 1970. Horst Mahler had been found not guilty at the first trial, but the Federal High Court had quashed this verdict. So Ulrike Meinhof and Horst Mahler were both in the dock in Room 700 of the Moabit Criminal Court, along with Hans-Jürgen Bäcker, accused by the prosecution of being the man who had shot down the library employee Georg Linke.

Ulrike Meinhof looked ill, sat there in silence and scarcely exchanged a glance with Mahler.

Then she made a statement lasting forty minutes, in a quiet, almost expressionless voice, objectively and without emotion. Now and then, turning to the audience, she asked, 'Can you hear me?' She explained the aims of the Red Army Faction: 'The anti-imperialist struggle, if it is to be more than mere chatter, means annihilation, destruction, the shattering of the imperialist power system – political, economic and military.'

Ulrike Meinhof went on to announce that the prisoners were going on hunger strike, and set out their demands: social insurance and pensions for all prisoners, a free choice of doctors, the right to strike, unsupervised sexual contacts, unsupervised visiting, an end to censorship of prisoners' mail, abolition of youth detention centres, the establishment of mixed-sex prisons. 'If the pigs give in to one or the other of those demands, so much the better. Then we can use our powers to fight for something else.'

Ulrike Meinhof's statement aroused only pity in most of the journalists in court. One of them wrote: 'Ulrike Meinhof speaks, mercilessly turning her sharp mind against herself. A self-made martyr, a self-elected Joan of Arc of proletarian internationalism, with no army behind her but the people who call themselves the RAF, a spectral image in her poor clever head . . .'

Directly after Ulrike Meinhof's arrival at the Moabit prison, the group members in their various jails began refusing food. Horst Mahler did not join them in the strike.

Barely a fortnight later, Monika Berberich, taking the witness stand in the Baader rescue trial, said that Mahler had been 'out of the RAF for some time, by common consent'. Mahler had been ejected because of his vanity, airs and graces and claim to leadership. Monika Berberich described him as 'an unimportant tattler and a ridiculous figure'.

When he was released from custody, Horst Mahler wrote of the RAF members in prison:

'A man who is convinced that he has been harmed by being kept in isolation really will have circulatory disorders, and his mind really will be clouded. A man who keeps telling himself that he is being slowly killed by the deprivation of sensory stimulus and human communication actually will die of it – perhaps by his own hand.'

12
'A Hypocritical Bitch from the Ruling Class'

Months before the beginning of the third hunger strike, Ulrike Meinhof was to have begun work on writing a basic history of the Red Army Faction. She wanted to call it 'On the Anti-Imperialist Struggle'. The project was known as 'Bassa' in the group's internal jargon, after the Cabora Bassa dam in Mozambique. Ulrike Meinhof made her first notes in handwriting.

'The formation of the RAF in 1970 was in fact of a spontaneous character. The comrades who joined the movement saw it as the only real way of doing their revolutionary duty.

'Nauseated by the proliferation of the conditions they found in the system, the total commercialization and absolute mendacity in all areas of the superstructure, deeply disappointed by the actions of the student movement and the APO, they thought it essential to spread the idea of armed struggle.

'Not because they were so blind as to believe they could keep that initiative going until the revolution triumphed in Germany, not because they imagined they could not be shot or arrested.

'Not because they so misjudged the situation as to think the masses would simply rise at such a signal.

'It was a matter of salvaging, historically, the whole state of understanding attained by the movement of 1967/1968; it was a case of not letting the struggle fall apart again.'

'Teresa is in charge of gathering material for Bassa,' decreed Gudrun Ensslin. 'She has a lot to do, but I don't see it taking years, I'd say a few months to a year, something like that.'

However, Ulrike Meinhof did not make much progress with her work. She did manage to write the statement about the hunger strike for the trial. Baader and Ensslin were obviously not happy with her outline of it, and criticized her harshly. Ulrike Meinhof reacted with self-doubt and self-criticism.

Of her relationship with Baader, she wrote:

'The essential thing, my disturbed relationship with you both and particularly Andreas, will arise from the fact that I wasn't animated by revolutionary violence, it was just a phrase shamelessly used, as compared to my situation now.

'My social development towards fascism, through sadism and religion, which caught up with me because I never fully resolved my relationship to it, I mean the ruling class, and I was once its darling, had kept killing things off inside me . . .

'The really bad part of my delusion . . . behaving to the RAF as I used to behave to the ruling class, toadying, I mean treating you like cops, which simply means I was like a cop myself a long time, in the psychological mechanisms of domination and submission, of fear and clinging to the rules. A hypocritical bitch from the ruling class, that's merely self-knowledge. Everything's just "as if" . . .'

* * *

In August 1974, Andreas Baader copied out Ulrike Meinhof's 'self-criticism' for the 'Info-system'. Thus the other RAF prisoners received the document, together with self-reproaches from other RAF members.

Margrit Schiller wrote: 'Hatred: I was always terrified of A. [Baader], which was only the other, nasty side of hate . . . defence against being taken over by someone who wouldn't be corrupted . . .'

Replying to her, Gudrun Ensslin described the characteristics of Andreas Baader's role in the group:

'The rival, absolute enemy, enemy of the state: the collective consciousness, the morale of the humiliated and insulted, of the urban proletariat – that's what Andreas is.

'Hence the hatred of the bourgeoisie, the press, the middle-class left, concentrated on him . . .

'Because 14 May [1970, the date of the freeing of Baader in Berlin] has turned out to mean just that – the struggle for power. It was the first battle we won, an armed rescue operation, our model.

'We could measure ourselves by Andreas, by what he is, because he wasn't the old order any more (open to blackmail, corrupt, etc), but the new order: clear, strong, implacable, determined . . .

'Because he governs himself by our aims . . .'

13
Either a Pig or a Man

On 2 October 1974, the Federal Prosecutor General officially indicted the five core members of the group: Andreas Baader, Gudrun Ensslin, Ulrike Meinhof, Holger Meins and Jan-Carl Raspe. The trial was to begin the next year, and to be held at Stammheim. The defendants were accused of five murders. The files on the case initially ran to 170. About 1,000 witnesses and 70 experts were being called to give evidence.

Early in November 1974, Andreas Baader and Jan-Carl Raspe were flown to Stammheim by helicopter. Marksmen were posted on the prison roof. With a large escort of heavily armed police, Baader walked from the helicopter to the prison van which was taking him from the landing pad to the building. Both men had grown very thin during their hunger strike. Holger Meins, who was originally to have been transferred to Stammheim with them, stayed behind in Wittlich; his health had been severely affected by the hunger strike, and he was not fit to travel.

The object of their hunger strike had been to get transferred to Stammheim to join Gudrun Ensslin and Ulrike Meinhof. Now the transfer had suddenly been ordered by the court responsible for their conditions in jail.

Prison Officer Bubeck of Stammheim had the impression that Baader was positively hoping to be forcibly fed. He was nothing but skin and bone. 'His eyes were wide with the fear of death. He wouldn't listen to the officer who met him when he made earnest attempts to explain the daily timetable on the seventh floor. He turned only to Dr Henck, the prison doctor, and his anxieties didn't seem to be set at rest until the doctor told him the procedure would begin the next morning.'

In line with regulations, the Stammheim prison officer had to ask the prisoners every time if they were willing to be forcibly fed. If they were, which seldom happened, they could sit on a chair in the room outside the cells to be fed. But usually the answer was no. Then the officers took the prisoners out of the cells and laid them on portable stretchers outside. Their arms and legs were fixed in place with straps fastened by Velcro. Paramedics pushed the heads and upper body of each prisoner down, and Dr Henck inserted a tube through the nose, down the oesophagus and into the stomach. He checked whether the tube was in place with a stethoscope. Then he stirred ingredients in a basin, including eggs and glucose, to make the thin liquid to be fed to them. A paramedic filled a syringe with the vanilla-coloured mixture and injected it down the tube and into the stomach. As Bubeck remembered it, the prisoners often shouted, 'Pigs! Murderers! Torturers!' while they were being forcibly fed.

At the beginning of a hunger strike, the prisoners gave the prison officers all the food they had in their cells. Biscuits, chocolate and soup cubes were packed in cardboard boxes and deposited in the 'food cell', out of the prisoners' reach. But more often than not foodstuffs that had been kept back and hidden among books were found during the regular inspections of the cells. But the more often hunger strikes were staged over the years, being employed as a 'weapon against your own body', the more that weapon wore out. The general public hardly knew the strikes were taking place, and the prisoners took to eating increasingly often in secret. Once Bubeck found that one of the defending lawyers had a dozen ham sandwiches with him. When he spoke to the lawyer about it, the man said he was a diabetic and had to eat frequently. Bubeck smiled at him: 'Not very tactful, is it, eating in front of Herr Baader while he's on hunger strike?'

At the end of October 1974, Manfred Grashof gave up his hunger strike, but resumed it a few days later.

In this situation Holger Meins, then close to death from malnutrition himself, wrote him a letter:

'You are not with us any more, you are saving your own skin and thus giving the pigs a victory, that's to say: if you deliver us up you are the pig yourself, a pig defecting, going behind our backs so that you can survive personally. In that case – I mean if you're not going on with our hunger strike – you'd do better and more honourably (if you still know what honour is) to say: There it is, I'm alive. Down with the RAF. Up with the pigs' system—

> Either a pig or a man
> Either survival at any price
> or a fight to the death
> Either problem or solution
> There's nothing between.

Rather sad. Having to write you something like this. Of course I don't know myself what it's like when you die or when they kill you. How would I? In a moment of truth in the morning, this was the first thing that went through my head:

Ah, so that's how it is (but I still didn't know how), and then (facing the gun barrel aimed straight between the eyes): ah well, so that was it. I was on the right side, anyway.

You ought really to know something about that too. Ah well. Everybody dies, anyway. Only question is how, and how one lived, and that issue's clear enough: fighting the pigs as a man for the liberation of mankind: a revolutionary, in battle – with all one's love for life, despising death. That's the way for me: serving the people – RAF.'

Gudrun Ensslin received a copy of this letter, and wrote to Holger Meins. 'You might as well stop blowing hot air up that character's military arse – what's it all for? What good does it do you – what good does it do the guerrilla movement? Anyway, that's not total war, that's total defensiveness.

'I'd just leave it. "Rather sad" . . . *No* sadness. *That's* the aim. *You* decide when you die. Freedom or death.'

14
The Death of Holger Meins

After almost two months on hunger strike, Holger Meins was a mere skeleton. Six feet tall, he weighed only just over six stone. On Friday, 8 November 1974, he had been in touch with his lawyers, asking them, 'Please send someone, and quick. I shan't be leaving my bed again.'

On the Saturday morning, his defending lawyer Siegfried Haag went to Wittlich. No one would let him into the prison. They said Meins was bedridden, and no lawyer was allowed to visit him in his cell for security reasons.

Haag telephoned his colleague Croissant, who told Judge Theodor Prinzing of the Stuttgart Second Criminal Division Court, 'Meins is in a critical condition. Please will you give orders for a doctor he trusts to be allowed to visit him. And please allow my colleague Haag into the prison.'

As presiding judge in the forthcoming trial of the Baader–Meinhof group, Dr Prinzing was responsible for the defendants' conditions of imprisonment. He gave permission for Haag to visit the prison, but refused to have an outside doctor called in.

Two of the prison officers carried Holger Meins into a room in the administration area on a stretcher. His eyes were half closed. Siegfried Haag, his defending lawyer, bent over him. 'I'm finished. It's over. I'm dying,' whispered Holger Meins.

The lawyer had seen enough to know that anyway. 'When I saw him lying there on the stretcher, I knew how things stood,' said Haag later. 'I put my ear close to his mouth; that was the only way I could hear him. Sometimes he managed to say something almost out loud if he made a tremendous effort. The visit lasted two hours; one reason it was two hours long was because I realized this was his last conversation, and he knew it too.'

Finally Holger Meins asked his lawyer for a cigarette. Haag lit it and put it between Holger Meins's lips.

Soon after Siegfried Haag had left the jail, the prison officers too noticed the prisoner's critical condition. They called in a doctor from Wittlich to help. By the time the doctor arrived at 5.15 p.m., Holger Meins was dead.

The prison doctor and the prison governor, who according to their express instructions should have informed the Ministry and asked the Stuttgart Criminal Division to have Holger Meins transferred to the intensive care ward of a hospital, had done nothing. The prison doctor had gone away for a long weekend, and there was no deputy to take his place.

When the news of Holger Meins's death on hunger strike was broadcast on the radio, protest marches, each with several hundred demonstrators, formed in Frankfurt, Cologne, Hamburg, Berlin and Stuttgart. In the Stuttgart district of Untertürkheim, they marched to Judge Prinzing's house.

The presiding judge of the Criminal Division told journalists that he had done all he could to preserve the life and health of Holger Meins. However, he could not say how far use might have been made of the available facilities in Wittlich prison.

It seemed obvious to the sympathisers that Holger Meins had been murdered. Graffiti sprayed on the walls of buildings and churches read, 'Avenge Holger Meins'.

15
Murder of a Judge

On 10 November 1974, a Sunday, at about 8.50 p.m., someone rang the doorbell of an apartment at No 10–11 Bayernallee, in the Neu-Westend quarter of Berlin. Over the intercom at the door, a man said he was delivering flowers from the firm of Fleurop. He was let in; people delivering flowers had been there several times over the last day or so, because the master of the house had celebrated his sixty-fourth birthday the day before. Günter von Drenkmann, president of the Superior Court of Justice and Berlin's senior judge, looked through the peep-hole in his door. Seeing the delivery man with the flowers, he opened the door a little way. He had put the safety chain on. But the group of young people who suddenly emerged from the stairwell forced the apartment door open. There was a brief scuffle. Suddenly three shots were fired; two of them hit the judge. Günter von Drenkmann collapsed, bleeding.

The assassins raced away in a Peugeot and a Mercedes, going in different directions. The judge's wife called the police. A few minutes later he was taken to a nearby hospital, where he died.

Günter von Drenkmann had never had any professional connection with the Baader–Meinhof complex. He had never had any decisions to make about RAF members' conditions of imprisonment, or appeals from their lawyers, and had never delivered judgment in a terrorist case. He had been a judge in civil cases, was a liberal lawyer and a member of the SPD. It later turned out that the judge had been shot by a commando unit of the 2 June Movement, obviously in the course of an attempt to kidnap him.

16
'Holger, the Fight Goes On!'

The little Hamburg cemetery had never before seen such a crowd of mourners as attended the funeral of Holger Meins. Many citizens did not want the terrorist buried near their relations. In the days just after the funeral, whenever the dead man's father visited the grave he found the wreaths and flowers scattered all over the place. Wilhelm Meins put them back on the grave. One day he found a note beside his son's grave-stone. 'You won't find him again. He'll be hung on a tree and then at last he'll really die.' Wilhelm Meins was given police protection for ten days. Then he was told there was no way they could protect him and the grave any more.

Wilhelm Meins had a concrete cover sunk three-quarters of a metre underground, above the coffin. 'So that they can't get him out.'

The day after the funeral of Holger Meins, *Bild-Zeitung* came out with a headline: 'REVENGE! 2,000 SHOUT IN HAMBURG AT THE GRAVE OF HOLGER MEINS'.

'The Baader–Meinhof terrorist Holger Meins was buried yesterday morning. He did not go to his last rest peacefully: over 2,000 Communists shouted "Revenge!" The sound echoed eerily over the cemetery. And when the pastor uttered the words of Christ, "Father, forgive them," someone shouted, "We will never forgive the swine . . ."'

The story was accompanied by a photograph of Rudi Dutschke, captioned, 'Left hand holding his beret, right hand clenched, he cries, "Holger, the fight goes on!"'

Rudi Dutschke rejected individual terrorism. However, he still considered the members of the RAF his 'comrades'. He had known many of them well in Berlin at the time of the student movement. Holger Meins, for instance, who wanted to use the camera as a political weapon, who had made an instructional film on the manufacture of Molotov cocktails, and who then went even further, much further, to end as a gaunt figure with a straggling beard and spindly fingers lying on his deathbed.

And Jan-Carl Raspe, who had been on the committee of the Socialist German Students' Union in 1967, and was concerned about the revolutionizing of bourgeois individuality in Commune 2.

Rudi Dutschke also knew what wounds some of these people had carried away with them, not wounds like his own gunshot injury, but still traumatic enough. And he knew that the bullets Josef Bachmann had fired at him, like the death of Benno Ohnesorg, had set not a few on the path of violence.

Meanwhile, new groups were forming outside jail. They mostly originated in the 'torture committees', and the initiative often came from very young people who had never met Baader and Ensslin in their lives, but who started along the path to illegality in a state of indignation at the real or imagined inhumanity of their conditions of imprisonment. At no time of the 'underground struggle' did the RAF have so magnetic a power of attraction as they did when imprisoned.

Once in prison, the group developed a political stature they had previously lacked. The larger-than-life security precautions endowed the prisoners with a political significance they had never come near achieving with their writings and actions. Between 1970 and 1972, the police had been looking for some forty people. Now, at the end of 1974, they were hunting 300. Criminal Investigation Office experts estimated that what was described as 'the sympathizers' scene' numbered over 10,000. The definition of a 'sympathizer' was becoming wider and wider.

The death of Holger Meins had given the Red Army Faction a boost.

17
'The Knife in the Back of the RAF'

On 29 November 1974, in Berlin, Ulrike Meinhof was sentenced to eight years' imprisonment for attempted murder during the springing of Baader from custody in 1970. She was then moved back to Stammheim, where Baader, Ensslin and Raspe had already moved into their cells on the seventh floor.

At this time, contact was limited to the women seeing each other on one side of the cells area, and the men on the other side.

Even before the hunger strike began, Baader had written to Gudrun Ensslin, 'We must realize that one or two people may die during this hunger strike – but certainly no more. And then its effect will alter everyone's situation anyway.'

However, the hunger strikes were crumbling. Gerhard Müller had called off his in Hamburg, and so had Margrit Schiller. She wrote to the others: 'A few weeks ago, some time during the action, I surrendered the ability to continue being a member of the RAF.' As she did not want to die, she could no longer count herself one of the group.

Time and again, Gudrun Ensslin had tried to maintain discipline in her circular letters.

At the end of October, and thus before the death of Holger Meins, Ulrike Meinhof and Ingrid Schubert had expressed sympathy for Irene Goergens when she abandoned her hunger strike. Gudrun Ensslin wrote contemptuously at the time:

'It's impossible . . . to fight and not take the consequences; you can't subordinate the principles, ie the struggle, to your own fucking need for survival . . .'

When an article appeared in *Die Welt* on the supposed 'idyll' of Stammheim, she wrote to Ulrike Meinhof:

'*You* don't get given any orders. That's because we don't take any prisoners, don't liquidate any victims.'

Further: 'Did you see the *Welt* article? If Stammheim's an idyll – can Ulrike Meinhof be anything? A victim, crazy, cracked – that's been your line since I don't know when, but anyway that's how you've been quite brazenly and constantly putting it over in opposition to us for weeks of this conflict.'

Finally, Gudrun Ensslin wrote: 'Ah, the costumes of weariness – how tired I am of them, how fed up, how utterly sick to death – those mumbling clergymen, the boy scouts, old aunties, ravening females, little sonny-boys, ancient non-beings smothered in make-up – how tired I am of all that: hunger!

> I'd like to know.
> Am I in the cinema, or what, some pious film?
> Am I a turtle for soup?
> Or am I Struggle?'

Andreas Baader obviously did not take his hunger strike too seriously. Once, after a lawyer had visited him in his cell, he vomited and brought up some chicken; on another occasion prison officers found 200 grams of chopped roast meat wrapped in a handkerchief carried by another lawyer, who said it was his own elevenses.

Baader was proving himself zealous in the common cause. He frequently used green ink, as denoting that he was the leader, in his notes to the others. He wrote to Ulrike Meinhof:

'But of course you're one of those liberal cunts . . . you'll liberate yourself only in the fight, and not by whirling *around* yourself in the fight like a spinning top. And of course what you're producing does it no good either . . .'

He issued a demand to the women in Stammheim as a whole, now they were no longer kept apart:

'There is no solution for you but production, searching, writing, fighting. Digging out weapons, finding them, acquiring them – yes!'

* * *

Gudrun Ensslin, Ulrike Meinhof and Carmen Roll were sometimes locked in together, which increased tension among the women. Gudrun Ensslin complained to Baader:

'Ulrike, if you want to know . . . really gloomy: a vampire, quivering with blood-lust.'

And further: 'Ulrike's two outbursts of laughter during work: necrophiliac, hysterical, really absolutely hideous and unequivocal . . . directed against me. Although I keep saying, and I say again: not really against me, but against you. But there we are: yes, her laughter really was against me too, because it was against the revolution . . .'

Thus, to be 'against' Gudrun Ensslin meant being 'against' Baader. Against Baader meant against the revolution, and against the revolution meant against Gudrun Ensslin.

She wrote to Ulrike Meinhof: 'You open the door to the cops – you are the knife in the back of the RAF, because you never learn . . .'

Baader wrote to Gudrun Ensslin: 'I really don't understand it. I mean, I don't see the problem that occupies you so totally in all your letters: those confused battles with her about the devil knows what. Really, you're two grotesque madwomen . . .'

The one thing that seemed to have any permanence in this situation was Ensslin's relationship with Baader. Among the few personal notes the CID officers found when raiding the cells, Gudrun Ensslin wrote:

'And of course I could write you a beautiful, crazy book now – child, crosses, white wall, black crape dress – "I had the best of comrades", and so on . . .' And elsewhere: 'I had understood nothing. What you saw, and what of course I saw too, a few months back –

Betrayal, yes, and more:

there's also the way . . .

of loving and fucking: politics . . .'

For his own part, Andreas Baader attacked Gudrun Ensslin along with the others when he wrote to the 'lady's maids', as he called the women next door to him in the high-security wing. The main target of his criticism, however, was always Ulrike Meinhof:

'You lady's maids really are the plague . . .

'And of course it's the pig struggling away in there.

'That simply doesn't need any further elucidation, it's in every step Ulrike takes, everything she does, and betrayal is only a word for it . . .'

And again, specifically to Ulrike Meinhof:

'It's hatred, then – don't fool yourself, you hate us – there are any amount of signs of it, which naturally, oh so casually, and at the vital moment give rise to passivity, self-withdrawal, the wrong sort of language and content, destructiveness, misunderstanding. The problem is that you, and the others, have now become a burden, you're appallingly disorientated pigs. I'll have nothing to do with what you call self-criticism, and you needn't think I must. You're the ones destroying us – something the law could never do . . .

'But what's to become of it all now?

'The way things are now, I've nothing to say to you. So keep your gob shut until you've changed something, or go to the devil . . .'

Towards the end of the hunger strike, Gudrun Ensslin thought up a new idea which she was anxious to suggest to the RAF staff:

'I have this brainwave – I'll put it to you first, Coachman [Baader], and then to Ulrike and Jan. Brainwave only in so far as it's another way we can work the hunger strike.

'We can say one of us will commit suicide every third week (or second or fourth week, it doesn't matter which), until we're all out of our isolation . . .'

18
Cooking Smells

The hunger strike lasted a hundred and forty days. Holger Meins had not survived it. The health of almost all the RAF prisoners had suffered. Günter von Drenckmann had been murdered.

As an organization, the RAF had presented itself to the outside world as a combat troop fighting 'torture by isolation'. The Red Army Faction had become its own focus of attention. From the beginning of 1975, its entire fighting energies – both outside and inside jail – were almost exclusively devoted to the freeing of the prisoners themselves.

The declaration calling off the hunger strike on 2 February 1975 signalled this development:

'To the prisoners of the RAF.

'We ask you to call off the strike now, although . . . it proved impossible to achieve its object, the ending of isolation.

'Take this as an order.

'We are depriving you of this weapon because the struggle for the prisoners . . . will now . . . be decided by our own weapons.'

Baader and Raspe told Dr Henck, the prison doctor, 'We are stopping the strike today.' The doctor thereupon went over to the other side of the high-security wing, where the women were imprisoned, and told Ulrike Meinhof the men's decision. 'You should start eating again too.'

'We will not,' replied Ulrike Meinhof. 'We want to see it in writing, from Andreas.'

Dr Henck got Baader to write the word 'Eat' on a large sheet of paper, in felt pen, and to sign it with an 'A'.

He gave this note to Ulrike Meinhof, and she started eating again.

When the hunger strike had been called off the four Stammheim prisoners were allowed to spend several hours together every day. By comparison with the conditions of imprisonment of other remand prisoners, they could no longer be said to be in isolation.

The prison day began. The cells in Stammheim were opened at 8.00 in the morning. In prison jargon this was known as '*Aufschluss*', opening up. This was followed by a period of free association between the remand prisoners, both men and women, in the corridor between the cells. Andreas Baader coined the term '*Umschluss*', roughly speaking 'rounding up' for it, and the word passed into prison vocabulary in Stammheim and other jails as well.

Generally, so Prison Officer Bubeck remembered, Jan-Carl Raspe was the first to come out into the corridor between the cells in the morning, shaved and with his hair combed, to get his breakfast. He would say good morning to the officers and start reading the four newspapers and journals to which each of the prisoners was allowed to subscribe. Raspe often cut out articles about the RAF and stuck them into a kind of press-cuttings scrapbook for his fellow prisoners. Baader was last to emerge from his cell, as Bubeck remembered it, 'unshaven, his hair untidy, racked for minutes on end by his smoker's cough, often surly with the prison officers and his comrades.'

The prisoners had radio and TV sets in their cells. There were cushions and blankets out in the corridor; the chairs made available by the prison officers were seldom used. Usually the prisoners wore no shoes, only thick woollen socks in which they would sometimes slide around on the shiny linoleum after taking a short run-up. Baader liked to wear an unbuttoned shirt hanging out of his trousers; the others wore T-shirts or sweaters. An officer sat on a chair by the grating over the corridor, watching the prisoners all the time they were out there talking, smoking, quarrelling or reading. The distance had been laid down by the court: seven and a half metres, so that the prison officers could 'see but not hear the prisoners'. However, it turned out that they did in fact hear the prisoners talking about all kinds of subjects, not just their trial. The prison officers told the court, with the result that, as Bubeck recollected, the distance was doubled to fifteen metres.

The prisoners, who had endless time to spend in their cells, were always looking for ways to undermine the prison system. Jan-Carl Raspe in particular was constantly making things. He constructed little immersion heaters to boil water for coffee outside the permitted times. He used the turntables of record players and biscuit tins to make small stoves on which he could fry eggs or even bake pizzas over a candle flame. 'Almost every night,' Bubeck remembered, 'cooking smells would spread through the seventh floor.'

Raspe liked a particular toothpaste that the prison officers had to get him. It was not the toothpaste itself he wanted but the tube; it was made of lead, which he used to forge the police seals placed on the prisoners' radios and record players after their regular inspections.

They also had almost daily visits from their lawyers. Andreas Baader's visitors' list, for instance, sometimes looked like a lawyer's engagement diary itself, except that this was not a case of a lawyer receiving his clients, but a client receiving his lawyers.

24 January 1975:
10.20 to 10.55 a.m. Siegfried Haag
10.58 to 11.10 a.m. Siegfried Haag
2.20 to 2.35 p.m. Siegfried Haag
2.35 to 3.20 p.m. Otto Schily
2.45 to 3.55 p.m. Marielouise Becker
3.20 to 3.32 p.m. Kurt Groenewold
3.32 to 3.45 p.m. Siegfried Haag

That month, Baader had fifty-eight visits from eight different lawyers. In all, from 8 November 1974 to the time when such contacts were banned in connection with the Schleyer kidnapping on 5 September 1977, Baader had 523 visits, 43 of them from private visitors.

The authorities felt the security situation was now defused. Those first-generation terrorists known by name were almost all in custody. A commission of experts drawn from the Conference of Interior Ministers regarded the authority to issue directives earlier given to the Federal Criminal Investigation Office in connection with the 'Baader–Meinhof complex', as having done its job. Special Criminal Police squads were dissolved, since it was thought that there were only 'a few scattered remnants' left at large underground.

19
The First of the 'Second Generation'

Meanwhile, one Stuttgart legal office had assumed particular importance: this was the office of Dr Klaus Croissant at No 3 Lange Strasse. Croissant had started out as an orthodox middle-class lawyer, with a normal office, normal clients, normal staff and normal cases.

In 1973, he and his colleague Jörg Lang had founded the 'Committee against Torture by Isolation', an association of people whose opinions were left-wing to leftish liberal, supporting changes in the conditions of imprisonment of RAF prisoners. They ranged from a *Stern* reporter to an SPD city councillor.

Early in 1974, Lang went underground. Gaps on the committee were being filled at this time by young people from the Red Aid group. One of them was Volker Speitel, a young graphic artist, who was later to be one of the most important witnesses called by the Federal Criminal Investigation Office and the Public Prosecutor's Office in connection with the Stammheim deaths.

Speitel, his wife Angelika, and Willy Peter Stoll, who was later shot in an RAF police hunt, had been living in a commune, taking more interest in Timothy Leary, the apostle of the drug scene, than in politics.

When their joint projects for alternative forms of living and working failed to take off, they got in touch with Red Aid. 'Chaotic as this group was, it at least filled the vacuum of my disorientated existence,' wrote Speitel later.

Some Red Aid members were inclined to favour active support of the

Ulrike Meinhof in the offices of *konkret*, 1961:
'She has a great political career ahead of her.'

Andreas Baader, 1965: 'You either loved him or you loathed him.'

Gudrun Ensslin, 1963:
Christianity does not stop at the church door.

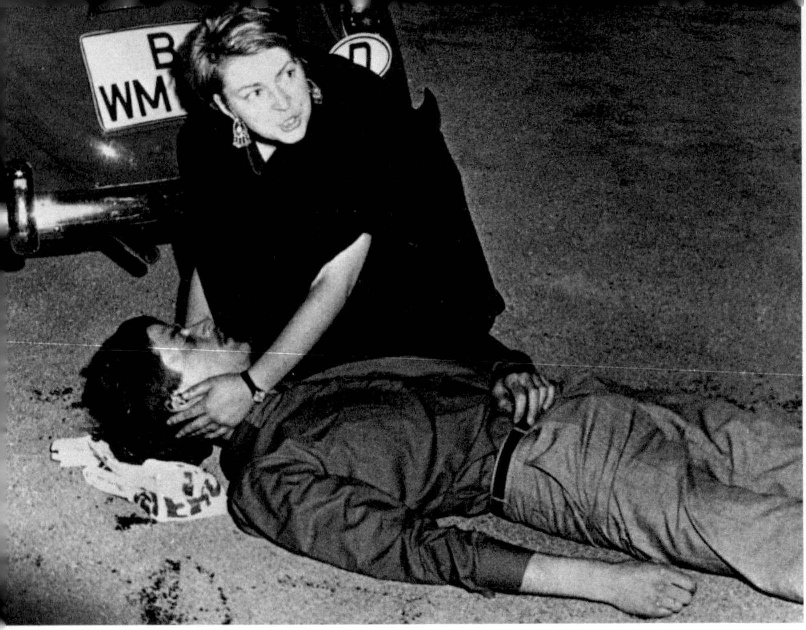

The student Benno Ohnesorg, shot by a policeman during the anti-Shah demonstration of 2 June 1967: 'I really see no difference between the police terrorist methods and the terrorism of the SA in the 1930s.'

'The Battle of the Tegeler Weg', Berlin, November 1968: 'We cannot rule out the use of violence on our own part.'

Andreas Baader and Gudrun Ensslin at the arson trial, October 1968: 'We have found that words are useless without action.'

Ulrike Meinhof wanted for attempted murder, 1970: with a leap out of a window she ended her journalistic career.

RAF attack on the officers' mess of the Fifth US Army Corps in Frankfurt, May 1972: 'Bomb attacks on the mass murderers of Vietnam are justified.'

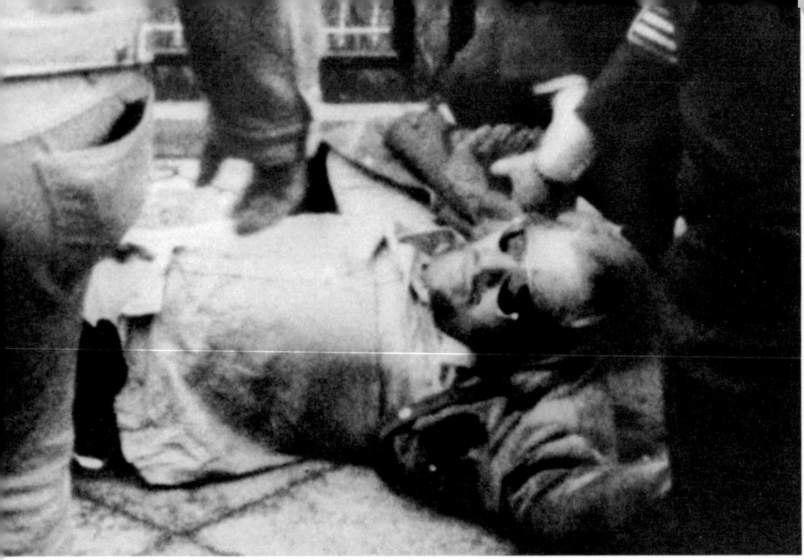

The arrest of Andreas Baader, 17 June 1972: 'They were sitting on a powder keg.'

(*Below left*) The arrest of Ulrike Meinhof, 15 June 1972:
'The feeling that your head is exploding.'
(*Below right*) Ulrike Meinhof and Gudrun Ensslin in handcuffs on their way to the trial:
'The knife in the back of the RAF.'

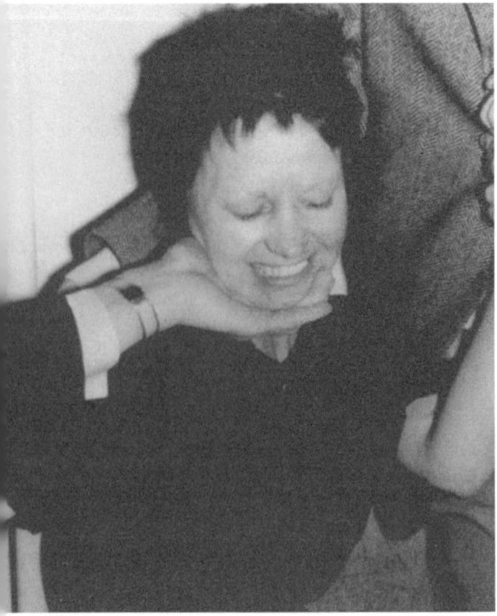

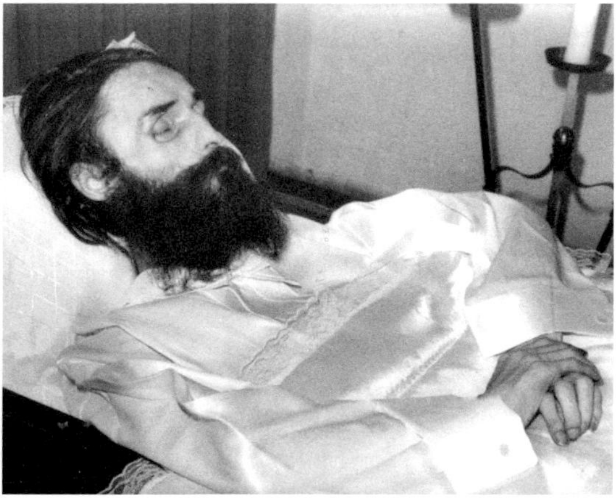
The laid-out body of the hunger striker Holger Meins, November 1974: 'You decide when you die.'

Rudi Dutschke at the grave of Meins: 'Holger, the fight goes on!'

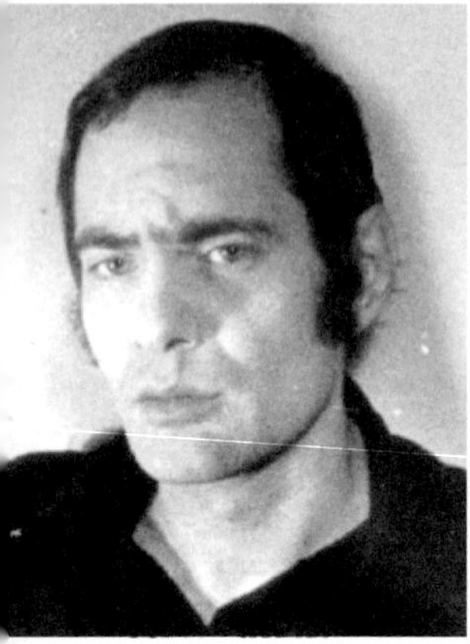

Minox photographs of Andreas Baader (*left*), Jan-Carl Raspe and Gudrun Ensslin (*below*), taken by the prisoners in Stammheim: 'If a camera was smuggled in, other things can come in too.'

Police reconstruction of Andreas Baader's record player, hiding a 7.65 calibre FEG pistol: 'The gun speaks.'

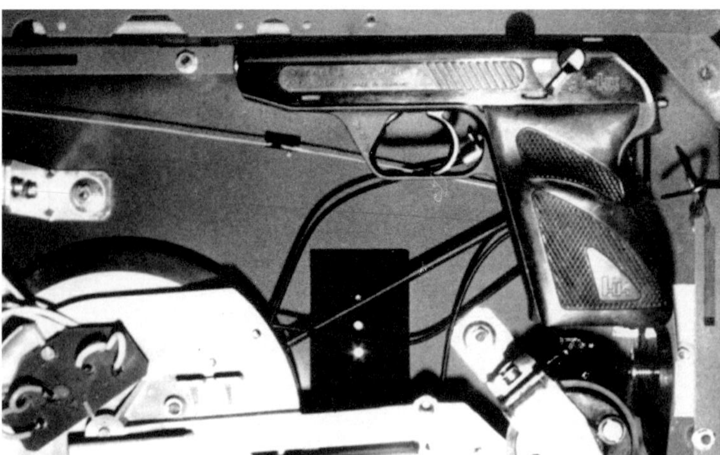

(*Above*) Peter Jürgen Boock: 'We are the next generation.'

(*Right*) Captain Jürgen Schumann, the pilot of the hijacked Lufthansa plane Landshut, the day before his murder, 15 October 1977.

The kidnapped president of the German Employers' Association, Hanns Martin Schleyer: 'prisoner of the RAF' for forty-four days.

(*Above*) Mourners and demonstrators leaving the funeral of Baader, Ensslin and Raspe walk past a line of police officers, with their hands above their heads as a gesture of protest, 27 October 1977.

Chancellor Helmut Schmidt and the widow of the murdered Hanns Martin Schleyer, 25 October 1977: 'The kind of situation in which no decision is exclusively right.'

RAF. Speitel knew little about the Red Army Faction, but he was impressed by the attacks on the American bases in Frankfurt and Heidelberg, and the decision to 'take to the gun' won his unqualified admiration.

During the long hunger strike in the autumn of 1974, the Red Aid group came closer and closer to the Committee against Torture by Isolation.

Since they were prepared to put up posters and distribute leaflets, they acquired more and more influence on the committee. Angelika and Volker Speitel began working in Croissant's office. They soon took over the provision of care for the prisoners, organized the RAF's 'Info-system', which passed through the office, assembled press cuttings, duplicated the prisoners' circular letters, got them books and collected contributions. This turned into a 'learning process' for Volker and Angelika Speitel and other members of their group.

Speitel wrote later: 'The prisoners offered suggestions and ideas even over the smallest details of office procedure, like photocopying and manning the switchboard. They devised us a process of political education.'

Then Holger Meins died. 'The death of Holger Meins and the decision to take to the gun were one and the same. Sober thought was impossible by now; it was simply the emotional drive of the last few months reacting.'

Volker Speitel went underground. Later, he said the lawyer Siegfried Haag had put him in touch with people outside the law. The first encounter took place in a Frankfurt bar, where Hanna Krabbe and Bernhard Rössner met him and took him to the 'base', a furnished attic room. Here Lutz Taufer, Ulrich Wessel and others were waiting. When Speitel walked into the little attic and had his first conversation with the outlaws, he was disappointed. 'All that was left of the old RAF structure was some explosives and hand grenades, and a manuscript about forgery techniques, and money. The police had managed to mop up almost the whole of the RAF. Apart from our own group, consisting of five people at that point, the RAF didn't exist at the end of 1974, or it existed only in prison.'

The Stammheim prisoners wanted to see some action at long last. From their point of view, the first generation of their successors, formed in Hamburg at the end of 1973 and captured by the police in a lightning swoop on 4 February 1974, constituted an awful warning. That group, later called '4.2' with reference to the date of their arrest, had spent weeks and months making plans, with local Counter-Intelligence men in Hamburg observing them at it and listening in on them around the clock.

That must not happen again. The new generation of the RAF meant to do 'less planning and more acting'. First of all, they compiled a list of potential targets. It began with the word 'Embassy', under which were listed London, Amsterdam, Vienna, Stockholm and Bern. Volker Speitel went to Switzerland and discovered that the German Embassy in Bern was practically impregnable in military terms; it was too well secured.

Meanwhile, the group began renting apartments for their illegal purposes and recruiting new members, particularly from the ranks of the 'torture committees'.

Speitel found that the illegality got on his nerves, or so at least he said later. He was afraid the group might plunge into rash ventures in the grip of their persecution mania. 'Somebody once said his fear of taking action was growing every day, so he would like to take action at once, and then he would be rid of his fear.'

Speitel left the underground again and went back to Croissant's legal office in Stuttgart.

20
A Politician Is Kidnapped

Elections were to be held in Berlin in the spring of 1975. For the first time, after a total of twenty-seven years in power or sharing power, the Social Democrats had to face the prospect of not returning to the Chamber of Deputies as the strongest party. This was actually more to do with the SPD's own symptoms of exhaustion than with their Christian Democrat opponents and those opponents' front-running candidate Peter Lorenz, a fifty-two-year-old lawyer. What the CDU mayoral candidate chiefly lacked was popularity. That, however, was soon to change.

Lorenz had adopted 'More vigour brings more security' as the slogan for his campaign. The Social Democrat Chancellor Helmut Schmidt mocked a CDU advertisement showing a picture of Lorenz under the headline 'Berliners live dangerously', remarking, 'If Peter Lorenz is responsible for that nonsense, he obviously must feel scared in his bed at night.'

Seventy-one hours before the election, at 8.53 a.m. on 27 February 1975, Peter Lorenz left his home in the Zehlendorf district. Three minutes later, 1,500 metres from his house, a four-ton truck blocked the road ahead of his Mercedes, and a Fiat rammed it. Lorenz's driver was knocked down with a broomstick, and the CDU mayoral candidate himself was dragged into a car standing ready.

The first sign of life from the kidnap victim came twenty-four hours later: a Polaroid photograph showing the politician with a notice around his neck saying. 'Peter Lorenz, prisoner of the 2 June Movement'. The kidnappers were demanding the release from custody of six people: Horst Mahler, Verena Becker, Gabriele Kröcher-Tiedemann, Ingrid Siepmann, Rolf Heissler, Rolf Pohle. All of them except Horst Mahler could be said to be vaguely connected with the 2 June Movement. Not a word about the RAF leadership, only a brief line of apology: 'To our comrades in jail. We would like to get more of you out, but at our present strength we're not in a position to do it.'

The authorities looking for the kidnappers were surprised. 'This is cold professional work,' commented Berlin Public Prosecutor Nagel.

The demands were nicely judged, and such that the state could meet them. No one accused or convicted of murder was on the list.

For the first time, a 'Larger Crisis Staff' was set up in Bonn, comprising leading figures from all the political parties. They had no constitutional mandate, nor any real authority to take decisions.

The politicians were in favour of complying with the kidnappers' demands. Chancellor Helmut Schmidt said, thirty years later, 'They took it for granted that the prisoners should be exchanged for the hostage Lorenz. I agreed to that myself, but next morning I realized it was a mistake; it simply invited repetition of the same manoeuvre.'

Among the kidnappers' demands was that the former governing Mayor of West Berlin, Heinrich Albertz, should accompany the freed prisoners on their flight.

On Sunday, 2 March 1975, Pastor Albertz held a church service in Schlachtensee parish hall, Berlin. He preached on the text: 'And the Lord said: Take now thy son, thine only son Isaac, whom thou lovest, and get thee into the land of Moriah, and offer him there for a burnt offering upon one of the mountains which I will tell thee of.'

At the end of his sermon, Albertz said: 'The names, the references, the confusion, the entanglements, the servants, the bared knife, the sacrifice, the torment, the hope, the obedience, the faith – today, here, on 2 March 1975 in Berlin – you can see them all in action for yourselves.'

A few hours later, Pastor Albertz flew to Frankfurt. He was led through the underground roads of the airport complex, guarded by policemen with submachine guns, to a room where the prisoners who had been brought together for the flight out were sitting. There were a table, some chairs, and a transistor radio. And hidden microphones.

Directly after his first meeting with the prisoners, an officer indicated to Albertz that microphones were concealed in the cell. Albertz raised the matter with the senior officer responsible. 'Is this true?'

The police officer shook his head. He did not look Albertz in the eye.

'You're an officer. I hope I can take your word for it,' said Albertz, and went to join the prisoners.

Take-off of the Lufthansa plane that had been laid on was shown live on television. Horst Mahler was not on the aircraft when it flew out. He had refused to be exchanged.

The plane finally landed in Aden, Yemen, where the prisoners disembarked. After his return, on 4 March, Pastor Heinrich Albertz spoke on television, giving the code-word that the prisoners were free by quoting, 'A wonderful day such as today . . .', a line from a German drinking song.

The following night, Peter Lorenz was released in a Berlin park. His kidnappers had given him some small change so that he could phone his family.

One of Lorenz's kidnappers, Till Meyer, heard later from the lawyer Klaus Croissant how the prisoners in Stammheim followed the course of the kidnapping on television, spellbound. 'How did the state react, and when; how did the Greater Crisis Staff, the Lesser Crisis Staff react; how did we react? All of this was earnestly and closely analysed on the seventh floor by Andreas Baader, Gudrun Ensslin and Ulrike Meinhof.'

As a result the prisoners in Stammheim laid plans to outdo the 2 June Movement with a really major operation.

Pastor Albertz learned from the head of the Berlin Senate offices that there had been hidden microphones in the cell at Frankfurt airport after all. However, he was told, it had been impossible to hear anything because a transistor radio was playing. Albertz did not believe this. During his conversations with the prisoners, the transistor had been switched on only briefly, for the hourly news bulletins.

In his report, the former governing mayor of Berlin said, 'I would like an explanation of this matter. I was in that cell as a pastor. To listen in on my conversations with the prisoners was an unwarrantable breach of trust shown to a man who had not undertaken that difficult task for pleasure.'

The bugs at Frankfurt airport were not the only ones installed at this time.

On 2 February 1975, the day of Lorenz's abduction, President Wagner of the regional Baden-Württemberg Office for the Protection of the Constitution called the Federal Office for the Protection of the Constitution in Cologne. He asked to speak to Rausch, head of Department 4. Wagner told the head of counter-espionage that he needed some technical assistance. Hidden microphones – bugs – were to be installed in Stammheim jail.

Rausch agreed without consulting his boss Günter Nollau, head of the Federal Office. On 1, 2 and 3 March 1975 two counter-espionage technicians installed the microphones in five cells in Stuttgart-Stammheim Prison.

21
Storming the German Embassy

In Stammheim, the last few metres of the wall around the multipurpose building erected for the Baader–Meinhof trial were being painted. Sound engineers were connecting up the tone controllers for the loudspeakers in the courtroom, and a squad of cleaners were putting a shine on the yellow plastic chairs for the spectators. Dr Theodor Prinzing, aged forty-nine, the presiding judge, told a small party of people, 'The trial is about to take place, or at least to begin.' It was shortly before twelve noon on 25 April 1975.

At this same moment there were about a hundred Swedes and Germans on the premises of the West German Embassy in Stockholm. Six of them were armed with pistols and explosives. The terrorists were:

Siegfried Hausner, aged twenty-three, who had started making bombs as a schoolboy, and had later been a member of the 'Explosives Study Group' of the Heidelberg Socialist Patients' Collective. Hanne-Elise Krabbe, aged twenty-nine, top of her class when she took her school-leaving exams in Nordhorn, and also a member of the Socialist Patients' Collective as a student in Heidelberg. Karl-Heinz Dellwo, aged twenty-three, a postal worker, who had been one of the militant squatters of Hamburg. Lutz Taufer, aged thirty-one, a member of the Socialist Patients' Collective. Bernhard-Maria Rössner, aged twenty-nine, who had come to the notice of the police as the instigator of a sit-down demonstration in Hamburg against 'torture by isolation'. Ullrich Wessel, aged twenty-nine, son of a millionaire, and one of the Hamburg RAF sympathisers.

In the consular department, the six brought out their weapons, seized an embassy employee who they obviously knew had the keys to the upper storey of the building, and fired off their guns. Most of the people around at the time fled into the open air, panic-stricken. The armed raiders held eleven of them, herded them up to the third floor of the embassy, then bound and gagged them and laid them on the floor.

A few minutes later the Swedish police arrived, occupied the ground floor, and prepared to attack the upper storey with gas cartridges. One of the terrorists called for the police to go away. 'Or we'll shoot the German military attaché.' The police stayed.

At 1.17 pm, the terrorists occupying the embassy telephoned the Stockholm office of the German Press Agency: 'The Holger Meins Commando is holding members of the embassy staff in order to free prisoners in West Germany. If the police move in, we shall blow the building up with fifteen kilos of TNT.'

The terrorists had already deposited explosives in Ambassador Stoecker's corner room, and laid blasting cables under the carpet. Once again, they told the officer commanding the Swedish police squad to move his men out. 'Within two minutes, or it'll go sky-high.' When there was no reaction, they ordered the military attaché, Lieutenant-Colonel Baron Andreas von Mirbach, to walk out on to the landing, his hands bound. Then they shot him. The lieutenant-colonel collapsed, hit in the head, chest and leg. Two Swedish policemen, stripped to their underpants to show that they were unarmed, dragged the dying man down the stairs. The policemen retreated and set up their headquarters in the ambassador's living quarters in the building next door. They sandbagged the building and distributed bullet-proof vests.

At 3.30 p.m. the terrorists again called the German Press Agency in Stockholm, specifying demands for the freeing of twenty-six prisoners in West Germany, including Ulrike Meinhof, Andreas Baader, Jan-Carl Raspe and Gudrun Ensslin.

When Chancellor Helmut Schmidt heard news of the occupation of the Embassy, he withdrew to his study in the Palais Schaumburg in Bonn for half an hour. Then he told the assembled members of the Larger Crisis Staff his decision. 'Gentlemen, all my instincts tell me that we must not give in.'

Towards 8.00 p.m. the Swedish minister of justice was told of the firm stand the government of the Federal Republic was taking. After a moment's hesitation, he said, 'We accept this decision.' The minister then telephoned the embassy and told the terrorists that Bonn had uncompromisingly rejected their demands. For a moment the line seemed to have gone dead. It appeared that the man at the other end was unable to grasp the news.

The Swedish minister of justice spoke to the terrorists in the embassy nine times that night, trying to offer them safe conduct in return for the freeing of their hostages. They refused. 'It's useless, we're not negotiating. If our demands aren't met we shall shoot a hostage every hour. Victory or death!'

At 10.20 p.m., one of the terrorists asked for the economic attaché. 'I'm here,' said Dr Hillegaart. He was led to an open window looking out. 'Hallo, hallo, can you hear me?' he called. Then three shots were fired. The sixty-four-year-old economic attaché slowly fell forward and lay there, half hanging out of the window. He was dead.

The Swedish police got a vehicle equipped with K 62 stun gas into position; this gas had been used for the first time to overpower two bank robbers in Stockholm in 1973. They were going to fire gas cartridges which burst on impact into the building from a distance of a hundred metres. But it did not come to that.

Thirteen minutes before midnight, a series of detonations shook the embassy building.

The third-floor windows, frames and all, fell out into the street. Guttering was flung into the trees; an office chair landed on the grass almost a hundred metres away. Outside, policemen were thrown to the ground by the pressure of the blast. At the same moment a wave of fire raced through the third floor of the embassy, flames rising above the roof. 'Help!' came shouts through the fire. Then Ambassador Stoecker, who had managed to loosen his bonds, came stumbling out of the inferno. Three of the terrorists followed him; they had lost or thrown away their guns, and put up no resistance when arrested. Two more fell to the ground in front of the building, injured. The sixth was found dying in the grass behind the embassy. The shock wave had flung him out of the building.

Police and firemen stormed the burning building and freed the hostages. Almost all of them were badly burnt.

Three people had died: the embassy attachés von Mirbach and Hillegaart, and one of the terrorists, Ulrich Wessel. Siegfried Hausner, severely injured, was flown back to Germany by special plane a few days later.

'It was only one or two days after the end of the Stockholm attack that one of the hostage-takers was flown to us by helicopter,' said Prison Officer Horst Bubeck later. 'His name was Siegfried Hausner, a young man in his early twenties, and he was badly burnt.' He was put in the Stammheim prison hospital, where the Ministry of Justice had set up a complete intensive care department for the prisoners when they were on hunger strike. But the prison hospital had neither the equipment nor the specialist staff to care for severe burns. According to Bubeck, Hausner had 'no chance of surviving, as the doctors saw immediately'.

On 1 May, when Bubeck came on duty at seven in the morning, he saw the dying man just once. Hausner was unable to speak, but fully conscious. His body, said Bubeck, looked 'like a single huge scar, burnt red and black all over. His hair had been singed off. His face was charred. His hands and fingers were all kinds of colours and badly swollen.' Only his eyes still seemed alive in their sockets.

Suddenly Hausner's eyes moved restlessly. A nurse offered the injured man one of the hospital's 'order forms' and a pen. Hausner squeezed the pen between his swollen fingers, which could hardly move, and wrote, 'My throat hurts – I'm an alcoholic! I think the smoke + heat have scratched the mucous membrane. 1. suck 2. gargle 3. ¼ or ½ litre of milk to keep the swallowing reflex going.' The slip of paper dropped from his hand. He reached for it again and wrote, 'Or a sip of tea or water.'

Hausner was given something to drink. The note went into the waste paper basket. Bubeck retrieved it, smoothed it out and kept it.

When Hausner died of an oedema of the lungs on 5 May, the prisoners on the seventh floor asked the prison officers, 'Well, have you finished him off?'

A few days after the attack on the embassy in Stockholm, on 1 May, the technicians from the Federal Office for the Protection of the Constitution came back to Stammheim and rendered more 'assistance' to their colleagues of the regional Baden-Württemberg Office.

Soon afterwards, in an operation agreed with the Federal Chancellory, technicians of the Federal Intelligence Agency (the Bundesnachrichtendienst, BND for short) went to Stammheim and installed bugs in 'two vacant cells'.

Now seven cells in Stammheim were bugged, five by the technicians of the Federal Office for the Protection of the Constitution, two by technicians from the BND.

The 'listening-in operation' in Stammheim remained a secret for two years. Then the two Baden-Württemberg ministers responsible, Traugott Bender of Justice and Karl Schiess of Internal Affairs, had to admit that bugs had been installed at Stammheim to monitor the prisoners. They stated at the time that conversations between the lawyers and their clients had been recorded 'in two justifiable cases of emergency:

'The first began on the day after the attack of 24 April 1975 on the German Embassy in Stockholm. Conversations were recorded for ten days, the last being on 9 May 1975.

'The second occasion when conversations were recorded was after the arrest of the former lawyer Haag and of Roland Meyer on 30 November 1976. In this second phase recording was carried out over twelve days in all, during the time between 6 December and 21 January 1977.'

The fact that secret service technicians had installed microphones first in five cells and then in another two suggests that other cells as well as the visitors' rooms for lawyers were bugged. There were only four such rooms on the seventh floor at Stammheim.

Two weeks after the raid on the Stockholm Embassy, the lawyer Siegfried Haag was arrested, charged with obtaining weapons in Switzerland for the terrorists who occupied the embassy. However, when his offices were searched and no evidence was found, he was released again on 10 May 1975. Haag went underground. In a press release he said that, 'In a state that tortures political prisoners by means of systematic long-term isolation, and subjects them to brainwashing in remote parts of their prison, in a state whose functionaries executed Holger Meins and Siegfried Hausner', he could no longer practise his profession as a lawyer. At the end he announced, 'It is time to address more important issues in the battle against imperialism.'

The battle was to go on underground while the founding generation of the RAF faced the court in Stammheim. Their trial began there a bare two weeks after Haag had gone underground.

PART FOUR

The Trial: The Baader–Meinhof Group in Court

1
The Multi-purpose Hall
(1st day, 21 May 1975)

A memorial of steel and concrete had been erected to them in their lifetime. The judiciary of Baden-Württemberg had a new courtroom built for the trial of the 'hard core' of the Baader–Meinhof group, in a potato field beside the most modern prison in Europe. This multi-purpose hall, constructed from prefabricated parts in the space of a few months, cost 12 million Deutschmarks. The windowless building was to be used as a workshop by the prisoners of Stammheim later.

Two hundred spectators could be accommodated in the courtroom itself, which was 610 square metres in size and lofty as a gymnasium. Neither the heating and ventilation pipes under the ceiling nor the steel structure of the roof were covered in. The walls were bare concrete. There were yellow plastic chairs for the audience, white tables for the judges, the prosecuting and defending lawyers, and the defendants. It was modern and functional. It could just as well have been the hall of a modern comprehensive school, or a sports hall with rather makeshift fittings, or a village parish hall.

The front wall bore an outsize version of the coat of arms of the *Land* of Baden-Württemberg.

In spite of the loud differences of opinion between the defendants and their lawyers on one side and the court and public prosecutor on the other, one thing had been agreed at the outset: the trial was to be recorded complete on tape, and its proceedings transcribed. Some of the tapes themselves were preserved and came to light again only in 2007.

The trial of Andreas Baader, Gudrun Ensslin, Ulrike Meinhof and Jan-Carl Raspe began here on 21 May 1975. It was a sunny day; people crowded around the fortress built for the trial as if it were a fair. Mounted police patrolled the perimeter of the building, which was protected with barbed wire. Aircraft were banned from the air space over the prison and the multi-purpose hall. The inner courtyard and the roof of the courtroom building were covered with steel netting, so that explosive devices dropped from the air could do no harm.

As the Stammheim trial approached, the Bundestag had revised the Code of Criminal Procedure. Baader's lawyers Klaus Croissant, Kurt Groenewold and Hans Christian Ströbele were barred from taking part in the main trial shortly before it began. When it did, Andreas Baader had no defence lawyer.

In the crowded courtroom, the presiding judge, Dr Theodor Prinzing, declared the proceedings open. 'And now I come to the criminal case against Andreas Baader, Ulrike Meinhof, Gudrun Ensslin and Jan-Carl Raspe.'

He named the defence lawyers present: Rupert von Plottnitz, Helmut Riedel, Marielouise Becker and Otto Schily. These were defending counsel who had the confidence of the accused. In addition, the court had summoned a number of court-appointed defence lawyers who were not in the confidence of the accused, to ensure the legal continuation of the trial in case one of the defendants' chosen defending counsel resigned his brief, voluntarily or otherwise.

The defendant Ulrike Meinhof asked to speak. Her subject was these court-appointed defending lawyers, or 'compulsory defence counsel'. 'None of them has the slightest right . . .' she began. The presiding judge interrupted her. 'Wait. This is not being recorded on the tape. Excuse me, please, Frau Meinhof, this is not being recorded on tape, and we must have it in the record of the proceedings. It's not my fault.'

'Let me finish what I was saying!'

Baader joined in. 'Yes, what is this silly business?'

'Herr Baader,' said Prinzing, 'I think Frau Meinhof is quite able to make her own statements.'

'Let us speak!' cried Ulrike Meinhof.

Baader turned to the presiding judge. 'This isn't your problem.'

Dr Prinzing reacted impatiently. 'Is this a collective defence, with the two of you speaking collectively and indiscriminately?'

'Stop your stupid jokes!' said Baader.

Dr Prinzing forbade him to continue speaking.

'And stop interrupting!' Ulrike Meinhof put in. 'Let us speak!'

'You have two methods,' said Baader. 'Either you interrupt us or you manipulate us with your tape recordings.'

'Obviously,' agreed the presiding judge, 'our technology renders you unable to make any statements.'

Then Ulrike Meinhof was able to make her point. 'They've been forced on us – state-appointed defence lawyers in league with the prosecution, and we may assume that everything they say is angled against us . . . And we also want it on record that the manipulation of these microphones leads one to suppose their purpose is to pick up everything we say.'

'But what would be the point of that, when the trial is public anyway?' inquired the presiding judge.

'We're saying,' said Baader, 'that the microphones are adjusted so as to pick up conversation between the defending lawyers and the prisoners, private conversation, as it were.'

Dr Prinzing said he thought he was mistaken. Baader said that after all, the microphone switches had been fitted to the dock. 'The arrangement's really perfect,' said Baader. Moreover, he added, someone had written 'Head off' beside his microphone.

'What was that?' asked the presiding judge.

'I said I've just discovered that someone has written "Head off" beside the microphone. What does that suggest to you?'

'I am afraid your meaning is too obscure for me. I don't know what you are trying to say.'

2
Baader without a Defending Lawyer
(2nd day, 5 June 1975)

Dr Prinzing wanted to move briskly on to questions on personal data, but Andreas Baader asked to speak. 'It can't have escaped your notice that so far I have no defending lawyer. We had no intention of going along with the way this case has been stacked against us. And it's impossible for anyone to appear for the defence in a trial where the law is being permanently altered the whole time, and where the legal process is unsatisfactory, and bent or made to look ridiculous by the Public Prosecutor's Office.'

The trial, he said, was an object lesson proving the Red Army Faction's analysis correct. And now here he was without any defence counsel. 'It has been very difficult to find a defending lawyer,' Baader added. 'It wasn't possible with the week's notice you gave me.' Conversations with lawyers who might conceivably appear for him had had to be conducted under supervision. 'So it was objectively impossible to establish if there was any lawyer who would accept the persecution which the public prosecutor and the BKA will obviously link to my brief.'

Baader petitioned for suspension of the trial until he had found defending counsel and was allowed unsupervised conversations with lawyers. He said he made that a condition: for three years, he claimed, the prosecution had checked every word of the case for the defence, by searching cells and lawyers' offices and confiscating mail. And, Baader added, 'by planting bugs in the cells used for lawyers' visits; we've known about those since the summer of '73'.

Baader's allegation that conversations between the defendants and their lawyers had been bugged only caused public head-shaking. The press could not imagine that authorities of the Federal Republic of Germany would use microphones and tape recorders to interfere with the sacrosanct confidential relationship between defendants and their lawyers. Andreas Baader's comment was generally considered a manifestation of the paranoid delusions of the Baader–Meinhof group. But in fact Baader was not so very wide of the mark.

However, that came to light only two years later.

3
Compulsory Defenders
(3rd day, 10 June 1975)

On the third day of the trial, Andreas Baader still had no defending counsel of his own choice. The court-appointed lawyers sat silently in their places. The defendants firmly declined to speak to these 'compulsory defenders'. The atmosphere of the trial was becoming tenser by the hour. To make matters worse, the presiding judge had not allowed the defendant Baader more than three-quarters of an hour for a conversation with the Darmstadt lawyer Dr Heldmann, who despite everything was prepared to undertake Baader's defence.

The Federal Public Prosecutor's office thought that Baader would be adequately represented by the two court-appointed lawyers 'assigned to him firstly for his own welfare, and secondly for the safeguarding of this trial . . . If he does not wish to make use of these gentlemen's services, that is his own affair.'

'Very well,' said Andreas Baader, 'then I have to say again, and keep on saying, that the lawyers over there can't defend me. They cannot appear for me, they have never talked to me and they never will talk to me.'

Finally the presiding judge tried to move on to the questioning on personal data. He was unable to do so. Instead, Marielouise Becker, defending, read out an application for the discharge of the court-appointed defending lawyers. Their sole function, as defence counsel who were in the confidence of the public prosecutor and of the court, said this petition, was to ensure the smooth running of the proceedings 'as puppets in this show trial staged by the imperialist state power and planned ahead in detail'.

The presiding judge requested one of the rejected court-appointed lawyers, whose name happened to be Linke, to comment. Linke said, 'Their preferred defenders, of course, are of the left . . .' [in German: *Linke*.]

Baader interrupted. 'Shut up, Linke.'

Prinzing intervened. 'Herr Baader, any more such remarks would oblige us to take measures to which we would much rather not resort. We want you to be present at this trial.'

The defendants and their lawyers shouted interruptions. Another of the court-appointed defenders, Künzel, rose to speak. 'The tone of this performance, and the claims that have been made, oblige me to make a few comments for reasons of legal accuracy.'

Gudrun Ensslin interrupted him. 'You're not speaking for me!'

'I am not speaking to Frau Ensslin, definitely not, because I –'

Baader bawled, 'All you have to do is keep your gob shut!'

'Herr Baader, I am not speaking to you at the moment,' said Künzel.

With difficulty, the presiding judge attempted to restore calm. Gudrun Ensslin, whose microphone had been switched off, was trying to make herself heard.

'Frau Ensslin, one moment, Frau Ensslin,' cried the presiding judge.

'Don't go covering anything up with drivel!' shouted Gudrun Ensslin.

'I am not trying to cover anything up with drivel. But the fact is that you will not allow anyone else to speak. A person who, perhaps, holds views other than yours. Kindly listen quietly, and then you can say what you think.'

The audience in the courtroom were now beginning to shout too. Dr Prinzing informed Baader, 'I am empowered to tell you that such conduct could force the court to continue this hearing without you for the time being. We would find this very unfortunate.'

Baader went on talking; his words could not be distinguished, because his microphone too had been switched off.

'Herr Baader, it is not your turn to speak at the moment, and please do not act up in that fashion. It is of no use.'

The defendants interrupted, shouting, and rose from their seats.

'One moment, no, no, you cannot leave this courtroom. You cannot leave this courtroom,' stammered the presiding judge. Amidst the general chaos, he tried to call on Otto Schily to speak. Schily suggested adjourning the trial for half an hour's break. The presiding judge could see no call for this.

'We will see how the defendants now conduct themselves. It goes down on record that the defendants are trying to prevent Herr Künzel here from speaking by means of shouting.'

'What are you really after?' shouted Gudrun Ensslin.

'Frau Ensslin!' With difficulty, the judge tried to keep his composure. 'If you go on disturbing the proceedings now, then as I have said, we will withdraw and consider what measures must be taken to deal with you.'

The court adjourned for consultation.

Five minutes later, the judges were back in their places.

Dr Prinzing turned to Baader. 'In the event of the continuation of such conduct, the court would be forced to decide to exclude you from this part of the trial. You can say what you like about that. Or you can keep quiet and conduct yourself properly from now on.'

'I'm making it quite clear once again,' said Andreas Baader, 'that as long as those compulsory defenders over there go on speaking, forced on us against our will as they are, we'll go on creating a disturbance. And for this part of the trial, I mean as long as they're speaking, I'd suggest that you do exclude us from this part of it, so that we don't have these scenes, these silly scenes, I mean this wrangling.'

The presiding judge tried to make himself heard, but Gudrun Ensslin drowned him out.

'And just so you understand what we mean by "we", if those swine over there open their big mouths again . . .'

'Of whose big mouths are you speaking?' inquired Dr Prinzing.

'That's exactly the point. It's you or us,' said Gudrun Ensslin.

'We will note the fact,' said the presiding jduge, 'that should the compulsory defender, as you call him, speak again, you intend to disturb the proceedings further.'

Baader, Meinhof, Ensslin and Raspe were led away by courtroom officials.

4
Baader Tries to Get a Hearing
(6th day, 18 June 1975)

Due to the effects of the hunger strike on their health, the issue of fitness to stand trial, and with it the issue of the defendants' conditions of imprisonment, now became the dominant themes of the proceedings. The accused were allowed back into the courtroom, and Andreas Baader, as spokesman for the group, put his political assessment of those conditions of imprisonment and the political purpose of 'torture by isolation' on record.

He read out a paper which left nothing to be desired in the way of unintelligibility: 'The basic problem, on this point too, is the antagonism that calls for the state machine to make re-education, or brainwashing, a legitimate project. That is, in order to subdue the subject the state machine must be able to constitute it. The cause at issue between the repressive state machine and the captured revolutionary, however, is that both know that in their irreconcilability, as in their relationship, they express the maturity of the development wherein the contradiction between productive forces and the circumstances of production becomes antagonistic in the final crisis of capital, and thus the expression of the trend whereby the legitimation of the bourgeois state has fallen apart.'

The presiding judge withdrew Baader's permission to speak.

Ulrike Meinhof spoke next. 'I declare that I am not fit to stand trial. That is, that at most, and this is putting it very high, I can just about follow what goes on here. And that naturally I am hardly in the position, here and now, to say anything when something absolutely should be said, when I want to say something. The purposes for which we were kept in isolation have naturally taken effect. And naturally the difficulties of association with which we have to contend are enormous. It is entirely absurd, entirely absurd to believe that these three years can have passed and left no trace on any of us. I therefore apply, simply because it is necessary and needful, for myself and every one of us here, to be given a medical examination by an independent doctor.'

Ulrike Meinhof further applied for the hearing to last at most two or three hours a day.

Her applications were rejected.

5
The Basic Rule of Terrorism
(23rd day, 5 August 1975)

While the presiding judge kept trying to get control of the trial so that examination of personal data could at last begin, the defendants and their lawyers made application after application for the trial itself to be dismissed. They were attempting to raise it to the political plane and convey to the public what the forces were that impelled their underground struggle. In their cells, they had prepared statements which they delivered at the trial, and which were constantly interrupted by the presiding judge, who found them excessively wordy.

It was a case of the collision of two worlds, bound together, if at all, only by the Code of Criminal Procedure.

Andreas Baader tried grappling with the state's official definition of the urban guerrilla movement. He quoted the Interior Minister of the

Rhineland–Palatinate, who had said, 'The basic rule of terrorism is to kill as many people as possible. Numb horror is the state of mind terrorists obviously wish to produce in more and more people throughout the world.'

'I would say,' commented Andreas Baader, 'that is the precise definition of Israel's policy towards the Palestinian liberation movement, that is the precise definition of the USA's policy in Vietnam until its defeat. That is the precise definition of the policy of the Chilean junta, and that is the precise definition of the policy of the Federal Prosecutor's Office, its basic rule being as many dead fighters as possible, as many dead prisoners as possible, executions in the open street, shooting to kill, and so on. Numb horror is, in fact, exactly the state of mind the Federal Prosecutor's Office wants to produce in more and more people by having more and more "dead sections" built in prisons, putting prisoners in them more and more often and leaving them there.'

Dr Prinzing warned Baader, 'You have to give grounds for the dismissal of these judges, not make general remarks.'

Baader continued, 'What Federal Prosecutor General Buback is doing is by exact definition terrorism, state terrorism. And thus the terrorist Buback . . .'

'Herr Baader,' the presiding judge interrupted him, 'I am withdrawing your permission to speak. If you are trying to accuse the federal prosecutor general of pursuing a course of state terrorism, that goes beyond what we . . .'

Here Baader wanted to say something, but the judge turned his microphone off.

Ulrike Meinhof spoke. 'Terrorism is the destruction of utilities such as dykes, waterworks, hospitals, power stations. All the targets at which the American bomb attacks in North Vietnam were systematically aimed from 1965 onwards. Terrorism operates amidst the fear of the masses. The city guerrilla movement, on the other hand, carries fear to the machinery of the state.'

The presiding judge interrupted Ulrike Meinhof and warned her, 'I cannot accept your giving reasons which have no relevance to the subject.'

'You might as well expel us from court straight away,' said Andreas Baader, 'since you're going to stop us saying anything.'

Ulrike Meinhof was allowed to go on. 'The actions of urban guerrillas are never, never directed against the people. They are always directed against the imperialist machine. The urban guerrilla fights the terrorism of the state.'

The presiding judge here silenced Ulrike Meinhof, whereupon the defendants rose to their feet, collected up their things and moved away from their seats. 'Please sit down; you have no right to leave the trial,' said the presiding judge.

Still standing, Baader answered, 'You won't even let us give our reasons for applying to have the trial dismissed, which means there's no point at all in our presence. In fact, you're robbing us of our last basic rights.'

'You're a washout!' shouted a member of the audience at the presiding judge.

Dr Prinzing turned Baader's microphone off, but he went on speaking without an amplifier. 'So maybe you're in charge of the microphones, but you're not in charge of this trial, not by a long way.'

On the instructions of the presiding judge, the defendants Baader, Ensslin and Meinhof were removed from the courtroom.

6
'A Fascist Arsehole'
(26th day, 19 August 1975)

Yet again the presiding judge wished to proceed to the hearing of personal data. But the defendants still had not been examined by a doctor in whom they had confidence. Their lawyers insisted that they could not be held responsible if the defendants were being doped just so that they would not fall off their chairs during the trial. The superficial opinion of expert witnesses such as Dr Henck, the prison doctor, was not enough to guarantee that the prisoners were fit to stand trial.

Rupert von Plottnitz, defending, told the court, 'We will not appear for the defence in this court any more until it is operating on a basis of definite findings instead of makeshift expedients.'

There was applause in court, and Marielouise Becker and Otto Schily rose to their feet, put their papers together, and stood in front of defence counsel's bench.

'The trial will continue even in your absence,' the presiding judge told the lawyers.

Unmoved, Rupert von Plottnitz too stood up, collected his files and ranged himself beside his colleagues.

'I protest against your remarks, as constituting an insult to our duty as defence counsel,' said Dr Heldmann, now defending Andreas Baader as the lawyer of his own choice. As he walked out of the courtroom together with the other lawyers of the defendants' choice, he turned to the presiding judge once more. 'We take our duties as defence counsel seriously in refusing to participate in the trying of defendants who may perhaps be unfit to stand trial. That is our duty as defence counsel.' The panel of judges, he added, could let him know as soon as they had a medical opinion.

The presiding judge was confused: 'Dr Heldmann is leaving the courtroom, the defendants are on their feet – what is the meaning of this?'

'You ought to expel us from the courtroom, that's what,' called the defendant Raspe.

'That's right, yes,' added Baader.

'You are to be seated!' cried the presiding judge.

'No, we're not going to take any further part in the trial. Have us expelled.'

'If you continue standing there like that, and are not prepared to . . .'

'Well, what do you want, then?' Andreas Baader interrupted him. 'You want us to go roaring about the place, or what? Do stop these silly . . .'

'You are to be seated and take part in this trial quietly.'

'We will not take part in the trial.'

'So you have said, Herr Baader. You are refusing to be seated.'

'Do you want us to make some sort of formal disturbance, or what?' asked Raspe.

'Expel us!' demanded Gudrun Ensslin and Ulrike Meinhof.

'I must inform you that you are now causing disruption of the trial. If you continue, you will have to be expelled.'

'So I should hope!' replied Baader. 'Go on, you old fool!'

'Do all of you feel the same way?' asked the presiding judge.

'Yes,' replied Gudrun Ensslin.

'Then you are refusing to remain here?'

The courtroom became restive. A row of people in the audience stood up.

'The public must either be seated or leave the courtroom. There will be no standing here. If those people do not sit down they will have to be removed from the court.'

After a short conversation with the other judges on the panel, the presiding judge announced that the defendants had disrupted proceedings and would now be expelled from the hearing. It continued without the defendants and their chosen lawyers.

'However, as we are now coming to the stage of examining personal data, we think the principle of a legal hearing is of such paramount importance that we will have the defendants brought in again, singly.' The presiding judge asked the prison officers to bring in the defendant Raspe first. 'By force if necessary; that can't be avoided.'

When cries of protest from spectators were heard in the courtroom, Dr Prinzing added, 'I would ask the members of the security forces here to keep a close eye on the public seating area, so that we can discover the identity of the disruptive element and measures can be taken accordingly.'

Sixteen minutes after his expulsion, Jan-Carl Raspe was dragged back into the courtroom by two prison officers. 'Please sit down,' said the presiding judge.

'I won't sit down.'

'Then I must draw the following points to your attention. We now intend to proceed to the examination of personal data.'

'That doesn't interest me.'

'At this point you have an opportunity to give your own account of yourself. The consequence of your failing to do so will be that we must proceed with the trial.'

'All I have to say is that I've been dragged in here.'

'Would you kindly use a microphone?'

'At the moment all I have to tell you is that I've been dragged in here by force. In the circumstances I'm not giving any account of myself.'

And Raspe thumped the dock several times. 'I'm going down again now, and naturally you'll be carrying on with this spectacle.'

'It is your duty, as a defendant, to remain here.'

'If you won't expel me from court anyway, I'll climb out over this balustrade somehow.'

Raspe tried to thrust his way out of the dock, but was prevented by the guards from leaving the courtroom. Thereupon the court decided to have Raspe removed again.

The presiding judge ordered the defendant Meinhof to be brought in. A few minutes later she was carried into the courtroom by four officers who were holding her hands and her feet.

'Please sit down, Frau Meinhof.'

'I've no intention of sitting down.'

'You have no intention of sitting down,' repeated the presiding judge. 'Would you at least make use of the microphone, so that we can hear what you have to say?'

'I don't want anything to do with this. I'm in no position to defend myself, and naturally I can't be defended either.'

'Will you give an account of your personal details?'

'In these circumstances I will not give any account of my personal details,' said Ulrike Meinhof, making her way out of the dock. She was restrained by the guards.

'I want to go,' she said.

'It is your duty, as a defendant, to remain here.'

'I'm not letting anyone force me, you arsehole!'

'Frau Meinhof, I observe that you have just addressed me as "arsehole", as "you arsehole".'

'Perhaps you'll take note of that . . .'

After private consultation with his colleagues, Dr Prinzing said, 'The defendant is expelled from court for the rest of today's hearing for calling the presiding judge "you arsehole".'

Andreas Baader was brought in. He refused to sit down. 'Get on with it and expel me, will you?'

'Herr Baader, this is not a question of your own wishes.'

'Then list all the disturbances, or do I have to call you names? I'm finding this very difficult. You want to force me to stay here?'

'It's not that I want to: I must.'

'What are you waiting for, do you want to provoke abuse or what?'

'I don't want to provoke anything. I would far rather you refrained from abuse.'

'I shall disrupt the trial. This manoeuvring of yours is a dirty trick.'

'There is no dirty trick involved. The rules of procedure oblige me to act as I do.'

'So what do you want? Are you set on having physical violence here, or what?'

'I want you to sit down and take part in the hearing in an orderly manner.'

'Hell, it's filthy manipulation, the way you're forcing me to spend five minutes insisting you expel me. I simply want to be out of here.'

'It is not a question of your personal wishes. Your duty as a defendant is to remain here.'

'Oh, all right, carry on with your ridiculous procedure. I shall create a disturbance as long as I'm in here.'

'So far you are creating no disturbance,' remarked the presiding judge.

'Well, let me tell you, Prinzing, you'd better expel me now or I'll find myself forced to abuse you.'

'Herr Baader,' said the presiding judge sternly.

'Are you set on hearing it, then? All right, you can hear it, you can have it all sorts of ways.'

'I do not wish to hear it.'

'Well, you can hear me tell you you're a fascist arsehole.'

While Gudrun Ensslin was led into the courtroom by prison officers and forced to stand in front of the dock, the presiding judge commented, 'Ah, a fascist arsehole.'

'Now will you expel me?' inquired Baader.

'And me too, you old swine,' added Gudrun Ensslin.

The presiding judge was about to say something, but Baader interrupted him. 'I'll say it again, Prinzing, loud and clear: you're an old fascist arsehole!'

The presiding judge ordered Baader's microphone to be switched off.

'We're not fit to stand trial, and owing to that we won't participate in this, you dirty bastard,' said Gudrun Ensslin.

'You have created a disturbance. I understood you to call me a dirty bastard; did I hear that correctly? Or was I mistaken? I would like to have that ascertained; is it right? And you, Herr Baader, have called me a fascist arsehole.'

Then the presiding judge asked Gudrun Ensslin if she would give an account of her personal details.

'Old swine,' was the answer.

The defendants were expelled again and taken back to prison. The presiding judge asked the court-appointed lawyers if there was anything they wanted to say about these incidents. There was not.

After personal details had been examined in this way, the representative of the Federal Prosecutor's Office was able to read out the indictment:

'I charge:

'Andreas Bernd Baader, unemployed; Gudrun Ensslin, student; Ulrike Marie Meinhof, journalist; Jan-Carl Stefan Raspe, sociologist, with having jointly committed nine separate offences:

'a) in that maliciously and by methods constituting danger to the public they did on two occasions murder in all four persons, and on other occasions attempted to murder at least fifty-four other persons;

'b) and in that, in this connection, they did employ explosive materials to cause explosions, thus endangering life and limb and causing danger to other objects of particular value . . . and in that, in this connection, they did form an association with the object of committing criminal offences . . .

'Even after their arrest, the defendants did not abandon their aims. While in prison, they attempted to reorganize the work of their group . . .'

The defendants were not in court to hear the charges.

7
Unfit to Stand Trial
(39th day, 23 September 1975)

The proceedings dragged on for over four months. The issue of the fitness of the defendants to stand trial came up again and again.

On the thirty-ninth day of the trial, the opinions of the three medical experts appointed by the court were submitted. They came to the unanimous conclusion that the defendants were suffering from weakness, a poor state of physical fitness, and disorders of speech and vision; they were between 14 and 23 kilograms below their proper weights, had low blood pressure and poor powers of concentration, and Ulrike Meinhof was suffering from actual inability to concentrate. Baader was also found to have an unusually low pulse rate.

The medical experts considered their fitness to stand trial was limited to a maximum of three hours a day, and suggested some relaxation of their conditions of imprisonment.

One of the doctors, Professor Rasch, thought that ten to fifteen prisoners should be brought together to form 'a group capable of interaction', and that this was the only way to reduce the damage done by solitary confinement.

The claims made again and again by the defendants and their lawyers had now been confirmed by expert witnesses.

* * *

'We on this panel must now get the legal consequences clear in our minds,' said Judge Prinzing. After three minutes, he adjourned the trial, telling those concerned it would continue in a week's time.

In Stammheim jail, one of the prison officers wrote his report for the prison files:

'26 September 1975. The cell of the above mentioned prisoner [Baader] has been in an indescribable condition for the last few days. The whole floor is covered with food and other objects. The officers on duty keep finding flies settling on foodstuff that is already half rotten. No notice is taken of any remonstrations by the officers guarding the prisoner.'

8
A New Law Comes into Force
(40th day, 30 September 1975)

Dr Prinzing, the presiding judge, announced, 'The trial will be continued in the absence of the defendants. The reason for this is that the defendants have . . .' But he could get no further. Several of the defending lawyers jumped up in a state of agitation and interrupted him.

'I would like to give the reasons justifying this decision,' shouted Dr Prinzing, through the noise. 'Please do not interrupt me. The defendants are . . .'

But again the presiding judge could not proceed.

'I asked permission to speak,' said Rupert von Plottnitz, defending.

'You will kindly be quiet. No one here has permission to speak. Herr von Plottnitz, you do not, you do not have permission to speak at this point.'

'We have a right to a hearing now,' said Dr Heldmann.

'You do not have a right to a hearing now, you have already had one, you have already had one.'

'I didn't even get a chance to say what I thought, you swine!' shouted Baader.

The presiding judge warned the defendants, threatening them with expulsion from the court.

'Go on, then, give me a warning, you old arsehole!' bellowed Baader.

The defendants Meinhof and Ensslin abused the presiding judge: 'You swine . . . you killer.'

Dr Prinzing tried to announce the expulsion of the defendants from court, but Gudrun Ensslin's voice rose above his. 'I see it's this judge's business to thin out the ranks.' The presiding judge told the prison officers to remove Gudrun Ensslin from the courtroom. The defendant Raspe interrupted, shouting, and was immediately given a warning by the presiding judge. 'Or you will fare the same.'

Ulrike Meinhof had jumped up too. 'We won't forget what you're doing here. And you won't succeed in holding this trial either, a trial with perjured witnesses, false versions of events constructed by the police, the whole disastrous bag of tricks. You have to face the fact that the reason we're not fit to stand trial is because we've been tortured for three and a half years. You can't get around that.'

The presiding judge had Ulrike Meinhof expelled from court too. As the prison officers led her away, Ulrike Meinhof yelled, 'You imperialist state swine!' at the judge.

Although the presiding judge told the clerk of the court to turn off Jan-Carl Raspe's microphone, he was unable to silence the defendant, and expelled him from court as well. Just before the defendants were led out, Gudrun Ensslin turned back once again. 'You won't be forgotten, Prinzing. You've made sure of that, made sure of what's coming to you.'

Ulrike Meinhof was suddenly quite calm again. 'You're well and truly through with your show trial now.'

When the dock was empty, Dr Prinzing began reading out the decision of the court. 'The defendants are unfit to stand trial according to Paragraph 231 of the Code of Criminal Procedure. The law makes provision to ensure that a defendant does not impede the course of the trial by intentionally induced unfitness to plead.'

Paragraph 231 of the Code of Criminal Procedure was tailor-made for the Stammheim trial. After the introduction of this new law, it was possible to continue the trial in the absence of the defendants if they themselves were responsible for their unfitness – at least in the opinion of the court. The idea was to ensure that the trial went ahead smoothly. For the Stammheim proceedings, Dr Prinzing made the following calculation: 'The evidence to be heard will turn out unusually extensive: the Federal Prosecutor's Office alone has named 997 witnesses and 80 experts whom they propose to call.' If the maximum of nine hours a week as suggested by the medical experts were observed, the trial would not come to an end within a reasonable length of time.

'Aren't you ashamed of yourself?' exclaimed Otto Schily, interrupting the presiding judge's exposition. But Dr Prinzing was not deterred. He quoted the statement of one of the prison officers who had heard Baader, when with the other three defendants, saying, 'We must be sick, we must seem broken.' He ended with the words, 'This panel does not consider the further presence of the defendants imperative, according to the present findings. They will be brought back into court as soon as they are fit to stand trial again.'

'Heil Prinzing,' cried Rupert von Plottnitz.

The presiding judge inquired, 'Is it down on record that Herr von Plottnitz has just remarked, "Heil Dr Prinzing"? I would like that down in the record of the trial.'

'This is incredible, incredible,' said Schily indignantly. 'You've certainly wrecked the idea of the constitutional state.' And turning to the federal prosecutor, he added, 'Congratulations, Herr Zeis, I really do congratulate you.'

Stammheim report of warder on duty, 30 September 1975:

'About 1.00 p.m. I opened Cell 711, to take Herr Raspe to see his lawyer.

'Baader immediately came towards me, saying, "You rotten swine, which of you told them outside we said we needed to look sick? We'll get that swine wherever he may live."'

Report, 1 October 1975:

'Baader, Raspe, Meinhof and Ensslin all together. Baader: "Miesterfeld [one of the prison officers], you're a swine, you got us into this."'

Report, 8 October 1975:

'The prisoners all together.

'Recorded from memory:

'1.30 to 2.00 p.m., Baader was abusing the lawyers, Plottnitz and Riedel, then they talked about the trial and conditions of imprisonment. Baader said, "Why doesn't that swine make changes to the conditions of imprisonment, then?" Otherwise the questions were written down or spoken so quietly they couldn't be heard.

'2.00 to 2.30 p.m., conversation conducted very quietly. The name Croissant mentioned quite often. Nothing concrete to be made out. Baader: "Miesterfeld, mind this, you swine, I don't want any informers . . ."

'3.00 to 3.30 p.m. When I relieved Officer Koutny, Baader told Meinhof and Ensslin, "That one there, he has a special job to do . . ."

'Question from Ensslin: "What's his name, then?" Baader: "He's certainly been put here by Bonn."

'Meinhof said something indistinct. Baader: "Those cops, that damn Miesterfeld, those overfed prison warder bastards." Meinhof, "Yes, they bear the prison trademark all right." Rest of the conversation barely audible. Mention frequently made of words like Cuba, CIA, oppressors, etc.'

9
Ulrike Meinhof on the Possibility and Impossibility of Defection
(41st day, 28 October 1975)

At the beginning of the forty-first day of the trial, the presiding judge told the court how he envisaged the further course of the proceedings, now that the defendants' unfitness to stand trial had been established. 'It is open to the defendants to participate in the trial as long as they feel they are in a state to do so.' The defending lawyers challenged the court on the grounds of bias again.

'In this connection we have to speak of a declaration of war against the prisoners by the judges, whom we challenge,' said von Plottnitz. 'However, in war there would always be the Geneva Convention, whose provisions would protect the prisoners from something that is to be considered legitimate in consequence of the judges' decision: the deliberate destruction of their health. The risk of the prisoners' health deteriorating if they continue to be kept in isolation, as mentioned in the medical report, does not bother the judges; after all, they long since shifted their own responsibility for the destruction of the prisoners' health on to the prisoners themselves.'

The presiding judge pointed out that the Federal High Court had rejected all complaints concerning the RAF members' conditions of imprisonment. The supreme court had also said that the extent to which they were largely kept in isolation – alone or in small groups – was admissible. The prisoners were dangerous, particularly in that every one of them freely admitted to supporting the aims of the Red Army Faction.

'This is opportunist justice,' said Ulrike Meinhof. 'It's absurd to claim we would disrupt prison life. How, when, where? How are we ever supposed to have disrupted prison life when we have never, and I mean never, spoken to any other prisoners in jail for three and a half years?'

Ulrike Meinhof then pointed out a dilemma that had occurred to many outside observers as well, though no one had expected a prisoner who was a hard-core member of the Baader–Meinhof group to bring it up.

'How can a prisoner kept in isolation show the authorities, always supposing he wanted to, that his conduct has changed? How? How can he do it in a situation from which every, absolutely every expression of life has already been cut out? The prisoner kept in isolation has only one possible way of showing that his conduct has changed, and that's betrayal. The prisoner kept in isolation has no other means of altering his conduct. That means that in a situation when you're in isolation, there are just two alternatives: either . . .'

The presiding judge interrupted her. 'Frau Meinhof, there is no further connection to be seen between this and the challenge to the court.'

Ulrike Meinhof went on. 'Either you silence a prisoner . . .'

The judge interrupted her again. She went on.

'. . . by which I mean he dies, or you get him to talk. And that means confession and betrayal. That's torture, that's nothing less than torture by isolation, defined by the need to extort confessions, to intimidate the prisoner so as to penalize and confuse him.'

Dr Prinzing stopped Ulrike Meinhof saying any more.

Obviously, the presiding judge had not noticed how far Ulrike Meinhof's remarks showed her to have moved away from the group. Doubt was equated with betrayal in the Red Army Faction. The mere idea of defecting was as bad as defection itself.

On 13 January 1976, the defendants in the trial read out long political statements in which they admitted to membership of an urban guerrilla group. They claimed 'political responsibility' for the bomb attacks with which they were charged, but would say nothing about the criminal aspect.

And only now did the actual trial begin.

At the end of January, Dierk Hoff the metal sculptor, from whose workshop the Red Army Faction's bomb came, testified against the accused.

In February, the letters claiming responsibility for the various attacks were read out. Then the court began hearing evidence relating to the attack on the US Army's Heidelberg barracks.

Early in March, witnesses gave evidence concerning the bomb attack on the Augsburg police headquarters, and then concerning the attack on the Bavarian Criminal Investigation Office in Munich.

During this phase of the trial, the defendants were very seldom in court.

10
'A Defence in Its Death Throes'
(85th day, 9 March 1976)

Defence counsel's bench was thinly populated. Most of the defending lawyers who had the prisoners' confidence had sent substitutes; only the 'compulsory defenders' had turned up almost in force.

Ulrike Meinhof asked to speak. While Andreas Baader left the courtroom, she moved to challenge the presiding judge: 'For the last two months the whole trial has, in practice, been directed and aimed against just one person, Andreas. The object of this was surely propaganda to prepare the way for his murder.'

The court withdrew Ulrike Meinhof's permission to speak.

Gudrun Ensslin associated herself with the motion. 'The reason is evident, right here in the empty seats before us.' Gudrun Ensslin indicated the sparsely occupied defending lawyers' bench. 'Prinzing's succeeded in smashing the defence. He did it by means of twelve exclusions, by disciplinary proceedings and by dismissing lawyers from the case. We know all about that. What we have here is a defence in its death throes.'

The presiding judge interrupted her. 'It is not now open to you to rake up old grievances which gain nothing in credibility by your repetition of them here at every opportunity.'

Gudrun Ensslin continued. 'We challenge you in your function as a judge in the service of the state. As such you've managed to bring the defence to its knees. What we have here now is a sick defence, an unprepared defence, a defence physically and mentally wrecked.'

Stammheim report, 6 April 1976:

'When lunch was distributed to the prisoner Baader in the multipurpose hall today, the prisoner took the plastic plate of rice, sauce and shashlik from me and immediately flung it at the cell wall beside me. My uniform shirt and trousers were quite badly stained by splashes from the food.'

On 20 April 1976, witnesses began giving evidence about the bomb attack on the Hamburg building of the Springer press, in which several print workers and office staff had been severely injured.

The defendants stayed away from the examination of the bomb victims.

11 '. . . Because You Want to Crack Up'

Almost four years had passed since the arrest of the defendants: four years of imprisonment, three of them spent in more or less strict isolation, then locked up together on the fourth floor of Stammheim jail.

The conflicts within the group intensified, particularly between Ulrike Meinhof and the others. Prison officers had sometimes seen Andreas Baader tear up things Ulrike Meinhof had written and hand them back to her, saying 'Shit.'

In March and April 1976, her conflict with Gudrun Ensslin escalated. Fragments of the two women's quarrel can be reconstructed from secret prison letters found later by Federal Criminal Investigation officers.

In one of these letters, Gudrun Ensslin described the manner in which the long-running disagreement between herself and Ulrike Meinhof was conducted. The issue was the files concerning the witness Karl-Heinz Ruhland, who had turned state evidence. Ulrike Meinhof was supposed to be getting them from Hans Christian Ströbele. This was in March 1976; Ruhland had just given *Der Spiegel* an interview.

Gudrun Ensslin saw Ulrike Meinhof's letter before it was sent, to check it over. 'Since Ulrike's stuff, visually, makes a poor –' here she corrected herself – 'a terrible impression, I type it out again before I send it off, leaving out a meaningless phrase she had at the end, because it didn't express our relationship with Ströbele any more. And I take out two or three of those feeble filler words like "just" whose function is to waste time and which are only a kind of luxury. They do have their uses: one merely needs to be able to master them, that is, they just have to convey precision.' The former student of German language and literature crossed out her own 'just' again; after all, she had that moment been criticizing Ulrike Meinhof's use of it.

Gudrun Ensslin sent the re-typed letter off without showing it to Ulrike Meinhof. She wrote to Baader: 'Afterwards I tell Ulrike I typed it and left something out. Why do I do that? The point of my telling [was] to torment Ulrike by paying her back in her own coin. An eye for an eye.'

In another letter to Baader, she wrote of Ulrike Meinhof, 'She's mistrustful, and more than that, suspicious. She doubts what I say because it not only might be a lie, in her opinion it is a lie.'

On relationships in the group, she wrote, 'The way it all works is like this: I can't cope with, I'm not up to, the burden of the mistakes, the crap I've allowed to go on over the years. And that's the point . . . because objectively, only an old swine could cope with them.' In the margin, Gudrun Ensslin scribbled, 'I've had enough.'

Those relationships, particularly between Ulrike Meinhof and Gudrun Ensslin, were obviously at their lowest ebb in the spring of 1976. While the group presented a united front to the outside world at the trial, the two women were bitterly at odds within the prison.

On 29 March, when Ulrike Meinhof's sister came to see her, Ulrike had complained (according to the records of the officers responsible for supervising the visit) that the other members of the group were giving her false information, or cutting her off from information completely.

In particular, criticism of her work as 'the voice of the RAF' and Gudrun Ensslin's arbitrary alterations to her letters and other writings, which she took as a form of censorship, added fuel to the fire.

'Fear is reactionary,' Ulrike Meinhof wrote at the head of one of her letters to the others.

'The one thing that for some time now has kept me from suggesting Jan checks my stuff instead of Gudrun is fear. I don't think she can stand it any better than I do. I can't or I won't go into that. It's nothing to do with me.

'But I can't stand it.'

To Gudrun Ensslin, she wrote, 'It won't do. Either you throttle me when I take a breath of air, when I get something into my lungs that will last for days and weeks, or it seems to me that *you* are choking. That's the set-up within which we're struggling as hard as ever, and I'm constantly on the brink of provoking it, as I do when I give way: only a fool is provocative. That's objective. So it's not a matter of a reproach, and it's not anyone's fault. But it all cries out for a solution.'

Gudrun Ensslin, to the others:

'This is the way I see it:

'1. there's the fact that I can't offer criticism too often,

'2. there's the fact that Ulrike won't take criticism from *me*, and whether she'll actually take it from anyone but Andreas – well, we'll see.'

Ulrike Meinhof answered her. 'I don't know why you do it, pouncing on mistakes of mine and keeping on about them. I can't stand it.'

To this Gudrun Ensslin replied, 'I'm not a witch. But I've come to be brutal at times.' As to Ulrike Meinhof's 'wallowing in the dirt', she wrote, 'The only thing you manage to convey with that rat-like trick is that you're doing it because you want to crack up.'

That, then, was Gudrun Ensslin's view of it: Ulrike Meinhof *wanted* to crack up. Perhaps 'cracking up' or self-destruction was indeed the only way Ulrike Meinhof could opt out of the fighting fraternity of the Red Army Faction. Doubts, 'wallowing in the dirt', could produce only 'lack of interest and coldness', as she put it, in Gudrun Ensslin, who let no doubts form in her own mind. To doubt was a personal failure, was betrayal. Or as she had already written to Ulrike Meinhof a year before: 'You open the door to the cops – you're the knife in the back of the RAF, because you never learn . . .'

Further argumentative writings on the seventh floor of Stammheim prison did not even pass directly between the two women themselves. In a letter to Baader, Gudrun Ensslin described a quarrel with Ulrike Meinhof in the courtroom building:

'Then I exploded, and I told her she had better stop attacking me and being elitist, and trying to stop me defending myself at the same time.

'So then she got up, seething, and went to the door, and I really bellowed with rage. I said wouldn't she realize she wanted to topple me – her method being the hammer blow and then to act innocence.'

Ulrike Meinhof wrote, 'There's nothing strange about my saying I can't stand it any longer. What I can't stand is being unable to defend myself. There are all sorts of things going on, I won't say anything about that, but I could hit the ceiling over her mean, sly ways.

'And it seems to me as if some kind of deal had been made long ago, but I'm not part of it any more.

'Gudrun knows I say nothing when she lies. And that's how it goes on, but I can't stand it.

'How am I ever to find myself if I'm forced at the same time to coexist with the horrible image of me she has in her head?'

When Gudrun Ensslin had read this letter, she wrote in the margin, 'Projection, paranoia, swine.'

12
The End of Solidarity
(106th day, 4 May 1976)

The defendants put in a joint appearance for the first time in a long while. At 2.09 p.m., Baader, Raspe, Ensslin and Meinhof came into the courtroom. Ulrike Meinhof had been officially excluded from the court for a month, from 10 March to 10 April, and thereafter she had stayed away from the trial of her own accord.

That day, 4 May 1976, the defending lawyers had brought with them a whole sheaf of applications to call witnesses, in order, as the defendants had previously phrased it, 'to put the trial on a political footing'.

Before Schily and his colleagues began reading out these applications, Gudrun Ensslin and Ulrike Meinhof left the courtroom together. It was

2.24 p.m. Half an hour later, Gudrun Ensslin came back. Ulrike Meinhof never set foot in the courtroom again.

She did not hear her defence counsel moving that the following people be called to give evidence:

Ex-President of the USA, Richard M. Nixon,

Former US Secretary of Defense, Melvin Laird,

and in addition the German politicians:

Willy Brandt,

Helmut Schmidt,

Ludwig Erhard,

Georg Kiesinger,

Walter Scheel . . .

The idea of applying for these people to be called to give evidence was to show that the US government, by military intervention in Vietnam and Cambodia, had committed violations of international law, that West German soil had been among the places from which they operated, and that accordingly it might be a relevant legal issue to consider whether, in its own turn, 'the use of force against certain military establishments of the USA on West German territory, such as bomb attacks on US bases in Frankfurt and Heidelberg, was justified'.

The lawyers were citing the full horror of the Indo-Chinese war in support of their applications.

When defence counsel had read them out, Jan-Carl Raspe asked to speak. 'We accept these applications,' he said, 'and they are partly our own idea. That is to say, in formal terms, we associate ourselves with them. We consider them correct. But of course we do not conceive of our policy in terms of international law . . . the only thing that can come of the absurd attempt to pass judgment on revolutionary politics is a system of lies and false witness . . .'

The presiding judge stopped Raspe speaking.

It was Andreas Baader's turn next. 'The applications are possible because they convey two connecting circumstances. First, they convey a notion, if such a thing is juridically possible, of the contradictions from which this policy [of the RAF] has developed . . . Naturally the applications will have no effect in the immediate future. In fact, as opposed to the concealed purpose behind these proceedings, a fascist military trial does at least have the dignity of the unambiguous nature of a measure which can admit to its methods.'

* * *

Gudrun Ensslin spoke after Baader:

'If there is one thing about the 1972 affair that depresses us, it is the lack of correlation between our head and our hands.

'We would have liked to be militarily more efficient. To put it simply once again: we are responsible for the attacks on the CIA headquarters and the headquarters of the Fifth US Army Corps in Frankfurt am Main, and on the US headquarters in Heidelberg.

'In so far as we were organized into the RAF from 1970 onwards, fought in it, and were involved in the process of the conception of its policies and structure, we are certainly also responsible to the same degree for operations undertaken by commandos – for instance, against the Springer building, of which we knew nothing, with the principle of which we do not agree, and which we disowned while it was in progress.'

Four years before, almost to the day, seventeen print workers and office staff had been injured in the RAF attack on the Axel Springer printing works in Hamburg. Ulrike Meinhof had written the letter claiming responsibility.

When Gudrun Ensslin now disassociated herself from this attack, no newspapers had been appearing in West Germany for a week. The printers were on strike for the first time in the history of the Federal Republic.

Ulrike Meinhof was the only one of the four Stammheim defendants not to make any statement on this central day of the trial. Nor did she listen to the prepared statements of her fellow fighters concerning the Red Army Faction's attacks. Ulrike Meinhof stayed in her cell.

If the police inquiries were correct in finding that Ulrike Meinhof was at least jointly responsible for the attack on the Springer building in Hamburg, then there can hardly be any doubt as to why she did not appear in the courtroom. She would have regarded Gudrun Ensslin's calculated disassociation of herself from the Springer incident as public notice that their solidarity was at an end.

Four days later, Ulrike Meinhof was dead.

13
The Death of Ulrike Meinhof

Saturday, 8 May 1976, the anniversary of the end of the Second World War. The printers were still on strike. The following Sunday was Mother's Day. All these circumstances were brought up later in the interpretation of what happened on the night of 8 May on the seventh floor of Stammheim jail.

At 7.34 on the Sunday morning, two prison officers unlocked Cell 719. Ulrike Meinhof was hanging from the grating over the left-hand window of her cell, her face turned to the door. Six minutes later the prison doctor, Dr Helmut Henck, was on the spot. He ascertained that 'the body was already completely cold', and saw 'numerous livor mortis marks' on the dead woman's arms. The corpse was not taken down from the window grating until 10.30. By then more than a dozen police officers had been in the cell, collecting clues and photographing every inch of it.

The officers conducting the inquiry reconstructed the way in which Ulrike Meinhof must have died:

She had torn one of the blue and white prison towels into strips, knotted them together, and twisted them into a rope. Then she pushed her bed away from the window, laid the mattress on the floor in front of the window, and put a stool on it. She tied the rope around her neck, climbed on the stool and put the other end of the rope through the close mesh over the window grating. Then she jumped.

There was no farewell note from Ulrike Meinhof. But she had written months before, in the margin of a paper on strategy, 'Suicide is the last act of rebellion.'

14
'Not the Place for Memorial Tributes'
(109th day, 11 May 1976)

Once again, on the first day of the trial after Ulrike Meinhof's death, there was a crowd of people outside the gates of the courtroom building, which were fortified with barbed wire. The agenda for this, the 109th day of the trial, hung in the show-case beside the entrance. The name of the defendant Ulrike Meinhof had been neatly crossed out.

'We will continue the proceedings against the defendants Baader, Ensslin and Raspe,' said the presiding judge. 'The proceedings against Frau Meinhof are at an end as a result of her death; her defence counsel's brief is thus terminated. I must thank you for your cooperation.'

The 'compulsory defenders' König and Linke rose and left the courtroom. Dr Prinzing turned to the spectators. 'I noticed just now that some of the spectators did not rise. I would like to call your particular attention to the fact that acts of provocation occurring here in this courtroom mean that you risk losing the opportunity to follow the rest of this hearing.'

The presiding judge then announced that the defending lawyer of Ulrike Meinhof's own choice, Michael Oberwinder, would now be permitted to appear for Baader. Directly afterwards, Dr Prinzing wanted to go on hearing the evidence of witnesses, as if nothing had happened.

Dr Heldmann spoke. 'I move for a ten-day adjournment of the trial. Ulrike Meinhof's death has brought about a completely new situation for defence counsel and this whole trial. The death of Ulrike Meinhof, which no one expected, has, one might say, ruptured the closest of family ties, namely those existing between the four prisoners. I have something else in mind as well: the cause of Ulrike Meinhof's death is not clear. The prisoners themselves, their defence counsel – and not only ourselves – have considerable doubts of the official version which claims Ulrike Meinhof committed suicide. No one had noticed so much as the hint of a sign of any such thing. And that again militates against the official suicide story. It is our strongest and most pressing concern – I am speaking of the defending lawyers still remaining here – to recognize the dangers that could perhaps arise from this incident, including threats to the lives of the other three prisoners.'

Jan-Carl Raspe appeared in court.

'I haven't much to say,' Raspe began. 'We think Ulrike was executed. We don't know how, but we know by whom. And we can work out the way it was calculated. I remember Herold saying, "Anti-RAF operations must always be carried out in a way that will cancel out the positions of their sympathizers." And Federal Prosecutor General Buback said, "The vitality of the security services lies in the people who are committed to them. People like Herold and myself will always find a way." It was an execution, conceived in cold blood, in the same way as Holger was executed.'

The presiding judge interrupted him. 'Herr Raspe, you know the court's attitude to these claims. The court will not in any circumstances accept such defamatory remarks.'

But Raspe was allowed to go on. 'If Ulrike had decided to die because she saw death as her last chance of asserting her revolutionary identity against the slow destruction of the will in the torment of isolation, then she would have told us, or at any rate she would have told Andreas. It was that kind of relationship.'

'This is not the place for memorial tributes,' Dr Prinzing told him sharply. 'All you may do here is make a petition.'

'I said before I didn't have much to say.'

'The question is what you aim to achieve with your remarks, Herr Raspe.'

'I'd have been through with them long ago if you'd let me finish speaking.'

'Ah, so you do not intend to make any petition . . .'

'Just a moment,' cried Raspe.

'. . . in which case I cannot allow you to continue speaking.'

'I associate myself with the motions proposed by defence counsel,' said the defendant.

The presiding judge was satisfied. 'That could have been said quite quickly and concisely. You may go on now.'

'It was the kind of relationship that develops between brother and sister, directed towards a political end. Arising out of the potential of these policies, the relationship was a function of them. That is to say, she was free within it, as free as one can only be in the fight for liberation. To claim now that there were stresses and an estrangement between

Ulrike and ourselves, using that crude, wicked slander to make the project of Ulrike's execution a possible weapon of psychological warfare, that's Buback's work, and that's Buback's stupidity.'

The presiding judge interrupted him. 'I have given you a final warning. Herr Raspe, you are not permitted to speak any more, on the grounds of persistent insulting language towards the federal prosecutor general.'

'Well, your sadism, the measures you take . . .' said Raspe, and he put his papers together and left the dock.

Gudrun Ensslin asked to speak. 'As you've just demonstrated, you're a judge under whose auspices two out of five prisoners have been killed . . .'

The presiding judge interrupted her. 'First and last warning.'

'. . . and if one of the remaining three now speaks out against the state machine that you sit here to represent, and as whose representative you sadistically act, you interrupt and refuse to allow him to speak . . .'

'You are not entitled to raise objections to a measure which affected Herr Raspe.'

But Gudrun Ensslin was allowed to continue speaking. She read out an account of Ulrike Meinhof's last day:

All four prisoners, according to Gudrun Ensslin, had been together for an hour in the morning and half an hour in the afternoon of that Saturday, 8 May. They had talked about the relationship between identity and consciousness, with reference to Gramsci and Lenin. The atmosphere had been good; they had laughed together. At the end of their afternoon meeting, Ulrike had changed her clothes again, and had not gone out to exercise on the prison roof; it had been too hot for her.

That evening, about 10.00 p.m., the two women had talked to each other again at the window. At one point late that night, Gudrun Ensslin had woken up because Ulrike was listening to music in her cell.

Next morning, shortly after her cell was unlocked, a prison officer had told her, 'Frau Meinhof is dead.' Then the prison doctor had come, and described the suicide as an irrational act. 'The group is too small,' he had said, 'there's bound to be tension in such a group.' The prisoners had rejected that idea. It was quite clear to them all that Ulrike had been a good deal better recently. To this, the doctor had said, 'These are people capable of the utmost self-discipline. It's unique; I've never seen anything like it before.'

The prisoners had then cut short the conversation and asked to see

Ulrike again. The prison administrators had refused. Shortly before 11.00 a.m., the tin bathtub containing the corpse had been hastily pushed out of the cells section.

Gudrun Ensslin rose and left the courtroom.

Otto Schily put his files together. 'The defence will not take part in the trial again until after the funeral of Ulrike Meinhof.' Then he left, accompanied by the other lawyers of the defendants' choice.

After the mid-day break, the presiding judge continued the trial with the examination of witnesses. Jan-Carl Raspe made another brief appearance in the courtroom.

'Herr Raspe?' asked the surprised Dr Prinzing.

'I just wanted to say that your manner and your function leave one no way of relating to you except waiting in a corner with a gun.'

'Do you want to make a petition?' inquired the presiding judge. 'No? Then we can continue with this case.'

Stammheim report, 13 May 1976:

'When medicaments were distributed at 10.00 p.m., Baader, having been given his sleeping tablet, refused to take it straight away. He amiably described me as an "old arsehole".'

15
'And Finally She Herself'

On 16 May, Ulrike Meinhof was buried in Berlin. Over 4,000 people followed her coffin to the Protestant cemetery of the Holy Trinity in the West Berlin Mariendorf district. Many of them had painted their faces white; some were masked. They carried banners reading, 'We bear mourning and rage that we will not forget,' and 'Ulrike Meinhof, we will avenge you.'

The theologian Helmut Gollwitzer raised the question of whether Ulrike Meinhof might have taken a different path if 'there had been more people ready to join her in fighting for a more humane society'. He went on:

'I see this woman whose life was hard, who made her life hard by allowing the misery of others to affect her so much, this woman with her hopes and endeavours and depressions, I see her now in the peace of the love of God. Amidst all the killing and violent death in our world, human life, and finally she herself, were to be found along the way she chose to take –'

After Ulrike Meinhof's death, additions were to be made to the Stammheim group. Prison Officer Horst Bubeck went up to the seventh floor several times on behalf of the judiciary to suggest which woman member of the RAF might be transferred here. In one case, Gudrun Ensslin said, 'If *she* comes there'll be a hunger strike.' Of another woman, it was said, 'If *she* comes you'll have three of us dead the day after tomorrow.'

In the end it was agreed to transfer Irmgard Möller to Stammheim. Soon afterwards Ingrid Schubert followed, and finally, on 3 June 1976, Brigitte Mohnhaupt was allowed to join the RAF founding members in the high-security wing. Bubeck and his colleagues breathed a sigh of relief. 'We were glad that at last we'd found people on whom the core of the RAF could agree. However, Frau Mohnhaupt was already serving a sentence for criminal offences and was due for release in early 1977. Day after day until then, she spent time with Baader and the other two on the seventh floor during their free association period – what a surprise when she subsequently became chief organizer of the Schleyer kidnapping, with the idea of putting pressure on the authorities to release the Stammheim prisoners.'

In effect, the judiciary had sent the successor of the RAF founders Baader and Ensslin straight to them for training in the high-security wing.

16
The Calf's Rope

For some people, Ulrike Meinhof's death was obviously not enough. A bowls club sent ten marks to the Stammheim court to buy ropes for the other prisoners. The judge had the money paid into court funds under 'miscellaneous'. The accompanying letter was given to the prisoners. Not all the letters that found their way into the cells of the high-security section of the prison were anonymous.

A year and a half later, when the Parliamentary Commission of Inquiry was looking into the circumstances surrounding the deaths of Baader, Ensslin and Raspe, the committee chairman Rudolf Schieler asked Horst Bubeck of the prison service what relations between the prisoners and their guards had been like.

On the whole, said Bubeck, it had not been a bad relationship, except that the prison officers always had to pay for it when 'something had happened' outside.

Schieler asked what he meant.

'Well, when some anonymous person sent a letter to the prisoners, with ropes or such things, telling them to go and hang themselves, and they got past the censor,' replied Bubeck.

'What did, the ropes or the letters?' asked Dr Schieler impatiently.

'The ropes and the letters,' said Bubeck.

The faces of the committee members showed incredulous amazement. 'The ropes got through too?' asked one of the politicians, into the silence.

'The ropes got through too,' Bubeck confirmed.

'The ropes?' inquired the committee chairman again.

'That's right, the ropes,' confirmed Bubeck.

The committee members looked at each other in horror. 'It can't be true!' one of them exclaimed.

'Oh yes, it's true,' said Prison Officer Bubeck. He hardly seemed to realize what it was about his story that struck the committee members as so sensational. 'And they took it all out on us . . . we got blamed for Meinhof's death. So yes, there were times they lit into the prison officers.'

'Incredible,' said one of the MPs.

The chairman, Dr Schieler, struggled for words.

'Herr Bubeck, what you are telling us . . . well, first of all, let me say we don't envy you the job you and your colleagues have to do. Nor is the job of a member of parliament always an easy one . . .'

Dr Schieler's colleagues laughed.

A CDU MP put in, 'But we still prefer it!'

When the laughter died down, the chairman went on. 'But what you are telling us now is a very considerable surprise; I mean your statement that such things as ropes, enclosed with a written suggestion that the recipients might use them to hang themselves, actually got past the censorship of the prisoners' mail.'

There was more laughter.

'They got past,' nodded Bubeck.

The chairman asked, 'Who's responsible for censoring mail in the prison, and for this business?'

'It wasn't the prison, it was the panel of judges.'

The committee members were increasingly baffled. It was possible, with some difficulty, to see the prison administration letting such things through, perhaps the doing of some minor official, but the idea of the presiding judge of the court allowing a rope to be delivered was beyond their powers of imagination.

'So it was the panel of judges,' said the chairman.

'Did they see the ropes too?' asked one of the members.

'Yes,' said Bubeck.

'They saw the ropes, and they let them go through?' repeated another member, incredulously.

'That's right.'

'What sort of ropes were they?' inquired the chairman.

The prison officer raised his arms and indicated a length of eighty centimetres or so. 'A hemp rope . . . like this . . .'

'Of the normal strength for hanging people, then,' said Dr Schieler.

'Not quite as strong,' Bubeck told him. 'More of an ordinary calf's halter, but . . .'

Dr Schieler finished the sentence for him. '. . . it would have done the job.'

'Yes, it would have done the job,' agreed the prison officer, 'though all the same, I ought to say that of course there were several such things in the prison anyway that hadn't been sent in.'

Several of the members simultaneously and in colloquial Swabian dialect gave their opinion of the whole examination. 'This is something else!'

'To whom were they addressed?' asked one of them.

Before Bubeck could answer, the chairman said, 'I must ask another stupid question: if a letter gets past the prison censorship, can't you then remove any objects accompanying such a letter that run counter to security in the prison, or is it forbidden to do so?'

A member of the committee cried, 'How about a weapon?'

Bubeck turned to him. 'If you were asking about a weapon, well, of course we wouldn't deliver a weapon, but with ropes we didn't have any . . .'

One deputy suggested, 'Perhaps they were sent pistols by post?'

There was laughter.

17
The Vietnam War and the Right to Resist
(121st day, 28 June 1976)

The defence had produced five witnesses, Americans who used to work in American military headquarters, but had since left the service. Initially, the court said it was prepared to hear these witnesses.

'May I ask you to specify the subject matter of the evidence?' said the presiding judge.

Michael Oberwinder, defending, told him, 'The particular point of the witness Winslow Peck's evidence will be a statement that the IG-Farben building in Frankfurt am Main was an important centre of US activities during the Indo–China War.'

Federal Prosecutor Dr Wunder challenged the admissibility of examining the witness. 'The defendants' real aim in bringing this proposed evidence is not to contribute to establishing the truth. Rather, they want to turn the case brought against them into a stage upon which they can perform as agitators.'

Dr Heldmann disagreed with the Federal Prosecutor: 'If the evidence we propose to bring shows that war crimes have been committed and the territory of the Federal Republic was used in that connection, then the Federal Republic itself is involved in acts of aggression in breach of international law. As a legal issue, that is of great significance to the outcome of this case: did the necessary preconditions exist for the use of emergency protective measures or the application of the internationally legal right to resist, on West German soil and against institutions of the aggressor against international law?'

The lawyer quoted the former public prosecutor general of Hesse, Fritz Bauer, who had written, 'The right to resist is not confined to a state's internal area. It crosses national frontiers. Not only is it everyone's right, it can also be used for everyone's good.'

Otto Schily gave an example: 'Imagine there had been a bomb attack on such an institution as the Reich Security Headquarters in the days of the Third Reich. Imagine a defendant had been tried, charged with being the perpetrator of this bomb attack. Would you refuse to let such a defendant bring evidence that went beyond the incident at the Security Headquarters and took in the Third Reich's murderous operations and policy of total extermination of Jewish citizens? Everyone who has ever studied law knows that in the area of the right to resist or the use of emergency protective measures, one may in some circumstances call upon such rights even if the ensuing action leads to the loss of a human life. It is a difficult and a grave issue.'

The court adjourned for three hours, and then Dr Prinzing announced, 'Examination of the witness on the subjects specified is not admissible.'

The witness Winslow Peck went home again.

The defence then tried to call a second witness, Barton Osborne. Oberwinder said that among other things, this witness would state that the computer in logistics headquarters at the Heidelberg base had been used to make calculations concerning operations in the surface bombing of civil areas in South Vietnam, and the bombing of the embankments of the Red River in North Vietnam. The aim had been to achieve the highest possible effectivity, in other words, the highest possible number of deaths among the civilian population.

Federal Prosecutor Dr Wunder challenged this witness too. The court, he said, should not have absurd or unintelligible evidence forced upon it. Nor did the West German legal system permit one to cite an alleged right to resist and to employ emergency measures as grounds for waging 'private wars at one's own discretion and under one's own management'.

* * *

Otto Schily spoke again. 'I think it is necessary to state clearly, once again, what is involved: the committing of genocide through the agency of military establishments based here on the soil of the Federal Republic of Germany. That is an issue you cannot duck . . .

'Perhaps, to give you a tangible idea of the matter at stake, I should remind you of those pictures of children burned with napalm which we saw in this country on television.

'The pictures are the same: the Jewish child in the ghetto going towards the SS men with his hands up, the Vietnamese children running, burned and screaming, towards the photographer after the surface bombing. And the evidence concerns this question: should such murderous operations be permitted or hushed up, or was there justification for taking action against the state machine and the mechanisms whereby those murderous operations were carried out? That is the issue.'

After another adjournment, the court announced that the evidence of the witness Osborne was not admissible either. 'The subjects of the evidence as specified are not of consequence from any legal viewpoint, or as the basis for grounds of justification. The Vietnam War is not the subject of this trial.'

18
Journeys to the Middle East

The prisoners in Stammheim had chosen the lawyer Siegfried Haag, who had gone underground shortly before the beginning of the trial, to reorganize the group. There was to be an end to spontaneous operations; the new generation of the RAF was to be active within an international context.

To create that context, Haag travelled to the Middle East with Elisabeth van Dyck of the Heidelberg branch of the Socialist Patients' Collective to refresh links with the PLO. But Yasser Arafat told them that he had changed his own policies now. The PLO no longer aimed to carry out 'military operations', as acts of terrorism were described, but to negotiate. Other groups were therefore dealing with the practical side of things. He suggested that Haag turn to Dr Georges Habash's Popular Front for the Liberation of Palestine (PFLP). There Haag was sent on to the 'outside operations' department of the PFLP under the leadership of Wadi Haddad, *nom de guerre* Abu Hani.

The German lawyer had to go on to Aden, where the PFLP had its training camp. Here he met the comrades who had been released in the blackmail operation after Lorenz's kidnapping, and was also able to take part in a short military training course.

In Germany, the comrades decided on a group trip to Aden for training, and to that end they met in Sprendlingen. They were to set off in pairs by different routes for South Yemen. As soon as they had assembled in a nature reserve frequented by walkers and joggers a police patrol car appeared. One of the group was wearing an anorak with its zip fastener pulled right up; he had hidden a pistol under it. The policemen got out and made straight for him. 'What have you got there?'

'What's the problem? We stopped here for lunch, that's all,' said one of the group.

The officers explained that they were looking for an exhibitionist said to be making a nuisance of himself in this area. Although they didn't give the impression of being about to expose themselves to small children, they'd like the man in the anorak please to show them what he had inside his jacket.

'I'm not doing any striptease act,' the man objected. But the police officers insisted on his coming to their patrol car with them. There they checked his personal details. There was nothing wrong with them, but the policemen insisted. 'Now let's see what you have under that jacket.'

At this the man unzipped his anorak, took out his pistol and said, 'Hands up.'

The police officers stood beside the car with their hands up, but one of them, turning swiftly, drew his own gun and fired. There was a frantic exchange of shots in which one of the policemen was hit in the head. A bullet hit Rolf Clemens Wagner in the buttocks. Peter Jürgen Boock shouldered the bleeding man and dragged him to a car park on the outskirts of the nature reserve. A woman was sitting at the wheel of her Renault R16 there. Boock held the pistol in front of her face. 'Get out of there!'

The woman screamed and clung to the steering wheel. A shot rang out and the windscreen shattered. Boock jumped into the passenger seat and tried to push the woman out of the car with his feet. When she finally let go of the wheel and fell to the ground, Boock shouted to the injured Wagner, 'Come on, get in!' Then he raced away. The owner of the car, still screaming, clung to the window and was dragged along until she couldn't hold on any more.

When a full-scale manhunt began, Boock and Wagner hid under fallen leaves and branches in a part of the woods. They were not found.

The conspirators all met again in one of the several apartments they used. Rolf Clemens Wagner was treated by a doctor, who tended him more or less voluntarily.

Boock was one of the last group to arrive in Aden some time later. There was a welcoming party waiting on the roof of the airport building. Siegfried Haag had had a toupee made and sported a piratical beard. Verena Becker was there, and Zaki Helou, Wadi Haddad's deputy. Peter Jürgen Boock thought later he remembered that Monika Haas from Frankfurt was in the group – the woman who was later suspected of having smuggled the weapons for the hijacking of the Lufthansa plane Landshut to Palma de Mallorca.

The few ordinary passengers passing through the airport, who all had to undergo a particularly meticulous checking procedure on arrival, were astonished to see these young Europeans welcomed like dignitaries on a state visit. However, the group had to surrender their passports on entering the country. When Boock complained about that to Siegfried Haag, Haag explained that it was because of an agreement between the Palestinians and the government. As long as the group was in the country the representatives of the PFLP would be in control of their movements in and out.

Only later did Boock discover who else knew exactly about the German group's movements: the representatives of the GDR Ministry of State Security, who were training the Yemeni secret service and had Aden airport under their control. You could even hear German spoken with a Saxon accent there.

On the next day the group went on to the camp. There was tea to welcome them, and then they talked until early in the morning. Siegfried Haag explained that he had waited for the others before beginning his military training. So far he had only been getting fit by long-distance running.

In blazing heat and over 90 per cent humidity, a large part of the group that was later to take part in the Schleyer kidnapping and other operations trained for guerrilla warfare; as well as Peter Jürgen Boock and Siegfried Haag, they were Rolf Heissler, Verena Becker, Sieglinde Hofmann, Stefan Wisniewski and Rolf Clemens Wagner. The legendary terrorist Carlos and his German aide Johannes Weinrich were there too – if not all at the same time.

Training began early in the morning with long-distance running, practice for close combat, and gymnastics. After lunch there was a break until one o'clock. Then came the study of weapons, guerrilla theory and the theory of house-to-house fighting. After the evening meal, when it was a little cooler, they practised marksmanship. In the evening they made plans for their return to Germany. At the very top of the list was the freeing of prisoners, especially those in Stammheim. The terms 'Big Money' and 'Big Get-Out' were coined. Siegfried Haag prepared papers in cipher; they were found on him later.

19
A Camera and Other Equipment

On 30 November 1976, Siegfried Haag was arrested near Butzbach.

Directly after his arrest, police officers searched the apartment of Elisabeth von Dyck, who sometimes worked in Croissant's office with Volker Speitel and others. The officers found photographs taken in the high-security wing of Stammheim jail. The fine-mesh window gratings could be seen in some of the pictures, which were taken with a Minox; others showed the prisoners themselves. They had photographed each other. Where there were photographs, the officers correctly deduced, there must be a camera too.

Next day officers of the Baden-Württemberg Criminal Investigation Office searched the cells of the prisoners Baader, Ensslin, Raspe, Schubert and Mohnhaupt on the seventh floor of the prison. They found two hotplates, made of toaster spirals, and 'three round pieces of olive-green vegetable substance', i.e. hashish. They found no Minox camera. Asked about the photographs, Ingrid Schubert said she had brought the camera with her when she was moved to Stammheim from another prison. 'I sent the camera and films out afterwards. The prison administrators know the opportunities for that sort of thing: private visits, visits from lawyers.'

On the next day of the trial, a week later, defence counsel were told to take off their shoes and open their trousers at the checkpoint going into court. The lawyers were indignant. 'I demand,' said Dr Heldmann, 'that the judges' panel at least keeps the extent of annoyance to the defending lawyers down to that level of unreasonableness which has unfortunately become usual here over the last year and a half.'

Otto Schily remarked that he supposed the next step would be to search a defending lawyer's rectum. The court briefly adjourned.

During the adjournment, Dr Heldmann wanted to go and see his client Baader. He came back, indignant, and told the court that Prison Officer Götz would not let him see Baader unless he was prepared to take off his shoes and open his trousers. 'I see there's been no change in the unjust practice of forcing lawyers to expose themselves!'

The judges and the prosecuting lawyers laughed. 'I don't really find it as funny as all that,' said Heldmann.

'Naturally, I can appear for the defence here only under certain conditions,' said Otto Schily. 'Some time there's always that well-known straw which breaks the camel's back.'

Dr Heldmann left, leaving a written message behind him. 'Perhaps the presiding judge will yet call to mind the level of civilization which our legal system once attained. Should he do so, I can be reached at my office.'

'I take note of what Dr Heldmann says,' said Dr Prinzing. 'Obviously these measures affect certain people's most treasured assets . . .'

'You can cut your jokes, sir,' Schily snapped.

Dr Prinzing quoted Ingrid Schubert's admission that she had smuggled photographs and a camera out of prison by getting her visitors to carry them.

As private visits to the prisoners were closely supervised, it was understandable that the prison administration must check the defending lawyers more strictly from now on. 'If a camera was smuggled out, other things can come in or out too. If they go out, they can also come in.'

The defending lawyer Arndt Müller, for instance, had visited his client Gudrun Ensslin two hundred and thirty-two times in all in prison. However, the Commission of Inquiry and the Public Prosecutor's Office came to the unanimous conclusion that it was impossible to smuggle anything in or out of the prison by such means. The searches were too thorough.

But there had been weak links in the chain, if only when entering the courtroom – even if the officers responsible denied it. However, Arndt Müller set foot in the courtroom building only forty-nine times altogether, when he met Gudrun Ensslin in the room set aside for conversations behind the courtroom itself. Only on these occasions would it theoretically have been at all possible to hand over hollowed-out files which could have contained either the Minox or other equipment.

At the arrest of Siegfried Haag on 30 November 1976, the police found papers with him setting out the RAF's operational plans for the immediate future. They mentioned a forthcoming commando raid with the cover name of 'Margarine', a 'Big Money' operation and another called 'Big Get-Out'. There was also a note saying, 'Check out H.M.'

The BKA investigators set about deciphering these references. And after the Minox photographs had been found on Elisabeth von Dyck, and the authorities were informed that items could get into the prison, the bugging devices on the seventh floor were switched on again.

The official version ran:

Between 6 December 1976 and 21 January 1977, conversations between defending lawyers and their clients in the high-security wing of Stammheim prison were recorded on twelve days in all.

20
A Judge and His Friends
(171st day, 10 January 1977)

Judge Prinzing was encountering serious difficulties at the Stammheim trial. Otto Schily, defending, had had some sensational information passed to him. According to what he had been told, the presiding judge had been making contacts of a very remarkable nature with Federal

Judge Albrecht Mayer, of the Federal Supreme Court's Third Criminal Division – the court responsible for dealing with complaints about the panel of judges at Stammheim, and which would also have to consider any appeals in the Baader–Meinhof case.

Dr Prinzing sometimes talked to Federal Judge Mayer on the telephone, and that was not all. He had sent photostats of papers concerning the trial to Mayer, not through entirely official channels.

Nor was that quite all either. Federal Judge Albrecht Mayer had passed the papers sent to him by Dr Prinzing on to the press.

As evidence, Schily could produce the copy of a letter from Federal Judge Mayer to the editor-in-chief of the daily paper *Die Welt*, Herbert Kremp.

Mayer and Kremp were members of the same fraternity.

'Dear fellow fraternity-member Kremp,' wrote the federal judge, and he reminded the *Welt* editor of a telephone conversation between them in the spring of 1973, in which he had made some suggestions to the paper concerning publication of material dealing with the Baader–Meinhof complex. 'I now turn to you again, on the same subject. Last week, the former gang member Gerhard Müller gave evidence in the Stammheim trial. I enclose:

1. extracts from photostats of the police interrogation of Müller,
2. an extract from the verbatim records of the trial taken on 13 July 1976.'

The judge made no bones about what he wanted Kremp to do with these documents. 'In the light of these new revelations, would not *Die Welt* like to take another look at the report in *Der Spiegel* of 4 September 1972? Not to do me any favour, but in order to make the stance and the practices of that journal clear once again . . . Perhaps the task might even tempt an editor-in-chief?'

Albrecht Mayer referred to the supposed smuggling of a secret letter out of jail by Otto Schily; the files sent to Kremp dealt mainly with this matter. On one of the verbatim records, Dr Prinzing had written in his own hand that Schily had always been absent from the trial when the subject of 'the secret Ensslin letter' came up.

The Federal judge gave his fellow fraternity member the telephone number at the Federal Supreme Court, to which he could ring through in case of any questions, and said that 'should the suggested article appear' he did not need a copy. 'I take *Die Welt*.'

Schily challenged the presiding judge, Dr Prinzing. His challenge was disallowed. However, one of the court-appointed lawyers, Künzel, moved to challenge the judge again. 'The reasons put forward in [Schily's] challenge should be aired, should be openly discussed. Otherwise this trial will bear a stain of which it can no longer be cleansed.'

This challenge too was rejected by the court. But Künzel's motion had hit the presiding judge where it hurt. He reacted with every indication of panic.

On the evening of 13 January 1977, Dr Prinzing telephoned Manfred Künzel, who had been a junior in his chambers years before. He told the surprised lawyer that he had the impression Künzel had been very reluctant to challenge. Then he remonstrated with the defending lawyer. To him, he said, that challenge had been the worst part of the trial in all its two years' duration. After all, it did make a difference from which side of defence counsel's bench a challenge came. Now the press would be in full cry after him again.

Künzel said he had been unable to understand Dr Prinzing's attitude to Schily's challenge. In answering the charge of having contact with judges in superior courts only by saying that he would make no statements about private conversations, he had helped to nourish the suspicion that such contact actually did exist.

'Put yourself in Frau Ensslin's position,' said Künzel, so often vilified as a 'compulsory defender' by the defendants. 'She must now be saying to herself that any future appeal is pointless, since there's been an interchange between the two courts with the aim of ensuring that no appeal against this court's judgment can succeed.'

Prinzing replied, 'Frau Ensslin doesn't care. This is all Schily's doing.'

'I don't see that, not when I visualize Frau Ensslin's position.'

'You're looking at this in the abstract,' said Dr Prinzing. 'I can tell you, from the concrete viewpoint, Frau Ensslin doesn't care.' The judge said he knew from the prison staff that the defendants were unmoved by the so-called files affair, and had shown hardly any interest in it. One of them had said, 'Just something the lawyers are up to again,' and that was all.

Dr Prinzing then complained of the stress to which the court and particularly himself were subjected by this affair. 'I'm almost at the end of my tether. And if I can't see it through, Herr Künzel . . .'

Dr Theodor Prinzing did not see it through. When Dr Heldmann, defending, made use of this nocturnal telephone call, of which Künzel had told him, as a reason to issue yet another challenge to the judge on the grounds of bias, even Prinzing's colleagues on the panel of judges could not save him. 'It does not depend,' they said, 'on whether Dr Prinzing is or feels himself to be biased. The deciding factor is whether, from the defendants' viewpoint, there may be reasonable distrust of the judge's impartiality. Such misgivings cannot be dismissed.'

And with this, the eighty-fifth challenge to the judge for bias was upheld. He was discharged from the case, and replaced by the associate judge, Dr Foth.

21
Filing

On 8 February 1977, Brigitte Mohnhaupt was released from prison. Volker Speitel and Elisabeth von Dyck fetched her from the jail. Soon afterwards she met Peter Jürgen Boock in an apartment on Baden-Powell-Weg in Amsterdam that was used by RAF members for laying plans.

It was one of the apartments also used in the Schleyer kidnapping later.

'First, I thought she was a fascinating woman,' Boock remembered later, 'and I have to admit we started an affair straight away. For quite a while neither of us could leave the other's side. And second, she'd been close to them for a considerable time, and I wanted to know all about it. I wanted to know what it was like in there, what they were doing, we spent days discussing the subject. She told me everything that went on there, who did what and how, sexuality was part of it too, who'd been sleeping together and what kinds of situations arose from that.'

The couple withdrew to the bedroom, lay in the double bed in each other's arms, and Brigitte began telling him about the Stammheim prisoners. Psychologically they were in poor condition, she said, most of all they feared for their lives; it wasn't imagination, it was a very real danger. It was true that none of the prisoners thought Ulrike Meinhof had been murdered, although it was always presented like that to the outside world. But they feared the worst for themselves. The prisoners simply didn't want another failed attempt to free them, said Brigitte Mohnhaupt as Peter Jürgen Boock remembered it. They wanted to stake everything on a single card now, and they'd thought of taking Federal Prosecutor General

Siegfried Buback hostage during hearings in the Stammheim courtroom fitted out for their trial. They'd need weapons for that. If another attempt to free them failed they'd take their own lives. They couldn't wait much longer, and while they still felt they were in good shape and strong enough, they would at least decide when they died for themselves. This wasn't a subject for discussion by the group as a whole, she said, the prisoners in Stammheim weren't having those on the outside tell them what to do. 'And you're not to tell the others about this,' he says Brigitte told him. 'Whatever happens. The story is, it was murder.' Peter Jürgen Boock was given the job of getting hold of three guns, explosives, and blasting caps, and smuggling them into the cells of the high-security wing.

Over the next few weeks Peter Jürgen Boock acquired the guns and explosives from various depots. The bullets were stuck between two strips of adhesive tape to keep them from clinking as they were being transported. The equipment was to be put inside hollowed-out file binders by the lawyers' assistants and then carried into the courthouse by the lawyers. The trial run with the Minox camera had already succeeded. Then the guns would follow, and all kinds of other things requested by the prisoners in 'the most secure prison in the world'.

In the course of 1976, the chambers of lawyer Dr Klaus Croissant in Stuttgart had been much in use for supporting the new group, called 'the Haag–Meyer gang' by the police and the prosecuting counsel. But the flow of information between inside and outside the jail had not worked as well as Baader and Ensslin imagined it would.

Now Brigitte Mohnhaupt's release from prison fitted the strategic concept very well. She was to 'clean up' the chambers.

Like the new boss of a business, Brigitte Mohnhaupt had indeed made a clean sweep. Now everyone was waiting for her orders, for she, with the blessing of the prisoners in Stammheim, was the accredited representative of the imprisoned RAF leaders.

Later it was considered that Volker Speitel had played a particularly important part in finding ways of smuggling items into the high-security wing of the prison.

After the death of the prisoners on the seventh floor, Speitel, who from 1976 had again been the person responsible in Croissant's office for the care of the prisoners, said that the lawyer Arndt Müller had taken various items into the 'multi-purpose hall' of the courtroom building.

In his evidence before the investigating judge of the Federal High Court on 4 January 1978 – two and a half months after the deaths in the high-security section of the prison – Volker Speitel stated:

'One day the prisoners persuaded Müller to smuggle out a sealed letter, which he was to give me. In this letter the prisoners told me what they thought about Müller: with his stolid calm, they reckoned he was the perfect person to take things in and out on a regular basis, and I was to see about fixing it. At the end of August and the beginning of September 1976, the prisoners discussed with me for the first time the problem of how certain other things could be brought in; they wanted a Minox or something similar. I did have a feeling that all this was more or less a trial run for something else, but they weren't saying anything about that, not at that point in time.'

The 'discussions' with the prisoners, said Speitel, were by means of secret letters.

Speitel claimed that the prisoners had known their lawyers were only cursorily searched as they entered the courtroom building. As the defending lawyers had to hand over their briefcases, only the files remained as a possible means of transport for illicit objects. File binders suitably prepared for this purpose could then have been exchanged in the courtroom or the cell acting as a waiting-room behind it. The defendants were not searched on their way back from the courtroom to the high-security wing, so they could have taken the file binders that had been converted into containers back to their cells with them.

The police officers at the entrance, Speitel said, never physically took and searched the file binders brought into the courtroom by the defending lawyers. The lawyers themselves simply leafed through these folders before the eyes of the policemen, who therefore failed to notice anything hidden inside them.

Once he knew about all this, Speitel claimed later, he had prepared the lawyer Arndt Müller's 'files' for the same purpose. He cut hollow spaces inside the files, hid objects inside them, and stuck the hollow spaces up again with bookbinding glue. In that way, according to Speitel, you could still leaf through the edges of the whole stack of papers without revealing the hollow space and anything hidden inside it.

'In all, three pistols went into the prison like that, and so far as I remember five sticks of explosive too. Then there was any amount of odds and ends like earphones, cables, radio sets, an electric iron, a hotplate. There was ammunition with all the guns, and they were fully loaded.' After his arrest Speitel said that light bulbs had also gone into the prison in the same way. The guns were a 38-calibre revolver with a nickel-plated barrel, a Heckler and Koch 9-millimetre pistol, and a Hungarian FEK 7.65 pistol. The side plates of both pistol grips had been removed. The side plates from the FEK were thrown away, those of the Heckler and Koch buried in an earth dump. They were to be delivered later.

22
An Unfounded Application by Otto Schily
(184th day, 15 March 1977)

Otto Schily, defending, rose to speak. 'I apply for the suspension of the trial and the questioning of Federal Interior Minister Maihofer, with a view to clearing up the question of whether conversations between the defendants in this trial on the one hand, and conversations between the defendants and their lawyers on the other, have been inadmissibly monitored in secret, recorded on tape, and handed over to State Security or other departments for assessment.'

The new presiding judge, Dr Foth, asked in a matter-of-fact tone, 'Are you perhaps prepared to name your points of reference, Herr Schily?'

Otto Schily mentioned the bugging of Interatom managing director, Dr Klaus Traube, a top man in the nuclear energy industry. Traube had come to the notice of the terrorist hunters in Counter-Intelligence because he used to mix with suspicious persons on the anarchist scene. The investigations of the secret service men led to nothing indicating that Traube was a real security risk. The affair showed how fast the Federal Republic was moving towards becoming a surveillance society. *Der Spiegel* had just exposed 'the bugging of Citizen Traube' and Schily quoted a statement made by the leader of the parliamentary Social Democrat party in the Bundestag: 'Herbert Wehner demanded that in future, monitoring measures such as were taken in the Traube case should not be taken in prisons either. Wehner's specific suggestion that such measures should not be taken in prisons must have a solid basis in information before Herr Wehner.'

The defence, he added, might put forward other points at the relevant time.

The federal prosecutor opposed Schily's motion. Senior Public Prosecutor Zeis said, 'I suppose we couldn't have expected Herr Schily not to try to make capital out of the Traube case. In his eagerness to propose motions in this courtroom which will affect public opinion, he is now going so far that he confuses a petition to receive evidence with a petition to inquire into evidence. The Federal Prosecutor's Office is of the opinion that even the elucidation of the matter, particularly in so unfounded an application, does not call for the witness he names to be examined.'

Dr Foth warned the federal prosecutor: 'I would ask you, too, to avoid stridency and derogatory expressions as far as you can.'

'Sir, I shall be very happy to do as you ask,' replied Zeis. 'However, I think that if it is being insinuated here that conversations between defendants on the one hand, and between defendants and their lawyers on the other, were monitored by means of some kind of listening device, then I think that the Federal Prosecutor's Office may also be allowed a word on the subject.'

23
'The Same Decisions Again in a Comparable Situation'

Two days after Otto Schily had made his 'unfounded application', the regional Baden-Württemberg Interior Minister Karl Schiess and Justice Minister Traugott Bender spoke to the press. They told journalists that there were two cases, within a fairly short period, of the monitoring of conversations between the defendants and their lawyers. In both cases, the Ministers referred to 'justifiable emergency' as specified in Paragraph 34 of the Criminal Code.

The reason for the monitoring, they said, had been 'strong suspicion' that certain incidents of hostage-taking, arson and murder had been planned by the 'hard core' of the group members in custody in Stammheim, and translated into action by way of their contacts with visitors.

In both cases, there had been grounds to fear that an incident involving hostages was imminent. The first time conversations were monitored was after the attack on the German Embassy in Stockholm in April 1975, and they had picked up clues on 29 April about a children's playground and a possible plan to take a hostage there.

The second time conversations were monitored was after Haag's arrest.

The Ministers did not mention the fact that the monitoring equipment had been installed as early as the first three days of March 1975 – more than six weeks *before* the attack on the German Embassy in Stockholm.

Nor did they say in how many cells the microphones had been fitted.

There were four cells available for conversations between the prisoners in Stammheim and their defence counsel. Five cells had been bugged in the first operation, which was the work of technicians from the Office for the Protection of the Constitution. In the second operation, performed by BND men, two more cells had microphones installed in them. Thus it is reasonable to suspect that conversations with lawyers were not the only ones monitored.

In their statement to the press, Ministers Bender and Schiess had written that they stood by their decisions and 'would make the same decisions again in a comparable situation'.

24
The Court-Appointed Lawyers Appear for the Defence
(185th day, 17 March 1977)

'The Federal Prosecutor's Office has had the gall to speak of a petition intended as propaganda,' said Otto Schily, defending. 'This is the terminology they like to use for sweeping facts under the carpet. And the defence hardly expected the gentlemen responsible to admit the truth in a hurry.

'What is happening at this trial can only be called the systematic destruction of all constitutional guarantees. So far as that goes, the trial has its significance for the state of this republic, in that it serves as an example. The defence cannot in any circumstances hold itself responsible for participating in this trial a moment longer, when it may perhaps seem to offer a kind of alibi by appearing.'

Schily proposed a motion to suspend the trial until the issue of the monitoring operations was completely cleared up.

The 'compulsory' defenders, or court-appointed lawyers, all associated themselves with the motion to suspend the trial. Manfred Künzel said, 'I join in moving for a suspension until this outrageous state of affairs has been explained.'

Senior Public Prosecutor Zeis spoke, less briskly than on the previous day of the trial. 'I would like to say, for the Federal Prosecutor's Office, that none of the prosecutors in this court had any knowledge of the events involved. Further explanation will be offered as soon as the Federal Prosecutor's Office knows the facts. Thank you.'

'Thank you very much,' said the presiding judge, and was about to proceed with the examination of a witness. Schily began to protest, but the presiding judge interrupted him. 'No, I am not allowing that now.'

The lawyer rose, collected his papers, and said, 'Very well, sir, then I leave this courtroom, under protest.'

'I can't stop you,' said Dr Foth, 'I think you should stay.'

Schily did not stay.

Künzel too spoke in favour of hearing no more evidence from the witness. 'It could turn out that no constitutional defence has really been possible since the moment when the first bug was installed.'

At this the presiding judge adjourned the trial.

Secret services that no one knew about and that had no official existence were also involved in the monitoring operations at the time, for instance the telecommunications branch of the Federal Border Police in Heimerzheim. This group, 500 men strong, was not given official recognition until 1994. In 1973 its monitoring specialists and the engineers' section of the Federal Ministry of the Interior were involved, for instance, in investigating the VHF radio that Baader had in Stammheim prison.

The engineers' section of the Interior Ministry was a particularly secret group of specialists and also worked for the BKA. As early as 1972 it was suggesting to its colleagues ways of making secret letters legible from up to 200 metres away by using parabolic mirrors.

This was a case of exemplary if strictly secret cooperation by the Federal German secret services. Even the Decoding Centre in Bonn (the Zentralstelle für das Chiffrierwesen, ZfCh for short), a subsidiary department of Federal German Intelligence, was involved, and helped to decipher the secret letters sent in code by the RAF members.

In the first monitoring phase in Stammheim in 1975, the monitors listening in had been next to the visitors' cells on the seventh floor and were running their tape recorders there. After that they moved openly to the courthouse where the trial was held, which had a room devoted to technology, with monitoring devices and tape recorders as well as telecommunications equipment. Experts from several services worked here, as an application of 1975 for an extension shows: people from the *Land* Criminal Investigation Office, the Protection of the Constitution Agency and the BKA, working in rooms 139 to 142.

25
Last Appearance of the Defendants
(187th day, 29 March 1977)

Dr Foth was able to produce a letter from the Baden-Württemberg Justice Minister Bender, giving more information.

'I can assure you first of all,' wrote the minister, 'that I fully understand the attitude of the judges and the defence.' On both occasions, however, monitoring measures had been employed 'as a method of crime prevention of a purely precautionary nature', and thus had no relevance to the Stammheim trial.

Andreas Baader had appeared in the courtroom, gone into the dock, and asked to speak.

'Do you want to make any statement about the matters we have been discussing, Herr Baader?' inquired the presiding judge.

'I don't know what you've been discussing,' said Baader.

'Well, just now we were discussing the monitoring that occurred in Stammheim prison. If there is anything you would like to say, you have the opportunity to do so now.'

'Right, then I would like . . .'

'I am all ears,' said Dr Foth.

'. . . I would like to make an application.'

'Go on.'

'I would like to apply – and it's for the first time too – I would like to apply for Brandt and Schmidt, as heads of government, to be called to give evidence.'

'Herr Brandt and Herr Schmidt,' repeated the presiding judge.

Baader then reeled off a long list of subjects on which he thought the two Social Democrat chancellors should be questioned. As heads of government, he thought they would confirm that the RAF had been persecuted 'since 1972, according to a conception of anti-subversive warfare contrary and hostile to the Basic Law'.

In addition, Baader applied to have the Baden-Württemberg Ministers Bender and Schiess called to give evidence in the bugging affair. Among other things, he said, they would be able to state that the report of an alleged plan made in Stuttgart to take a hostage from a children's playground was an intentional falsification.

Andreas Baader then left the courtroom. This was his last appearance in court.

Jan-Carl Raspe came in. He wanted to make an application too.

'Very well, go ahead,' said the presiding judge.

'We apply to have Maihofer called. To settle the question of whether the prisoners' cells were bugged too. And we further apply to have Schüler as head of the Chancellery and thus co-ordinator of the West German secret services called, and also Wessel as chief commissioner of intelligence, to prove that both were informed of the fact that the monitoring systems on the seventh floor were being maintained by the BND until very recently. And further that the BND had free and continuous access to the seventh floor.'

The former presiding judge, Dr Prinzing, so Raspe said, had also been informed of the monitoring of conversations in the cells. The judge had several times quoted, verbatim, remarks made by Baader and Gudrun Ensslin only in their own small circle. In addition, these quotations had sometimes been attributed to the wrong person.

'For instance,' said Raspe, 'the remark, which is faked anyway, that one of us said, "We must seem to be sick and look weak." And what Prinzing said to Künzel, about Andreas saying, "Here's another bit of fishy business!" when the application was rejected, that's clear proof of it too.'

Raspe went on. 'Of course it would be absurd to suppose the Federal Prosecutor's Office didn't know anything about the bugging, when it's clear to everyone that the whole big drama of the manhunt, our conditions of imprisonment, the liquidation of prisoners and the trial is in the hands of the Federal Prosecutor's Office. It was the Federal Prosecutor's Office that said, after the murder of Ulrike . . .'

Dr Foth interrupted him. 'The presumption of innocence applies to the Federal Prosecutor's Office too. If you are going to speak of matters like murder, you should perhaps get it clear in your mind that all citizens are entitled to be presumed innocent until . . .'

'Oh, well,' said Raspe, 'if we're speaking of the presumption of innocence in a department of that kind . . . Anyway I didn't make it personal.'

'You spoke of murder, and there is usually a murderer behind a murder, is there not? If that is what you really mean. Otherwise, it is a death.'

'We're sure it was murder. But anyway, it was the Federal Prosecutor's Office that claimed to have inside knowledge of the prisoners and publicly spread the rumour of differences of opinion and tension between us after Ulrike's death.'

Jan-Carl Raspe left the courtroom. This was his last appearance at the Stammheim trial too. When he had gone, Public Prosecutor Dr Wunder spoke. 'As to this monitoring business now under discussion, our conscience is as clear as it is humanly possible to be.' He turned to defence counsel and added, 'Please will you tell Herr Raspe that.'

The spectators in the courtroom burst out laughing.

Soon afterwards Gudrun Ensslin appeared. She seated herself in the dock and said, 'I want to give you a brief account of the demands we're making in the hunger strike we started today.'

'We are not discussing hunger strikes at the moment,' the presiding judge interrupted her.

'We began a hunger strike today.'

'You began what?'

'A hunger strike.'

'I can't let you talk about that. We are not discussing your conditions of imprisonment during this hearing, and that's that.'

'Very well, it's clear that this is not the place for any kind of political statement. They've become superfluous.'

Gudrun Ensslin rose, slipped out of the dock and left the courtroom. She was never to enter it again either.

26
The Murder of the Federal Prosecutor General

On 7 April 1977, at nearly 8.30 a.m., an offical blue Mercedes drew up outside Federal Prosecutor General Siegfried Buback's house in Fichtenweg, Karlsruhe, to fetch him. The driver, Wolfgang Göbel, aged 30, had changed the number plates before setting out. Siegfried Buback was one of the people at highest risk in West Germany.

On the way to the Federal High Court, the car stopped at a red light. Siegfried Buback was in the front passenger seat; Georg Wurster, aged 33, head of the motor transport pool of the Federal Prosecutor's Office, was in the back of the car. The driver, Göbel, had stationed the car in the lane which would take it straight ahead. It was 9.15 a.m.

Suddenly a heavy Suzuki motorcycle came up close to the Mercedes in the right-hand lane. Its driver and pillion passenger were wearing motorcycle suits and helmets that covered their faces. When Buback's car started to move, the motorcycle passenger fired an automatic weapon at the window and the door of the blue Mercedes. The bullets smashed through glass and metal. The official car of the Federal Prosecutor's Office rolled on and came to a stop by a bollard. The driver, Wolfgang Göbel, had been shot dead. Federal Prosecutor General Buback died on the grass verge by the roadside. Georg Wurster, badly wounded, was taken to hospital, where he too died.

The search for the killers began at once. It drew a blank. That afternoon, the government's 'Smaller Crisis Staff' met in Bonn. The Federal Prosecutor's Office took over the investigation, and gave orders for stricter conditions of imprisonment for the Stammheim prisoners.

Around this time Boock and Brigitte Mohnhaupt had gone to Baghdad, where they were to meet the 'Old Man', Wadi Haddad, the godfather of all European terrorists. It was almost a romantic trip. They woke up in the morning in a little house with the sun shining in. Boock opened the window and picked an orange from a tree growing right outside. He peeled it in bed. 'It was animal pleasure, improbable really, incredible and unreal.'

Then they met Wadi Haddad, or 'Abu Hani', as he was known, who had brought his whole troop with him, and the couple were welcomed like dignitaries on a state visit. There was a lavish meal, and then they came to the point. The liberation operation was almost within reach now. It was just a matter of finding countries prepared to take the prisoners. 'Not a great problem,' said Abu Hani. 'We can settle that quite quickly. North Korea is a possibility, Yemen, Iraq, perhaps Algeria, but only in an emergency.' Somalia was another possibility as a stopping-off place, but not for the long term. And in fact Iraq was problematic too, since after all the entire Palestinian structure was situated there. Better not endanger the Palestinians by making trouble for Iraq. So that really just left Yemen.

The couple went back to Amsterdam by way of Malta, Paris and Brussels. On the afternoon of their arrival they had a phone call from Germany. 'He's dead. It worked out.' The caller was referring to the assassination of Federal Prosecutor General Siegfried Buback.

Brigitte Mohnhaupt set about writing a letter claiming responsibility. She hunched over the typewriter, her hair falling over her face, and then, as she usually did in such situations, put a strand of hair in her mouth and went on typing. The couple argued over every sentence. Boock thought she ought to avoid using 'impossible' language. 'But Brigitte kept on treating me like a child, saying, "What you want is sheer populism. And the people who'll be reading this already have some political nous. Anyone really interested will understand what it's all about."'

A few days later a letter claiming responsiblity was put into the letter-box of the German Press Agency in Frankfurt. 'History will always find a way for such representatives of the system as Buback. On 7.4.77 the Ulrike Meinhof Commando executed Federal Prosecutor General Siegfried Buback . . .'

Otto Schily and other lawyers issued a statement condemning 'this senseless and brutal murder with the utmost horror and revulsion'. Such a 'perfidious act of murder', said the statement, was 'a grave crime against the constitutional state'.

The murdered Federal Prosecutor General Siegfried Buback was given a funeral with military honours, with more guards and security measures than almost any other such occasion before it in the history of the Federal Republic of Germany. The nightmare of terrorist violence was answered by the nightmare of an ever-present police force. The pictures showed, with painful clarity, how terrorism had changed the Republic in the last seven years.

The new generation of the RAF obviously had no scruples left, and hardly even pretended to believe in political legitimation. Yet a line led straight from the early 'Urban Guerrilla Concept' of the first generation of the RAF to the murders and kidnappings of the year of terror 1977.

27
The End of a Ghost Trial
(191st day, 21 April 1977)

The penultimate day of the trial. Neither the defendants nor any of the defending lawyers of their own choice appeared in the courtroom.

Dr Foth allowed the court-appointed lawyers to sum up.

Eberhard Schwarz's summing-up lasted forty-five minutes. He urged the suspension of the trial.

Andreas Baader's second 'compulsory defender' made his plea next. Dieter Schnabel spoke for thirty minutes, and asked the court to come to a just decision.

Peter Grigat, defending Jan-Carl Raspe, also spoke for thirty minutes, and applied for the suspension of the trial.

Raspe's second court-appointed lawyer, Stefan Schlägel, spoke for half an hour as well, applying for the suspension of the trial on the grounds of defects in the proceedings.

As Manfred Künzel had not appeared to defend Gudrun Ensslin, Dr

Augst was the only defence counsel to sum up on her behalf. He too applied for the suspension of the trial.

Then things moved very fast. In order to observe the provisions of the Code of Criminal Procedure, the presiding judge sent an officer to the defendants to ask if they wanted to make use of their final opportunity to speak during the main trial.

Before four witnesses, the prisoners stated that they had nothing to say.

'In the light of that statement, I will close the proceedings for today,' said Dr Foth. 'We will continue on Tuesday, 28 April 1977, when the verdict of the court will be delivered.'

28
The Verdict
(192nd day, 28 April 1977)

The presiding judge, Dr Foth, delivered the verdict:

'In the name of the people!

'The defendants Andreas Baader, Gudrun Ensslin and Jan-Carl Raspe are found guilty of jointly committing the following crimes:

a) three murders in conjunction with six attempted murders,

b) one further murder in conjunction with one attempted murder.'

In addition, the court found the three defendants guilty of twenty-seven other attempted murders, in conjunction with bomb attacks.

Baader and Raspe were each found guilty of two more attempted murders, and Gudrun Ensslin of one more attempted murder.

'The defendants are found guilty of having formed a criminal association.

'Each of the three defendants is sentenced to life imprisonment.'

29
The Safest Prison in the World

Two days after the verdict was delivered, Dr Nusser, the governor of Stammheim prison, visited the prisoner Baader in his cell. 'The Ministry of Justice has decided to bring a certain number of prisoners together,' said the governor. 'Those concerned are prisoners here in Baden-Württemberg, and prisoners that other regions are asking us to take.'

In fact, the idea was to create a sizeable group of RAF prisoners, something for which the prisoners were then on their fourth hunger strike. The hunger strike was immediately called off.

Considerable structural alterations began in May, so that more prisoners could be accommodated in the 'short section'. A self-contained high-security block was to be created, containing Cells 715 to 726.

The conversion of the seventh floor took about six weeks. It was done by the prison's own carpentry, painting, locksmith's, electrical and construction services. These all used the labour of prisoners from various different sections of the prison. From time to time during the conversion work, therefore, there would be five prisoners doing construction work in the high-security area, two doing carpentry, five employed on locksmith's work, and up to six painting.

The fact that other prisoners, usually kept strictly segregated from the RAF group, were suddenly going in and out of the terrorists' area was not known in the Stuttgart Ministry of Justice.

In the middle of June 1977, after the rest of the work had been done, the wooden partition which had hitherto divided the corridor between the men's and the women's cells was taken down. Bits of it lay about the corridor until everything that could be incorporated into something else had been re-used. 'It looked like something out of the Wild West,' said the prison electrician Halouska later.

During this time the prisoners' daily four hours of association with each other took place on this building site. Prisoners at work on the conversion, the men in charge of the prison workshops, the Baader–

Meinhof prisoners and their guards were often all there at the same time.

Conversations developed between the imprisoned RAF leaders and the prisoners employed on the conversion work. One of them, working for the prison paintshop, told his foreman when they knocked off that while he was at work, the Baader–Meinhof prisoners had asked him for 'paint, filler and palette knives' to do up their cells.

The RAF prisoners' cells were repainted too at this time. The prisoners Baader, Ensslin and Raspe, standing about in the corridor during their association period, talked to the other prisoners as they mixed the paint and showed them colour samples.

Building materials such as plaster, paint, wood and tools were left lying about the corridor. Once Jan-Carl Raspe appropriated a hammer and two screwdrivers. The locksmiths' foreman noticed, went to Raspe's cell and found the missing hammer there. Raspe did not return one of the screwdrivers until Deputy Governor Schreitmüller and Inspector Bubeck threatened to have his cell searched by Criminal Investigation officers. After some thought, he produced the second missing screwdriver that afternoon.

Almost all the building materials used on the seventh floor, such as sacks of plaster, were obtained outside and delivered by a builders' merchant. The sacks were neither searched at the prison gates nor checked before they went up to the seventh floor. Some of the prisoners working on the conversion were also employed in work outside the prison.

During the frenetically busy period of the conversion, the prison administration was fully conversant with conditions on the seventh floor; both the prison governor and his deputy checked personally, several times, on the progress of the work.

When Inspector Bubeck of the prison service was asked about this later by the Commission of Inquiry, he said, 'Naturally I saw the problems arising from the prisoners being able to make contact with other prisoners at work up there, and the problems that might arise later. There was a lot of discussion of how to get around all this, but nothing came of it.'

The Justice Ministry had also been informed of the problems, according to Bubeck. Later, however, Under-Secretary Dr Kurt Rebmann, now Federal Prosecutor General, the person responsible at the time, told the Commission of Inquiry that he had known nothing about it.

'I've only just learnt myself that they were using prisoners. I wouldn't have thought it possible. But they did. Well, all the same, there couldn't be any contact because they were in their cells. So let's put it like this: I don't suppose that what we have is the terrorists sitting about together, and along come the prison officers, along come other prisoners and set about hacking plaster off the walls.'

'But that's just what did happen!' several members of the Commission cried.

'At least, you didn't suppose it was possible,' suggested the chairman of the Commission.

'It certainly transcended the powers of my own imagination.'

The members of the Commission of Inquiry laughed.

At the end of June 1977, the Stammheim terrorist block had thus been made so secure that there was nothing to stand in the way of its occupation by a sizeable group of prisoners.

Ingrid Schubert had already been transferred to the high-security wing of Stammheim on 3 June the previous year. Brigitte Mohnhaupt had been transferred at the same time, but she was released from jail on 27 January 1977. Irmgard Möller had arrived on 1 January 1977. When the section was extended, three prisoners from Hamburg came to join the Stammheim group. So now there were eight prisoners on the seventh floor.

As it turned out later, but not until after the deaths of Baader, Ensslin and Raspe, the prisoners had stashed away tools, builder's materials and probably paint. It must have been at this time that they made the hiding places in their cells where they later concealed pistols, ammunition and explosives.

30
Three Respectable Young People

A few weeks after sentence was pronounced in the Stammheim trial, Susanne Albrecht, daughter of a Hamburg lawyer, visited the family of the banker Jürgen Ponto, who lived in Oberursel in the Taunus. Ponto, the head of the Dresdner Bank, was godfather to one of her sisters; she herself did not know him very well, but she had stayed overnight with the family a few years before.

On 1 July Susanne came visiting again, this time unannounced. She talked to Ponto's daughter Corinna for some time, and asked some casual questions about alarm systems, the staff of the house, and the number of dogs kept. Less than a month later she called the Pontos and asked if she could speak to 'Uncle Jürgen'. Ponto was out, and his wife asked Susanne to call back about eight-thirty in the evening. When she called at ten-thirty, and asked if she could drop in, although it was so late, Frau Ponto said, 'Susanne, my dear, you did say you'd call at eight-thirty. We're going to bed now.' She asked Susanne to come and have a cup of tea at four-thirty the following afternoon.

Late in the afternoon of 30 July 1977, Jürgen Ponto and his wife were sitting on the terrace of their house when the bell rang. Susanne Albrecht was at the garden gate with two well-dressed companions, a man and a woman. Ponto's chauffeur asked who was there over the intercom.

'It's Susanne.'

Ponto was talking on the telephone, but he handed the receiver to his wife and told the chauffeur, 'Ask Susanne to come and sit down in the hall.'

The chauffeur pressed the buzzer, and then turned to Frau Ponto. 'There are two more young people with her.'

'What do they look like?' asked Frau Ponto.

'Very respectable.'

Susanne Albrecht was wearing a brown skirt, a flowered blouse, and a light brown jacket to pay this visit, and her companions were well dressed too. The young man was wearing a needlecord suit, a white shirt and a tie, and his hair was cut short. The woman wore yellowish beige culottes, a matching jacket and a headscarf. They were the RAF members Brigitte Mohnhaupt and Christian Klar. All three had pistols with them.

Ponto went into his study and shook hands with them. 'Well, you're quite a committee,' the banker greeted his guests, suspecting nothing as he led them over the terrace and into the house. He accepted with pleasure the bunch of wild roses that Susanne Albrecht had brought and looked around for a vase. Then everything happened very quickly.

'You come with us – this is a kidnapping,' shouted Klar, aiming his pistol at the banker. Ponto, raising his arms, took a step towards Brigitte Mohnhaupt. 'Are you out of your mind?' he asked, bewildered. Klar fired once at point-blank range at the master of the house. Brigitte Mohnhaupt fired five times.

Two of the shots hit the banker in the body, three bullets shattered his skull. Ponto collapsed on the living-room floor before his wife's eyes.

Susanne Albrecht, who had fired no shots and later claimed that she had even taken the ammunition out of her gun before going there, ran out with her companions to the waiting getaway car, driven by Peter Jürgen Boock.

Jürgen Ponto died at 6.30 p.m. in the Neuro-Surgical Hospital of Frankfurt am Main.

Two weeks later, express letters were sent to several newspapers. 'In a situation where the Federal Prosecutor's Office and the security services are preparing to murder their prisoners, we don't have much time for long statements. As for Ponto and the bullets that hit him in Oberursel, we will say that we didn't realize clearly enough how powerless such characters, who set off wars in the Third World and wipe out whole nations, are in the face of violence when it confronts them in their own homes.'

The statement was signed, 'Susanne Albrecht, of an RAF commando'.

After making some more preparations in Cologne for the next and greatest operation, the one they hoped would finally set the Stammheim prisoners free, Peter Jürgen Boock and Brigitte Mohnhaupt went to Baghdad again. They wanted to discuss the necessary details for the 'Big Get-Out' with Abu Hani. One point to be cleared up was how much money they should ask for in addition to the prisoners – and how much of it the PFLP would get. Flight routes had to be discussed, and the passwords to be given to the prisoners. They were to be spoken at the time of their liberation as a signal meaning: all in order here on board, no armed men with us, you can let the hostages go.

After discussing all the details of the operation, which was to be carried out in four to six weeks' time, Boock and Mohnhaupt went to Paris, where there was already an apartment to act as a communications centre.

31
The Rocket Launcher

That summer of 1977, the second generation of the Red Army Faction, successors of the leaders and founder members now imprisoned at Stammheim, consisted in essence of Brigitte Mohnhaupt, Sieglinde Hofmann, Elisabeth von Dyck, Christian Klar, Willy Peter Stoll, Peter Jürgen Boock, Susanne Albrecht, Adelheid Schulz, Rolf Clemens Wagner and Stefan Wisniewski.

In the weeks after the failed attempt to kidnap Jürgen Ponto which had ended in murder, the group worked out a new plan: they were going to attack the Federal Prosecutor's Office itself. Peter Jürgen Boock built a multiple rocket launcher similar to the type nicknamed a 'Stalin organ' in a Hanover apartment converted into a workshop. The device consisted of 42 galvanized steel tubes about 60 centimetres long, which were screwed to stretchers mounted on top of each other, sandwich fashion. Home-made rocket-like missiles with four-section fin assemblies 15 centimetres in length were fitted into the tubes, and filled with explosive and contact fuses. Carpet was stuck around the entire rocket launcher, which weighed about 150 kilos.

Basically speaking, it had been made from parts available in any ironmongery shop. Boock had given various group members who were passing through the job of buying separate pieces. 'You couldn't very well go into a place selling sanitary wares and ask for forty-five tap extensions measuring fifty or eighty centimetres each. That would be enough for a whole high-rise building. We had almost all the ironmongery stores in Hanover sold out in no time.'

It had taken Boock almost three months to build the rocket launcher, from the first idea to its execution. Then the weapon was tested in a gravel pit near Göttingen. The first rocket flew up and far above the edge of the pit. Boock had greatly underestimated both its flight path and the height of its trajectory. There was such force behind the rocket that it brought down an entire tree.

On 25 August, a married couple giving their name as Ellwanger made an appointment to visit the painter Theodor Sand and his wife, who lived at

Number 9 Blumenstrasse, Karlsruhe. They said they wanted to buy one of the artist's pictures for their new bungalow in Bergzabern.

At ten on the dot next morning, the Ellwangers turned up at the artist's home, which happened to be exactly opposite the Federal Prosecutor's Office building. Seventy-four-year-old Frau Sand opened the door and let in the dark-haired young man and his 'wife', who was wearing a blue suit jacket and skirt. They looked at the sixty-eight-year-old artist's pictures, and talked knowledgeably and animatedly about art.

Towards mid-day 'Herr Ellwanger' asked if he could use the lavatory. When Theodor Sand turned to show his guest where the door was, the visitors suddenly attacked the two old people. Theodor Sand thought he had a couple of mental patients to deal with. He resisted, shouting, and fell to the floor with his attackers.

'Frau Ellwanger' and her alleged husband drew pistols and pointed them at the artist and his wife. 'This is a Red Army Faction operation. It's not meant for you, it's against the lawyers in the Federal Prosecution building.'

'There are shorthand typists and other staff working in there as well,' Frau Sand pointed out.

'Yes, you're right, but they're on the lower floors.'

The 'Ellwangers' made the two old people sit in two armchairs in the sitting room. They tied their arms and legs with string and sticky tape, put the chairs back to back and tied them to each other.

Shortly afterwards, a Renault R4 bearing the legend 'A. Krieg – Instant Customer Service' on its side drew up outside the building opposite the Federal Prosecutor's Office. A group of young people carried metal objects into the Sands' apartment in bags and a cardboard carton labelled '12 x 30 Pampers, Normal'.

The maker of the rocket launcher, Peter Jürgen Boock, began to put it together, while the others, pistols at the ready, waited and tried to explain themselves to the old people. This was a 'lofty task', they said; they were doing it 'as a sign to the comrades imprisoned in Stammheim'. They would rather have been dealing with a younger couple, but it so happened the Sands' apartment was ideal for their purposes. One of the women guarding them took five hundred-mark notes out of her bag and wanted to give them to the old couple, saying there might be some damage to the apartment. The Sands refused the money, and would not drink from the brandy bottle offered to them either.

* * *

It took Peter Jürgen Boock several hours to put his rocket launcher together. Even as he was constructing it beforehand, he said at his trial later, he had had misgivings. At first he had not known what it was to be turned against. They had told him someone else would get the device into position, but he hadn't agreed to that. He had wanted, he said, to keep the murderous thing under his own control so that he could sabotage it when it was used. It was only with difficulty that he had managed to come along on the commando operation; in spite of his recognized technical capabilities he was regarded as an uncertain factor because of his considerable consumption of drugs.

As he was erecting the rocket launcher in the Sands' apartment, his misgivings grew and grew – or so he said later. Behind the windows of the Federal Prosecutor's Office he could see secretaries, legal officials, people young and old who might be employees or might be visitors. He thought of the results of firing the thing, and felt something like a lump of ice growing inside him. Boock could no longer see any connection between his earlier motives for joining the RAF, i.e. to free the prisoners from the situation they were in, and what he was about to do now. People would be killed. The operation could make him a multiple murderer. As he aligned the tubes with the windows opposite, he decided to sabotage the ignition. He dragged the construction of the device out as long as possible. When it was nearly ready, he did not wind up the clock to set off the ignition, so that the launcher would not fire.

And certainly the rocket launcher failed to work. When sentence was passed on Peter Jürgen Boock later, his evidence was dismissed as simple self-preservation. The judges decided that the fact the clock really had not been wound up was pure accident.

The Stammheim prisoners were increasingly dissatisfied with the activities of the group outside. They criticized the Ponto operation as sheer amateurism, and they were pressing harder and harder, in terms that sounded like an ultimatum, for a successful operation to free them. 'If you can't manage to get us out we shall take our fate into our own hands,' the secret letters smuggled out kept saying. 'The others,' according to Boock, 'must have thought that by that they meant something other than Brigitte and I did. We knew exactly what they were saying. We'll take our fate into our own hands meant, we'll put an end to it, we'll do the hostage-taking, we'll kill ourselves, we'll mount a suicide operation.'

Boock and Brigitte Mohnhaupt knew that there were guns and

explosives hidden in the cells; after all, they themselves had acquired them and got them smuggled into Stammheim. Brigitte had also told Boock where the prisoners had prepared hiding places. For instance, the wash-basins in the cells were hollow inside. You just had to remove the basin itself and enlarge one of the ventilation holes to have a hollow space ready for use at any time. Then the floorboards were taken up. There was unplastered grey concrete underneath. You could scratch holes in it, mix the powdered scrapings with toothpaste and use the mixture as mortar.

Meanwhile Jan-Carl Raspe had perfected a communications system. He had soldered loudspeakers to microphones and converted the prison's own cable connections between the permanently installed loudspeakers of its intercom radio for his own purposes. The amplifiers of the prisoners' record players provided enough energy for very good communication from cell to cell.

More and more pressure was put on the group outside. A few weeks before 'Big Get-Out' was due to start, the prisoners sent a secret letter saying they wondered whether the group could still call itself part of the RAF. They would deny them that title if something didn't happen soon. In a dilemma, caught between rejection by the founders of the RAF and actual responsibility for their suicide, the group decided on swift action.

32
'We're Dealing with a Large-Scale Problem'

On 1 September 1977, Chief Commissioner Herold of the Federal Criminal Investigation Office told the Interior Committee of the German parliament, the Bundestag, about the results of inquiries into the murder of Ponto and the failed attempt on the Federal Prosecutor's Office in Karlsruhe.

Even at the time of the arrest of the lawyer Siegfried Haag on 30 November of the previous year, said Herold, there had been indications that new attacks were being planned: 'For the first time there were signs that a capital crime of considerable extent was imminent. This impression was reinforced by the detailed papers found when we picked up Haag, which seemed to be plans for a murder. We assumed that this would be the "execution" we had long feared. But at the same time there was a reference to another, subsequent operation code-named Big Money. That could have meant anything from a bank raid to a kidnapping. However, one of the papers gave us another clue suggesting that we couldn't rule out a kidnapping. It ran: "Check out H.M., discuss Big Money, where to 'bunker' the character?"

'If one examines all the factors and asks, who is H.M. or M.H., who has such initials – we made a thorough search of *Who's Who?* – and if one then asks, which of these people could have something to do with "big money", one comes up with a certain person whose name I will not give here and now.'

A week before, the new Federal Prosecutor General, Kurt Rebmann, had himself given the name belonging to the initials H.M. at a meeting of the Law Committee: Hanns Martin Schleyer, President of the Employers' Association.

One of the members of the Committee asked Herold in what connection the name of Susanne Albrecht had first come up. 'Is it true that Frau Albrecht was reported by the security services to have gone underground in June 1977? Was the link between Frau Albrecht and the Ponto family known in the appropriate quarters? Did anyone draw the possible conclusion from this relationship that the Ponto family ought to be told about Susanne Albrecht's way of life?'

Dr Herold replied, 'It isn't a case of Susanne Albrecht being one of just a few suspects or dangerous people in this country; we are dealing with a problem on a large scale. I've already said here that the number of highly dangerous people investigated on a more or less permanent basis by our computer inquiries is about 1,200. Susanne Albrecht was one of those 1,200.' And beyond this circle, which could at any time become active and dangerous and had indeed done so during the last few years, said the BKA chief, there was another, wider circle of some 6,000 sympathizers.

'We are not, thus, dealing with a problem of individual figures; unfortunately we're dealing with a large-scale problem. No one in the Federal Republic can keep watch on 1,200 highly dangerous persons, and no one can counter all possible danger by taking precautionary measures.

Everyone knows that about twenty officers are needed to keep complete round-the-clock watch on one person. Multiply 1,200 by 20 – the whole German criminal police simply does not have those forces. That shows the particular and pre-eminent importance of permanent, routine surveillance, operating like a dragnet, of that circle of people, in the form of surveillance by computer.'

Then the BKA chief went on to mention the extent of international terrorist links. 'It is clear enough that these revolutionary groups calling themselves the Red Army Faction are part of a worldwide Red Army, part of an international force promoting civil wars.' There were certain indications, he said, that the Red Army Faction 'is already prepared to begin the skirmishing phase, that is, a phase of concerted attacks on the nerve centres of this state, in order to split the defence of the state, disorientate it, keep it tied up to no effect, and then go on from there in the overall concept of demoralization, of the encouragement of like-minded people, of hope for imminent changes.

'They have a logistical basis for this prepared to an extent that should not be underestimated.'

In fact the core group was much smaller than the BKA and the general public assumed. It consisted of Brigitte Mohnhaupt as the person trusted by the Stammheim prisoners, Peter Jürgen Boock, Stefan Wisniewski, Sieglinde Hofmann, Rolf Heissler, Rolf Clemens Wagner and Christian Klar. These people could give direct orders 'on the spot' to other members of the group such as Friederike Krabbe, Sigrid Sternebeck, and others. Boock said: 'Whichever of them happened to be present anywhere automatically held command.'

Under pressure from the prisoners in Stammheim, they forged ahead with plans for an abduction somewhere in the Cologne area. The hostage they wanted, as the security services had also correctly suspected, was Hanns Martin Schleyer, head of the Federation of German Industries and the Confederation of German Employers' Associations, and a member of the board of Daimler-Benz.

The drama began to take its course.

It was a matter of principle, both for a small group which, in its hubris, thought it could declare war on the state, and for the state itself. The victim was a figure symbolizing the economy, capitalism, the system. A man positively destined for the role.

33
'Wannsee Conference'

All was ready for the great blow to be struck. The core group met for the last discussion of the operation at an apartment in Junkersdorf. It had been rented because the apartment block had an underground garage in which the kidnap victim was to be transferred to another vehicle; after all, he couldn't be driven straight from the scene of the crime to his hiding-place. The apartment was empty except for a bedside light and a radio.

The commando party sat on the floor in a circle, with an old bucket lid in the middle of the circle acting as an ashtray. The dim lamp lit only the floor; faces were left in darkness, and finally blurred in a fog of cigarette smoke. Words echoed in the empty apartment, and so they all lowered their voices. At first they discussed the last secret letter from Stammheim. The ultimatum issued by the RAF founders for something to be done at last, or they would do something irrevocable themselves, allowed only one answer. In Boock's words: 'In fact we quite quickly reached the point where we told ourselves that to go on waiting in case a better opportunity turned up wouldn't make any difference. We must take a tough line and see it through. A tough line meant killing Schleyer's companions so as to get hold of him.'

One of those present had scruples. 'I don't want to put myself under such pressure. There must be another way. I can't go along with this.'

'Okay, then you go into the next room while we carry on discussing it,' said one of the leaders. 'This is none of your business any more.' The man concerned stood up and left the room. Thereupon Peter Jürgen Boock was picked to drive the kidnap car. 'We need someone who can drive relatively calmly under all that stress and pressure, and we don't have so many of those.' So he slipped into the role. 'But I'd happily have done any other job at the time.'

They had brought large sheets of paper and coloured felt pens from their headquarters in the University Centre. They sketched the planned location of the abduction and the expected course of events on the sheets of paper: 'Who was going to do what, who would stand where, how to communicate with each other, what we had to keep an eye on.' They went over the entire operation again and again. 'But what really happened didn't come into it.'

'It was a totally unemotional debate,' Boock remembered later. 'In Baghdad afterwards I said to another RAF member: "That was our Wannsee Conference."' Just as the Nazi functionaries debated their plans for the Final Solution, he said, they had coldly discussed the murder of Schleyer's companions. 'With a kind of sober objectivity, although we were aware of the enormity of what we were discussing.' But that, Boock thought later, was probably the only way to approach what they had planned to do. 'If we'd approached the full dimensions of that enormity in words, it would hardly have been possible any more.'

They expected Schleyer's driver to be an armed bodyguard, and that disposed of the subject. 'In other circumstances I'm sure I'd have asked why we actually had to shoot the driver, what was the point, we can let the man go, I'd have said. Give him a kick in the arse, and that would be it.' But there was no room now even for such minimal moral considerations. 'I never took part in such an unemotional, icy cold discussion in that way before,' said Boock, 'and I never did again either.'

After that they went back to the University Centre. Boock prepared the weapons, and began packing them into a baby's pram, in which the longer guns too could be unobtrusively taken to the location of the attack.

Stefan Wisniewski was to act as leader of the operation. That kind of thing was usual in their raids. 'It was quite clear,' Boock remembered. 'You don't have time for discussion.'

Brigitte Mohnhaupt was not to take any part in the operation. That too was the usual RAF line. 'It was obvious that Brigitte wouldn't take part, in line with the principle that there must always be one of the leaders left to re-form the group if something goes wrong. She was thunderstruck to think she couldn't be there. She wanted to join in, but the majority decision was no.'

PART FIVE

Forty-Four Days in Autumn

1
The Kidnapping
(Monday, 5 September 1977)

There had been plenty of warnings.

After the murder of the Chairman of the Board of the Dresdner Bank, Jürgen Ponto, on 30 July 1977, the investigators discovered that three weeks earlier, on 6 July, a young man had seen documents relating to Ponto and Schleyer at the Hamburg Institute of International Economics. This man had said he was writing a thesis on leading economists. He had filled in the application form for outside visitors accordingly. It was only when Jürgen Ponto was dead that Federal Criminal Investigation officers discovered the alleged doctoral candidate was a former assistant in Klaus Croissant's Stuttgart office named Willy Peter Stoll, and had gone underground some while ago.

Hanns Martin Schleyer, President of the Employers' Association of the Federal Republic of Germany and of the Federation of German Industry, and on the board of Daimler-Benz, was given the classification Security Risk 1. Thereafter, he had a bodyguard of Baden-Württemberg Criminal Investigation officers. His office and apartment in Cologne and his house in Stuttgart were kept under surveillance. A Criminal Investigation officer advised Schleyer, 'Close your balcony door when you go to bed'. As a further precaution, he was told he should fit a wide-angled peephole to the door of his Cologne apartment, reinforce the lock, and install a police emergency call device with three trip buttons.

The street Am Raderthalgürtel was along Schleyer's route from his office at the Economic Institute of German Industry on the Oberländer Ufer to his Cologne apartment. On the afternoon of 1 September, a resident noticed two young women sitting there for over an hour and a half in a blue Alfa Romeo. Next day, he saw the two women at the same spot again. They seemed to be busy doing something to the car. Their behaviour struck the man as suspicious; he called the police and gave them the car number. Soon afterwards two police patrolmen arrived and asked for the two women's papers. They did not check any other personal details because of a fault in the police computer. Nor did they have the car number checked, assuming that their colleagues at police headquarters had already checked it after receiving the telephone call. However, headquarters had obviously left that job to the men on patrol.

It was only after Schleyer's death that the investigators discovered the blue Alfa had been used by one of his kidnappers, Adelheid Schulz. The car number was a duplicate, fixed up by the usual RAF system.

5 September 1977 was a Monday. Hanns Martin Schleyer rose early in the morning, at five o'clock, in his two-storey house at Number 17 Ginsterweg, Stuttgart. The rest of his family were still asleep when his driver came to collect him in his official Mercedes an hour later.

At 6.30 a.m., he took off for Cologne in Daimler's twin-jet Falcon aircraft. He was met by his Cologne chauffeur Heinz Marcisz, who took him to the office on the Oberländer Ufer. A cup of coffee, his mail, then 'morning prayers', his weekly conference with the departmental heads. 2.00 p.m.: a meeting of the executive committee of the Employers' Association with the employers of Joint Metal, to discuss the next round of wage talks.

The keyword was 'Mendocino'. The idea came from Willy Peter Stoll, who together with Stefan Wisniewski liked to warble 'Mendocino', the popular song of the time. The group had prepared their weapons and the pram that morning, cleaned the apartment, sent the last of their things off, decided how to distribute statements on the commando raid, and made phone calls to Paris. The infrastructure of Operation Big Get-Out was still the same. The central organization was a good twenty-five members strong, and there were a number of sympathizers on the periphery of the group who could be called on from case to case.

One group member was posted near the Federal Employers' Association building to let a second, standing further along the route, know when Schleyer was leaving. The second person was to call the commando group in a café and give the keyword as soon as the car drove past with the President of the Employers' Association in it: 'Mendocino' was the cue for the kidnapping to go ahead.

It was left to the members of the commando group to decide for themselves whether or not to wear bullet-proof vests. Boock put his on at first, then took it off again in the café. 'It felt too rigid. And I was in a frame of mind where I couldn't have cared less about such things.' Stefan Wisniewski kept his bullet-proof vest on.

The scene was surrealistic: the four of them sitting in the café, their guns out of sight, ordering coffee and cakes. It was early afternoon, and several housewives and elderly ladies were seated at the other little tables. None of the group were masked, and would not be. 'After all, no one but Schleyer himself was going to survive,' said Boock later. Several of the group had taken tranquillizers, one had taken a stimulant. Some were tired, others strung up. There was one iron principle that they all observed: 'Don't eat anything, always go into action on an empty stomach.' They had read, somewhere in the works of Che Guevara, that if you've eaten anything and you take a shot in the belly, you're dead. In Boock's words, 'First clean underwear, second an empty stomach.'

Boock ordered a doughnut, nibbled a corner of it and left the rest. He drank cocoa to soothe his stomach. Then the phone rang. The café proprietor picked it up and asked if there was a Herr Müller on the premises. Stefan Wisniewski took the receiver. 'Mendocino', said the voice at the other end of the line. 'Mendocino', said Wisniewski. 'Here we go.'

They knew they still had ten minutes to wait. Someone began counting. Then Willy Peter Stoll and Stefan Wisniewski got into the yellow Mercedes. Sieglinde Hofmann and Boock followed in the Volkswagen minibus. They turned into Vincenz-Statz-Strasse and got the yellow Mercedes into position. It was to act as an obstacle and bring Schleyer's convoy to a halt. Boock left the VW minibus in which Schleyer was to be driven away on the Alleenring, and helped his companion Sieglinde Hofmann to unload the pram. Then they went ahead to the corner of the street. From there they had a good view of the Mercedes. They adopted a casual stance, like two acquaintances who had happened to meet: 'Hi, how are you? And I see you have the baby with you too . . .'

Late in the afternoon, Schleyer left his office to be driven to his apartment at Number 10 Raschdorffstrasse, in the Braunsfeld district of Cologne. His chauffeur Marcisz was at the wheel again; the car's number plate was K–VN 345. Following it, in an unmarked police car, were the police officers making up Schleyer's bodyguard: Reinhold Brändle, aged 41; Roland Pieler, aged 20; Helmut Ulmer, aged 24.

At about 5.25 p.m., the convoy was driving west down Friedrich-Schmidt-Strasse, which passes Raschdorffstrasse, where Schleyer lived, on the right. Raschdorffstrasse was a one-way street. The two cars had to make a detour to reach Schleyer's apartment.

'There they are,' said Sieglinde Hofmann. Boock took his gun out of the pram and hid it under his jacket. Sieglinde Hofmann pushed the pram a little further. The trap was set.

Directly after turning into Vincenz-Statz-Strasse, which runs parallel to Raschdorffstrasse, Schleyer's driver suddenly had to stamp on the brakes. There was a blue pram standing in the road in front of him, and beside it, parked half on the pavement, a yellow Mercedes with Cologne number plates. The car with the three policemen in it ran into the back of Schleyer's car.

As the two cars collided the shooting began. The commando moved in with all guns blazing. Later, Boock could hardly remember who had been firing at what. 'It was almost like the sound of a single shot, really deafening. That was because we'd used two HK-43 assault guns without silencers.' Within a few minutes an entire magazine of 30 cartridges had been fired from one of the guns. There was a minute of total silence, and then Schleyer's escort began returning fire. Boock saw Sieglinde Hofmann go down on her knees. He couldn't tell if she had been hit or not. 'I ran over. I don't know if I was firing as I ran, or only when I was level with the cars. At the same moment Willy Peter Stoll came up, jumped on the bonnet of the escort vehicle and fired his entire magazine into it.' He had run straight across Boock's own line of fire, and was almost hit by his bullets. Then silence fell again.

Stoll was still standing on the car bonnet with the catch of his large-calibre repeating rifle off. The magazine was empty, but Boock could still hear it clicking. Into the silence, one of the commando group said, 'It's gone wrong. They're all dead.' Boock himself thought that no one could have survived the shoot-out, and went back to fetch the VW minibus. As he reversed it the sliding door, which was not locked, sprang open, and Boock could see Willy Peter Stoll and another member of the group dragging Schleyer out of his car. The others jumped into the bus as well and forced the president of the Employers' Association down on the floor. Stoll had flung himself into the passenger seat beside Boock: 'Come on, get moving!' As Boock put his foot down, he saw that the lights had turned red at the next junction, and a line of slow-moving cars was waiting for them to change. He raced along the pedestrian walkway and filtered on to the junction between a lamp post and the lights. With traffic flowing to right and left, he drove straight across the street. Just ahead of them, a truck was trying to reverse into the street. Boock almost ran down the man with the little signalling flag and continued in his wild career.

Sieglinde Hofmann had filled a syringe with a short-term anaesthetic and injected Schleyer with it. The president of the Employers' Association was babbling, half unconscious, 'No need for that.' 'We decide what's needed around here,' Boock snapped at him.

Horst Herold, commissioner of the BKA, was to have been away from his office until 7 September. He was planning to spend a few days with his colleague of the Protection of the Constitution Office. The two of them were going to take long walks in the beautiful hilly countryside of Bavaria, philosophizing about concepts of terrorism and how to counter it. When news of the kidnapping of Schleyer came, Herold quickly packed his case and left his hotel room. From his official car, he called Gerhard Boeden, head of his Terrorism Department, and had himself informed of the details of the attack.

The back windows of the VW minibus were curtained, but in the haste of their flight the kidnappers had forgotten to draw the curtains. They drove on at high speed to the underground garage of the Wiener Weg tower block, where the Mercedes was waiting to continue the journey. The car park next to it was full, so the Volkswagen Bully had to be parked a little further away, and the president of the Employers' Association, now semi-conscious, was dragged to the Mercedes. A ventilation hole had been cut in the partition between the back seat and the boot. They stowed Schleyer away in the boot, and Stefan Wisniewski got in with him, pistol at the ready. Boock sat at the wheel, Sieglinde Hofmann slipped into the passenger seat, and Willy Peter Stoll lay across the back seat. They wanted it to look as if there were only two people in the car.

They were almost out of the underground garage when it occurred to Sieglinde Hofmann that they had forgotten to leave the note written earlier, claiming responsibility for the RAF, in the VW minibus. They reversed, and placed the note in the vehicle. Schleyer, it said, had been abducted by an RAF commando; further statements and demands would follow. Then they raced away towards Erftstadt-Liblar.

As they drove into the underground garage of the tower block at 8 Zum Renngraben, one of the two in front asked, 'Everything okay? Is the air circulating?' Stoll passed the question on to the boot. Schleyer and his guard were to stay there for another two hours, waiting to be taken up to the 'people's prison' later. When Schleyer stirred, Wisniewski wanted to give him a second anaesthetic injection, but the kidnap victim said he didn't want it, he would keep absolutely quiet as he was. Wisniewski agreed not to administer it, but warned him, 'I'm lying right here behind you with a loaded gun. So don't go thinking you can get out of here alive. Make any noise and we're both dead.'

Boock, Sieglinde Hofmann and Stoll went up to the third floor in the lift. Brigitte Mohnhaupt was waiting for the commando group and its victim in apartment 104, which had been carefully prepared for the abduction. One room in the three-roomed apartment was furnished as an ordinary living-room, another as a bedroom. Schleyer was to be accommodated here. They had put some air-beds on the floor of the children's room among empty cardboard cartons and general junk.

Boock badly needed to go to the lavatory, and told Willy Peter Stoll, as he passed him, 'My God, don't you ever do a thing like that again.' He meant the moment when Stoll had come into his line of fire. Suddenly he realized that his hands were unsteady. He looked down, and was surprised to see how fast they were shaking. He was freezing, his fingers were cold as ice, although it was hot and stuffy inside the apartment.

Later he lay down on one of the air-beds and didn't move for an hour. Willy Peter Stoll was in an even worse state. It looked to Boock as if he were in deep shock, perhaps because he himself had almost been shot by his comrade, or perhaps because he had shot Schleyer's companions with his own gun. He never got over it, and afterwards Boock sometimes felt that Stoll had lost his mind over the operation. Willy Peter Stoll was shot by the police later during an attempted arrest in Düsseldorf.

A good hour after midnight they took Schleyer out of the car boot and brought him up. The anaesthetic had worn off, and the kidnapped president of the Employers' Association, pale and shaking, was able to walk by himself. He obediently followed all their instructions. They put another mattress on the floor beside the double bed in the bedroom and told Schleyer to lie down on it. Microphones hidden under the bed had been connected to a recorder in the kitchen. It was to be left running the whole time and record everything Schleyer said. As usual in a 'people's prison', they were also planning to question their victim later. The television was permanently switched on. At 9.30 p.m. they watched Federal Chancellor Schmidt on ARD: 'As I speak to you, I am sure that the perpetrators guilty of this act are also listening in somewhere. At this moment they may feel a triumphant sense of power, but they should not deceive themselves. In the long term terrorism has no chance, for terrorism is opposed not just by the organs of state but also by the will of the whole nation.'

The apartment had a surface area of 77.66 square metres. One Frau Lottmann-Bücklers had rented it on 18 July 1977 after seeing a newspaper ad. She filled in a form giving her personal details on the spot. She had been born on 13 October 1956, she said, and was a dressmaker by profession. No one checked up on her data.

'Frau Lottmann-Bücklers' had also furnished the apartment. The shelf unit on the wall cost 998 marks, the bedroom furnishings cost 1,969 marks, of which she paid 1,469 marks in cash. She bought a refrigerator and an electric stove at a Hertie store, paying 583 marks for the two items together, also in cash. Then there was a Samurai brand TV set and several small things, including a doormat with a stag motif on it. Investigators later found such doormats with pictures of hunting scenes in a whole series of apartments used by RAF members, and they concluded that there was an allusion to the name of the Interior Minister of North Rhine-Westphalia at the time, Burkhard Hirsch (Hirsch meaning 'stag' in German).

The kidnappers had constructed a dungeon inside a built-in cupboard in the corridor and lined it with plastic foam. The cupboard was 160 centimetres wide by 71 centimetres deep by 250 centimetres high, and contained a chair and a chain. Boock showed Schleyer this dark box and said, 'No one will hear you in there. That's where we'll put you if you don't act normally. Then we'll have peace and quiet in the living-room.'

Schleyer spent the first part of his abduction in this apartment, probably ten days, because after 16 September, as the police later discovered, no electricity was used at apartment no. 104 in the high-rise block, about 30 minutes' drive away from the scene of the kidnapping in Cologne.

2
A Thorough Search

The prisoners in Stammheim heard the news of Schleyer's kidnapping over their radios. They also saw the Second Channel programme *heute* ('Today') on TV in their cells when it transmitted a report of the kidnapping at 7.23 p.m.

It was not until the main television news went out at 8.00 p.m. that warders unlocked the cells and removed the prisoners' radios and TV sets.

An hour later, Baader, Ensslin and Raspe were moved to other cells on the seventh floor. A group of Stuttgart Criminal Investigation officers had been detailed to search the cells in Stammheim jail occupied by the Baader–Meinhof prisoners. Federal Prosecutor Widera ordered the operation.

Two officers began searching Jan-Carl Raspe's cell. At first they were in some difficulty, as the lighting in the cell did not work. They had a table lamp brought in. The cell was very untidy. Working in a clockwise direction, the police officers searched its chaotically scattered contents. Apart from a light bulb lying among books on a shelf they found nothing which, as the report said, 'might point to any other criminal activity'.

The light bulb was handed over to a member of the prison staff. Just before the two officers had completed the operation, one of them was called away. There was more to be done in Stuttgart: a police raid on Klaus Croissant's office.

Three officers searched Andreas Baader's cell that night. The light was dim in this cell too, and would not even have been bright enough for reading. Finally the prison officers brought in a standard lamp. The policemen were able to read anything they held directly under it; the rest of the cell was still dark. The officers put a neon tube in the ceiling fitting, but it did not work.

One of the officers searched the lavatory, wash basin, and the part of the cell where food was standing about. Another officer took the bed apart. He found tools of all kinds underneath it, a screwdriver and a quantity of electric plugs and cable. The police officers handed a radio and a record player from Baader's cell over to the administrative staff of the prison, requesting that they be closely examined.

As Chief Superintendent Josef Ring stated in evidence later, there had been 'a thorough search'. 'I gave express instructions for all books to be searched, and all objects found in the room, and all the furniture. I didn't expressly ask for the walls to be searched. However, of course that's part of a thorough search, as my colleagues knew.'

The officer leading the search party personally checked the contents of some fifty spice containers in Andreas Baader's cell.

They checked only the cells currently occupied, not the other, empty cells in the high-security section. Just how 'thoroughly' they had searched these cells was to emerge six weeks later.

Nothing was impounded that night except for a lamp Andreas Baader had made out of a thermos jug.

On his four shelf units, Baader had 974 books and 75 LP records, a harmonica, an Olivetti typewriter, a box of Pelikan water-colours, two pairs of sunglasses, hair spray, eye shadow, two fur coats, an electric alarm clock with batteries, a record player with amplifier and loudspeakers, numerous tubes of medicaments, spices, cutlery, plates . . .

Jan-Carl Raspe had a record player too, also cables and electrical equipment; the men searching the cells did not stop to think about the significance of this. He had a microphone as well. And cough syrup, spices, vinegar, baking powder, Soluvetan digestive tea, an electric hotplate . . . He also had 550 books, almost all on politics and history.

In Gudrun Ensslin's cell, the officers found items of food such as cocoa, rolled oats, raisins, mustard, and also detergent, Samson rolling tobacco, rusks, a Mum roll-on deodorant, a Schick lady's razor, an eyebrow pencil, an electric hotplate, a typewriter, a tea infuser, a bottle of perfume, a record player, a blue toothbrush, a violin and a music stand . . .

Gudrun Ensslin had about 450 books in her cell, including numerous works by Lenin and Marx, but also Willy Brandt's *People and Politics*, Heinrich Hannover's *The Murder of Rosa Luxemburg and Karl Liebknecht*, Thomas Szasz's *The Myth of Psychotherapy*, Hans Magnus Enzensberger's *The Short Summer of Anarchy*, and Bertolt Brecht's didactic dramas, among them *The Measures Taken*, which along with *Moby Dick* was part of the standard reading matter of the RAF prisoners.

The search of the cells ended at 2.45 a.m.

3
The Hard Line
(Tuesday, 6 September 1977)

The Second Channel's television programme *heute* had made it known that the police were looking for a white Volkswagen minibus, number plates K-C 3849. At 7.45 p.m., the caretaker of a Cologne apartment block at Ib Wiener Weg telephoned. The wanted car was in the garage underneath his block. Fearing it might be booby-trapped, a police squad opened it up with the aid of a cable winch. Inside the vehicle, the officers found a copy of a letter to the Government, demanding that they halt all investigations immediately – 'or we'll shoot Schleyer at once, before there can be any negotiations for his release'.

The police searched the multi-storey building, looking for an apartment used by the conspirators. One of the apartments was let to a 'Lisa Riess'. Parking slot 127 in the underground garage, where the Volkswagen bus was standing, was hers as well. Towards midnight, a remote-controlled mini-tank imported from Northern Ireland, fitted with a searchlight, a video camera and an automatic rifle, was placed in position outside the apartment.

Police officers forced the door and steered the tank through the apartment by remote control. The place was empty except for an air mattress, a walkie-talkie radio, a chair and a bedside table.

The kidnappers had stocked up on medicinal drugs to stabilize the circulation, so that they could treat the president of the Employers' Association if necessary. He was robust, but all the same he was sixty-two years old, and corpulent. There was also a doctor ready on call. Plenty of food had been laid in so that they need not leave the apartment for days. They had bought baby-food for Schleyer; the whole fridge was full to the top with it. 'Alete brand for preference,' said Boock later, 'because anyone can digest that even if he has stomach trouble or he's so upset that he keeps throwing up.'

The group had planned in advance exactly who would be guarding Schleyer when. They had read that when a hostage-taking lasts for a long time, too much intimacy and familiarity can develop between guards and their hostage. So the guards were to keep changing. They had expected Schleyer to react angrily, and they were surprised to find him so co-operative. 'He worked out how we were thinking and even pointed out mistakes – in his own interests, of course,' said Boock. 'All the same, he told us from the start that he wasn't giving us information that might affect the security of the Federal Republic in any way. And he would not lend himself to being part of any blackmail deal with the Federal Government either.'

The first of the kidnap commando to be relieved was Willy Peter Stoll. Adelheid Schulz appeared in the Zum Renngraben hide-out in the morning.

'Where is he?' she asked Brigitte Mohnhaupt, who pointed to the bedroom. 'In there.'

Adelheid Schulz opened the door and said, in the broadest of Swabian accents, 'Never expected to find yourself in the People's Prison, did you?'

Schleyer looked at her as if she were a ghostly apparition, and Peter Jürgen Boock could hardly control himself for laughing.

They began their 'interrogations' on the first or second day. These sessions were to be recorded on the equipment installed in Schleyer's room. They had prepared a script in which questions about matters that were unimportant, but could be checked, alternated with harsher questions. That way they hoped to find out whether Schleyer was telling them the truth or trying to trick them. In fact they themselves had no clear idea of just what they wanted to discover from him. As a result Schleyer gave them what were almost university lectures on management and economics. In answer to many questions he simply shook his head. 'Look, these ideas of yours bear all the hallmarks of your own attitude.'

In principle the interrogations were carried out in pairs. One interrogator asked the questions, the other supervised the conversation in the background and only occasionally joined in. They had planned a tough schedule, but they managed to stick to it only on the first day. 'The man was quite unlike the stereotypes and our own ideas of him,' says Boock. Schleyer was jovial, cracked jokes, told stories about his wartime experience as a POW, and pointed out that this wasn't the first time he'd been a prisoner. Only when the conversation turned to his Nazi past did he really seem affected, at least as Boock saw it.

They had originally meant to provide a chemical toilet for him when he had to answer the call of nature, but then they let him use the normal lavatory in the apartment. 'Only don't try getting to the front door. First, you won't manage to anyway, and second there'll always be someone there with a gun. And if you let out so much as a squeak, that's it. Even if it sends us all sky-high. You've seen the kind of risk we took to get hold of you, so don't get any ideas.'

They were using the familiar '*du*' to address Schleyer, and he was soon using it to them too. He recognized Christian Klar and one or two of the others from the commando group. He did not know Boock, and asked him his name a couple of times, but Boock didn't give it away. At first the kidnappers had shielded their faces behind hoods, but that soon turned out to be too uncomfortable, so they faced Schleyer unmasked.

The group members felt safe because they had nothing to lose. Either the plan would work or they'd be dead. The only other thing that might happen was arrest, but as they saw it, prison meant the same as death.

At night they drew up statements for the Federal Government and the press. This was mainly the women's work. They had spent months devising a communications plan for the mother of all operations. There were plenty of people they could rely on. The main base of their support consisted of about twenty-five auxiliaries who were ready for anything, and were longing to be admitted to the inner circle.

No one was to know everything. Division of labour outside that inner circle was all-important. If one head of the hydra was chopped off, another would grow in its place.

Three or four people had been given the job of disseminating news. They were told only a short time in advance that they were to carry messages, but never what the messages were. The rule was for one person to be given a message by the commando group and another to deliver it. Then even if the courier was arrested delivering the message, he could never have said just where it had come from.

Horst Herold had himself driven at high speed from Bavaria to Bonn. That same night he met Chancellor Schmidt there. Then he went to BKA headquarters in Wiesbaden. From there he returned to Bonn, tired out but equipped with a comprehensive programme for a manhunt, its details called up from his BKA computer.

'In fact, all I had in my mind was the thought of bringing the business to a satisfactory end; I was perfectly cool,' Herold remembered later. 'Perfectly cool, while the others were in a state of agitation; even Schmidt seemed worn out, and Maihofer and Vogel and all of them. But I was not at all agitated.'

Helmut Schmidt and Horst Herold, the two former Wehrmacht officers, agreed that there could be no question of capitulation.

Herold wanted to play for time, keeping the kidnappers waiting, forcing them to give him information he could feed into his computer, so that a picture of the abductors could be gradually built up until they finally got some clues to the victim's whereabouts.

'From hour to hour,' said Herold later, 'our picture of the kidnappers became clearer. In fact it was clear as day. We knew all about it, we just had to get hold of them, that was the only thing. The way it used to be, when you were after a murderer the difficulty was not knowing who he was. If you knew who he was, then you'd got him. But here it was the other way around. That was a new departure, so to speak.'

Herold suggested keeping quiet about the letter found in the kidnap vehicle, to make the kidnappers get in touch again.

On the afternoon of 6 September, the daughter of a Protestant dean in Wiesbaden found an envelope addressed 'To the Federal Government' in the family's letter-box. She put it on her father's desk, unopened. Twenty minutes later the dean came home and opened the letter. He glanced at it. The telephone rang, and a stranger's voice spoke to him. 'There's a letter for the Government in your letter-box. Send it on.' Then the caller rang off. The dean called the police in Wiesbaden and the Federal Criminal Investigation Office; the BKA had the letter collected at once. The envelope contained two photographs of Schleyer, one showing him in front of the RAF symbol, with a placard saying 'Prisoner of the RAF'. The other was a private photograph which the kidnap victim obviously had had on him.

The letter, written without the customary initial capitals for all nouns used in German, said, 'on monday, 5.9.77, the siegfried hausner commando took prisoner the president of the employers' association and the federation of german industry, hanns martin schleyer.'

The kidnappers demanded 'the immediate cessation of all investigations, or schleyer will be shot at once'. As conditions for his release, their demands were as follows:

'1. the release, in exchange, of the red army faction prisoners andreas baader, gudrun ensslin, jan-carl raspe, verena becker, werner hoppe, karl-heinz dellwo, hanna krabbe, bernd rössner, ingrid schubert and irmgard möller, to go to a country of their choice. günter sonnenberg, unfit for prison custody since his arrest because of his gunshot wound, is to be freed at once and the writ against him cancelled . . .

2. the prisoners are to be brought to frankfurt airport on wednesday at eight in the morning . . . at ten o'clock in the morning one of the prisoners will inform the commando by direct transmission over german television that all is going according to plan for their flight out . . .'

As a 'guarantee of the lives of the prisoners' while they were being flown out, the kidnappers wanted them to be accompanied by 'payot, secretary general of the international federation for human rights at uno' and Pastor Niemöller. Each prisoner was to be given 100,000 marks.

'we suppose,' the letter concluded, 'that after demonstrating at the time of stockholm how fast he comes to his decisions, schmidt will bestir himself to make his attitude to this fat cat of the elite of international economics clear just as quickly.'

A handwritten letter from Schleyer himself was enclosed. 'I have been told that if investigations continue my life is in danger. The same would apply if the demands are not met and the ultimatums observed. On the whole I am well; I have not been injured, and I think I shall be freed if the demands are met. However, the decision is not mine. Hanns Martin Schleyer.

The kidnappers had dictated the text to him. He had hesitated over some phrases, and said, 'That doesn't sound as if I'd said it myself.'

'How would you have put it, then?'

Schleyer made a suggestion.

'Fine, then write that.'

Above all, the kidnapped president of the Employers' Association was trying to avoid any impression that he was asking the Federal Government to give in to blackmail. He was prepared to refer to the subject only indirectly. The kidnappers went along with that.

Shortly after 7.00 p.m., Chancellor Schmidt strode into the office of the opposition leader in the parliament building in Bonn. 'Herr Kohl, I must speak to you privately.' Helmut Kohl's colleagues left the room without a word. Briefly, Schmidt described the contents of the kidnappers' letter, and agreed tactics with the leader of the Christian Democrats.

The first requirement was to gain time: an actual exchange of prisoners had to be avoided at all costs. As a first step, all RAF prisoners were to be completely isolated in prison from each other and from the outside world. There was no legal basis for such a procedure, but it was indicated in this case to avert 'the existing danger to human life' and permissible according to 'the legal notion of justifiable emergency'.

From this moment on, all the RAF prisoners were completely isolated. They could not receive visits from their lawyers either.

An expert engineer from the regional Criminal Investigation Office had been to Stammheim that morning. He was shown the loudspeakers, amplifiers and record players removed from the prisoners' cells the night before. The engineer, Heinz Nabroth, examined the equipment, but – allegedly – found nothing suspicious about it. And yet even a layman, as it transpired after the death of the prisoners, could see that the amplifiers had been modified to a considerable extent.

The Commission of Inquiry in Stuttgart later came to the conclusion that, 'No great degree of expert knowledge was necessary, when the equipment was taken apart, to see that it had been altered.'

There were signs of some rather rough and ready welding, which made it obvious that the equipment had been used not just for listening to music, but to enable the prisoners to communicate with each other.

The Criminal Investigation Office's engineering expert cleared the equipment, and it was returned to the prisoners in their cells.

Herold's entire staff had moved at top speed from Wiesbaden to Bad Godesberg. A good half dozen of his closest colleagues, including Assistant Commissioner Steinke, moved into the BKA offices there. Gerhard Boeden's office was made ready for Herold. This was where all the threads of the investigation were to come together, and the provincial Criminal Investigation Offices were to be kept informed and their work coordinated from the same place. In the Schleyer case the independence of the provincial police forces, usually jealously guarded, was to yield to the supremacy of the Federal Criminal Investigation Office, at least *de facto*. The biggest concerted investigation in the history of the Federal Republic was beginning. No stone was to be left unturned to find the kidnapped president of the Employers' Association. And all information was to be fed into Herold's computer.

The structures of command in the police were altered virtually overnight. The provincial police forces involved no longer made their own decisions on the spot. Everything went through the BKA and the Federal Prosecutor's Office. But chaos had entered into the equation on the very first day. The federal prosecutor, concluded a secret Criminal Investigation study in Cologne, had asked the BKA to investigate, which led to a 'gap in communications', and from then on the local police had no more legal responsibility, although the duties were all theirs. It still remained to be seen just how wide that gap in communications was.

4
'Spindy'
(Wednesday, 7 September 1977)

At 9 a.m. the commanding officer of the police service held a discussion with his departmental heads in Hürth, at the offices of the Bergheim chief district administrator, on the course of action they should follow.

Commissioner Biemann ordered a search for possible hiding places to be carried out at once. At 10 a.m., the departmental heads were sending out all available officers in the district. The head of the Criminal Investigation Department (Kripo) also mobilized all his officers. Around 1 p.m. the requisite instructions from Cologne arrived, but by this time the local police was already out and about.

This was normal routine work for the officers. They were hunting for suspect properties and persons. The pattern was clear: they must search in particular for suspicious tenants in complexes of high-rise buildings near the motorway and with underground garages.

In the Erftstadt-Liblar area, the officer responsible, Superintendent Ferdinand Schmitt, set off for the building at No. 8 Zum Renngraben. He rang the bell of the caretaker's front door on the first floor. The caretaker couldn't tell him about anything suspicious, but he referred him to his mother-in-law, who dealt with rental agreements for the management of the apartments. The police officer, being familiar with the area, knew her and went straight off to see her.

'Well, the fact is, Herr Schmitt,' she said. 'with so many people moving in and out I don't make written notes about them.'

'Think about it, please,' the police officer replied. 'Herr Schleyer has been abducted, and several men were killed during the abduction.'

The woman suddenly had an idea. 'Sit down at my desk here for a moment.'

The officer sat down opposite her.

'There was a woman with long dark hair sitting just where you're sitting now, in June or July. She rented an apartment at 8 Renngraben. And after I'd told her she had to make an advance payment of 800 marks for rent, she picked up the bag standing at her feet, put it on her lap, took wads of fifties, hundreds and five-hundreds out of it and put the money on the desk.'

'Can you remember her name?' asked Schmitt.

'No, but the caretaker will be able to tell you.'

'May I make a quick phone call to him?'

When the police officer asked the caretaker for the woman's name, he said, 'Herr Schmitt, I'll have to remind you of the Data Protection Act. On principle I can't give you any information about the tenants.'

The police officer pointed out that this was a special situation, and after some further hesitation the caretaker said, 'Her name is Annerose Lottmann-Bücklers. Divorced, a fashion designer by profession. She moved here from Bismarckstrasse in Wuppertal.'

Superintendent Schmitt thanked the man and went to the police station, feeling galvanized: it all fitted together.

'It was well known that the kidnappers who had abducted Herr Schleyer financed themselves by raiding banks and getting hold of other people's property in all kinds of ways. No normal woman would go to rent an apartment carrying so much cash on her, would she? And that's why I was firmly convinced that those people had come here from Cologne. They could drive along the Federal motorway from Cologne, turn off at the Erftstadt junction, come here to Zum Renngraben, that would be exactly 1.6 kilometres.'

The tenant by the name of Lottmann-Bücklers was obviously a hot trail. Within forty-eight hours of the kidnapping of Hanns Martin Schleyer, the local police had tracked down an apartment that met all the criteria, and had been rented in a rather suspicious manner.

At 3 p.m., the Erftstadt police sent a telex to the police chief of the Bergheim administrative district mentioning Apartment 104 in the high-rise block at Number 8 Zum Renngraben. Within just under two hours, then, this obviously hot tip should have been passed on to the centre of operations. The telex first went on from the regional administrative offices in Bergheim to Department K (for Kripo), where further investigations were to be made. However, no one checked the name of Annerose Lottmann-Bücklers, or whether the personal details she had given when renting the apartment were correct.

If that had been done, it would have emerged immediately that the address in Wuppertal given by the woman, Bismarckstrasse 8, could not be right, for the simple reason that the numbers of the buildings there begin with 11. And she was not known at that address anyway. However, a woman in Hamburg calling herself Annerose Lottmann-Bücklers had applied four times for an identity card, twice saying that she had lost one, and once alleging that hers been stolen. In addition, if Herold's PIOS computer had been consulted, more indications that something was wrong with that name would have come up. In all, Herold's 'super-brain' would have been able to supply almost half a dozen connections with the RAF. But if no one consulted the computer, it could hardly come up with any answers.

Information was indeed coming in to the police from all sides, but in this case it was not just a vague clue offered by some ordinary citizen. A police officer had been investigating – and had discovered something obviously explosive.

At 10.00 a.m., Commissioner Herold of the BKA had a message sent to the kidnappers by way of the radio:

'The Federal Criminal Investigation Office is instructed to check that Herr Schleyer is still alive . . .' Unmistakable signs of life would have to be produced, said the message. The police would ask certain questions over the radio during the afternoon.

Towards 2.00 p.m. the BKA went on the radio again and said the kidnappers were to send a tape of Schleyer answering personal questions whose answers only he himself could know. 'What is Edgar Obrecht's nickname? What is the name of the Eulers' grand-daughter, and where does she live?'

Horst Herold had adjusted to the kidnappers' own conspiratorial mode of conduct. Questions such as these, and their answers, were put to the kidnappers and their hostage several times over the next six weeks, not just as a means of getting some sign of life from the victim, but to help in identifying his kidnappers.

As soon as the BKA had put out its radio message asking for some sign that the hostage was alive, one of the kidnappers – later on, the court assumed in passing sentence that it was Peter Jürgen Boock – told Schleyer, 'And after that – it's part of their delaying tactics – they'll want you to answer questions, so they can be sure you're still alive.'

'Has that been announced?' asked Schleyer.

'Yes, over the radio. They did the same thing with Lorenz, it was the same game . . . the question is, do we go along with it, or do we give them their definite proof some other way . . . for instance,' the kidnapper went on, 'a message over South-West Radio for Herr So-and-so, travelling somewhere. That'd be one idea, maybe we should alter it that way.'

The kidnappers recorded this conversation on tape, but the recorder was standing so far away that only parts of the dialogue came over. The police found the tape in 1982, in an earth dump at Heusenstamm, labelled 'Conversation with Spindy'. As *Spind* is a German word for a wardrobe, Schleyer's temporary residence in the built-in cupboard had obviously moved his kidnappers to give their victim this nickname.

Boock had a different explanation for the name. The kidnappers, he said, had called Schleyer 'Spindy' because the corpulent president of the Employers' Association was shaped like a spindle.

Late in the afternoon, a Protestant pastor in Mainz found a package containing two letters from Schleyer, a videotape, and a letter to the Government from the kidnappers in his letter-box. On the tape, Schleyer read one of the letters aloud; his voice sounded tired. He referred to the radio message putting the questions. 'To simplify this matter, perhaps it will do if I say that at the end of that broadcast I heard an appeal go out for a Herr Vijot from Belgium, travelling from Brussels to Karlsruhe in a white Volvo, to call his home. And my wife will remember our conversation at breakfast on Sunday morning, when she was so keen to have security devices installed in our Stuttgart house.'

In his letter, Schleyer wrote, 'I have been told in broad outline what has happened so far, and I would like to thank everyone who is helping me in my difficult situation. I am convinced that my kidnappers will do as they say, although delay will be harmful. In the circumstances, I am reasonably well; I send particular greetings to my family, whom I confidently hope to see again soon.'

In their own letter, the kidnappers again demanded that the hunt for them be called off at once, and that preparations be made for the exchange of prisoners. They were also demanding an appearance on evening television by one of them to announce the completion of the preparatory measures. Moreover, they wanted the videotape of Schleyer shown on all TV news programmes.

The Federal Government had no intention of entering into this game with the mass media. A strict news blackout had been imposed only the day before. The chancellor and his closest advisers were determined to prevent the kidnappers from communicating on equal terms with the Government, in public and with state authority – as had happened in the Lorenz kidnapping.

* * *

The manhunt, now in full swing, went on with as much secrecy as possible; simultaneously, Chief Commissioner Herold of the Federal Criminal Investigation Office was trying to stall the kidnappers, playing for more time to close in on them.

At 8.44 p.m., a suffragan bishop in Mainz found the tape recording of Schleyer's voice demanded by the BKA in his letter-box. An hour later, the BKA put out a television announcement on the Second Channel. 'The Federal Criminal Investigation Office received this information only a few minutes ago. A further statement will follow.'

On the tape, Schleyer answered the BKA's questions, and added, 'My guards say that this sign of life will be the last I can give before my release; they are pressing for the Government to come to a decision.'

Once again, the BKA played for time. At 11.15 p.m., they put out a bulletin on the Second Channel saying that because of its late delivery, transmission of the videotape was not possible yet. Shortly before midnight, the BKA addressed the kidnappers again on TV and suggested bringing in an intermediary, 'to avoid the confusion caused by parallel cases of disinformation and the troublesome loss of time'.

Night duty report, Stammheim, 7 September 1977:

'No incidents.'

5
Wild Ideas
(Thursday, 8 September 1977)

In the morning, the BKA met one of the kidnappers' demands for the first time; it published their second letter, although after a thirty-eight hour delay.

At 10.15 a.m., the 'Larger Crisis Staff' met and agreed to the suggestion made by the Government spokesman Klaus Bölling, that the press, radio and television be asked to say nothing about the contents of the video and tape recordings, copies of which the kidnappers had sent to the media.

That afternoon, the German Press Council also appealed to the media to exercise restraint in their reporting of the Schleyer kidnapping. Over the next few weeks, almost all newspapers and magazines observed this voluntary form of self-censorship.

At mid-day, the BKA addressed the kidnappers again over the radio, repeating their suggestion of a go-between, since 'communication by radio and television has proved inappropriate'.

At about 5.00 p.m. the 'Smaller Crisis Staff' met again; the meeting went on, with one short break, until 10.00 p.m. The chief commissioner of the BKA told the chancellor what the advantages of using a go-between would be. 'First, to keep contacts with the kidnapper secret, thus avoiding publicity. Second, to make communication more difficult for our opponents. It's easy enough for us to give a mediator information, but much harder for the kidnappers. Third, it would increase our chances of finding out exactly who they are. And fourth, we'd gain yet more time to find out where Schleyer is being kept.'

Herold recalled the name of Payot, mentioned by the kidnappers in their first letter. Denis Payot was not, as the kidnappers obviously supposed, a United Nations official, but president of the Swiss League for Human Rights, a lawyer practising in Geneva, and the signatory of many declarations about the 'torture by solitary confinement' of the RAF prisoners. Herold was given the go-ahead to use Denis Payot as a mediator.

Late that evening, the chancellor addressed the meeting: 'I would now ask you, gentlemen, to express any ideas you may have as to what we should do, however wild they may seem.'

Herold had an idea. 'I would suggest that we let the prisoners fly out to some desert airfield, supposedly in Yemen. We let them leave the plane and send a message home. Then we arrest them.' The BKA chief had also thought of the best place to carry out such a piece of deception: Israel. The Israeli secret service Mossad would be sure to cooperate.

* * *

Chief Federal Prosecutor Kurt Rebmann's turn came as the fifth or sixth speaker. He remarked that this was a 'state of emergency transcending the law', and suggested shooting the Stammheim prisoners one by one until Schleyer's kidnappers freed him. They would only have to make a change in the Basic Law, which could be done within hours by the Crisis Staff, in which legislative and executive responsibility were combined. Chancellor Schmidt, says one eye-witness, listened to Rebmann's remarks with an icy expression on his face, and was quick to call the next speaker. Later, after the end of the meeting, one of the participants apparently said, 'If we'd done that, we'd have been lowering ourselves to the level of the RAF.'

The television journalist Christoph Maria Fröhder, to whom this story had been told years after the event, took a TV portrait of the chief federal prosecutor as the occasion to ask Rebmann about it. 'Members of the Schleyer and Mogadishu Crisis Staff say you recommended a pitilessly hard line at the time, they say you even suggested shooting a prisoner in retaliation for every hostage. Was that suggestion connected only with the circumstances of the time, or is it still valid today?'

As the camera rolled, Rebmann replied, 'No, at that time, I might say, it arose from the situation. Federal Chancellor Helmut Schmidt did once ask us all simply to make suggestions, even if we hadn't thought them through properly yet. The idea was that we could just let the fancy roam. So at the time I brought up that idea in the course of the discussion, but of course it wasn't meant entirely seriously; I didn't expect the legislators to pick up on it, and there's no doubt that we'd have needed a legal basis for any such measures.'

All day, the police of the whole Cologne area wore themselves out looking for other possible hiding-places. Meanwhile their colleagues of Criminal Investigation worked on the suspect properties reported to them and those known to themselves. The information was collected into four files and 'investigated under cover'. The special nature of the Erftstadt-Liblar information obviously did not earn it preferential treatment.

Late in the afternoon of 8 September the police chiefs of the Cologne district were summoned to the office of the president of the local administrative district. Commissioner Biemann was one of those taking part in the conference, which went on until 8 p.m. It was decided to continue searching for suspicious persons and properties over the weekend. After the results of the search had been evaluated by the head of the Kripo, a list would be sent on to the Schleyer Special Commission of the BKA, 'Soko 77'. At the same time preparations would go ahead for what was called the *Exekutivschlag*, the 'Executive Strike'. When that password was given, a lightning operation checking up on the people and properties named in the lists was to begin.

Night duty report, Stammheim, 8 September:
'No incidents.'

6
'A Man Would Like to Survive . . .'
(Friday, 9 September 1977)

On the morning of 9 September there was another discussion at 8.30 a.m., this time arranging the details of the 'Executive Strike'. Finally, at around 10 a.m., Commissioner Biemann and Kripo Commissioner Breuer sat down with some of their colleagues for a final session going through the lists of people and properties that had been compiled, and evaluating them. The final list of suspect properties was ready at last late in the afternoon of 9 September. Over 48 hours had now passed since Superintendent Schmitt had been tipped off about apartment 104 at Number 8 Zum Renngraben in Erftstadt-Liblar.

At 5.30 p.m. the final list was sent through by telex, under the number 827, to the co-ordinating staff at Cologne police headquarters. Contrary to previous plans, the co-ordinating staff and not the office of the head of the administrative district was to be in charge of the assembled reports.

The telex was all of three pages long, and contained a list of four communes, several people of leftist sympathies, and several 'anarchist apartments'. Eight buildings were listed under the heading of 'Relevant Suspicious Properties'. In fourth place was: 'erftstadt-liblar, zum renngraben, 3rd floor, apartment 104, a frau annerose lottmann-bueckler said to have moved into the apartment on 21.07.77. Management of building applied to as matter of urgency. Advance rental of dm 800.00 paid at once in cash. Frau l.-b. took the money out of her handbag which apparently contained a whole stash of banknotes.'

The same afternoon, Commissioner Biemann and his colleagues worked out plans for the 'Executive Strike' operation, calculating the number of police personnel and the means of transport that would be needed. To be on the safe side, all the submachine guns and walkie-talkie radios from all the police stations were collected in Hürth. In telex No. 840, sent on 9 September, the police commissioner announced the concept of the operation, the numbers of officers and the means of transport needed and other operational details. The plan was for a police unit to move into each of the suspect properties. It was to consist of 'a high-ranking officer who knows the area as leader, nine police officers and four Criminal Investigation officers, with the necessary vehicles, drivers, and operational equipment.' The term 'Executive Strike' as the cue for the operation had now changed to 'Full Check-Up'. When it was given, investigation of the suspect properties was to be carried out at high speed.

The property at Number 8 Zum Renngraben was to be specially reconnoitred by the officer in charge of Erftstadt police station, in civilian clothes, in preparation for Executive Strike. According to the plans, he was to lead the operational unit there.

In the morning, another letter from the kidnappers arrived by express mail; this one was sent to the Bonn office of the French news agency AFP. Another Polaroid photograph of Schleyer was enclosed. The letter demanded a decision from the Government by 8.00 p.m. that evening. At noon next day, said the letter, still with an absence of initial capitals, 'the flight out of all the prisoners in a fully fuelled lufthansa long-haul aircraft' was to be shown live on television.

By way of credentials, the kidnappers added a remark from Schleyer himself: 'how lucky that the mirror which fell on arndt's cot at our home in offenbach didn't kill him.'

Yet again the Government and the BKA stalled, playing for time. The AFP agency was asked not to publish the letter, and so was the *Frankfurter Rundschau*, which had also received a copy.

These delaying tactics had not gone unnoticed by either the kidnappers or their hostage. Every hour Horst Herold gained with his strategy of obfuscation increased the kidnappers' danger of discovery. So they made Hanns Martin Schleyer write letters to old and influential friends, letters in which he himself tried to urge a quick decision.

In the afternoon, a letter was handed to the doorman of the Düsseldorf offices of Friedrich Flick AG, addressed to the executive partner Eberhard von Brauchitsch.

'I am still alive,' wrote Hanns Martin Schleyer, 'but I wish I knew more about the Government's decision. They are the only ones who can pull the strings, but they've imposed a news blackout. The demand for a mediator is sheer nonsense, since my kidnappers won't reveal themselves or expose our "holiday resort" even to a "mediator", so three-sided contact is impossible. In my situation, of course uncertainty is dreadful. If Bonn is going to reject the demands, I wish they would do it quickly, although "as it was in the war", a man would like to survive . . .'

Night duty report, Stammheim, 9 September:

'22.00 hours, night duty check by A.J. Walter. 23.05 hours, when medicaments were given out, Baader wanted to take Ensslin "a bowl of porridge" – request refused, as they are still in solitary confinement.

'Otherwise no incidents.'

7
The Go-between
(Saturday, 10 September 1977)

Meanwhile, the Federal Criminal Investigation Office had contacted the Swiss lawyer Denis Payot, asking him to act as mediator. Payot agreed, and held a press conference late that evening, at which he introduced himself. 'I have no mandate from the German police. My mandate has been signed and comes from the Federal Government itself, headed by the chancellor of the Federal Republic of Germany, Herr Schmidt.'

At the time, Denis Payot was 35 years old, with thick glasses and dark blond hair, and had a small and not particularly flourishing law practice in the watchmakers' quarter of Geneva. Later, after the six dramatic weeks of the Schleyer kidnapping, he was paid a fee of 180,000 Swiss francs by the West German government, including expenses.

Half an hour before midnight, the kidnappers called the Swiss lawyer for the first time. A woman's voice on the line said, 'I am a member of the RAF.' As credentials, she passed on a statement by Schleyer that could come only from him. 'In June I met Herr Karl-Werner Sanne and the United States representative at the Organization of International Industry.'

The caller demanded, 'By 6.00 p.m. on Sunday, one of the prisoners is to appear on German television and state that preparations for their flight out are in progress . . .' After that, the kidnappers would give proof that Schleyer was alive. They would then allow six more hours before the plane took off. On arrival at their destination, Andreas Baader would say something containing a remark from which the kidnappers could conclude that the prisoners had arrived safely. Then they would release Schleyer. 'There can be no compromise.'

It was now the weekend. The kidnapped president of the Employers' Association had been held in apartment 104 on the third floor of Number 8 Zum Renngraben since Monday night. The police were still looking for the hostage's hiding-place by means of 'cautious questioning of sections of the population known to them', although its details had gone on record five days earlier. At the same time, operational instructions were handed out to every police unit: 'Observe, cordon off, investigate, search with the co-operation of occupants, or by force if necessary, Property Number . . . with regard to the possible holding there of the hostage Schleyer. Identify and check up on persons affected. Investigate suspect items, impound or confiscate them in return for a receipt if necessary. If advisable, take photographs of the building both inside and outside . . .'

Night duty report, Stammheim, 10 September:

'20.05 hours, gave Baader a Fortral. 23.05 hours, Baader given Dolviran by medical orderly. No incidents. Very quiet.'

8
Playing for Time
(Sunday, 11 September 1977)

That night Payot passed on the third and latest ultimatum to Bonn.

A telephone call was immediately made to the German Ambassador in Geneva, Dr Sanne. He was asked if he had met Hanns Martin Schleyer in June, as the kidnappers claimed. Sanne looked at his engagements diary and said that the date had in fact been 14 July, and an American representative had also been present at the meeting.

Next day the Federal Criminal Investigation Office used the discrepancy between June and July as an excuse for telling the kidnappers, via Denis Payot, 'This information . . . is not proof that Hanns Martin Schleyer is currently alive. The BKA therefore requests the kidnappers to send with their next communication some form of proof which can be checked to show that he is alive at the time of sending.'

Also, said the BKA, the arrangements for the exchange given in the message were not precise enough. 'In the absence of any knowledge of the flight's destination and route, and without any definite agreements concerning the use of air space and landing permission, it would be impossible, on account of the experience of air personnel in the Lorenz kidnapping case, to find a crew for this possibly very dangerous assignment.'

Arrangements for the lightning operation to check and search the properties on the Bergheim list were made at 6.30 p.m. on 11 September 1977 by the Cologne District Administrator's office, under the name of Operational Order Number 2, keyword Full Check-Up.

At the Erftstadt police station they were now firmly convinced that Schleyer was being held in apartment 104 of the building at Number 8 Zum Renngraben. Rolf Breithaupt, then in charge of the Erftstadt police, said later, 'It all clearly fitted.' When he and his wife drove past the high-rise building, the chief superintendent pointed briefly up. 'He's in there.'

Breithaupt, a giant of a man at 1.90 metres tall and weighing over two hundredweight, had visited the property twice to reconnoitre it and then make plans for storming the place. He wore civilian clothes and carried a service pistol in a holster. On the third floor he walked slowly from apartment to apartment, with his colleague Kanzinger backing him up. He stopped at the door of apartment 104 too. 'I was only that far from Schleyer,' said Breithaupt later, showing the distance with his hands.

This was probably the day when Peter Jürgen Boock was in the apartment alone with Schleyer. A moment of absolute calm. There was nothing to do, no more interrogations, no statements to be drawn up. The two of them were talking quietly. Suddenly the sound of the door bell of one of the neighbouring apartments was clearly heard. Then the door bell of the next one rang, then the one after that. The ringing came closer. Finally the door bell of apartment 104 also rang. Boock wondered frantically what to do. 'If that's the cops. . . .' He reached for his submachine gun and cocked it, to show Schleyer that he must keep completely quiet. The kidnap victim understood how serious the situation was, and did not move. The footsteps outside moved away.

'Okay,' said Boock, putting down his gun. 'I think it's all clear now. We can go on talking.'

'Would you have shot me?' asked Schleyer.

Boock hesitated, and thought at the same moment that he ought not to hesitate at all at this question. It would only arouse hopes in Schleyer that could lead him to do something wrong. So Boock said very firmly: 'Yes.' But he didn't think that Schleyer believed it.

'Should the idea of letting me go ever enter your head,' replied Schleyer softly, 'I assure you I will use my influence on your behalf.'

Boock replied, 'Should the idea of running for it ever enter your head, you can be sure I'll shoot.'

Superintendent Ferdinand Schmitt, who had made the crucial inquiry, wanted to see the case to the end himself. 'I'm going in now,' he told his colleagues, but Breithaupt as his superior officer reminded him of the instructions from Cologne and Bonn – no acting on their own initiative, no risks to be taken. Breithaupt says, 'We always assumed that the BKA or GSG 9 would search the apartment.'

Night duty report, Stammheim, 11 September:

'19.30 hours, medical orderly gave Baader an injection. 23.02 hours, medicaments distributed by medical orderly. 23.45 hours, Baader asked for a Dolviran – given one. 2.20 hours, Baader asked for a Dolviran – given one. Otherwise no incidents.'

9
'The BKA Will Begin Preparations'
(Monday, 12 September 1977)

In the morning, a man of about twenty-five left a packet addressed to 'Herr von Brauchitsch, Flick KG' at the Breidenbacher Hof hotel in Düsseldorf. The envelope contained a tape recording and a letter to the Government. It began with proof that Schleyer was alive, a piece of information transcribed without capitals in the usual RAF style: 'today was my cousin anni mueller's birthday, she was born in würzburg in 1904.'

The kidnappers said they would extend their ultimatum until midnight. 'Only the prisoners themselves can give the federal government the names of countries to which they might fly.' The kidnappers said they would not respond to any more messages given to the Swiss lawyer by the BKA unless concrete steps towards an exchange were taken.

Schleyer's voice was on the tape.

'I have now – it's about midnight on 11 September 1977 – been told of the new demands made through Monsieur Payot. I am rather surprised that unilateral demands are being made again, and among other things demands for a sign that I'm alive, although I gave one quite clearly only on Saturday night. On the other hand, the main demand, the one that means life or death for me, i.e. what the decision of the Federal Government is, has not been made known . . .'

After long meetings of both the 'Smaller' and the 'Larger' Crisis Staffs, a new message to the kidnappers was drawn up, to be conveyed to them by the Swiss lawyer late that evening. 'The BKA will begin preparations. To this end the prisoners will be asked questions.' Each individual prisoner would be given a questionnaire in prison, asking if he or she was prepared to be flown out, and if so, to what country.

At midnight the kidnappers' fourth ultimatum ran out.

10
'We Don't Intend to Build up Our Potential Again'
(Tuesday, 13 September 1977)

Alfred Klaus of the BKA was given the job of visiting the Stammheim prisoners and giving them the questionnaires.

When he was taken up to the seventh floor in the morning, he met Federal Prosecutor Löchner. Shortly after 9.00 a.m., Andreas Baader was taken to the BKA man and the state prosecutor in the visiting cell at the entrance of the high-security section.

He began by trying to get information out of the policeman, but Klaus was unforthcoming. Then Baader said he wanted to discuss two points.

'If there's an exchange, then the Government needn't expect the released prisoners to come back to West Germany. We don't intend to build up our potential again. As to that, however, I can only speak for those of us who are here in Stammheim, or have been here. And what I've said won't hold good if our sentences are quashed or there's a significant political change. The Government's only alternatives are to kill the prisoners, or to release them some time or other. Flying us out would mean a lowering of tension for some time.'

Then Baader went on to his second point. 'It's in the Government's interests to avoid further escalation. So the Government ought to make an effort to find a country willing to take those prisoners whose release is being demanded.'

The BKA officer, who had listened to Baader's propositions in silence, put the questionnaire in front of him. Baader pushed it away. 'I don't want to give any information here.' Klaus talked him into at least putting his demands in writing. His impression was that Baader was very nervous, and thrown off balance by the lack of any news.

Klaus also had a feeling that the details of the kidnapping of Schleyer and the conditions bound up with it had not been agreed with the prisoners.

Under the question in the duplicated questionnaire: 'Are you prepared to be flown out?' Baader wrote: 'Yes.'

He named 'Algeria/Vietnam' as possible destinations, and added: 'We think the Government must ask the countries in question to accept us.'

Gudrun Ensslin was taken to the visiting cell the same day. To the question of whether she could suggest a destination, she replied: 'Yes – after there has been a joint consultation of all the prisoners whose release or exchange is demanded by the commando.'

Klaus visited the other prisoners on the seventh floor in their cells. He was startled by the chaotic state of the cells occupied by Verena Becker, Irmgard Möller and Jan-Carl Raspe. There were books lying around everywhere, and the prisoners obviously slept on mattresses on the floor. Raspe too made the answer to the question about a destination conditional on a joint conversation between the prisoners, and so did Irmgard Möller. Verena Becker wrote 'Yes' under the question: 'Are you prepared to be flown out?' and 'No' under the question: 'Can you name a destination?'

When Klaus had given the questionnaires to the other prisoners, Baader asked to see him again, and added Libya, the People's Republic of Yemen and Iraq as possible destinations.

That morning, appeals from several lawyers against being barred from contact with their clients arrived at the Constitutional Court in Karlsruhe.

At about the same time, the kidnappers called Denis Payot's office in Geneva. 'We ask Monsieur Payot to reject the role assigned to him by the Federal Government, whose sole and only function is to delay and postpone a decision, so as to gain room to manoeuvre for a military solution.'

Marking time in the so-called secret negotiations, they said, was absurd when one considered the aim of the operation: the release of the prisoners. 'The Government has not taken a single concrete step over these last nine days to signal that they really are prepared to exchange Schleyer. The BKA's announcement that the hunt would be called off was a joke. Every newspaper carries photographs of road-blocks and reports of apartments that have been stormed,' said the caller. 'We are giving the Government a last deadline: they must meet our demands by midnight tonight.'

At this the Criminal Investigation Office said it would have the questionnaires filled in by the prisoners taken to Payot by special messenger. The Smaller Crisis Staff decided that 'as a positive sign to the kidnappers' they would start exploratory talks with the governments of Algeria and Libya, named by Andreas Baader as possible destinations. Payot was to tell the kidnappers this too.

The keyword 'Full Check-Up' to start the search of all possible hiding-places for Schleyer, including the Erftstadt apartment, was never given. Instead, on 13 September at 6.32 p.m., the first clause of the operational order was changed to the effect that 'searches of properties may be carried out only if there is a search warrant in accordance with §105, paragraph I, of the Criminal Code'.

But no decision to carry out searches was made either in Erftstadt or in the supervising centre at the offices of the chief district administrator in Bergheim.

Schleyer was now spending his eighth day in apartment 104, which had already fallen under suspicion six days ago.

Tentative attempts made by the head of the Kripo to discover, from the Soko special commission and the offices of the chief district administrator in Bergheim, what had become of the list of properties were speedily dismissed. The officers in charge of the Soko unit firmly requested Kripo Commissioner Breuer to 'desist from further questions because,' it was claimed, 'dealing with them takes up too much time and organization.' In addition, the Cologne regional authority stated on 13 September that properties listed for checking in Telex 827 had been evaluated by the Soko and placed before the chief federal prosecutor for 'investigation with regard to measures that might lead to criminal proceedings (searches)'. Obviously no such thing had been done, but the local police officers in Erftstadt, who were firmly convinced that Schleyer was being held captive in apartment 104, could at least feel vaguely hopeful that something was going on, if the Soko was investigating on its own initiative all the time in their area, although without telling the local officers. Thus, in theory at least, there was a chance that the BKA or GSG 9, a special operational unit of the Federal Border Police, might be planning something under cover.

But they were not. The telex with the information about Schleyer's hiding-place had been mislaid somewhere.

Night duty report, Stammheim, 13 September:

'For incidents, see separate report.'

In this report, which ran to almost three pages, Prison Officer Wolf recorded conversations between the prisoners.

The prison officers had often seen the ban on contact between the prisoners on the seventh floor – and with it the prevention of opportunities to communicate among themselves – being circumvented: if the prisoners stood on stools in their cells and put their mouths close to the air-slits in the doors, they could call out to each other. The prison officers were not happy about this. To prove to their superior officers that the prisoners really were exchanging information, Prison Officer Wolf went to sit in a cell on the other side of the grating outside the high-security section that night. From there, he could hear what the prisoners were saying.

At 7.15 p.m. he made a note that the occupant of Cell 715 called out, 'What can you hear, what have you heard? It's empty underneath me.' It was Baader, telling his fellow prisoners that the cell under his was unoccupied, so he couldn't listen in to any news from the sixth floor.

Raspe, in Cell 725, said, 'Empty underneath me too.'

Baader asked again, 'Jan, how about you? Nothing?'

'Didn't hear anything yesterday evening either,' Raspe shouted.

Baader replied, 'I don't get this.'

Irmgard Möller called through the slit in the door of Cell 718, 'Say that again.'

'I don't get it. Meetings and so on, who's messing about?' asked Baader.

At 7.20 p.m. the officer cautioned the prisoners and made a note of it: 'Cautioned them for the first time.'

Five minutes later Baader called, 'Hey, Gudrun, Jan, she's answering everyone, Gabi. Possible countries in sequence: Algeria, Libya, Yemen, Iraq.'

The officer noted: 'Rest of conversation difficult to understand.'

At 7.30 p.m. Gudrun Ensslin joined in their laborious shouted conversation from Cell 720.

'Provoking another warning,' noted the prison officer.

'A very long week,' called Jan-Carl Raspe.

Baader said, 'Pure drivel on the other side!'

Then they wondered whether a helicopter had landed or not. 'Could be,' said Raspe.

At 7.35 p.m., Baader dictated something about a hand-over to the others. He spoke so fast that the officer couldn't write it all down. Then he was able to copy Baader's cryptic remarks again: 'Amazing, Wehner's talking about perversion.'

Then Baader asked the officer for sleeping pills and Dolviran.

Raspe wanted soap to wash himself.

Soon after that Baader called again, 'Hey, Jan, are those crisis staffs still at it?'

Raspe obviously knew something more. 'That conversation with Schmidt takes place this evening.'

'Who's involved?' Baader called.

'The European Commission has declared solidarity with Federal Germany,' shouted Raspe through the slit in the door.

Baader shouted, 'Oh, so they say they're all agreed! Jan, this could go on for ever. I've heard stuff about summary justice, execution. The guy underneath me always listens to the radio commentaries. They were against it.'

At 11.50 p.m. the prisoners were warned to keep quiet again.

The officer noted down, 'Baader in a bad temper.'

Quarter of an hour after midnight Baader demanded Dolviran.

Soon after that all fell quiet. The officer wrote, 'No more incidents until end of the shift; all quiet.'

These conversations were reported to Inspector Bubeck by telephone. He arranged to have mattresses put across the cell doors as a temporary measure: next day they would think of something else.

That same day, 13 September 1977, Andreas Baader was moved from Cell 719 to Cell 715.

After the deaths of the Stammheim prisoners, an empty hiding-place into which a gun would have fitted was found in the window wall of this cell.

When he had been moved to Cell 715 he called the prison officers again and asked them to bring him his coffee things. An officer looked around in Cell 719 – and found a black Minox camera and its film cassette inside the box of coffee filters. The film had not been exposed.

11
A Journey, a Cry for Help and a Communications System
(Wednesday, 14 September 1977)

At midnight the fifth ultimatum had run out.

Just after midnight the telephone rang in the Stuttgart home of Hanns-Eberhard Schleyer, Hanns Martin Schleyer's son. His wife picked up the phone.

'Good evening, Frau Schleyer, I would like to read you the commando's statement. Would you like to . . .'

Frau Schleyer had had the kidnappers on the phone once already the previous day. 'You're the same person who rang yesterday, if I remember correctly, aren't you?'

'That's right, yes. Would you like to write this message down?'

'A very funny question,' said Frau Schleyer. 'What is it, then?'

'I'll be happy to read you out this statement. Though only if you're interested?'

'Rather a curious question, don't you think?' replied Frau Schleyer.

She picked up a pencil and took down the caller's words. 'Marking time in the so-called secret negotiations . . .' said the caller.

'Mm, yes.'

He went on dictating. '. . . is absurd, considering the aim of the operation.'

'Isn't the aim of it absurd too?' asked Frau Schleyer.

'. . . is absurd, considering the aim of the operation: the release of the prisoners. As for the infamous calculation of the Government . . .'

'The what?' asked Frau Schleyer.

'. . . the infamous calculation of the Government.'

'You dare use the word infamous? I don't believe it,' said Frau Schleyer, and she took down the rest of the statement.

At 8.00 a.m., Minister of State Wischnewski took off on a flight to Algeria and Libya, as a signal to the kidnappers that the Federal Government was genuinely going to try to find a country willing to accept the RAF prisoners.

At about mid-day, the kidnappers rang Denis Payot in Geneva again. They suggested televising the prisoners' departure by air that night on both German television channels, two hours after normal close-down.

That afternoon, a packet containing a videotape arrived at the Bonn office of Agence France Presse. The tape was of Schleyer sitting in front of a placard showing the RAF symbol, and saying:

'I am turning to the public, and I hope there are enough independent journalists who will be ready to publish these reflections of mine.

'The very circumstances that led to my capture on 5 September clearly show that the precautions taken by the Criminal Investigation Office were unsatisfactory, their surveillance totally inadequate, and that many circumstances contributed to making it very easy for my kidnappers to attack me. None the less, I have repeatedly said that I entirely go along with the Government's decisions – whatever they may be. But now that the Government and the political parties have begun negotiations, telling my family and myself and the public again and again that what they want in the final analysis is for me to be released alive, my own wish to survive has naturally increased, and I am following the measures taken by the BKA more and more closely. In my view those measures consist of tricks which are supposed to gain the BKA time to find my kidnappers.

'However, if they track my kidnappers down, that means my death; my kidnappers will be forced to kill me . . .

'I am deeply concerned that this approach may mean the mistakes which have been made will have to be covered up by my death. And there have been many such mistakes over the last few days.'

The use of a go-between, he added, the repeated requests for more signs of life, the alleged transport problems of the exchange of prisoners, all reinforced his suspicions. In self-protection, he wanted to say so publicly.

'As for the rest, I would like to tell my family that in the circumstances I am reasonably well, I am in good health and in full possession of my mental faculties, and not under the influence of drugs . . .'

If he were exchanged for the prisoners, he said, he could go home to his family safe and well.

* * *

That day, padding to prevent contact between the prisoners in Stammheim was fitted to their cells: sheets of chipboard covered with plastic foam which were heaved into position outside the doors of the seventh-floor cells at night, to stop the prisoners calling out to each other.

It is doubtful whether the prison officers really thought this would prevent all communication.

During their years of joint residence on the seventh floor, prisoners and warders had to some extent come to know each other. Horst Bubeck, for instance, knew that Jan-Carl Raspe, to whom Gudrun Ensslin had given the name of 'Carpenter', was remarkably good with his hands.

The prison officers and the regional Criminal Investigation officers who had frequently searched the cells also knew that Raspe in particular had a great many electrical parts, cables, plugs, and so forth. They had even found a microphone in his cell, which he was allowed to keep. Allegedly, the officers had no idea what the prisoners did with these things.

Only after the death of the prisoners on the seventh floor did BKA officers and a Federal Mail engineer reconstruct the uses to which the prisoners had put all this material.

The prison authorities should really have been forewarned, for only three years before some ingenious prisoners in Stammheim had developed an inter-cell communications system. They had used the transmission system bringing radio programmes into the cells until 10.00 p.m.; they tapped it at night and fed in a programme of their own, using a radio set and a cassette recorder.

'A few tips for you today, listeners. If you can't stand the boring food, if you don't get enough chance for sport, or you have any other problems, keep on complaining, keep on writing letters. The more the better. This is Stammheim III saying goodbye for now.' And so on.

When the prison officers discovered the Stammheim radio pirates' location and means of operation, the transmission system was short-circuited at night, and thus rendered useless for unofficial broadcasting.

In 1974, one of the prison officers, the electrician Halouska, helped to clamp down on the imprisoned broadcasters' activities.

Three years later, in the summer of 1977, at the request of the prisoner Irmgard Möller and with the knowledge of the prison administration, Halouska disconnected the radio wires in her cell from the transmission system covering the whole building. This meant that the earthing at night was no longer effective, and the circuit on the seventh floor could be secretly used.

The wires ran from Irmgard Möller's cell to the far end of the section, where Gudrun Ensslin occupied Cell 720, and then crossed the corridor to Andreas Baader's cell opposite, Cell 719. Raspe's cell was separated from Baader's by the stairwell, so he could not be contacted via the loudspeaker cable, which stopped short at this point.

However, there was a second distribution network in the high-security section, the alternating-current circuit for the infirmary area, which ran parallel to the normal power supply. It was meant for electric shavers, and the current was switched on only at certain times. When the electricity was switched off, this electric shaver circuit could be used for communication too. These two circuits, running on both sides of the section, were not linked. Only if the radio wires were connected up to the shaver circuit would communication all over the section be possible. All that was needed was a 'bridge', and it was possible to construct one in Baader's cell, 719, and Cell 718. A junction cable which would do the job was found there after his death.

All the prisoners' cells in the high-security section were thus wired up to each other, and all that was needed for a working intercom system was transmitters and receivers.

These were present in every cell: the amplifiers and loudspeakers of the prisoners' stereo systems, which could be run off the mains as well as by batteries. The prisoners had been allowed to keep their stereo equipment even when the ban on contact with each other came into force.

Any loudspeaker and headset can be used as a microphone if it is connected up properly, and an interposed amplifier will provide the power.

After the death of the prisoners, engineers found equipment adapted in this way in their cells. They said that with a little practice, it was possible to construct a perfect intercom system out of the material in the cells within ten to sixty seconds. The adaptations made to the loudspeakers, amplifiers and electrical circuits could not be explained in any other way. The Federal Mail engineer, Otto Bohner, who inspected the system after the death of the prisoners, was surprised that the adaptations had not been noticed before, although regional BKA officers, one of them an engineer, had searched the record players, loudspeakers and amplifiers more than once.

12
Outside and Inside
(Thursday, 15 September 1977)

An hour before midnight, Schleyer's kidnappers telephoned Denis Payot in Geneva again, suggesting a flight path over Italy, Yugoslavia, Libya, Egypt or the Gulf States.

'In any case, we would exclude a route passing over Israel, Morocco or Ethiopia,' said the caller. For the rest, he added, the Federal Government was to ask the countries named as destinations by the prisoners to take them in.

Meanwhile it had become clear to the kidnap commando that the apartment in Erftstadt was no longer safe. They now knew that the police were going from building to building, checking up on apartments which fitted Herold's criteria for properties that could be used for subversive activities. The group had already prepared a new hiding-place in Holland, but the rental agreement for the apartment in The Hague had not been signed yet. Brigitte Mohnhaupt travelled to the Netherlands to hurry the arrangements along.

Their victim was to be moved as inconspicuously as possible; they called the process 'potting on'. They wanted an outsize case or some kind of basket for the purpose. Each of the group had seen something of the kind somewhere, but no one knew where you went to buy one. They thought of everything from a tin trunk to a portable cupboard, until in the end they found an enormous wicker basket.

Schleyer had to climb into the basket and was taken down to the underground garage in the lift. There they loaded the basket into an estate car that took it to the green border with Holland. On the other side another estate car had driven to the border. The basket and its contents were transferred. Then it drove along the motorway to The Hague.

The transfer must have taken place on 16 September at the latest, because from that day on no more electricity was used in the Erftstadt apartment, as the meter showed in later reconstructions.

Eleven days had passed, eleven days in which Schleyer could have been liberated from an apartment that was known to the police.

13
'. . . And Wanted the Radio Turned Down'
(Friday, 16 September 1977)

The kidnappers called Payot again. They complained that the only reason why the countries named by the prisoners as destinations had not yet said they were prepared to accept them was lack of effort on the part of the West German Government. 'We would like to know exactly at what level and with whom contact has been made.' Delay, they added, would hardly be in Herr Schleyer's interests.

The Criminal Investigation Office answered briefly, 'Contact made at ministerial level.' They then asked for another sign of life from Schleyer.

The kidnappers responded that night, gave the requested sign of life, and suggested ways of releasing Schleyer. Once the plane carrying the prisoners had landed safely, and their fellow travellers Payot and Pastor Niemöller were back, Schleyer would be released within forty-eight hours. He would be able to call his family by phone as soon as he was released.

Most of the members of the kidnap commando group were to be withdrawn and go to Baghdad. Flights were hastily booked, tickets bought, passports prepared.

Stefan Wisniewski, as operational leader of the commando, was to stay in Europe along with a few of the other group members and guard Schleyer. New quarters were prepared for them from The Hague, this time in Brussels. From there, Peter Jürgen Boock flew to Baghdad by way of Cairo. For him, it came as a relief. 'It was like we'd been on speed all this time. First the preparations, then the operation. And then you're finished, your nerves are in shreds, you're exhausted.' He had asked Brigitte Mohnhaupt if she felt that way too, and she had said yes, it was exactly the same for her.

Friederike Krabbe and Monika Helbing, who had rented the Erftstadt apartment as Frau Lottmann-Bücklers, had flown to Baghdad ahead of them to find accommodation. When Boock and Mohnhaupt arrived, the RAF already had two places to choose from.

At first they stayed in the smaller apartment, then they moved into the larger one, which was in the middle of the diplomatic quarter of Baghdad.

As soon as they arrived, Brigitte Mohnhaupt had a brief meeting with Abu Hani, with whom the next steps were to be discussed: arrangements for receiving members of the group, financial questions. The group had originally intended to demand 100,000 marks from the Federal Government for each of the prisoners released – so with eleven prisoners on the list it would come to a million marks in all. But Abu Hani had said, 'If they'll pay that, they'd go up to ten million. If they really want the exchange made, the amount won't come into it.' Later Brigitte complained to Boock of 'that old materialist'. It was the political dimension that mattered after all, she said; this wasn't a bank raid. In the end they demanded a million marks for each of the prisoners, as Abu Hani had suggested.

Night duty report, Stammheim, 16 September:

'21.50 hours, Baader asked for a Dolviran and wanted the radio turned down.

'23.00 hours, with medical orderly, gave Baader medicine. No incidents. Very quiet.'

Obviously the prisoners could follow radio programmes from the cells below them – and the prison officers were aware of it.

14
A Routine Day in a Kidnapping
(Monday, 19 September 1977)

Questions and answers designed to show that Schleyer was still alive went back and forth, and still no decisions were made.

Denis Payot told the BKA he was not prepared to accompany the prisoners on their flight. If need be, he said, he would fly to their destination separately so that he could convey Baader's message to the kidnappers.

The kidnappers were getting impatient. They told the BKA, 'All we have to say is that we are not going to spend another fortnight negotiating. That's just for your information . . .'

Night duty report, Stammheim, 19 September:

'At 23.05 hours, Baader and Raspe given medicine by the medical orderly. No incidents.'

15
A Special Law
(Tuesday, 20 September 1977)

Minister of State Wischnewski returned from Aden.

That same morning, the justice ministers of the *Länder* met in Bonn to exchange notes on their experiences with the contact ban imposed on the prisoners. Some courts had ruled that lawyers might visit their clients in spite of the ban. However, they had not been allowed into the prisons. That was clearly a violation of the law: the executive had gone over the heads of the courts. The contact ban, for which there was no legal basis, had been ordered on the grounds of an appeal to Paragraph 34 of the Criminal Code, legitimizing actions normally contrary to the law in an emergency. The principle expressed in Paragraph 34, known as 'justifiable emergency', allows infringements of the law if higher legal values are thereby protected. Most lawyers agreed that only a citizen and not the state itself can appeal to 'justifiable emergency'.

This was perfectly clear to the justice ministers. In addition, several Baader–Meinhof lawyers had applied to the Constitutional Court to give an interim ruling. The highest court in the land was to decide whether, in the case of the contact ban, an appeal to justifiable emergency could be reconciled with the Basic Law at all. This put the Federal

Government and the regional justice ministers in a very awkward situation. If the judges in the Constitutional Court decided that the state's application of Paragraph 34 in this particular case and in general was lawful, there would have been considerable consequences in constitutional law: 'justifiable emergency' would have been approved as the equivalent of an Enabling Act in exceptional situations, and nobody really wanted that.

On the other hand, if the decision of the judges in Karlsruhe went the other way, the Government would have received a resounding slap in the face while in an extremely tense situation, and nobody wanted that either.

In this dilemma, the regional justice ministers, together with Federal Justice Minister Vogel, decided to take a third way, though it was hardly less problematic. A law was to be passed in a hurry creating a legal basis for the contact ban, of whose necessity they were all, except for the Berlin representative, convinced.

The process of legislation in the Bundestag is complicated and wearisome. Months if not years usually elapse between the introduction of a bill and its becoming an act. It was different with the law on the contact ban. Once introduced, the bill took all parliamentary hurdles at unprecedented speed. Within a week, a law had been passed giving the justice ministers the right to cut the prisoners off completely from contact with each other and the outside world. The application of the law assumed that danger to a person's life and limb or freedom existed, and there were good grounds for suspecting that such danger proceeded from a terrorist association. The ban on contact might last for a maximum of thirty days, and must be confirmed by a court after two weeks. However, isolation could be reimposed if a judge thought the relevant pre-conditions again existed.

16
A Shoot-out
(Thursday, 22 September 1977)

That afternoon, the kidnappers called Payot again: what answers had Minister of State Wischnewski brought back with him from Algeria, Libya, Iraq, the People's Republic of Yemen or any other countries?

The Criminal Investigation Office replied: 'We expect answers to our questions from the four destination countries shortly.'

Soon after 5.00 p.m. the BKA received a report that the presumed terrorist Knut Folkerts had been arrested in Utrecht after a shoot-out. A Dutch policeman had been killed and two more severely injured.

The BKA officer Georg Pohl was sent to Holland to make Folkerts an offer. 'A new identity, a million Deutschmarks, and the prospect of emigration to the United States. No reaction, he didn't even deign to answer me.'

Folkerts confirms this, but has something else to add. 'At the time of the Schleyer kidnapping, I was offered a million marks and free passage out of the country. The other half of this offer was the threat of hanging.' Which of course the BKA officer denies.

17
Investigations
(Saturday, 24 September 1977)

About mid-day, one of the kidnappers called Payot's law office. 'We are just wondering how long Monsieur Payot is going to play this game. We are coming to feel we have no time and no inclination to play it ourselves. End of message.'

The Criminal Investigation Office was lying in wait for calls to Payot. His office phones were being tapped.

The BKA had also wired the telephone lines to find out where his calls came from. This expensive operation produced the information that all calls to Payot were made from public telephone kiosks, most of them near Cologne railway station. If the police unobtrusively turned up at the kiosks in question, the caller had disappeared.

Several calls had also been made to Payot from the Gare du Nord railway station in Paris. The BKA obviously got this information from the French authorities. Moreover, out of over a hundred letters from the kidnappers during Schleyer's six weeks of captivity, at least fourteen were sent from France. The stamps on these letters, the investigators discovered, had all come from the same stamp machine at the Gare du Nord. The saliva with which the stamps had been moistened was always that of the same person.

To get on this person's trail, everyone between the ages of twenty and thirty-five who travelled on the seventy trains a day running between Cologne and Paris was checked with particular care.

By now the police knew the people likely to get letters from the kidnappers, mainly newspaper offices, radio stations, news agencies and private persons such as Eberhard von Brauchitsch. All the letters were marked 'Urgent – for immediate attention!'

The main post offices of West Germany were told to look out for such letters and give them to the police. On 13 September, postal workers in Dortmund were successful. They fished five letters from the kidnappers out of 500,000 items of mail. Three other letters which had also been posted in Dortmund got through the net. Only these three items reached their destination without a detour by way of the BKA first.

18
A Journey around the World
(Sunday, 25 September 1977)

The BKA sent a message to the kidnappers: 'Of those countries so far approached at ministerial level, Libya and South Yemen have refused, two have not yet given a final answer. In the circumstances, the country named last by Baader, Vietnam, has also been approached. We will send further information about progress.'

Late that evening, Minister of State Wischnewski flew to Vietnam.

Meanwhile, the core group of the RAF had landed in Baghdad. A few days after their arrival, an old acquaintance suddenly turned up. Johannes Weinrich had once belonged to the 'Revolutionary Cells', but then joined the legendary terrorist Carlos and his group. The core members of the RAF felt rather cool about him, and he did not meet with a very friendly welcome. Even Weinrich's looks did not appeal to Boock and the others. He was like a successful young businessman in his faultless suit, with a small bag dangling from his wrist. Weinrich quickly came to the point: 'Abu Hani wonders why you don't ask him to join you in an operation.' Schleyer's kidnappers had not previously thought of this idea. They had intended to wait until Helmut Schmidt finally gave in. If the crisis couldn't be resolved in the foreseeable future, they thought he would probably resign, so they had only to play for time.

'Well, thanks for telling me,' Brigitte Mohnhaupt answered dismissively. 'I'll think about it. And I'll mention it at the next routine discussion with Abu Hani.' She indicated to Weinrich that he could go now. Boock was surprised that Abu Hani had sent the German assistant of the legendary Carlos to see them rather than one of his own men.

At the next meeting with Abu Hani they did broach the subject of an operation that might be carried out with his aid, and to their great surprise he immediately came up with two ideas. 'Preparations have been made for both,' he told them. 'You only have to choose.' One operation would be a hostage-taking in the German embassy in Kuwait, the other the hijacking of an aircraft taking holiday-makers from Palma de Mallorca back to Frankfurt.

They rejected the plan to occupy the embassy in Kuwait at once; the experiences of Stockholm were still too fresh in their minds. The hijacking was not really much to their liking either, or at least not in the form suggested. More than once the prisoners in Stammheim had indicated that they were not particularly keen on being freed by means of blackmail after the hijacking of an aircraft carrying civilian passengers or holiday-makers. However, the group agreed to this idea, and sent a member back to Europe at once to tell the commando group with Schleyer about this new development.

A few days later Abu Hani came to see Boock again. 'We've been trying something out,' he said. 'If you want to take weapons through electronic security controls, you line the inside of a case or a cosmetics bag with lead foil. Then they can't see what's inside it, and it will show up in the X-ray device as a black hole.' Did Boock have a better idea, he asked.

'Weapons?' asked Boock. 'Weapons could mean all kinds of things. Do they have to be used for real or just as a threat?'

Abu Hani thought for a moment. 'They really need to be there to keep things under control, as a threat. If they have to be used for real then things are going wrong anyway.'

Boock realized that it was hand grenades they needed, and thought about it. 'In that case I'd make them out of plastic or glass.'

A few days later Abu Hani came back and presented Boock with a hand grenade of the Russian kind. It was made of glass painted olive green, and looked just the same as a real hand grenade with a steel jacket. However, it had only the explosive force of a harmless banger, not the devastating effect of a splintering metal jacket.

Later it was discovered that the hand grenades smuggled on board the Landshut by the hijack commando group were made of plastic. When one of them exploded during the operation to liberate the hostages at Mogadishu, its effect was indeed very slight.

Some time later Boock received a message saying that Abu Hani wanted to meet him in Algiers. With Brigitte Mohnhaupt, who was to be responsible for co-ordination between the hijackers of the aircraft and the group members guarding Schleyer, he flew to the Algerian capital by way of Cairo and Tripoli. They stayed in a house belonging to the Algerian secret service, five or six kilometres outside Algiers.

Brigitte Mohnhaupt conducted negotiations with Abu Hani, in the main over the division of the increased sum of money to be paid as ransom in addition to the freeing of the prisoners. Then she used a specially secured and allegedly bug-proof telephone belonging to the Algerian secret service to phone one of Schleyer's guards in Paris.

Brigitte Mohnhaupt had been conducting most of the discussions with Abu Hani by herself. Then Rolf Clemens Wagner arrived from Paris to discuss ways of co-ordinating the holding of Schleyer with the hijacking, and brought with him medication urgently needed for Boock. The two of them now talked to Abu Hani, discussing the joint commando statement, how to exchange hostages for the prisoners and the money, and the division of the 15 million marks demanded. Then Wagner left again. Soon afterwards Rolf Heissler also arrived from Brussels, received his final orders, and went back to join the group guarding Schleyer.

Brigitte Mohnhaupt flew back from Algiers to Baghdad with Boock. There she called the group together in the big house and told them what kind of operation was going to take place in the next few days. 'There was squabbling almost at once,' says Boock, 'because a few people were brave enough to say: look, this kind of contradicts our own statement. But Brigitte Mohnhaupt got very heated and came up with the old killer argument again: "So what do you want? Do you want to get them out or do you want them to die in jail? What do *you* think we ought to do? Show me an alternative!" Everyone fell silent, and the subject was closed.'

The decision in favour of hijacking the aircraft, wrote group member Rolf Heissler later in a privately circulated document, 'was one we didn't make lightly. After long discussions, we agreed on Operation Kofre Kaddum, to be carried out by the Martyr Halimeh commando.'

The PFLP set to work at once. Forged Iranian passports were produced in a forger's workshop in Baghdad for the PFLP members who, it was planned, would attack the plane. Souhaila Sayeh was now Soraya Ansari, Zohair Akache got a passport in the name of Ali Hyderi, Nabil Harb became Riza Abbasi, and Nadia Shehadah was Shahnaz Gholam.

The alleged Persians had been born in the Lebanon and Israel. 'Shahnaz Gholam' aged twenty-two; was a Lebanese Christian by birth. 'Riza Abbasi', aged twenty-three, had been born in Beirut. 'Ali Hyderi' was born in 1954, in the Palestinian refugee camp of Burj-el-Brajneh, on the outskirts of Beirut. His parents had fled from Israel in 1948.

Souhaila Sami Andrawes Sayeh ('Soraya Ansari') was born on 28 March

1953 in Hadath in Lebanon. Her Palestinian family came from Haifa, but had to leave after the founding of the state of Israel. Her parents settled in East Beirut, and became quite prosperous. Souhaila was brought up a Christian and went to one of the best schools in Lebanon, a girls' school run by French nuns in Beirut. In 1965 her parents moved to Kuwait. Souhaila had to go to a Muslim school, but left it a short time later to become a nun. For that purpose she would have had to move to the Arab part of Jerusalem, but immediately before she left the Six Days' War broke out. Souhaila stayed in Kuwait and left school, with a school-leaving certificate that was one of the three best out of those gained by 10,000 candidates for higher education in her year. However, she did not get a university place because she was not a Kuwaiti citizen, and did not have good enough connections. She went back to Lebanon, where she studied English language and literature.

Gradually, she became politicized by family members who told her about their old home in Palestine.

At the beginning of 1977, Souhaila travelled to Aden for military training on the instructions of the PFLP. She was twice invited home by the leader of the PFLP camp, Zaki Helou, and met his German wife Amal – Monika Haas. She went back to Kuwait, but in October was sent to Baghdad again. Here she met the PFLP members Zohair Akache, Nabil Harb and Nadia Shehadah, of whom she had met only Nadia already, at Beirut University. Abu Hani in person came and delivered her a lecture on the political situation and the planned operation. The hijacking of the aircraft was given the name of Operation Kofre Kaddum, while the hijackers themselves were to be known as the Martyr Halimeh Commando. Kofre Kaddum, she learned, was a Palestinian village that had been razed to the ground by Israeli soldiers. The name of the commando group was intended to evoke memories of the failed hijacking of a French plane in Entebbe. Two Germans, Wilfried Böse, cover name Mahmud, and Brigitte Kuhlmann, cover name Halimeh, had been among the commandos shot by the Israelis. The new hijack commando was thus to be called Martyr Halimeh, and its leader, Zohair Akache, was to appear under the name of Captain Mahmud.

The passports were complete forgeries, the names pure fiction. Separately, and travelling light, the four of them left Baghdad for Mallorca.

The four did not have weapons with them; those were to be brought to Mallorca by a different route. Only eighteen years later did the Federal Prosecutor's Office bring charges against a woman and a man who, they thought, had acted as couriers for weapons and explosives. According to the investigations made by agents in Karlsruhe, the PFLP had given the job of smuggling these weapons to Mallorca to Monika Haas, the wife of Wadi Haddad's deputy, Zaki Helou, and an accomplice with the cover name of Kamal Sarvati, later identified as a certain Said Slim.

19
Jan-Carl Raspe and the Word 'We'
(Tuesday, 27 September 1977)

On this day, the kidnappers sent letters to various newspapers and news agencies, to Payot and Eberhard von Brauchitsch:

'No more proof that Schleyer is alive will be given except in connection with concrete indications of the exchange.' Even if the Government was trying to keep the result of Minister of State Wischnewski's negotiations from the kidnappers, said the letters, they knew for sure that there were countries which would be ready to accept the eleven prisoners.

On his chief commissioner's instructions, Alfred Klaus flew to Stammheim by helicopter. He arrived at 6.30 p.m.

Quarter of an hour later, Raspe was brought into the visiting room. 'I have something to add to the questionnaires,' he said. 'I can put a few more countries on the list.' Then he gave the BKA man a sheet of paper with a prepared typewritten statement:

'If the Government is really trying to make this exchange, and supposing the countries already named – Algeria, Libya, Vietnam, Iraq, South Yemen – will not take us, we would suggest several other countries: Angola, Mozambique, Guinea-Bissau, Ethiopia. 27.9.77, Raspe.'

Alfred Klaus took the list, looked at Raspe, and said, 'The word "we" and your listing of the five countries already named by Baader must mean you've been in touch with each other.' Raspe looked confused, but said nothing. He signed the original and the copy of his statement, and asked Klaus to send it on to the crisis staff.

'Have you anything else to say?' asked the BKA man.

Jan-Carl Raspe replied, 'The length of time all this is taking leads one to suppose that a police solution is intended. That would mean you were on course for a political catastrophe; I mean dead prisoners.'

As for the rest, he said, the prisoners' isolation from the outside world was now total. He couldn't see why they weren't at least allowed to communicate with each other inside the prison, particularly as their isolation was obviously going to be made legal and thus put on a different plane. 'If no decision is made, we may continue in this state for another three months.'

'My own view,' said Alfred Klaus, 'is that a message from the prisoners for the kidnap operation to be ended would remedy that.'

At the end of the conversation, Raspe said, 'Whether we're accepted by the countries named depends on how hard the Government is trying.'

When Raspe was taken back to his cell, Alfred Klaus told Inspector Bubeck, who had been present during the conversation, that the prisoners could obviously communicate with each other. Thereupon Bubeck took the BKA man into the corridor outside the cells and showed him the padded panels which were supposed to make verbal contact from cell to cell impossible at night.

20
The Arrest of Volker Speitel
(Sunday, 2 October 1977)

At midnight the contact ban law, which had been passed by the Bundestag, came into force. Two minutes later, the Federal Justice Minister imposed the ban on seventy-two prisoners, and sent telexes to that effect to the legal administrative bodies of the *Länder*. A state of affairs which had already been in existence for three weeks was thus legalized.

The BKA sent another message to the kidnappers, demanding another sign of life from Schleyer, and saying, 'In the present state of the negotiations, there can be no question of bringing the prisoners together.'

The kidnappers, added the BKA, obviously entertained entirely false expectations of the willingness of those countries named as destinations to accept the prisoners. However, the Federal Government was prepared to make further efforts.

A few days earlier, Volker Speitel, who had acted as courier between the Stammheim prisoners and the 'illegal' groups outside, had gone to Denmark along with other sympathizers to prepare a demonstration against the contact ban. After the demonstration, one of his women companions said later, they were going on to Greece to organize a similar operation there. Speitel had called Croissant's Stuttgart office on 30 September and learned that the police were looking for him.

None the less, Volker Speitel boarded a train on 2 October 1977 and went back to West Germany. He was arrested soon after crossing the border.

21
Medication
(Monday, 3 October 1977)

Night duty report, Stammheim:

'23.10 hours, medication given to Baader and Raspe.

'1.25 hours, Baader asked for Optipyrin. Given at 1.30 hours.'

After the contact ban came into operation on 5 September, the prisoners on the seventh floor, particularly Baader and Raspe, seem to have had all the medication they cared to ask for. Fortral capsules, Optipyrin capsules, Dolviran tablets, Tradon pills, Xitix tablets, Paracodin cough mixture, Adalin tablets, Dolantin injections, Novadral pills, repository Impletol injections . . .

Adalin, Dolviran, Optipyrin and Paracodin in particular, said the Commission of Inquiry later, 'can also be taken to induce a sense of well-being'.

It was the classic mixture of uppers and downers: strong analgesic stimulants and hypnotics.

Andreas Baader used to take a special mixture of Dolviran tablets, barbiturates and Coca-Cola in Berlin in the early sixties. The prison officers in Stammheim served him his drugs every evening. Later, at the post mortem on him, the forensic experts found traces of all kinds of pharmaceutical preparations in his urine: phenobarbital, secobarbital, salicylic acid, salicyluronic acid, pyrarolon derivatives, paracetamol, p-aminophenol, carbromal and metybolite with bromide, codeine, marphine, pantazocine, dihydrocodeine, nicotineo and caffeine.

However, said the doctors, one could not conclude from this that the prisoner's mind was confused.

22
Searches: A Tower Block and a Lawyer's Office
(Tuesday, 4 October 1977)

About 2.00 a.m. the investigating judge of the Federal High Court issued a warrant for the detention in custody of Volker Speitel and the woman companion arrested with him in the express train from Denmark.

On the same day, police officers began searching the Am Kölnberg tower block in Meschenich. After two days, they came upon Apartment 1919, which had been rented by one Cornelia B. on I June. On 23 September, she had given notice in writing that she would be leaving on 30 September, and gave her new address as the Park Lane Hotel in London. The investigators concluded, from the reports of handwriting experts and by showing photographs to employees of the estate agency letting the apartments, that Angelika Speitel had been the tenant of No 1919.

She was Volker Speitel's wife. Allegedly, it was not until months later that he stated he had known the Am Kölnberg apartment was used by Schleyer's kidnappers.

However, when they were searching the block between 4 and 6 October, BKA officers showed the neighbours photographs of Angelika Speitel.

Four days' surveillance of the car in the underground garage had produced no results; it was now opened up, with the help of a winch, in case there were explosives hidden inside. In the boot, the investigators found a button from one of Hanns Martin Schleyer's cuffs. The officers deduced that the president of the Employers' Association had been taken to his first hiding-place in the boot of this car after the attack.

The same day, 4 October, Klaus Croissant's law offices in Stuttgart were searched again. The previous search had been less than a week before, and afterwards the offices were sealed.

No official explanation was given for the second search. However, it is worth noticing that in his evidence – which he allegedly did not begin to give until very much later – Volker Speitel mentioned some special hiding-places in the filing room of Croissant's offices. Other details from his interrogation also allow one to conclude that Volker Speitel actually began to talk on 4 October.

He himself, his lawyer and the Federal Prosecutor's Office have always denied this. Had Speitel begun to talk earlier, it might have been suspected that he had told the authorities there were guns in Stammheim before the prisoners' deaths. No full record of Speitel's interrogation was ever published.

On 4 October, Andreas Baader was moved from Cell 715 in Stammheim, to which he had been moved on 13 September, back to his former cell, Cell 719. No official reasons were given. Later, however, after the death of the prisoners, an empty hiding-place into which a pistol would have fitted was found in the window wall of Cell 715. During his time in Cell 715, Baader's record player along with its amplifier and loudspeakers, all allegedly carefully searched, had been returned to him. When he moved back to Cell 719, his old cell, he was allowed to take these items with him, and they were not searched again at that time. After his suicide, the investigators found a structure made of straightened-out paperclips inside the record-player. Baader had obviously used it to fix the pistol, a Hungarian FEK, in place.

Deputy Prison Governor Streitmüller said later, 'Now we know that Baader probably had the pistol inside his record player. So the weapon obviously moved back and forth between us and Baader. Today we can only shake our heads over it, but at the time it didn't occur to anyone that the gun might be in there.'

Jan-Carl Raspe was also moved on 4 October, two days after the arrest of Volker Speitel, who had acted as courier to bring in the gun. He was moved from Cell 718 to cell 716. It was in that cell, as it turned out later, that a second weapon was hidden in a hollow space in the wall, the nine-millimetre Heckler and Koch which Raspe later used to fire the fatal shots at himself.

These coincidental events worked almost like a cunningly laid plan: first Baader is moved from his cell (719), in which no pistol is hidden, to another cell (715) which does contain a pistol. His record player is confiscated and searched. Then it is returned to him. He is able to hide the pistol inside it and take it with him without any trouble when he moves back to his old cell (719). At the same time, Raspe is moved from Cell 718 to the very cell (716) where a second pistol is hidden.

And the moving of the prisoners back and forth had another strange consequence. The prisoners' communications system, which consisted of two sets of cables, the wiring for the prison radio system and the wiring for electric razors, could be connected and thus made fully functional only in two cells, and those two were Cells 718 and 719. After his first move Baader was in Cell 715 and could not link up to the system, but Raspe could in Cell 718. When Baader was back in 719 he could keep communications going instead of Raspe.

So by pure chance the moving of the prisoners in the high-security wing helped Baader and Raspe to get their hands on guns, and allowed them to communicate with each other and the other prisoners at any time.

The padded panels were put over the cell doors in Stammheim only at night. By day, said the official statement, they would have blocked off too much air from the cells.

The prisoners had briefly gone on hunger strike in protest against the contact ban. No one outside the prison knew about this, neither their lawyers nor their families. The contact ban was in force.

That day, 4 October, Andreas Baader called out to the others, 'We start eating again now.'

23
Four Identical Appeals
(Wednesday, 5 October 1977)

Governor Nusser of Stammheim prison telephoned the municipal court of Bad Cannstatt, Stuttgart, and told Judge Bertsch that Raspe wanted to appeal against the contact ban. The judge was taken up to the seventh floor the same day. Jan-Carl Raspe saw him, and formally put his appeal on record.

Next, Baader was brought to see the judge. He registered an identical appeal.

On the afternoon of the same day, Judge Werner Heinz went to Stammheim prison. About 3.00 p.m., he saw Gudrun Ensslin. After a short conversation, the judge was given the wording of her appeal, made out in her own hand and dated the previous day, 4 October.

Next day the judge heard that Irmgard Möller too wanted to appeal against the contact ban. He went back to Stammheim again.

It does not seem to have occurred to anyone that the prisoners might have communicated with each other.

Night duty report, Stammheim, 5 October:

'Dr Bertsch, judge in Bad Cannstatt municipal court, Stuttgart, with Raspe and Baader until 19.30 hours.

'23.00 hours, medication given to Baader and Raspe.'

24
Unjustifiable Surveillance
(Thursday, 6 October 1977)

The prison doctor, Dr Henck, who had by now developed quite a good relationship with the prisoners, visited Jan-Carl Raspe in his cell. He found the prisoner in what struck him as a state of total depression; Raspe complained of sleeping problems, and found speaking difficult. He had tears in his eyes and mentioned thoughts of suicide.

Dr Henck was alarmed. The fear that the prisoners might commit suicide had in fact been lurking at the back of his mind for some time, but now the danger seemed to be acute. He thought of the prisoners as aloof, cool, and above all self-controlled. It was something quite new for the doctor to hear Raspe speak of sleeping problems.

The prisoners on the seventh floor had dimmed the light in their cells, and this struck him, with his psychiatrist training, as a sign of 'introversion, regression, withdrawal into the self'.

He could reconstruct the way in which the contact ban affected the prisoners. Even before it was officially imposed, conditions of imprisonment in the high-security section had been very strict for several weeks. After the brawl on 8 August, instructions had gone out for regulations to be tightened up as a 'house punishment'. 'You could go on like that to the point of absurdity,' Baader had said to him. Dr Henck said later that the prisoners in Stammheim had felt the contact ban was a continuation of this house punishment, and thus they suffered from it more than the prisoners in other jails.

After visiting Raspe, the doctor wrote a memo to the administrative staff of the prison. 'From the overall impression I received, we must assume that there is a genuine predisposition to suicide among the prisoners. I would like this to be noted, and I would like some suggestions as to how any possible suicides can be prevented.'

Assistant Governor Schreitmüller asked the doctor and Inspector Bubeck to come and see him that afternoon. He wanted to know what measures they thought could be taken with the contact ban still in force.

'Would it be justifiable to put Raspe in a padded cell or keep him under constant surveillance at night with the light on?'

Dr Henck thought that neither alternative could be put into practice. 'They would simply increase the pressure on Raspe.'

For the time being, they decided, Dr Henck should visit Raspe once a day.

A few months earlier, the Stammheim staff had been less considerate when it came to checking up on the prisoners at night, as the reports of the officers on night duty show.

On 16 August 1977, the report noted, 'Cells 719 (Baader), 720 (Ensslin/Möller), 721 (Schubert) had to be opened, as the prisoner did not respond to a call. 23.08–23.45 hours.'

18 August: 'The Baader–Meinhof prisoners checked at 11.00, 2.00 and 5.00 hours: cell doors opened.'

19 August:

'2.04–2.11 hours, checks carried out.

'5.08–5.12 hours, checks carried out.'

20 August:

'1.51–2.05 hours, checks carried out. Cells 767 and 720 opened, as the prisoners did not respond to calls. 4.58–5.05 hours, checks carried out. No sign of life from the prisoner Möller: doctor fetched from sick bay at 5.05 hours.'

21 August:

'Cell 720 (Ensslin/Möller) opened, as the prisoners did not respond to calls. 2.04 to 2.07 hours, checks carried out. No sign of life from the prisoner Ensslin: doctor fetched at 2.07 hours . . . 5.03 to 5.09 hours, checks carried out.'

Even more frequent checks were made on the prisoners the following night:

19.10 hours, Verena Becker; 19.13 hours, Gudrun Ensslin; 21.26 hours, Becker; 21.28 hours, Ensslin; 23.25 hours, Becker; 23.08 hours, Raspe; 23.10 hours, Baader; 23.15 hours, Ensslin; 23.17 hours, Irmgard Möller; 0.45 hours, Becker; 0.58 hours, Ensslin; 2.10 hours, Becker; 2.12 hours, Raspe; 2.13 hours, Baader; 2.15 hours, Ensslin; 2.17 hours, Möller; 4.04 hours, Becker; 4.06 hours, Ensslin; 5.25 hours, Becker; 5.27 hours, Raspe; 5.29 hours, Baader; 5.31 hours, Ensslin; 5.32 hours, Möller ('showed no sign of life, doctor arrived 5.37 hours').

And so it went on almost every night until the contact ban was imposed. When the prison doctor diagnosed suicidal tendencies in Jan-Carl Raspe, the checks made by the night duty officer were not resumed, out of 'consideration for the prisoners'.

Or were there by now other ways of keeping them under surveillance?

In Palma de Mallorca, a black-haired young man entered the lounge of the Saratoga Hotel at about 11.00 p.m. on the evening of 6 October and asked for a single room. The hotel was almost fully booked, and the man, who produced an Iranian passport in the name of Ali Hyderi, had to make do with an expensive four-bed room. Next morning he again asked if there was a single room now vacant. The receptionist could only offer him a double room.

'Anything else vacant?' asked the guest. 'I'm expecting someone about midnight tonight.'

The receptionist shook his head again. 'But you have a double room, perhaps this person can share it with you for a night?'

'It's a lady,' said Hyderi.

About midnight the lady arrived; she too produced an Iranian passport made out in the name of Soraya Ansari.

25
'None of Us Intend to Kill Ourselves'
(Friday, 7 October 1977)

Shortly after mid-day, a prison officer gave Baader a written ruling from the prison administration forbidding the prisoners to buy fruit privately. Baader threw this document at his feet and said, 'These are things you'll have to pay for. I give you just a few days more.'

'Look, you might read the signature on that,' said the officer.

'You're the bottom link in the machinery of murder, and it's you I'm holding liable.'

Shortly afterwards the prison doctor, Dr Henck, visited the prisoners on the seventh floor. 'A few more days, and there'll be people dead,'

Baader told him. Gudrun Ensslin said, 'There's sadism bursting out everywhere now.'

The same day, Andreas Baader wrote to the Higher Regional Court:

'Putting together all the measures adopted over the last six weeks and some remarks of the prison officers, one can conclude that the administration, or the officers of the security services, who – so one officer says – are permanently present on the seventh floor now, are hoping to incite one or more of us to commit suicide, or at least to make suicide look plausible.

'I state here that none of us – this is clear from the few words we were able to exchange at our doors two weeks ago, and from the discussions we have had over the years – none of us intend to kill ourselves. Supposing, again in a prison officer's words, we should be "found dead", then we have been killed in the fine tradition of all the judicial and political measures taken during these proceedings.

'Andreas Baader, 7.10., 19.00 hours.'

26
Suicide Threats and Confidence in the Politicians' Sense of Responsibility
(Saturday, 8 October 1977)

A handwritten letter from Schleyer arrived at the Geneva lawyer's office in the morning. A Polaroid photograph was enclosed. It showed the kidnap victim holding a placard which bore the inscription, '31 Days A Prisoner'.

Hanns Martin Schleyer wrote: 'I take this opportunity to thank my wife for her reassuring letter in *Bild am Sonntag* of 21.9.77. I can assure my wife that I am in good physical and mental health, so far as that is possible in the circumstances. The uncertainty is the worst thing to bear. In my first statement after the kidnapping, I said that the decision about my life was in the hands of the Federal Government, and I thereby accepted that decision. But it was decision I meant; I was not thinking of vegetating in constant uncertainty, in which state I have now been for over a month.

'My family and friends know that it is not so easy to get me down, and I enjoy robust health. But even I can't cope much longer with this state of inaction . . . One must take the conditions in which I am living into account, after all. A decision from the Government – such as I asked them to make at the very start – is urgently called for.

'All the more so as I am firmly convinced that the people holding me will not go on like this much longer. There can be no doubt of their determination, after the murders of Buback and Ponto.

'Like my wife, I have confidence in the sense of responsibility of the politicians who are answerable in this case, and I still hope to be reunited with her soon.'

About 2.00 p.m., Alfred Klaus of the Federal Criminal Investigation Office had a telephone call from Stammheim. Inspector Bubeck was on the line. 'Baader's asked for you to visit him. He wants you to be here by 4.00 p.m.'

Klaus was taken to Stammheim by helicopter. At 5.45 p.m., Baader entered the prison visiting room. He seemed nervous, and asked, 'Do you have anything to tell me?'

Klaus replied, 'I thought I'd come to hear you say something.'

Hectically and disconnectedly, Baader said, 'If this wretched game, if the increased isolation of these last six weeks don't come to an end soon, well, the prisoners will decide. This political calculation won't work out. The security services will be confronted with a dialectic of political evolution which shows them as tricksters who've been duped themselves. The prisoners don't intend to accept the present situation any longer. In future, the Government won't be able to do what they like with us.'

'What kind of world are you living in?' asked the BKA man. 'Don't you think these ideas of yours are out of touch with reality?'

'This is a threat,' said Baader. 'The prisoners will come to an irreversible decision within the next few hours or days.'

Klaus's impression was that Baader's nerves were giving way as a result of isolation and uncertainty.

After seven minutes, Baader rose and left the visiting room. Out in the corridor, he stopped and turned back. 'If the Government's intending to exchange the prisoners, we won't be taken just anywhere, we want to take part in negotiations about the destination and the method of exchange.'

Then he had himself locked in his cell again.

Alfred Klaus flew back to Bonn and wrote a memo about his conversation with Baader. 'In the circumstances, the prisoners' decision he mentioned can only mean suicide. It's not sure if he meant that seriously, or if the prisoners have been able to discuss it amongst themselves.'

A second couple, apparently of Iranian origin, had now arrived in Palma de Mallorca. They produced passports in the names of Riza Abbasi and Shahnaz Gholam, and moved into a double room in the Costa del Azul hotel, not far from the Saratoga, where their compatriots were staying.

Abbasi visited travel agencies almost daily. He was extremely keen to fly to Frankfurt by Lufthansa. He finally managed to book two first class tickets for Lufthansa Flight 181 on Thursday, 13 October 1977.

At the same time, Ali Hyderi was buying two more tickets, economy class, for the same Frankfurt flight.

27
'A Living Dog is Better than a Dead Lion'
(Sunday, 9 October 1977)

That morning, Gudrun Ensslin had told the prison officers she too wanted to see Klaus of the BKA. He turned straight round and went back to Stammheim. He saw the prisoner in the afternoon, again in the seventh-floor visiting room. Gudrun Ensslin had brought some notes with her, and told Inspector Bubeck, who was also present, to write down what she had to say:

'If the brutality here, which will not end even with Schleyer's death, and the reprisals, in the sixth year of our imprisonment in isolation last any longer – I am speaking of hours, days, I mean not even a week – then we, the prisoners in Stammheim, will take the decision out of Chancellor Schmidt's hands by deciding for ourselves, in the way still open to us.'

Gudrun Ensslin had dictated so fast that Horst Bubeck had trouble getting it all down. From the first few words, it had been perfectly clear to the BKA man that she was threatening suicide if the Government did not meet the kidnappers' demands.

He remembered Gudrun Ensslin's secret letter to her fellow prisoners of three years before, during their long hunger strike: 'I have this brainwave . . . another way we can work the hunger strike . . . one of us will commit suicide every third week (or second or fourth week, it doesn't matter which) . . . '

Gudrun Ensslin went on dictating rapidly:

'This is something that concerns the Government, because the Government is responsible for the facts which account for it – five and a half years of torment and murder, the show trial, the constant electronic surveillance, torture by drugs and solitary confinement – the whole wretched ritual carried out to break our will and consciousness, and it is also responsible for the way this inhuman conception has been taken to extremes over the last six weeks: total social and acoustic isolation, and all the harassment and torments that are supposed to finish us off. This cannot be a threat – that would be paradoxical, but I think the consequence must necessarily mean escalation, and with it the question "Why?" being asked in West Germany, if the concept that could never be discussed before, terrorism, is properly employed. It also means, that is, it is the premise of the decision – that whatever the Government may decide no longer has the same meaning for us as that from which they proceed.'

Gudrun Ensslin then sketched in the alternative, obviously intent upon seizing the initiative herself in the stalemate of the front-line confrontation between the Government and Schleyer's kidnappers. If the prisoners were exchanged and assured that the Federal Government would not try to extradite them from the country to which they went, Hanns Martin Schleyer would be released.

This, she said, would have yet another advantage for the Government. 'The Government can assume that we, that is the group whose release is concerned, will not return to the Federal Republic, either legally or illegally.'

Here Gudrun Ensslin again raised the subject of the proposition Andreas Baader had put to Klaus on 13 September.

The best way to ensure Schleyer's safety, she went on, would be to withdraw the writs for the prisoners' detention in custody and get them permission to go to some foreign country. As to whether the prisoners would accept money from the Government, as demanded by Schleyer's kidnappers, the eleven prisoners would come to a joint decision on that point.

When Gudrun Ensslin had finished dictating her text, Klaus asked her, 'What kind of decision is it you're going to take out of the Chancellor's hands?'

'I should have thought that was clear enough from what I've said,' replied Gudrun Ensslin. Klaus inquired whether she had heard about his conversation with Baader the day before.

'Yes,' said Gudrun Ensslin. She seemed calm and composed.

After this conversation, Alfred Klaus learned from the prison staff that the isolation of the prisoners on the seventh floor was by no means complete. For instance, with the windows open they could hear radio programmes coming from the cells below them. And it was possible for them to converse with each other during the day through the doors of their cells, because the padded panels were not put in front of the doors except at night.

Jan-Carl Raspe also asked to speak to the BKA man that afternoon. He was taken into the visiting room where Klaus was waiting for him at 3.15 p.m.

'I want to remind you of my warning of 27 September,' said Raspe. 'It's dead prisoners, not prisoners released from jail, that would mean political catastrophe. That's the Government's business, in that they're responsible for our present conditions of imprisonment, which are designed for the treatment of prisoners as if they were moveable puppets. If the Government won't come to a decision the prisoners will take the decision out of the Government's hands.'

'Are you planning to kill yourselves, like Ulrike Meinhof?' asked Alfred Klaus.

'I don't know,' said Raspe. He thought for a moment. 'There are other methods too, hunger and thirst strikes. Death's bound to follow after seven days on thirst strike. No medical fiddling around can get over that.'

'A living dog is better than a dead lion,' remarked Klaus. 'That's from *Ecclesiastes*.'

Jan-Carl Raspe mentioned the conditions of imprisonment on the seventh floor again, and that ended their official conversation.

'I am now speaking to you in a purely private capacity,' said Klaus, as Raspe rose. 'Surely it would be a historic action if the prisoners could bring themselves to preserve life, rather than destroying it.'

Raspe said something indistinguishable, and left the room abruptly.

A few minutes later, Irmgard Möller was brought into the visiting room.

'I just want to state that we are determined not to endure the barbarity of the measures taken against us any longer – measures said to have been taken on the orders of the crisis staff, even to the awful acoustic isolation of the way our cells are padded.' Like Gudrun Ensslin, Irmgard Möller had prepared her statement in writing. She described their isolation over the past five years, three years in solitary confinement and two in a small group. 'And for six weeks in a total social and acoustic vacuum, in which no human being can survive.'

She concluded by saying, 'At the same time, our calorie intake has been halved. Arrangements for access to food have been made so that our only alternatives are either to go hungry or to eat the prison diet, which the prisoners on the seventh floor have ascertained beyond any doubt has drugs added to it.'

Irmgard Möller said nothing about the demands to exchange the prisoners for Schleyer.

Alfred Klaus remembered calling his Chief Commissioner, Horst Herold, directly after these conversations and telling him about the prisoners' suicide threats. Herold, however, denies ever having heard anything about suicidal thoughts on the part of the Stammheim prisoners. That evening Klaus noted in a memo for the files: 'In the circumstances, we may suppose that they meant suicide . . . With regard to her own person [Ensslin's] we cannot rule out the possibility that she meant what she said. It is less likely that her fellow prisoners will carry out their threat – particularly as an alternative to release.'

Governor Nusser, informed of the conversations by Bubeck, took the prisoners' suicide threats very seriously too. He sent a letter to the Ministry of Justice in Stuttgart next day, marked, 'Very urgent, delivery by special messenger, for immediate attention.'

He wrote: 'The statements made by the prisoners can be taken as threats to go on hunger and thirst strike, but can also be interpreted as suicide threats. In the latter case, I should point out that it is impossible to impose effective measures to prevent prisoners kept in total isolation from committing suicide. Check-ups at night might perhaps do the trick if scrupulously carried out, which would presuppose constant opening at least of the flaps in the cell doors, thus making unimpeded contact possible, as well as constant lighting in the cells and surveillance of the prisoners, which in practice would prevent them from getting any sleep, thus also aggravating the situation to an intolerable degree.'

Nothing was done.

Night duty report, Stammheim, 9 October:

'22.30 hours, night duty check by H. Spitzer.

'Baader given cough mixture, Optipyrin and Dolviran by medical orderly at 22.00 hours.

'23.00 hours, Raspe given his medication (cough mixture, sleeping tablets).'

28
'Don't Tempt Providence!'
(Monday, 10 October–Tuesday, 11 October 1977)

Dr Henck, the prison doctor, also found ideas of suicide coming up repeatedly in his conversations with the prisoners. On one visit, Baader spoke of 'collective suicide'. Gudrun Ensslin expressed herself in just the same way; however, she then added, 'But suicide here is out of the question.' Henck was surprised to find that in spite of the contact ban they both used the same form of words, 'as if in a photographic reproduction'.

He could not rid himself of those fears lurking at the back of his mind. The guards too noticed that the prisoners were becoming increasingly nervous and aggressive. On 13 October, the prison doctor told the Prisoners' Advisory Board about the situation on the seventh floor. By chance, he happened to meet Governor Nusser there. 'Don't tempt Providence!' said the governor, horrified.

According to the law relating to prison custody in Germany, 'special security measures' are permissible if the mental state of a prisoner indicates a risk of suicide. The prisoners on the seventh floor could not be put in together – that was prohibited by the contact ban. The prison doctor still thought that putting them in padded cells was a step which would increase the ill effects of psychological pressure even further. Dr Henck suggested moving Baader from Stammheim to Bruchsal, Ensslin to Munich, and Raspe to Freiburg. But apparently this would be too expensive.

The prison governor wrote a letter to the Ministry of Justice, describing the pros and cons of every possibility. He himself, he said, could think of 'nothing warranted' that could be done. Traugott Bender, Baden-Württemberg's justice minister, replied asking him to do 'all that was warranted' to prevent suicide. Which, in its turn, the prison governor found 'not excessively helpful'.

29
Gudrun Ensslin Wants to Talk to a Politician
(Wednesday, 12 October 1977)

About 10.00 am, Gudrun Ensslin told a prison officer she wanted to talk to Under-Minister Manfred Schüler. 'I assume he plays a leading part in the decision-making process.' Schüler was head of the Federal Chancellery, and responsible for the co-ordination of the secret services.

About mid-day, she said, 'If the under-secretary can't come, I would talk to Minister Wischnewski.'

That afternoon Inspector Horst Bubeck of the prison service told her that Klaus of the BKA would shortly be coming back to Stammheim. 'I don't want to see a policeman, I want to see a politician,' said Gudrun Ensslin.

About 7.00 p.m., Alfred Klaus was asked by Commissioner Herold to go to Stammheim and talk to the prisoners. Klaus set off in an official car.

30 Hijacking of a Lufthansa Jet (Thursday, 13 October 1977)

At 9.00 a.m., Gudrun Ensslin was taken into the visiting room, where Alfred Klaus read a statement out to her:

'You are asked to inform the prisoner Ensslin that Under-Secretary Schüler does not in principle decline to talk to her. However, there would be no point in such a conversation unless the prisoner will first state what subject she wishes to discuss, and unless that subject goes beyond the content of the conversation she had with Herr Klaus on 9 October.'

Gudrun Ensslin had been copying down the text of this statement in silence. She thought for a moment, and then said, 'All that means is that Schüler won't talk to me at all.' She looked at the BKA man. 'I see your boss has the power of decision in Bonn in his own hands now.'

'How do you make that out?' asked Klaus.

'There is no other subject for such a conversation.'

'I could think of a number of alternatives,' said the BKA officer. 'However, I'm not empowered to put them to you.'

'The only two alternatives that exist were fully covered, so far as anything can be actually said, in the statement of 9 October,' replied the prisoner.

'You ought to give me a clear answer to what the under-secretary says,' Klaus insisted.

Gudrun Ensslin thought again for a little while, and then asked him to write down, word for word:

'As I understand it, this communication proceeds from an absurd calculation, namely that there could be differences between the prisoners and the commando, which of course is nonsense.'

Alfred Klaus assumed that Gudrun Ensslin thought the idea was to try driving a wedge between the prisoners and the kidnappers and playing them off against each other. 'Do you want to talk to Under-Secretary Schüler now, or not?'

'In the circumstances, I don't,' replied the prisoner. Then she hesitated, and asked to be allowed to speak to the others. 'Then they can say what they think straight away, and I won't have to get a telephone message out for you again, as I did at the weekend.'

On the way back to her cell, Gudrun Ensslin tried to call something to Baader. He was still asleep, and so did not respond.

Alfred Klaus rang the Chief Commissioner of the BKA. 'The other prisoners aren't being informed. Come back,' Horst Herold told him.

Meanwhile, on the holiday island of Mallorca, a large number of German tourists were getting ready to come home, including a group of young women who had been dancing the evening happily away at a 'Miss World' contest in a discotheque the night before. One of them was Diana Müll, aged nineteen: 'We'd been celebrating at the end of our holiday, and it was hard to get up in the morning.' They almost missed their flight; the doors of the Lufthansa jet that bore the name Landshut were already closed when the girls turned up. The owner of the disco, who had booked a great many of the flights and was a persuasive lobbyist, said: 'Open the doors again at once and let these women on board.' The group climbed in.

There was a good-looking young man sitting close to Diana Müll. She found herself looking at him again and again, 'because he was wearing such a funny jacket, a check jacket'.

About 13.00 hours, German time, the Landshut, named after a town in East Bavaria, flight number LH 181, took off from Palma de Mallorca for Frankfurt. There were eighty-six passengers on board the Boeing 737, and two corpses in zinc coffins in the freight compartment.

The crew consisted of Captain Jürgen Schumann, his co-pilot Jürgen Vietor, and stewardesses Hannelore Piegler, Gaby Dillmann and Anna-Maria Staringer.

As soon as the plane had taken off, the stewardesses served light refreshments.

Hannelore Piegler, as purser and senior stewardess, served the passengers in First Class. She thought the dark-haired couple in the first-class seats were Spanish. Her colleagues Gaby and Anna-Maria served the passengers in Economy, which was almost full.

Suddenly Hannelore Piegler heard loud, confused voices from the main cabin, with hoarse shouts rising above them. She pulled back the curtain dividing First Class from Economy, to go to the back of the plane. At this moment she received a blow which sent her tumbling against the cabin door.

Two men ran past her into the cockpit. They pulled the co-pilot out of his seat and dragged him back into the gangway. The two dark-haired women were standing there, holding hand grenades up in the air.

The co-pilot, the stewardesses and the first-class passengers were herded into the rear of the aircraft and threatened with a pistol by one of the black-haired men. The other man had stayed in the cockpit. Over the loudspeaker, he shouted, in English, 'Hands up. Follow the instructions . . .'

Passenger Diana Müll: 'He took the microphone and shouted into it like a madman, saying this was a hijack. And then the stewardesses came forward, Frau Dillmann for instance, all in total panic.'

Stewardess Gaby Dillmann, now Frau von Lutzau, says: 'We were all herded back like cattle, into the rear part of the cabin, and we had to put our hands above our heads. Then we were told this was a hijacking and we were to keep quiet, anyone who didn't keep quiet would be shot. We'd be shot for talking, or lowering our hands, well, basically we'd be shot unless we just breathed very quietly and kept our hands up. We all did what they said, meek as little lambs. What else could we do? Act like heroes and get shot? What good would that do? And then we thought, the RAF . . . because we knew there'd be huge difficulties, with the Federal Government guarding them like some kind of precious treasure in a high-security jail. And those were the people they wanted. But we knew at once it would be difficult. We really thought, there are so many of us and so few of them, it had to happen that way, it was only logical, a law of humanity.'

The hijackers told the crew to sit down in Economy, and moved the passengers around. Young men were placed by themselves in window seats.

Shortly afterwards, the fourth kidnapper came storming into the cabin, shouting that he had taken command on board, and was now the captain of the aircraft. His name, he said, was Captain Martyr Mahmud.

* * *

At 14.38 hours, air traffic control at Aix-en-Provence in the south of France reported a deviation from its route by the Lufthansa Boeing jet. Two hours later, the plane came down at Rome's Fiumicino airport.

At 17.00 hours, the leader of the hijackers spoke over the aircraft radio, demanding the release by the Federal Government of the eleven RAF prisoners.

In Chancellor Helmut Schmidt's words: 'This affair now had an additional dimension. Up to this point the life of one human being, Dr Schleyer, had been in great danger; now it was a case of over ninety human beings whose lives were in great danger. This was on a larger scale. And no one knew where the aircraft would be going.'

At this moment, Alfred Klaus the BKA officer had just returned to Bonn from Stammheim. He had a call from Governor Nusser of Stammheim prison at 4.20 p.m. 'Frau Ensslin wants to speak to you.'

Nusser passed the receiver over to the prisoner. 'Well,' said Gudrun Ensslin, 'if we say we want to speak to you, or to Wischnewski, then in the first place, and perhaps in spite of all our past experience, it's a question of a difference between politics and the police, entailing possibilities other than that of escalation – the rationale of all politicians who are condemned to be policemen, and a police force free to meddle with politics.'

It was, she said, a matter of explaining to the under-secretary what the release of the eleven prisoners would mean.

'You've known for six years that none of us would dream of discussing that with a policeman – all I can think of in that context is the deadly arrangements made for the transport of badly injured prisoners, finally the noose at the window . . .' Klaus could not make out what she was saying, and thus could not give any clear account of it.

Finally, Gudrun Ensslin said, 'So if there's going to be any talking, regardless of the tricks we expect from you . . . well, if there's any point in biting a sour apple, then you're to talk only to Andreas.'

Late that afternoon, the Protestant and Roman Catholic prison chaplains visited Andreas Baader in his cell.

'Herr Baader,' said Pastor Kurmann, the Protestant chaplain, 'we've not been asked to come, we're here on our own initiative to offer you the chance of some conversational contact.'

'What's the point of that? What do you expect to come of it? That won't have any consequences that'll change our situation here in prison for the better.'

'You may be right there,' said the Catholic priest, Father Rieder, 'but a personal conversation with us, particularly just at present, could bring you some relief, so it might change things for the better from the psychological viewpoint.'

'Well, if you want to do something, then you can tell your institution about our impossible conditions of imprisonment, our total isolation, the way they're systematically making us crack up.'

The very point of their visit, said the chaplains, was to get to know about the prisoners' situation. However, such conversations could be conducted only in the presence of both clergymen.

'Oh, I see. You have to check up on each other,' said Baader.

Meanwhile, prison officers had come along with the supper trolley, and the chaplains took their leave. 'You know we're ready to talk to you, Herr Baader, and if you want to call on us then just let us know.'

At Fiumicino airport, the Lufthansa plane was standing a good 1,000 metres away from the airport buildings. Armoured vehicles surrounded the aircraft. The hijackers' leader poured out long tirades, delivered in English, over the microphone in the cockpit. The Italians in the airport tower noted down the following extracts from his remarks: 'This is Captain Mahmud speaking. The German airline's jet has been taken over. The group I represent demands the release of our comrades in German prisons. We are fighting against the imperialist organizations of the world.'

Interior Minister Werner Maihofer, in Bonn, was told what had happened. He got in touch with his Italian opposite number, Francisco Cossiga, and told him the hijackers would probably make common cause with the kidnappers of Schleyer. Whatever happened, the Lufthansa jet must not be allowed to fly on. 'Shoot out the tyres.'

Cossiga, of the Italian Christian Democratic Party, hesitated. He said he would have to discuss such a question with other politicians first. He called the Italian Communist leader Enrico Berlinguer, whose party was tolerated at this time by the Christian Democrat minority government. Berlinguer, a distant relative of Cossiga's, was horrified by the prospect of a bloodbath on Italian soil. Christian Democrat and Communist agreed that the plane must take off again as soon as possible.

The Boeing was refuelled. Captain Schumann asked the tower for weather reports from Cyprus and permission to land at Larnaca.

At 17.42 hours the Boeing took off again with the ninety captives, who were entirely at the mercy of the hijackers. There was complete silence on board. 'If anyone so much as whispered,' the co-pilot remembered later, 'one of the terrorists would come storming up and bawl them out.'

Passenger Diana Müll: 'Captain Mahmud was furious. He'd ram his elbow into people's heads or hit them with the butt of his pistol.'

Stewardess Gaby Dillmann: 'The passengers obeyed. What could anyone do? If someone's holding a pistol in front of your face, you do as he tells you.'

In Bonn, the Smaller Crisis Staff met and decided to stick to their hard line, even after the hijacking.

Minister of State Wischnewski got in touch with the commanding officer of GSG 9, the special anti-terrorist unit of the Federal Border Police, Ulrich Wegener. 'Listen, a plane has been hijacked, a Lufthansa aircraft on its way from Mallorca to Frankfurt. Get your men ready to go in.'

'When does the operation begin?'

Wischnewski didn't know that exactly himself. 'Just get moving!'

Later, Wegener said, 'That was no trouble at all. Being ready and operational within a very short time was all part of the job in our role in emergencies.' More of a problem for Wegener, as it turned out, was which men to take. 'Everyone wanted to be in on the operation when it began, no doubt about that.'

At 19.55 hours, a Lufthansa plane was cleared for take-off at Frankfurt airport. Officials of the Federal Ministry of the Interior and the Federal Criminal Investigation Office were on board. At a stopover at Cologne/Bonn airport, a group of fit young men in trainers, jeans and sweaters boarded the plane; this was at about 22.00 hours. There were thirty of them, armed with guns, hand grenades, ladders and explosives. The men of GSG 9 had done five years' training for emergencies. They had learned how to storm aircraft within seconds, were experts in hand-to-hand fighting, and had gone down from airborne helicopters by rope.

Just before take-off, Wegener told his men what it was all about. The hijacked Boeing was to be captured and the hostages freed. This was going to be a suicide mission, and he wouldn't hold it against any man who didn't want to go along.

The men all grinned. This kind of operation was just what they had been waiting for.

About 20.30 hours, the Lufthansa jet, the Landshut, landed at Larnaca airport in Cyprus.

Gaby Dillmann: 'The temperature was over 50 degrees; it was like being in an incubator, the air was so hot and humid. People freaked out, and then they were carried to the openings. I felt it was like a farmer having to get his cattle alive to the abattoir somewhere.'

'Captain Mahmud' ordered the plane to be refuelled. In Gaby Dillmann's words, 'That madman was the driving force of the whole thing. The others obeyed him unconditionally. There was some kind of hierarchy, and nothing could break through it.'

Co-pilot Vietor: 'The Andrawes woman was . . . she was like one of those female concentration camp guards. She liked tormenting people. While the young man, well, he was really a very polite young fellow who never blew his top, and the little girl, as we called her, the pretty one, you could get along with her all right later, not at the start, you could talk to her later.'

Mahmud gave the order to take off at 22.50 hours.

The Boeing flew on eastwards into the twilight, making for the Persian Gulf.

Twenty-three minutes later, the plane carrying the GSG 9 men landed at Larnaca.

31
A Decision of Government Policy
(Friday, 14 October 1977)

An hour after midnight, Denis Payot in Geneva had a telephone call from Hanns Martin Schleyer's kidnappers. They wanted him to be available to receive a longer statement about 2.00 a.m. Payot informed the Federal BKA, and got the tape recorder with which they had supplied him ready.

Schleyer's kidnappers proved their credentials by answering questions the BKA had put to them ten days before.

'What did Eberhard Schleyer want to be when he was eight years old?'

The correct answer was, 'The Pope.'

'Who was the lady who wanted to sing to him in Prague?'

'Margot Hielscher.'

They were also asked to give the tenth word from their letter of 26 September to Agence France Presse, which was 'Schleyer'.

The first part of the statement was read out in English:

'This is to inform you that the passengers and crew of the Lufthansa 737 aircraft, flight number LH 181, from Palma to Frankfurt am Main, are completely under our control. The lives of the passengers and crew and the life of Dr Hanns Martin Schleyer depend upon your acceding to the following demands.'

Besides the release of the RAF prisoners, demanded by the Siegfried Hausner Commando, two Palestinians imprisoned in Turkey were also to be flown out. In addition, the kidnappers wanted a ransom of fifteen million dollars.

The second part of the statement was read in German. 'The ultimatum of the Kofre Kaddum operation of the Martyr Halimeh Commando is identical with the ultimatum of the Siegfried Hausner Commando of the RAF. Now that Schleyer has been a prisoner for forty days, there will be no more extensions of the deadline. Nor will there be any further contacts. Any delay will mean Schleyer's death . . .'

The speaker specified the banknotes in which the fifteen million dollars were to be handed over: seven million in hundred-dollar notes, three million in thousand-Deutschmark notes, three million in Swiss francs, two million in Dutch gulden.

The ransom was to be packed in three Samsonite suitcases and handed over by Schleyer's son Eberhard. He was to be at the Intercontinental Hotel in Frankfurt next day, 15 October, at twelve noon, wearing a beige suit, with a pair of sunglasses in his top jacket pocket. He was also to carry the latest number of *Der Spiegel* in his left hand, and he was to bring his passport with him. A contact man would approach him in the hotel and identify himself with the words, 'Let us save your father.' To this, he was to reply, 'We will save my father.'

After that he must follow the instructions of the kidnappers' representative.

The caller then made another long statement about the 'Kofre Kaddum' operation, saying that there was a link between the 'old Nazis' in the Federal Republic of Germany and the 'new Nazis' in Israel.

Chancellor Helmut Schmidt discussed the situation with Interior Minister Maihofer, Minister of State Wischnewski, Chief Commissioner Herold of the Federal BKA, and several under-secretaries, until five in the morning.

Meanwhile the hijacked plane landed in Bahrain on the Persian Gulf.

The GSG 9 men who were pursuing it received instructions to turn back to Cologne, but shortly afterwards these instructions were altered, and they were told to land at Ankara in Turkey first.

By now Captain Schumann had taken off from Bahrain again, and was flying the Boeing towards the sheikhdom of Dubai. When he reached Dubai, the runway was blocked. Schumann circled the airfield. 'Some time the fuel will give out,' he remarked. 'Some time we'll have to land. Maybe we'll be lucky.' Suddenly 'Captain Mahmud' put a pistol to the nape of his neck and shouted, 'You must land now, you must land now . . .'

The co-pilot, Jürgen Vietor, had taken over at the controls. 'There's no arguing with that,' he said, and brought the aircraft down lower. Jürgen Schumann spoke to the tower. 'We must come in now. We're landing.'

At the last moment, and on his own authority, the Dubai airport commandant had the runway cleared of the fire engines which had been brought up to form a blockade. The plane landed.

There was still an atmosphere of terror on board. Co-pilot Vietor: 'My wife had once given me a Junghans watch, they have a kind of stylized display, a star shape with a J inside it. Like the Star of David. And a J in it, and he saw that. You're a Jew, he said, I'm going to shoot you.'

Stewardess Gaby Dillmann: 'I had to kneel down in front of him too, and he hit me. And he said I was a Jew and I was – I was to confess it – and I was blazing with fury when I looked at him, and I wouldn't knuckle under. So then he couldn't help laughing, and he said: Okay, okay, you get up. It hadn't given him any fun because I wasn't all submissive.'

Sheikh Mohammed bin Rashid, aged twenty-nine, minister of defence and the third son of the ruler of Dubai, had himself driven to the airport at 200 kph, and made radio contact with the Lufthansa jet. He asked the hijackers to free the women, children, and sick passengers, and addressed them as 'my Arab brothers'. He also tried a more peremptory tone. Captain Mahmud rejected any kind of compromise.

It was beginning to get hot inside the cabin.

Gaby Dillmann: 'That night was really like being in hell. It's hard to imagine it, eighty people, and there were a lot of old people among them, they were close to death.'

Diana Müll: 'In the end I think the temperature was 60 degrees inside the plane. All you could do was stay in your seat and not move. And when someone ran along the plane it was very dramatic, the air swirled up, and we closed our eyes and tried not to breathe, until a moment had passed since that person went by and the air . . . the air settled again. It was worst of all when the air swirled up, it was almost past bearing.'

The clothes of the passengers and crew members, crowded together as they were, were sticking to their bodies. The stewardesses distributed the few remaining drinks to the passengers in plastic beakers.

Suddenly the purser, Hannelore Piegler, remembered that it was her Norwegian colleague Anna-Maria Staringer's birthday. 'What a day for a birthday,' she said quietly. 'I won't wish you Happy Birthday now, but if we ever get out of here alive, we'll make up for it later.' Martyr Mahmud had overheard. He offered his own greetings, in English: 'I wish you all the best for your birthday next year!' He went to the cockpit, made radio contact with the tower, and ordered a birthday cake, coffee and champagne.

Shortly afterwards the catering staff of Dubai airport supplied a pastel-coloured birthday cake, with 'Happy Birthday Anna-Maria' written on it in icing. All the passengers were given a small piece of cake, coffee and champagne. Captain Mahmud was in high spirits. He took the microphone and announced that the explosives were being removed from the sides of the aircraft. The relieved passengers applauded. Mahmud accepted the applause with a grand gesture. Then he went to the microphone again. 'We're removing the explosives, but only for five minutes, of course. Then they go back in place again.' The smiles on the passengers' faces faded away.

The crew had the idea of sending the German chancellor a telegram by radio, saying, 'We put our lives in your hands, and ask you most fervently to save us.' The stewardesses had used one of the Lufthansa picture postcards available on the plane to draft this message. Suddenly they realized that the card showed their own aircraft. Gaby Dillmann wanted the leader of the hijackers to autograph it. Mahmud smiled wearily, and came up with an idea of his own. He gave orders to have 'With compliments of the SAWIO, "Struggle Against World Imperialism"', written on the Lufthansa picture postcards, which were then to be distributed to the passengers.

Meanwhile two of the hijackers searched the passengers' hand baggage, which had been stacked in First Class. One of them suddenly came running down the gangway, holding a passport. A woman was taken to the front of the plane. Mahmud shouted hoarsely at her; there were kicks and blows. She came back from the first-class cabin, tear-stained, and went shakily back to her seat.

Mahmud followed her, a broken ballpoint pen in his hand. 'I've discovered Jews on board. Do you know what that is?' He held up the remains of the Montblanc pen, pointing to the small white star on its cap. 'That's a Jewish star, the Star of David. I shall shoot these Jews tomorrow, they'll come to me voluntarily tomorrow. I shall stand them in the open doorway of the plane and shoot them, with a bullet in the head from behind. They'll fall out of the plane of their own accord.'

Negotiating with Mahmud, the Dubai minister of defence had persuaded him to allow medicine, ice and drinks to be taken on board. The stewardesses distributed ice bags to the passengers so that they could cool their legs, which were swollen with sitting for so long. Mahmud repeatedly flew into fits of rage, threatening to shoot passengers out of hand. Then he would be perfectly calm again, and deliver long-winded lectures on the justice of the Palestinian cause, and how the village of Kofre Kaddum had been destroyed and its inhabitants slaughtered by Zionists.

As the plane stood at Dubai airport, letters from the kidnappers were going out to the press and to Hanns Martin Schleyer's son in Germany. The envelopes contained the joint statements of the Siegfried Hausner Commando and the Palestinian hijackers, which had been read out to the Geneva lawyer over the telephone the day before. The BKA's investigators established that the letters had all been written on the same typewriter.

In the morning, the two Stammheim prison chaplains had visited the prisoners Irmgard Möller, Gudrun Ensslin, Jan-Carl Raspe and Verena Becker – whose cell was in the 'long wing' of the prison – to offer to come and talk to them. Few words were exchanged. Jan-Carl Raspe stooped as he stood in the doorway of his cell, and Pastor Kurmann noticed that his face was twitching nervously. Verena Becker seemed very awkward and unsure of herself. When they made their offer, she nodded her head slightly and said hesitantly, 'Yes.'

Gudrun Ensslin struck the two chaplains as the calmest of all the prisoners.

The same day, Governor Nusser and Inspector Bubeck went to see Baader. They wanted to find out what purpose he thought a conversation with the head of the Chancellery, Manfred Schüler, would serve. Baader would not answer the question. Then he laughed and said, 'If Schüler doesn't come soon, he may have to travel a very long way to talk to me. Anyway,' he added, 'it must be a politician who comes, not a policeman.'

The West German cabinet met for a special session in Bonn in the morning. Justice Minister Hans Jochen Vogel set out the legal issues involved in an exchange of prisoners. On the one hand, there was the immediate and very real danger threatening the lives of the eighty-six hostages in the plane and Hanns Martin Schleyer, on the other the danger to an unknown number of people if the prisoners were released. In law, according to Paragraph 34, 'justifiable emergency', acceding to the kidnappers' demands, was neither inadmissible nor mandatory: the decision was one to be made on the grounds of government policy.

In the Government documentation of the incidents surrounding the kidnapping of Schleyer and the hijacking of the Lufthansa jet, the strategy adopted was later described thus: 'After extensive consideration of all relevant points of view, the Cabinet has decided that everything possible shall be done to save the hostages – without releasing the prisoners – including the use of all possible means of negotiation, and a police rescue operation.'

At 15.50 hours, Hans-Jürgen Wischnewski took off for Dubai in a Lufthansa Boeing 707. The state secretary, known as 'Ben Wisch' because of his good contacts with the Arab world, had with him a case containing ten million deutschmarks. On landing in Dubai, Wischnewski was going to ask permission for the GSG 9 unit to go in.

Rüdiger von Lutzau, boyfriend of the Landshut air hostess Gaby Dillmann, was in the co-pilot's seat. He had volunteered for the operation. The psychologist Wolfgang Salewski, who had been advising the Government on their dealings with Schleyer's kidnappers over the past few weeks, was on board too.

Unnoticed by anyone in the hijacked plane, the 707 landed on an outlying runway at Dubai airport half an hour before midnight.

That evening, Denis Payot received an express delivery package from Schleyer's kidnappers: it contained a videotape with a statement from the president of the Employers' Association: 'In my present situation, I really ask myself, must something drastic happen before Bonn finally comes to a decision?

'After all, I have been in the hands of the terrorists for five and a half weeks now, just because I have supported the West German state and its free democracy for years, laying myself open to attack on its behalf.

'Sometimes the statements that are being made – by politicians, among others – seem to me like a mockery of those activities of mine.'

At about the same time, the federal justice minister was seeing Schleyer's son Hanns-Eberhard in Bonn. Vogel told him that it was up to him whether he went to meet the kidnappers' emissary next day in the Intercontinental Hotel in Frankfurt with the fifteen million dollars, as they had asked. 'The money is available,' said Vogel. 'It weighs about 130 kilos.'

However, he added, Hanns-Eberhard Schleyer would be putting himself in immediate and very real danger. The larger crisis staff would have to decide whether or not the money was actually to be released when they met next morning.

'I can't see any alternative,' said Schleyer. He added that he would hold himself in readiness, on condition that the Government would also meet the kidnappers' other demands, i.e. the release of the prisoners, and on condition that no violent action was taken against the hijackers while he was away in Frankfurt.

The crisis staff would have to decide about that tomorrow morning too, said Justice Minister Vogel.

Hanns-Eberhard Schleyer was taken to the BKA annexe at Godesberg, where he talked to Horst Herold, who again pointed out the dangerous nature of the undertaking. However, said Herold, the money was ready at the Federal Bank. The police in Frankfurt had taken all the necessary measures. Then Schleyer went to a hotel in Bonn, with BKA officer Wolfgang Steinke, and spent the night there.

While the hijacked Boeing was still in the air, Chief Commissioner Herold of the Criminal Investigation Office had enlisted the help of colleagues in the Spanish police to have all 20,000 hotel registrations recorded in Palma over the last few days sent to Germany by air. Computer programmers worked round the clock in Wiesbaden feeding personal details into the BKA computer. Then Herold ran a data tape on which aliases were stored. The alleged Iranian passports came up, and examining the personal details of the holders of these false passports, the BKA investigators were able to discover the hijackers' real names.

'Captain Mahmud', whose Iranian passport bore the name of Ali Hyderi, and whose real name was Zohair Youssif Akache, was known to the police. He had enrolled as a student of the Chelsea College of Aeronautical and Automobile Engineering in London in 1973, and received his diploma in aeronautical engineering two years later.

He first came to the notice of Scotland Yard in December 1974, when he suddenly attacked police officers at a peaceful pro-Palestinian demonstration in Trafalgar Square. He was known to be a member of the PFLP, and was in danger of being deported, but was finally allowed to remain and continue his studies. A year later, Akache attacked the police during another pro-Palestinian demonstration. This time he was arrested and ended up in Pentonville prison. After going on hunger strike, he was deported to Beirut.

He was back in London at the beginning of 1977. Under a false name, he moved into a hotel opposite the Royal Lancaster, where the former prime minister of North Yemen was staying. On 10 April, the ex-prime minister, with his wife and a member of the staff of the Yemeni Embassy, got into a Mercedes outside the hotel. Akache had been in wait behind the car. He walked around the vehicle, opened the right-hand front door, and fired a pistol fitted with a silencer at the three occupants. They died instantly. Akache managed to fly out of London the same day. Scotland Yard had had him under surveillance before the assassination, but had not sent his personal details and description through to Heathrow Airport.

Near Baghdad, he was trained for further action by the Special Operations department of the PFLP under Wadi Haddad. The other members of the Kofre Kaddum operation were trained here too.

32
The Organs of State Do Their Duty
(Saturday, 15 October 1977)

At 7.50 a.m., Captain Schumann sent a telegram by radio to the West German chancellor. 'The lives of ninety-one men, women and children on board the aircraft depend on your decision. You are our last and only hope. In the name of the crew and passengers. Schumann.'

* * *

At 12.04, a six-seater Hawker Siddeley jet landed in Dubai. Ulrich Wegener, head of the GSG 9 unit waiting in Ankara, and other security experts were on board. The defence minister of Dubai refused to countenance a rescue operation by the German anti-terrorist squad, but began preparing for an operation conducted by the armed forces of the United Arab Emirates.

Meanwhile, Hanns-Eberhard Schleyer decided to appeal to the Constitutional Court as a last chance of rescuing his father. His written application was prepared by colleagues in his Stuttgart legal offices.

In his father's name, he applied for the issue of an interim injunction forcing the Federal Government and the regional governments involved to free those prisoners whose release was demanded, in order to save the life of Hanns Martin Schleyer.

But the die had been cast long before.

The same night, the Constitutional Court rejected the application. 'As the organs of state do their duty in effectively protecting life, it is, in principle, their own responsibility to make decisions . . . in view of the situation in contitutional law, the Constitutional Court can prescribe no specific decision to the organs of state responsible.'

The Government had told the Constitutional Court judges that an operation to rescue the hostages on the plane was being prepared. 'One result of this was that our decision was not announced until early in the morning, although we had made it some six hours earlier,' the president of the Federal Constitutional Court in Karlsruhe, Ernst Benda, said later.

Early in the afternoon of 15 October, shortly after Hanns-Eberhard Schleyer had telephoned the Constitutional Court, a new message for the kidnappers from the BKA was conveyed to Denis Payot. The countries of Vietnam and South Yemen, named by the hijackers as possible destinations, had firmly declined to receive terrorists. 'Somalia, also named by the commando, has not yet been named by the prisoners.'

As Baader had said they did not want to be flown out to just any country, but to be involved in determining their destination, the prisoners had to be consulted again. This consulation had begun, said the BKA.

It was the twenty-fifth communication the BKA had sent to Schleyer's kidnappers.

* * *

Once again, Alfred Klaus of the BKA was flown to Stammheim by helicopter. At about 6.15 p.m., he put a new questionnaire before each of the prisoners in turn:

'Through the Martyr Halimeh Commando's demands of 13 October, the kidnappers have named Vietnam, South Yemen and Somalia as possible destinations. Vietnam and South Yemen have already firmly declined to accept terrorists. Somalia is currently being asked. Are you prepared to be flown out to Somalia?'

Gudrun Ensslin signed the questionnaire and replied, 'Yes.'

Jan-Carl Raspe wrote, 'My final decision will depend on a joint consultation between all the prisoners to be released; with this proviso, I am prepared to be flown out.'

Irmgard Möller wrote: 'Yes, provided the Federal Government does not ask for us to be extradited.'

Andreas Baader hesitated over his answer, and said, 'I know the People's Republic of Vietnam is prepared to take us. I'd prefer to be flown out there. I can say it now: one of our lawyers got an assurance from the Vietnamese through diplomatic channels that they'd receive us.' He paused for a moment. 'Though not in connection with a hostage-taking operation.' Baader seemed nervous and unsure of himself.

He wrote on the questionnaire: 'Only if the commando really did name Somalia.' Then he said, 'If we're going to be sold back again once we're in Somalia, we might as well stay here.'

He came back to the subject of the conversation he wanted to have with Under-Secretary of State Schüler. 'I feel it's very important for me to discuss the political dimension of the exchange of prisoners with him.' At the doorway of the visiting room, he turned back again. 'Please, in any case, pass it on that I want that conversation.'

None of the prisoners had asked what the Martyr Halimeh Commando had to do with anything.

No one was surprised that despite the contact ban, they were obviously speaking to each other, and able to receive information from outside.

Night duty report, Stammheim, 15 October:

'Herr Klaus of the BKA with the prisoners Baader, Raspe, Ensslin, Möller and Becker from 18.10 to 18.45 hours. Inspector Götz present too.

'23.00 hours, Baader and Raspe given medication.'

33
Preparations to Storm the Plane and the Death of a Pilot
(Sunday, 16 October 1977)

Even as the twin-jet Hawker Siddeley landed in Dubai at noon the previous day, the GSG 9 leader Ulrich Wegener had been looking to see if there was any chance of storming the hijacked Boeing. Behind the plane, he saw sand dunes among which his men could take cover – if they got permission to attack from the defence minister of Dubai. When he met Minister of State Wischnewski in the airport tower, Wegener said, 'Something could be done here.'

Wegener had met two acquaintances at the airport, Major Alistair Morrison and Sergeant Barrie Davis of the SAS, the British special anti-terrorist unit. A few weeks before, they had visited Wegener and his GSG 9 unit at their Hangelar base in Bonn. They had been demonstrating their new stun grenades, whose dazzling flash and loud detonation rendered opponents incapable of fighting for at least six seconds. The SAS men had brought a collection of these grenades to Dubai with them.

Meanwhile, Wischnewski had been negotiating with the defence minister of Dubai over the possibility of sending in the GSG 9 men. He came to meet Wegener. 'The decision's come through at last. They want to do it themselves. There's nothing going for us here. The Sheikh wants to send in his own British-trained paratroopers.' One of the SAS men had just been discussing the chances of storming the plane with Wegener. 'It won't work,' he said. 'They've never trained for this kind of thing.'

'Then we'll just have to start training them,' said Wegener.

At 5.30 a.m., the leader of the hijackers contacted the tower. His voice was hoarse, and he sounded exhausted. He wanted the plane refuelled by 6.00 a.m., or he was threatening to shoot the pilot.

During the night, the power had failed inside the plane, and with it the air-conditioning on board. Captain Schumann had made it clear to the kidnappers that without any air-conditioning, and standing out all day in the blazing sun, the aircraft would become a mass grave. Mahmud had agreed to ask the tower for a generator, and Lufthansa employees pushed one into position underneath the plane. The air inside the Boeing, which you could have cut with a knife, slowly cleared.

Captain Schumann tried to send a signal indicating how many hijackers were on board through an order for cigarettes. 'Can you get us four packs of cigarettes, please, four packs? Different brands. Two of this and two of this, maybe.'

They understood his coded message in the tower. In a radio interview, the Dubai defence minister spoke with warm approval of the secret information provided by the captain of the aircraft. Mahmud heard him over the radio. The hijacker had also realized that the men who brought out the generator were Germans.

In the morning he suddenly confronted the pilot and ordered him out into the gangway. 'Put your hands up,' he shouted. Schumann rose and clasped his hands behind his neck. 'On your knees!' ordered Mahmud, pointing his pistol at Schumann's head. 'And now I'm going to tell you all who's responsible for the power failure and our miserable conditions these last few hours. The man to blame is kneeling here – your captain. He could have spared you all that. He's a traitor. He's been sending news out! Isn't that right? Admit it!'

'Yes,' confessed the pilot.

'You've all heard him admit his guilt!' yelled Mahmud. 'And now, in front of all your passengers, you'll confess you've had military training.'

'Yes,' said Schumann.

'The men who came out to bring us that generator were your Army friends, weren't they? Admit it!'

'No, no, really they weren't. They were our airline's men.'

'Well, now let's see what you learned in the Army. Stand up!' shouted Mahmud. 'Stand to attention! About turn! March! One, two, one, two, one, two!'

Jürgen Schumann marched up and down the gangway.

'So you've been sending information out by radio, during the flight and here in Dubai, right? Your co-pilot will be able to confirm that, right?'

'The co-pilot knows nothing about it. I did it on my own,' Schumann protested.

Mahmud took the onboard microphone and told the tower to refuel the plane again. Otherwise, he said, he would shoot the pilot, and then shoot a passenger every five minutes.

* * *

Meanwhile, Ulrich Wegener began training a troop of men on an Air Force field three kilometres from the tower. A Gulf Air Boeing 737 stood there. Twenty Bedouin soldiers and their English instructors were taught how to capture an aircraft by the GSG 9 leader. They trained under Wegener's command for hours. It worked surprisigly well. 'They're not a perfect team yet,' Wegener told the British officers, 'but it might come off.'

Just before twelve noon German time, Mahmud got into radio contact with the tower again. The plane was now about to take off, he said. If all the preparations were not made immediately, he would be forced to shoot a passenger every five minutes. Diana Müll was to be the first: 'He put the pistol to my temple and then counted down from ten. At first I thought I'd look Mahmud full in the face so that he would see how I died. But then I told myself no, you can't do it. That way, the last thing you see will be that . . . that ugly face, that brutal face. No, I thought, I don't want that. Then I looked at the sunlight outside, and, well, then he'd counted down to one. And then the tower shouted: we'll refuel you.'

The generator was removed. At 15.19 hours local time, the Landshut was in the air again.

Mahmud gave the co-pilot precise instructions: 'Fly in a left-hand curve and make for Oman.' Vietor could tell that the hijacker was reading from a note describing the entire flight route. The woman hijacker who survived, Souhaila Andrawes, said later, 'We thought all our demands had been met, the political situation looked good for us. The idea was for us to fly to Aden, where the operation would end, and we would give ourselves up to the Yemeni auhorities.'

Peter Jürgen Boock also knew that Abu Hani had given the hijackers detailed instructions: 'The first commando was really supposed to have finished its job in Aden; it would have left the plane to be replaced by a larger and more heavily armed commando unit which would then, so to speak, take over the hostages. There were also plans, if the situation went on much longer, for the new commando to leave the plane with the hostages and disappear, as it were, somewhere in the Yemeni desert and thus out of reach – as an additional means of putting on pressure, a new potential threat.'

The Boeing turned towards the island of Massira, belonging to the Sultanate of Oman, but the island's airport was closed for landing. The plane flew on towards Aden.

After three-quarters of an hour's flying time, Mahmud announced over the onboard microphone, 'We expect shooting when we land. There will be soldiers there. We are now going to tie you up. Please note that this is only for your own protection.'

The women passengers were told to take their tights off. One by one, the men had to step out into the gangway. One of the women hijackers threatened them with a pistol with its safety catch off. The other woman bound their wrists behind their backs with the cut-up tights, tying them so tightly that their hands swelled and discoloured. One of the men asked 'Martyr Mahmud' if their bonds could not be loosened. Mahmud agreed, and told the two women to loosen the knots. They set to work without a word.

Mahmud returned to the cockpit. The second man hijacker, the 'pretty boy', as the stewardesses called him in conversation among themselves, had fixed plastic explosives to the cabin walls in front of the first row in Economy; he pushed detonators into the explosive, and took the ignition cable through into the first-class cabin.

Captain Schumann got in touch with Aden airport. 'You can't land. The airport is closed,' the air traffic controller in the tower told him.

'This is an emergency. We're out of fuel. We must come down as soon as we reach the airfield. Please fetch someone in authority. We have ninety-one people on board. We shall crash if we don't get permission to land at once.' Schumann tried begging, tried commanding, shouted at the air traffic controller.

A few minutes later, another voice answered from the tower. 'We're sorry, the runway's blocked. There is no way you can land here.'

The background to the Yemeni refusal to let the plane land became clear only later. The country's socialist regime had good connections at the time with Eastern Europe, particularly the GDR. The Stasi was active here; the GDR advised South Yemen on security. And the GDR was also intervening in the hijacking of the Landshut – as Minister of State Wischnewski knew: 'We were aware that the GDR was in a very strong position there, so from the air, while we were circling, I sent an urgent request to Bonn to make contact with the GDR as well as the Soviet Union.'

The East German ambassador, Scharfenberg, received a telegram from East Berlin that day, telling him to use his influence with the Yemeni government to work for a peaceful outcome to the hijacking. At this the South Yemeni regime declined to give the terrorists the support they expected. Not even the PFLP representative in South Yemen, Zaki Helou, was allowed access to the hijack commando.

Later, Peter Jürgen Boock learned the details: 'He was prevented from even getting close to the airport. That told him there wasn't going to be any contact. He was extremely indignant, even afterwards, because it meant going right against all our agreements with the Yemeni government, and he hadn't even been given any kind of explanation why. So they'd eliminated him from the whole thing very abruptly, and there he was, four or five hundred metres from the airport, unable to do anything. The way he worked it out later was that the secret services of the Eastern bloc had probably moved into the driving seat long ago, and they'd put enough pressure on the Yemeni government to make it break the agreements.'

The Boeing had fuel for just twenty-five minutes' flying time left in its tanks. Aden was sixty kilometres off, and the next airfield, at Djibouti, impossibly far away.

Below them, the pilots saw two intersecting runways in the desert sand, marked on the map as the Sheikh Othman Airfield. They could see no buildings on the ground, nor could they find out what the runway was like. They decided to fly on to Aden in spite of being refused permission to land.

The stewardesses told the passengers how to act during an emergency landing. Watches, brooches, false teeth and all sharp objects were collected in a plastic bag. The co-pilot, Vietor, had taken over the controls. He circled the airport. Below him, he could see that all the tarmac roads and runways were blocked with tanks. The tower was no longer responding.

Jürgen Vietor managed to bring the aircraft down on a sand track beside the runway itself, which was dotted with tanks. Several hundred soldiers ran towards the plane and surrounded it, guns raised. It was dark now. Schumann asked for the megaphone and tried to explain the situation to the Yemenis.

Mahmud took the megaphone from him and addressed the soldiers in Arabic. Then he turned to the pilots. 'It's no good, we'll have to take off again.'

'That's sheer madness. We can't possibly take off again after an emergency landing like that.'

Mahmud allowed Captain Schumann to get out of the plane and check the bodywork. Vietor, the co-pilot, saw Schumann going down the steps and shining a flashlight on the left-hand side of the undercarriage of the aircraft. The wheels were buried in the sand up to their axles. Schumann called out, 'The left-hand side's all right. I'm going round to look at the right-hand side now.' Then Vietor lost sight of the chief pilot. He felt as if an hour passed by, and still the pilot did not reappear.

Mahmud became restless, and then shouted something in Arabic to the soldiers, who were still standing around the plane, pointing their guns. He turned and told the hostages, in English, 'If the pilot doesn't come back, I'm blowing the plane up. If he does come back, I'll execute him.'

Gaby Dillmann, the stewardess, got the impression that the captain of the aircraft had been taken and held by the soldiers surrounding the plane when he made this outside check: 'I can't explain it to myself any other way. Anything else just wouldn't have been like him.'

Then Schumann emerged from the darkness. Mahmud gave orders for the steps at the back to be let down. Schumann came down the aisle in First Class towards Mahmud.

'Down – on your knees!' shouted the hijackers' leader.

Schumann obeyed. He had clasped his hands above his head. Mahmud put one foot on an empty seat. 'This is a revolutionary tribunal. You put everyone here in danger of being blown up. You've betrayed me once already. I'm not forgiving you this second time. Are you guilty or not guilty?'

In a calm, quiet voice, Jürgen Schumann replied, 'Captain, there were problems over coming back to the plane.'

Mahmud struck him in the face with his left hand. 'Guilty or not guilty?' he shouted.

'Sir, let me explain, I couldn't come back to the plane.'

Mahmud struck the pilot so hard that his head jerked to one side. Then he pulled the trigger of his gun. Schumann fell to the floor. He was dead.

Gaby Dillmann was on the point of collapse: 'It was so terrible, he really had been shot at the front of the cabin, right in front there, close to the children. That was really awful. Although I don't think he knew it was an execution. You could see he was very frightened when he came in. I hid at that point, I put a blanket over my head and I thought: I'm not here, I'm not really here at all. And then, after he'd been shot, I started crying because no one made a sound. We'd been told that if anyone cried or screamed or did anything else that person would be shot at once. And now Mahmud had his corpse. It was terrible that it was *him*, but it wasn't ourselves. He had his corpse, he'd been wanting one all this time. Something to show: look, we mean serious business.'

At 16.21 hours, German time, the plane carrying Minister of State Wischnewski took off from Dubai.

South Yemeni air space was closed. The Boeing 707 landed at Jeddah in Saudi Arabia.

34
Magic Fire
(Monday, 17 October 1977)

Soon after daybreak, the hijacked Boeing was refuelled at Aden. It took off again at 2.02 a.m. German time. The hijackers had wiped away Jürgen Schumann's blood with moistened cloths. They had scraped bits of his brain off the gangway carpet into a dustpan, which they threw out of the opened cockpit window before take-off.

Jürgen Vietor was at the controls. The plane was on course for Mogadishu.

Two and a half hours later, at 4.34 hours German time, the co-pilot brought the plane down on the airport runway of the Somali capital. According to Vietor: 'They didn't know a thing about it. We arrived out of the blue, flew over the airport, swung the plane around to the left and landed.'

An hour later, the Somali government got in touch with the German embassy. The hijackers were issuing an ultimatum: the prisoners in Germany were to be released by 15.00 hours.

Gaby Dillmann remembers: 'When we landed in Mogadishu, Jürgen Vietor said, "We're not flying anywhere else. This is it. The plane's in no state to go any further." In fact we were glad. Because I had this feeling that we were always flying away from something. Which was right, because now we were flying away from the GSG 9 unit. But I wasn't to know that. All the same, I still felt we were flying away from the final outcome.'

By now a second GSG 9 unit had set out from Bonn. In Colonel Wegener's words: 'I was delighted to hear that the plane had landed in Somalia. We were just about sure they couldn't go on anywhere else from there.'

The plane with the GSG 9 men on board had set off for what in the first place was an unknown destination. When they reached Crete, orders came over the onboard radio to fly on to Mogadishu: 'Immediately, immediately . . . every minute counts, you must get moving . . . just get to Mogadishu as fast as you can.'

GSG 9 officer Hümmer, one of those on board, says: 'We were clearly told on the authority of the Federal Government that the operation to free the hostages would be up to us. It was great to know we had our chance now.'

The hijackers had stowed the body of the murdered pilot, Jürgen Schumann, upright in the cloakroom locker at the back of the Landshut. Co-pilot Vietor says: 'It was already smelling a bit, and they weren't very happy about that themselves, so they opened the right-hand door at the back, there's an emergency chute outside every door. They pushed Captain Schumann out down the chute.'

An ambulance came to pick the corpse up.

The main RAF group in Baghdad had followed the news of the hijacking and the subsequent aimless flight of the Landshut over the Deutsche Welle channel. After weeks of infuriating and unsuccessful waiting for a change of mind on the part of the Federal Government, they suddenly felt optimistic about the success of the operation. 'We all thought it had worked,' Peter Jürgen Boock remembered later. 'We thought Helmut Schmidt couldn't come up with any kind of police or military solution to the crisis. There was Schleyer on the one hand, the holiday-makers on the other. The exchange was going ahead.'

But their euphoria died down when the Lufthansa plane had to take off from Aden again. They had all been sure that the hijacking would end there. 'When news came that the plane couldn't stay, when it had to take off under threat of military action, it suddenly became clear that things were going terribly wrong.'

Minister of State Wischnewski, who had not been given permission to land by the authorities in Aden, arrived in Mogadishu at 12.00 noon. The Somali authorities, like their counterparts in Dubai, were not happy about working with representatives of the Federal German government. After all, the hijackers were brothers of the great Arab nation. At the time, the PLO had an office manned by sixty staff members in Mogadishu.

According to Wischnewski: 'Our reception in Mogadishu was decidedly cool – the word reserved isn't really strong enough. No one but me was allowed to leave the plane. They all had to stay inside. But I was taken to the president at once.'

While Wischnewski waited for his audience with the president, he spoke over the phone to Chancellor Helmut Schmidt, who said: 'I've been talking to the Somali dictator, the man's name is Siad Barre. Siad Barre will go along with us. We didn't promise him anything, we just held out the prospect of something later without actually promising it, we suggested he could get a large amount of aid for his country.'

After that Wischnewski himself got his interview with the Somali dictator:

'I put everything I had into convincing him. I was bold enough to say, "Mr President, there are two things we have to do between us. First, we have ninety human lives to save, and second, we have to preserve the full extent of your sovereign power. As far as the latter goes, I am able to assure you that if we take prisoners, then they are your prisoners." All he said to that was, "Oh, do you want to take prisoners too?"'

The hijackers had noticed the arrival of the second aircraft. 'Who are those people?' Mahmud asked the tower.

'A representative of the Federal German Government has just landed.'

In a hoarse voice, but quite calmly, Mahmud said, 'Tell the German representative there's nothing for us to negotiate about. I don't want to speak to him unless he can tell me the prisoners in Germany have been released.'

The tower asked if lunch was to be taken on board.

'We won't be needing any more to eat. Our deadline runs out in three hours' time, and after that everyone in the plane will be either dead or free.'

At about 8.10 p.m. the previous evening, the 'Smaller Crisis Staff' had decided to send Assistant Minister Dr Hegelau to Stammheim, representing Under-Minister Schüler, for the conversation Baader and Ensslin were demanding. Alfred Klaus of the BKA was to accompany him.

It was wet and windy next day, so the two officials could not go by helicopter as planned, but had to drive. Hegelau had never seen Baader before, and knew little about the details of the Stammheim trial and the Red Army Faction's operations. The BKA man briefed him on the essentials during their drive, and described various milestones in Baader's life. 'He's rather nervous and confused at the moment,' he finished.

Shortly before 2.00 p.m., the two negotiators arrived at Stammheim. They were taken to Governor Nusser at once, and then Inspector Bubeck came to collect them. They took the lift up to the seventh floor. Bubeck had the door of Cell 719 unlocked, and told Baader he had visitors. 'I'll be with you in five minutes,' said Baader. 'I've got something to do first.' He had himself locked in again. While Inspector Bubeck was waiting to see the light over the cell door come on, as a signal that Baader was about to emerge, the light over the door of the cell opposite came on instead. A prison officer unlocked the cell. Gudrun Ensslin came out into the corridor and turned to Bubeck. 'I want to talk to the two prison chaplains.'

Bubeck promised to pass the request on. Gudrun Ensslin was locked in again.

Meanwhile, the light above Baader's door came on too. He was let out of his cell and taken across the corridor to the visiting room. Alfred Klaus greeted him briefly. 'I passed on your request for a conversation. Assistant Secretary Dr Hegelau, representing Under-Minister Schüler, has come to see you.'

'I really wanted to speak to Schuler himself,' said Baader, speaking rapidly and not very clearly. Hesitantly, he sat down. 'It's really too late for this conversation,' he said. 'The chance of exerting any influence has been lost now.' He mentioned the hijacking of the Lufthansa plane. 'Up till now the RAF has rejected this form of terrorism.' They, the prisoners, he said, had never condoned operations involving innocent civilians, and did not condone them now. The Government must realize that the second or third generation would step up the brutality.

'There are two lines to take in the fight against the state,' said Baader, 'and through its attitude, the Federal Government has helped this extreme form to break through.'

'Where does terrorism begin, in your opinion?' asked Dr Hegelau.

'With this kind of terrorist violence against civilians,' said Baader. 'This is not the doing of the RAF, which has been aiming at a form of political organization for some time. You can read about that in our writings. As opposed to what's going on now, the RAF has pursued a policy of moderation.'

'Do you seriously mean that – after there have been eight deaths in the last few months?' asked Klaus.

'The brutality was provoked by the state,' said Baader, and he referred to the rocket launcher that had been trained against the Federal Prosecution building. 'That device was installed by members of our second, third or fourth generation. We don't personally know Schleyer's kidnappers and other people the police are after. If the BKA's saying these operations were masterminded from prison, that can't be so except in the ideological area. The armed combat has internationalized itself. It could be the Japanese or the Palestinians who are going to decide the course of events now. I don't know enough about it any more. I can only repeat that if the prisoners here are released, we won't come back to West Germany. We would indeed continue our struggle against this state, campaigning against it in the context of all international liberation movements. But it's absurd to suppose we'd go on fighting as international terrorists. International terrorism isn't the RAF's scene.'

Dr Hegelau asked, 'What sort of influence do you still have – say, as a symbolic figure?'

'I can see two possible ways ahead,' said Baader. 'One's further brutalization, and the other's a regulated struggle as opposed to total war. I know a few things that would make the Government's hair stand on end. But I'm sure there is still some chance of influencing the groups, here in the Federal Republic anyway.

'One could try to prevent a development towards terrorism here, although there are currents of other kinds too. In the final analysis, that's why I wanted this conversation. Terrorism is not the policy of the RAF. And anyway the release of the ten prisoners doesn't mean any escalation of armed violence. The public's being fed lies about that.'

'Why do you say the release of ten and not eleven prisoners?' asked the BKA man.

'Günter Sonnenberg's brain injury has left him a vegetable, so I'm not counting him any more.' Sonnenberg had been shot in the head when he was arrested.

Baader went on to talk about the group's original motivation. The main impetus, he said, had been given by the Vietnam War. Looking back, he still saw it as a cogent reason for the RAF's operations. However, he admitted that the group had made mistakes. He brought up another question: who would benefit by the escalation of terror and brutality, which in his eyes was the state's fault? Perhaps there were a good many people who actually wanted it. In any case, he said, it would bring a large illegal movement into existence.

Finally, Baader said, 'At the moment there is minimal community of interest between the state and the prisoners. Gudrun's already said all there is to say about that. Even the Federal Government will find prisoners released a lesser evil than dead prisoners.' The prisoners would have to die one way or another, he said.

The conversation lasted for over an hour. After Andreas Baader had been taken back to his cell, the assistant minister telephoned the Chancellery.

In the afternoon, the Protestant chaplain, who was visiting a convent in Leonberg, received a phone call from his Catholic colleague Dr Rieder. Gudrun Ensslin wanted to talk to them both.

About 3.40 p.m., a prison officer escorted the chaplains into the seventh-floor visiting room. Shortly afterwards, Gudrun Ensslin was brought in.

She sat down at a table.

'There's something I'd like to ask you to do,' said the prisoner. 'I'm assuming you'll be able to help me. Inside a file labelled "Lawyer" in my cell, there are three loose sheets of paper, with writing on them. They should be sent to the head of the Chancellery if they do away with me, or if I'm executed. Please would you see that they get there? I'm afraid that otherwise the Federal Prosecutor will suppress or destroy them.'

'But Frau Ensslin,' said the Protestant chaplain, 'do you really think someone wants to do away with you or execute you?'

'Not anyone here in this prison. The operation will come from outside. If we don't get out of here, terrible things are going to happen.'

'All hell will break loose do you mean?' asked Dr Rieder.

'You could put it that way, yes.' Gudrun Ensslin was perfectly calm, and spoke without agitation or nervousness.

'Who do you really want to liberate?' the Catholic chaplain asked her.

Thereupon, Gudrun Ensslin started talking about the inhuman jungle war in Vietnam, lasting almost thirty years, which had brought unspeakable suffering to millions of people, and whose effects were still incalculable.

In other countries, she said, there had been freedom movements and revolutions. The only means of bringing about social change which would lead to the liberation of the oppressed had been the use of violence. Such steps had been taken only half-heartedly in Germany, if at all. The existing military and economic links between the Federal Republic and the USA meant the masses were much oppressed and kept in a state of dependency, and this would inevitably lead to another and terrible atomic war. 'That must be prevented by any means, including force if necessary; that state of things must be changed.'

The conversation lasted an hour. At the end of it, Gudrun Ensslin again asked the chaplains to make sure, whatever happened, that the three sheets of paper reached their destination.

'Who would you want informed?' asked the Protestant chaplain.

'My lawyer and my parents.'

Gudrun Ensslin shook hands with the chaplains on parting. 'I hope we can continue this conversation another time,' said Pastor Kurmann.

'Theologians hope.' Gudrun Ensslin turned, smiling, and went back to her cell.

Inspector Bubeck accompanied the two chaplains down in the lift and then took them to see Governor Nusser. The chaplains told him about their conversation and the three pieces of paper which were to be sent on to the Chancellery in the event of an 'execution', to use Gudrun Ensslin's word.

'What did you say when she used that expression, "execution"?' asked Bubeck, joining the conversation. 'Didn't you say that sort of thing was absurd, something like that doesn't happen here?'

'Yes, I did,' said Dr Rieder.

The prison governor asked if the word 'execution' could also be taken as a threat of suicide.

Both chaplains said, 'No.'

The three sheets of paper mentioned by Gudrun Ensslin never came to light.

Minister of State Wischnewski was negotiating feverishly with the Somali government to get permission for the GSG 9 unit to go in. Rüdiger von Lutzau, Gaby Dillmann's boyfriend, was in the cockpit of Wischnewski's Boeing 707. It was his job to listen in to radio communication between the Landshut and the tower and write everything down.

General Abdullahi, the Somali chief of police, spoke to 'Martyr Mahmud'. 'The German government won't accept your conditions . . . the Somali government urges you to release the passengers and crew. We promise you safe conduct . . .'

The hijacker replied, 'I understand your news, general: the German government rejects our demands. That doesn't alter anything. We shall blow the plane up as soon as the deadline runs out, that is, in exactly one hour thirty-four minutes . . . if you happen to be in the tower then, you'll see the plane explode into a thousand pieces . . .'

Mahmud told the passengers that their government was going to let them die. Gaby Dillmann begged him to let her speak to the German envoy. Mahmud gave her the onboard microphone.

Gaby Dillmann spoke English. Only many years later did the tape recording with her words come to light.

'I want to say we're going to die because the German government has failed us. And we *are* going to die. They've tied us up already. Theirs is what we'd call a suicide mission in Germany. They don't care about their own lives or the lives of any other human beings. The German government doesn't care about our lives at all either. We're going to die now. I've tried to bear it as well as possible, but the fear is just too much. All the same, we'd like you to know that the German government did nothing to save our lives. They could have done everything, everything. We just can't understand it.'

Rüdiger von Lutzau had difficulty in making out her words, they were so distorted as they came over the radio. He wasn't even sure who was speaking. 'Right, so this is probably the last message I'll ever be able to send. My name is Gaby Dillmann, and I just want to tell my parents and my boyfriend – his name is Rüdiger von Lutzau – I want to say I'll be as brave as possible, and I hope it won't hurt too much. Please tell my boyfriend that I love him very much, and tell my family that I love them, I love them too.'

Only now did Rüdiger von Lutzau realize that he was writing down his fiancée's words. Gaby Dillmann hesitated, and then pressed the speaker key again. 'Say thank you to everyone for me, and if there's any chance left in these last one and a half hours, please, I beg you, try everything. Think of all those children, think of all the women, think of us. I can't understand it, I really can't. Can you live the rest of your life with this on your conscience? I don't know. We're all going to try to be as brave as we can, but it isn't easy. I pray to God, please, if there's any chance at all, any kind of way, help us. If there's any chance at all please help us.'

Rüdiger von Lutzau wrote every word down.

The four Palestinians had fixed explosive to the cabin walls again. As had happened before, they told the men on board to come out into the gangway one by one, and tied their hands behind their backs. Then they bound the women's hands with cut-up tights too. They collected all bottles of alcoholic drinks, knocked the necks off against the backs of the seats, and poured the contents over the carpets and the passengers.

Passenger Diana Müll: 'The idea of burning so miserably, maybe being blown sky-high at some point, burning alive was so dreadful for me that I told my friend: I'm going to wait for the right moment, and when it looks as if the end's coming, then I'm going to stand up and spit in his face. And she said to me, you can't do that, he'll shoot you. Yes, exactly. To me that was, well, the better way.'

The Somali minister of information spoke from the tower. 'Our government is currently trying to speak to the German government. We've already told you their position, but we are still trying. Now, in this situation, my government would like to ask you to extend the deadline by at least twenty-four hours . . .'

'We don't want to shed blood,' replied Martyr Mahmud from the plane, 'but as the imperialist fascist West German regime rejects our demands we have no choice. They don't care about their own people, so we shall have to blow up the aircraft with all on board . . . there's no alternative to blowing up the aircraft in exactly twenty-three minutes from now.'

The Somali minister of information asked if the deadline could not at least be extended by half an hour, to clear the area around the Landshut. Mahmud agreed to discuss this proposition with his comrades.

A few minutes later, the tower asked for the hijackers' leader again. The German chargé d'affaires in Mogadishu had some important news.

'I am listening, representative of fascist imperialist West Germany. Go on, read out your message,' said Mahmud.

'As you know, we have a high-level delegation from my government here. This delegation is led by a minister who has been discussing the present situation in detail with President Siad Barre. As a result of this conversation, it has become necessary to make a telephone call to the chancellor of the Federal Republic of Germany.' For technical reasons, however, said the chargé d'affaires, they had not yet been able to put the call through. After it, he would have some new and very important information to give.

'I see,' said Mahmud. 'But you've had almost ninety-six hours for all that. You capitulate in the last ten minutes – how do you think I'm going to take that, from the representative of the fascist imperialist West German regime?'

Michael Libal, the German chargé d'affaires, brought the conversation to an end. 'That's all I can tell you at the moment. Please wait.'

The hijackers extended their deadline by half an hour so that the Somalis could clear the area around the plane. The Somalis took their time about it. Twelve minutes after the expiry of the new deadline, Mahmud asked the tower, 'Have you closed all the runways?'

'No, not yet. We'll clear them. Please wait, sir.'

'Try and be as quick about it as possible.'

'Yes, sir, thank you very much for your co-operation.'

Wischnewski had to play for time: 'Then we told them that the Federal Government was giving in, but we'd need several hours now, the people had to be brought to Frankfurt first, but we'd keep them constantly informed of the plane's position, to make sure of the time.'

Soon afterwards the German chargé d'affaires got in touch again. 'Can you hear me, Herr Martyr Mahmud?' Wolfgang Salewski, the psychologist sent with Wischnewski by the BKA was standing beside him. Everything said to the hijackers had been discussed with the psychologist beforehand.

'I can hear you very clearly, I have very good hearing, representative of the West German fascist regime,' replied the hijacker.

'We've just had news that the prisoners in the German jails, the prisoners you wanted released, are to be flown here to Mogadishu.' However, he said, because of the great distance involved, the plane could not arrive until morning.

'You dare ask me to extend the deadline until morning – is that it, representative of the West German regime?'

'In principle, yes,' said Libal.

'What's the distance between the Federal Republic and Mogadishu, representative of the West German regime?'

'Several thousand miles.'

Mahmud wanted to know exactly, and the German chargé d'affaires promised to check.

'Okay, four minutes to go before the deadline runs out,' said Mahmud. 'If you're trying to trick us, or play games with us . . . I'd rather play with explosive. But if you're being serious, and you're concerned about the people on board this plane, then we're ready to negotiate.'

'As I've told you, we are now prepared to fly the prisoners here to Mogadishu.'

'Okay, you may be showing concern, but your government isn't. And you're showing concern now because you think we've sworn to do something and you think we'll do it, too. And if your government, the government of the West German regime, thinks this is going to be another Entebbe, you're dreaming.'

The tower produced the information that it was 3,200 nautical miles from Frankfurt to Mogadishu: seven hours flying time. The hijacker said he was prepared to extend the deadline to 3.30 a.m. Somali time, 1.30 a.m. German time.

Mahmud left the cockpit and went into the cabin. He said, hesitantly, 'We're going to untie you now. Something's happened which might save us all. But it's not time to rejoice yet.' The women hijackers set about untying the passengers. The hostages uttered exclamations of joy, and of pain as well: the tightly knotted tights had bitten deep into their flesh, cutting off the circulation at their wrists. Mahmud said, in his slightly imperfect English, 'In the last ten minutes, they promised me everything that I am asking for now for five days.'

The Lufthansa aircraft carrying the first GSG 9 commando squad had returned to Cologne Bonn airport from Turkey the previous day. On

Sunday, orders had gone out from Bonn for two more units of the group to be ready for action. On Monday, the plane took off for its initially unknown destination. It refuelled at Crete, and was now circling above Djibouti. After Chancellor Helmut Schmidt had received permission in his phone call to President Barre of Somalia for the commando squad to land, the operations centre got into radio contact with the GSG 9 plane:

'Are you ready to copy? . . . Message: Federal Chancellor to Minister of State Wischnewski. Federal Chancellor to Minister of State Wischnewski. First: Minister of State Wischnewski has full powers to negotiate with Yemeni government. Full powers of negotiation also extend to discussions of development aid to South Yemen.'

'Message received and understood, message received and understood.'

When the plane with the GSG 9 men reached Somali air space, operational HQ got in touch again.

'Okay, so no circling around waiting anywhere this time. Fly a bit carefully, ten minutes either way don't matter, just make sure you come in quietly under cover of darkness.'

'Okay, message understood.'

'Landing as discreet as possible. Landing as discreet as possible.'

An Israeli radio ham recorded this radio communication. Chancellor Schmidt learned about it from a newspaper: 'The worst of it was that a radio ham in Israel was technically capable of listening in. And that a West German newspaper printed it with a big headline on the front page. I called the editor-in-chief, the editor-in-chief of that newspaper at the time, and threatened him with dire consequences, I forget exactly what, if he didn't withdraw all copies of that edition at once. Which he did.'

After dark, at 19.30 hours local time, 17.30 hours German time, the Boeing 707 landed at the airport of the Somali capital, 2,000 metres away from the Landshut, coming down on a remote part of the runway. All its lights were off. No one on board the hijacked plane had noticed the 707's arrival.

It took the GSG 9 men two hours to unload their equipment and weapons.

Meanwhile Ulrich Wegener took stock of the terrain around the Landshut. Keeping in the cover of some sand dunes, he crawled on his stomach to within a few metres of his target: 'Getting close to the plane wasn't any problem. All the shades were down, the blackout whatsits, the plane was okay, the air-conditioning was running inside. And everything was quiet. There were some very good hills around that we could use for our reconnaissance teams and our marksmen. I'd more or less sketched out my plan in the course of the afternoon.'

The German chargé d'affaires and the psychologist Wolfgang Salewski were talking almost non-stop to the hijackers on board the Landshut, partly to distract them, partly to keep Mahmud inside the cockpit.

A group of GSG 9 men crept up to the plane from behind. They had ladders, guns, and highly sensitive sound detectors with them. Part of the group stationed itself underneath the plane and fixed the sound detectors in place, to keep track of every movement inside the aircraft.

The hijackers had given the senior stewardess some sheets of notepaper on which she was to write down the names of the passengers, divided into eleven groups of seven people each. Each group was to be exchanged for one of the released prisoners.

Lieutenant-Colonel Wegener took his deputy aside: 'If this thing goes wrong we might as well close GSG 9 down.' He went over to Wischnewski and said, 'Tell the chancellor that this is it.' The minister of state phoned the crisis staff in Bonn and got permission for the unit to go in.

He and the GSG 9 leader checked the time together. No one else knew about it. Then Wischnewski got the Somalis to alert the fire service and have ambulances and hospital beds ready. The airport was converted into an emergency hospital. 'It wasn't easy in a developing country,' said Wischnewski later.

Ulrich Wegener climbed back into the GSG 9 aircraft and had himself connected to Chancellor Helmut Schmidt over the dedicated line on board. 'Reporting that we're ready to go in.'

'Right,' said the Chancellor, 'and these are your orders to start the operation.'

Wegener said, 'Chancellor, there's one thing I have to point out to you, sir. Of course we're going to do our best, and the operation will be successful, no doubt about that. But there's one thing I can't guarantee, and that's that we'll get all the hostages out of the plane uninjured.'

Wegener never forgot Chancellor Schmidt's reply: 'Herr Wegener, no one can ever guarantee a thing like that. I know you will do your very best and so will your team. Give your men my regards.'

Later, Schmidt said: 'If we hadn't been able to prevent the terrorists from blowing up the plane in Mogadishu, I'd have resigned next day.'

On board the Landshut there was a more relaxed atmosphere, in anticipation of the promised exchange of prisoners. 'The leader still did a bit of shouting now and then,' Gaby Dillmann remembered. 'We were to hurry up with . . . oh, I don't know what. Then he gave back our passports and purses, valuables and handbags. Suddenly there was a weird kind of normality, just with a little crack in it, almost normal.'

Operational HQ in Germany came through to the GSG 9 unit over the radio: 'Waiting for your report, waiting for your report.'

'Okay.'

'Then,' said Wegener later, 'we began closing in on the plane, divided into assault teams, reserves and back-up. I made my way over there behind the first team, approaching the plane, there was some moonlight that night. It wasn't pitch dark, but quite dark. We could only move slowly. It was terribly hot, even at night, and terribly humid too, our clothes were sticking to us, and we had to keep something on because we were lugging all kinds of equipment with us.

The reserve troops were in position under the plane, the paramedics were in place too, and so were the explosives specialists.'

The German chargé d'affaires spoke from the tower again. 'Our information is that the Lufthansa plane took off at 19.20 hours GMT in Germany. By our calculations, it should land in Mogadishu at 4.08 hours GMT. We're now expecting concrete suggestions about the exchange of the hostages from you. Over.'

'That's after the deadline runs out,' said Mahmud. The German chargé d'affaires explained that there had been some difficulty in bringing the prisoners together.

Mahmud got the Somali chief of police to confirm what the German had said. Then he gave instructions for the conduct of the exchange.

'First, we don't want any reporters or television cameras present at the exchange. Second, what about the comrades coming from Germany? Third, we want the Somali representative to search the plane which is now standing on the runway at Mogadishu and make sure there's no one on board.'

'Understood.'

'No one's to approach the Lufthansa aircraft commanded by the Halimeh unit without previous permission.'

'Understood.'

'When the Germans land to bring us our comrades you must inform us first.'

'Yes, understood.'

'And then they are to approach the plane one by one and be searched by the Somali representative,' said Mahmud.

'Understood.'

'And further, the plane bringing our comrades must leave the airfield as soon as our demands are met, must get out of here . . . The commander of the Martyr Halimeh unit will ask one of the comrades to come to our plane for identification, so we can be sure about the other comrades.'

'Understood.'

'After this check-up, the comrade will go back to the Somali lines on the airport.'

'Understood.'

'We'll make further arrangements with the comrades coming from Turkey.'

'Would you repeat that?' Mahmud was asked by the tower. Mahmud repeated what he had said.

'Understood,' came the reply from the tower, 'if they come . . .'

At this moment Lieutenant-Colonel Wegener gave his men the order to storm the plane. The cue was: 'Springtime Magic Fire.' It was 2.03 hours Somali time, 0.03 hours Central European time.

The stun grenades went off outside the cockpit windows, incapacitating 'Martyr Mahmud' for a moment. The GSG 9 men themselves had briefly covered their eyes. Within seconds Wegener had the door at the front of the plane open. Two more troops of men stormed into the plane through the doors of the emergency exits. Another group, their faces blackened, made their way into the cabin from the rear of the plane. They were firing blanks into the air and shouting, 'Keep your heads down! Where are the bastards?' Some of the hijacked passengers shouted, 'At the front, at the front.' Then the GSG 9 men began firing live ammunition. The woman hijacker called 'the Little One' by the passengers died at once. The other woman, 'the Fat One', tried to barricade herself inside the toilet and fired through the door. The Border Police unit riddled the door with bullets. Mahmud was shot in the cockpit. The youngest hijacker, 'the Pretty Boy', fired his pistol until he too was hit and collapsed. The plastic explosives went off without doing much damage; only the stewardess Gaby Dillmann had her leg injured when one of the hand grenades went off. She was lucky. It was one of Peter Jürgen Boock's plastic grenades which had only slight explosive force.

Gaby Dillmann: 'When the hand grenade started rolling I thought: what am I supposed to do? You don't want to hold your breath if there's an explosion, you want to let it out – or was that right? Anyway, I breathed out, and something exploded, and then I looked, OK, my spine's in working order, I thought, then I moved my foot, which had been hit: wow, my toes still seem to be all there, I said. But even if I'd lost that foot, the main thing was I was still alive.'

One of the women members of the hijacking commando squad survived, badly injured. Years later, Souhaila Andrawes said: 'I felt I was wounded, and I thought I was dying. I remember that one of the German soldiers grabbed hold of my hand. That probably told him I was still alive.'

GSG 9 officer Hümmer: 'We had to assume Andrawes might still be holding hand grenades. So she had to be hauled out backwards until her hands showed, so that we could take a look at them. In that situation she came round.'

Gaby Dillmann: 'Then they said: "Get out of here, get out of here," and we ducked, we kept our heads low and we just . . . someone grabbed hold of me and pulled me in the direction of the emergency exit. And before I could look round I was outside. And I thought: dear God, we've done it. I don't believe this! I just don't believe it! The nightmare's over.'

Operational HQ came over the radio from Germany: 'Give result, give result . . .'

Colonel Wegener: 'The entire operation was practically over after seven minutes, including evacuation of the plane. Then I went out to the passengers and talked to them, and gradually I realized there was no one dead.'

The report of the operation's success went back to the Lufthansa HQ: 'Frankfurt, Frankfurt, GSG reporting, one, just one slightly injured, one slightly injured.'

'Okay, okay, got it, GSG . . . one slightly injured . . . all okay. Thank God.'

The Border Police commandos hauled the passengers out of the aircraft over the wings. Within a few minutes, the operation, code-named 'Magic Fire', was over. Three of the hijackers were dead and another badly wounded. At 0.12 hours, German time, Minister of State Wischnewski reported to Bonn, 'The job's done.'

35
The Night of Stammheim
(17–18 October 1977)

Just before 10.00 p.m., Jan-Carl Raspe had called the guard's cubicle over the intercom installed in all the cells, asking for toilet paper. The officer on duty, Rudolf Springer, said he would bring a roll when the medication was given out. Raspe was happy with this.

At 11.00 p.m., Prison Officers Zecha and Andersson, on duty in Cell Block I, came up to the seventh floor with Kölz, the medical orderly. When Springer unlocked the barred door of the high-security section to let them in, the automatic alarm went off at the gate below. Springer had informed the guard beforehand that medication was about to be distributed.

The officer on guard downstairs, watching a monitoring screen connected with the seventh-floor alarm system, could see the group of officers, which had now been joined by Woman Prison Officer Frede, entering the corridor outside the cells. Meanwhile, the alarm signal went on flashing down at the gate, and the alarm gong sounded at regular intervals.

The guard could switch the gong off if he wanted, for instance if he was on the telephone. Once activity in the section was over, the alarm system was automatically reset, and went off if anything started moving again in the area monitored by the video camera.

Meanwhile, Springer had moved the sound-absorbent padded panels away from the cell doors. Then he opened the meal flap on Raspe's door; it stood out horizontally on the exterior of the door, like a tray. The prisoner had draped reddish-brown cloth over the inside of the door. Raspe removed the clothes hanger from which the fabric was hanging from the door and hung it on the screen standing nearby. Most of the prisoners on the seventh floor had had screens of this kind made for them in the prison workshop, so that they could not be seen the whole time through the flaps in their doors.

Rudolf Springer put the roll of toilet paper on the meal flap. Raspe came over and asked for his medication. Paracodin cough mixture and an analgesic, Dolviran tablets or Optipyrin capsules.

The medical orderly gave him what he wanted.

'Thanks very much,' said Jan-Carl Raspe. The officers had seldom known him so friendly and polite, although unlike Baader, he had always refrained from swearing at them.

The meal flap was closed again.

There was nothing draped over Baader's door. When they had opened the flap, the officers could see him sitting on the floor of his cell in front of a plate with four half eggshells on it. Baader stood up, chewing, wiped his mouth, and went over to the doorway. He asked for a Dolviran tablet or an Optipyrin capsule, went into the cell, ran a glass of water, and came back to the door again. The medical orderly put an Adalin tablet into his hand. Baader swallowed it, washing it down with the water.

The officers thought he seemed more composed than usual.

The meal flap was closed again, and the sound-absorbent panels put back into place in front of the doors. Then the five prison officers left the section. Officer Springer unlocked the barred door and went back to the cubicle outside the high-security section. From here, he could watch the corridor and the cell doors on the monitor.

The other officers went back on duty in Cell Block I, except for Woman Officer Frede, who stayed on the seventh floor. She went to the duty room, and lay down there to sleep at about half an hour after midnight.

Rudolf Springer had a radio in his glazed cubicle. A news bulletin came over on German Radio at 0.38 a.m., and shortly afterwards all the German Broadcasting Corporation stations, which shared a joint night programme, put out the same news:

'The eighty-six hostages hijacked by terrorists in a Lufthansa Boeing jet have all been safely freed . . .'

Rudolf Springer went over to the barred door of the terrorists' section and listened. All was quiet.

In his night duty report, Springer wrote:

'23.00 hours, Baader and Raspe given medication.

'Otherwise no incidents.'

Exactly what happened in the high-security section between 11.00 p.m. and 7.41 a.m., a period of just under nine hours, will probably never be known; it remains matter for conjecture, speculation and myths.

To the investigators on the spot – detectives, medical experts, public prosecutors – the clues delivered a simple and unambiguous message:

Jan-Carl Raspe had a small transistor radio in his cell. When he had heard news of the rescue of the hostages in Mogadishu on South German Radio, he passed it on to his fellow prisoners over the communications system they had set up weeks before. During the next few hours, Andreas Baader, Gudrun Ensslin, Jan-Carl Raspe and Irmgard Möller agreed on a suicide pact.

Baader had been in Cell 715 from 13 September to 4 October. While in this cell, he had removed the 7.65 calibre FEG pistol from its hiding place in the window wall, and he took it with him when he was moved back to Cell 719. He hid the gun in his record player, which had now been returned to him.

After the making of the suicide pact, he took the pistol out of the record player, and while standing – so as to simulate a fight – he fired two shots, one into his mattress, the other into the cell wall beside the window.

Then he picked up the empty cartridges ejected from the pistol and put them beside him. He reloaded the pistol, crouched down on the floor of the cell, and put the barrel of the gun to the nape of his neck. He held the handle with one hand, the barrel with the other, and pressed the trigger with his thumb. The bullet entered his head at the nape of the neck, and came out through his forehead, just above the hairline.

Jan-Carl Raspe took the 9-mm Heckler and Koch pistol out of a hiding place behind the skirting board of his cell, Cell 716, and sat on his bed. Then he put the barrel of the gun to his right temple and fired. The large-calibre bullet went through his skull, grazed a wooden shelf, and rebounded from the wall.

Gudrun Ensslin, in Cell 720, cut a piece of loudspeaker cable with her scissors, pushed a chair in front of the window, tied the insulated two-wire cable to the narrow-mesh grating, put a noose around her neck, and kicked the chair aside.

In Cell 725, Irmgard Möller took one of the prison-issue table knives, pushed up her sweater, and stabbed herself in the chest four times. The knife touched but did not injure her heart sac.

Irmgard Möller was the only survivor.

She herself had another tale to tell:

'I lay awake a long time that night, reading by the light of a candle in a can. At four in the morning I called out to Jan, "Are you still awake?" He answered me. He sounded wide awake, not depressed, in fact he sounded very lively. The candle had gone out. I put out a second candle myself at about 4.30 . . .

'I lay on my mattress dozing with my head turned to the window. We didn't often undress at night, so it wasn't surprising I had my clothes on. And anyway, we thought we were going to be released.

'I heard thudding, squealing sounds at about five o'clock.

'They were very quiet and muffled, as if something was falling over, or someone was pushing a cupboard aside. I didn't identify the thudding sounds as shots at once. They didn't worry me. I didn't associate them with an attempt on our lives. The squealing didn't come from near my door or the side of my cell, it could have come from down below, or the opposite side of the section.

'After that I went to sleep again. And suddenly I sagged and lost consciousness. It all happened very fast.

'The last thing I remember, physically, is a loud rushing noise in my head. I didn't see anyone, or notice anyone opening the cell door.

'I came round on a stretcher in the corridor, curled up in a whimpering little heap, freezing cold, covered with blood, and I heard voices – they sounded pleased and spiteful – saying, "Baader and Ensslin are dead."'

Irmgard Möller told the public prosecutor: 'I neither tried nor meant to commit suicide, and there was no suicide pact.'

That night, there were five prisoners in the corner cell of the floor below, Cell 619, right underneath Baader's. None of them heard a shot.

And yet four shots were fired in the night on the seventh floor of Stammheim prison, Stuttgart.

36
Post Mortem
(Tuesday, 18 October 1977)

The Stammheim prisoners were found at breakfast time, just before 8.00 a.m. Jan-Carl Raspe was still alive. He died in hospital. Andreas Baader and Gudrun Ensslin were dead. Irmgard Möller was taken to hospital for an operation.

At 8.18 a.m. the homicide squad arrived at Stammheim prison. Half an hour later, they were joined by officials of the regional Criminal Investigation Office. At 9.00 a.m., Detective Superintendent Müller had the cells opened to take his first look. He gave instructions for no one to enter the cells until the forensic examinations were over. Some Polaroid photographs were taken from the doorways, and that was all.

The main RAF group, who were still in Baghdad, heard news of the storming of the Landshut, the liberation of the hostages in Mogadishu and the death of the Stammheim prisoners over Deutsche Welle. They had gathered in the house placed at their disposal by the Palestinians. 'Everyone sat there as if numbed,' remembered Peter Jürgen Boock. 'Some people were crying. The others blamed the state . . . now those bastards had done it, they'd killed them . . .' But then Brigitte Mohnhaupt spoke up. Apart from Boock, she was the only one who knew how the guns had got into Stammheim and what they had been intended for. Boock had the impression that Brigitte couldn't stand all the weeping and wailing any more. She said, energetically and agressively, 'I suppose you lot can only suppose that they were victims. You didn't know them. They're not victims and they never were. You don't get made a victim, you have to make yourself a victim. They were in charge of their situation themselves right up to the last minute. So what does that mean? I'll tell you: it means they did it themselves, not that it was done to them.'

There was an icy silence. Everyone was taken aback, none of them wanted to believe what they'd just heard. Some of them started talking, but Brigitte Mohnhaupt dismissed their protests. 'We're not arguing about that now. I'm not talking to you lot about it. It's none of your business. I can only tell you that's how it was. So stop seeing them as something they weren't.'

That closed the subject. And the legend of the murders in Stammheim was born outside the group, not in its inner circle. Later, several RAF members made statements saying that they had learnt from Brigitte Mohnhaupt, on that day, that the prisoners in Stammheim had committed suicide. Monika Helbing, for instance, told the Federal prosecutors in the Supreme Court: 'It was soon after the announcement of the deaths in Stammheim and the death of Dr Schleyer that we, Elisabeth von Dyck, Friederike Krabbe and I, first met Brigitte Mohnhaupt in our big house in Baghdad. She was reproaching herself for failing to free the prisoners. During that conversation she said that the prisoners in Stammheim saw no alternative to killing themselves, not out of despair either, but to promote the policies of the RAF. Brigitte Mohnhaupt interpreted the death of the prisoners as a "suicide action" in which the prisoners planned to promote the aims of the RAF by means of their own deaths.' Because of that conversation, she said, none of their group of three still had any impression that the prisoners might have been murdered.

Susanne Albrecht too said on record what Brigitte Mohnhaupt had told her before the 'night of Stammheim'. 'From what Mohnhaupt said, I gathered that the Stammheim prisoners intended to commit suicide if the operation to put pressure on the government to free them went wrong. But it was supposed to look as if the state had murdered the prisoners.'

Schleyer was still alive. It was clear, within the group, that those who were responsible for guarding him at the scene of his captivity would have to decide his fate.

Shocked by the death of the Stammheim prisoners, horrified by Brigitte Mohnhaupt's revelations, the group gave the tensions of the last few weeks free rein. Even at the time of the hijacking of the Landshut, some had had scruples, reservations that they hadn't entertained over kidnapping the president of the Employers' Association. About half of the group assembled in Baghdad no longer agreed with the action as a whole, and an even larger proportion were against shooting Schleyer. Some thought they ought to keep him in captivity for longer. Once the jubilation of the successful freeing of the hostages in Mogadishu had died down, they reasoned, Schmidt wouldn't be able to stay in office if the group succeeded in keeping Schleyer in their hands. Others thought they ought simply to let Schleyer go now, so that he himself could sort things out with the other side. After all, he had told his guards that he wouldn't give any information about them, and indeed that if he was allowed to go free he'd do something on their behalf.

In the present situation, the hardliners in the group had more difficulty than usual. Once they had stifled all doubts by asking: 'Do you want the prisoners freed or not?' That argument wouldn't work now, so there was also resistance to the leadership of the group. Brigitte Mohnhaupt and Peter Jürgen Boock were primarily to blame for the death of the prisoners, they said. After all, those two had smuggled the guns into the prison for them. In addition, the Stammheim prisoners themselves had said clearly, at quite an early stage, that they didn't want to be freed through the hijacking of an aircraft.

The spokesmen waxed aggressive without coming to any conclusions. The hardliners didn't have many arguments to use against their critics. 'I think,' said Boock, 'they themselves weren't clear about what could be done now.' They had only the standard question available: 'Are you still RAF members or aren't you?' It was always the same: 'Bastard or not, problem or solution, cop or freedom fighter?' The deadly alternative that was as good as a ban on thinking and discussion.

'Even if we've made mistakes,' said one of the hardliners, 'this isn't the time to tinker with the substance of the group. Now it's a matter of getting through this lean period as an integrated unit, and if you talk like that now, you're questioning the group's coherence as a whole. And then you're not RAF members any more.'

Nor was it any help that, for instance, Monika Helbing, who had rented the first hiding-place for Schleyer under the alias of Lottmann-Bücklers, burst into tears. She had ventured to draw a comparison with quasi-Fascist methods: 'The chain of operations in 77 has brought us to a state that we had once claimed to fight against.' Thereupon the others attacked her, until she couldn't and didn't want to defend herself any more. 'Throw me out, then,' she sobbed. 'I don't care. I don't want any more to do with a group which acts like that.' The judgement of the hardliners went along with that. 'We always said her heart wasn't in it. She doesn't really want to be one of us.' And with that the subject was closed.

At 9.06 a.m., Federal Chancellor Helmut Schmidt was told the news of the deaths of the Stammheim prisoners. His reaction: 'I felt stunned; I was shocked, horrified. We had just had a tremendous success, and this was like a blow below the belt. We were absolutely staggered. There hadn't been a lot of jubilation after midnight, it was more of a sense of deep relief. The relaxation of tension showed itself in a number of different ways, some people shed a few tears – and seven hours later, here was this.'

It was obvious to the chancellor that the events in Stammheim jail would be bound to arouse suspicion, particularly abroad. Federal Justice Minister Vogel suggested inviting international experts to conduct the post mortems on the dead prisoners. The regional Ministry of Justice in Stuttgart agreed. However, it was over half a day before the foreign forensic experts arrived: Professor Wilhelm Holczabek from the University of Vienna, Professor Hans-Peter Hartmann of the University of Zürich, and Professor Armand André of the University of Liège.

Thus it was not possible to begin examining the bodies until the afternoon – too late to determine the exact time of death. The German forensic experts, Professors Joachim Rauschke and Hans-Joachim Mallach, stood outside the cells from 9.30 a.m. onwards, involved in sometimes agitated argument with the police and prison officers, which got them nowhere. They were not allowed near the bodies.

About 4.00 p.m. everyone had arrived: besides the forensic medical experts and two public prosecutors, the dead prisoners' former defence lawyers, Otto Schily, Dr Hans Heinz Heldmann and Karl-Heinz Weidenhammer were present. The cells were examined in turn, first Irmgard Möller's and Jan-Carl Raspe's, then Andreas Baader's and Gudrun Ensslin's.

The German forensic experts dictated, for the record: 'The body of Andreas Baader is lying almost in the middle of the room, about midway between the bed and the bookshelves . . .

'There are two holes in the scalp, showing around the central line of growth of the hair, one in the lower region of the back of the head, the other just above the hairline on the forehead . . .'

In Gudrun Ensslin's cell, the experts dictated: 'The body is hanging straight down. Both arms are hanging limp beside the hips and thighs, the head is bowed forward and tipped slightly to the left. There is a deep constriction mark on the throat . . .'

The examination of the bodies in the cells finished about 8.15 p.m.

The dead prisoners were taken to the Bergfriedhof in Tübingen for the post mortem. Once again, the foreign experts and the lawyers were present.

Professor Mallach and his assistants dissected the corpses, while his Stuttgart colleague Professor Rauschke dictated the findings on tape. The foreign experts watched, gave advice, and discussed the findings. The lawyers put very few questions. They could hardly understand what Rauschke was saying into the microphone, and followed the French translation being made for Professor André from Belgium.

The provisional findings of the post mortem were signed by Rauschke and Mallach, the professional experts responsible. Their foreign colleagues received copies later, and did not have to sign them. However, all five experts had agreed in Tübingen on the statement they would release to the press: 'The findings so far, in the cases of all three corpses, do not exclude suicide, but on the contrary are compatible with suicide.'

37
The End of a Kidnapping

It was the death of the prisoners in Stammheim that finally triggered the murder of Hanns Martin Schleyer. The closing chapter of the 'German Autumn' had begun.

The core members of the group which had kidnapped him were still in Baghdad, and that was where the decision was taken. Peter Jürgen Boock was present: 'It was obvious that he'd be shot now, and then we got in touch with Abu Hani, told him that the moment had come when we were going to do it. Oddly enough, Abu Hani was against it. But then we told him that with so many comrades dead we couldn't and wouldn't let him live.'

The death sentence was sent to Brussels by telex. In Boock's words: 'There were telex machines for public use in Brussels; they were in the Post Office. So we sent a telex saying, "We'll have to wind up our business now. The last cargo was spoilt. Do you see it the same way?" I think it was a one-word answer that came back: "Okay." So they'd obviously come to the same conclusion.'

A woodland path near the border between Belgium and France saw the last scene in the martyrdom of Hanns Martin Schleyer. Two men from the kidnap commando took him to his place of execution.

They were probably Stefan Wisniewski and Rolf Heissler. Peter Jürgen Boock, still in Baghdad at the time of the murder, learned later how it was carried out: 'Rolf Heissler told me how it was to end. It was most unusual to ask questions about that sort of thing in the group, for instance to ask: did you fire the gun or did he? I explained it to myself by supposing that he was trying to prove something else too: I was part of a commando group myself this time, he was saying, and I played my part to the end.'

Boock kept Heissler's account to himself for almost thirty years. Only in 2007 did he say what he had heard: 'They got out of the car, opened the boot, took Hanns Martin Schleyer out and laid him down in the grass, and shot him on the spot. The whole thing lasted less than a minute. Open the boot, take him out, shoot him, put him back in, close the boot, drive back.'

There are no eye-witnesses to the murder. Only the two murderers. And one hearsay witness – although that witness had it from a primary source: 'At the time Rolf Heissler told me both of them had fired their guns. He and Stefan Wisniewski, the two of them.'

The final statement was as cynical as the deed itself. Silke Maier-Witt was the messenger of death: 'I was to wait in the telephone kiosk for instructions, and then I was to pass on that final statement. This is the RAF speaking, something like that. Today we put an . . . oh, to the life of . . . I can't say exactly how the words went any more, but I . . . it was kind of horrible.'

On the afternoon of 19 October 1977, the French newspaper *Libération* received a communiqué from the kidnappers of Schleyer:

'After 43 days, we have ended Hanns Martin Schleyer's miserable and corrupt existence.

'Herr Schmidt, who from the start has been reckoning with Schleyer's death in his power calculations, can find him in a green Audi 100 with Bad Homburg number plates in the rue Charles Peguy in Mulhouse. His death is of no significance in our pain and rage at the slaughter of Mogadishu and Stammheim. The fascist drama staged by the imperialists to destroy the liberation movement does not surprise Andreas, Gudrun, Jan, Irmgard and ourselves.

'We will never forgive Schmidt and the imperialists who support him for the blood that has been shed. The fight has only just begun. Freedom through the armed anti-imperialist struggle.'

The police found Schleyer's body in the boot of the green Audi. His face was distorted, his grey hair cut short. He was wearing the clothes he had on when he was kidnapped six weeks before. Schleyer had been killed by three bullets in the head. The doctors found remains of grass in the dead man's mouth, and there were fir needles clinging to his clothing. The investigators deduced that Schleyer had been murdered out of doors. He had been forced to kneel, and had fallen forward after the fatal shots were fired.

Hanns Martin Schleyer was laid to rest in Stuttgart on 25 October 1977. Everyone who had been responsible for the anti-terrorist measures that autumn assembled in the Stiftskirche.

They all felt guilty.

Federal President Walter Scheel said: 'Hanns Martin Schleyer died for all of us. We still have a chance to banish the danger of terrorism, and by we I do not mean just us, the Germans. We bow to the dead man. We all know that we are in his debt. In the name of all German citizens I ask you, the family of Hanns Martin Schleyer, to forgive us.'

On 27 October, Andreas Baader, Gudrun Ensslin and Jan-Carl Raspe were buried in a communal grave in Stuttgart's Waldfriedhof. Citizens protested against the three terrorists' being laid to rest in a cemetery. Some said the bodies should have been thrown on the municipal tip. However, Manfred Rommel, mayor of Stuttgart, said, 'I will not accept that there should be first and second-class cemeteries. All enmity should cease after death.'

Over a thousand policemen with submachine guns surrounded the cemetery. Demonstrators, many of them masked, held up placards bearing the inscriptions, 'Gudrun, Andreas and Jan were tortured and murdered in Stammheim', and, 'The fight goes on'.

The vicar said: 'Jesus was crucified between two men whose lives had been spent achieving their aims by violence. One of the last things he said was: "Father, forgive them, for they know not what they do." And that saying encompasses both judges and defendants at all times and in all places, all of us.'

Ever since, the idea of the 'German Autumn' has remained synonymous with assault by a group of political desperadoes on the power system of the German postwar state; synonymous also with the reaction of the state, its hard-line attitude and the price it paid. There is no one in a position of responsibility at the time who has not wondered, over the following decades, if he or the state had acted correctly.

Federal Chancellor Helmut Schmidt said later: 'We found ourselves inextricably entangled in these horrifying events. It is the kind of situation in which no decision is exclusively right. It's like something in Greek tragedy, where the characters are caught up in the tragedy and cannot free themselves from guilt.'

Germany in the autumn of 1977 saw the end, for the time being, of a nightmare of violence. The names Baader, Meinhof and Ensslin entered into German postwar history. Like many of their generation, they had opposed the old form of Fascism and what they thought was its new face. They had tried to change that murderous world by violence, they had made themselves lords over life and death, and they were as guilty as many of their fathers' generation had been. Quite a number of members of the RAF realized that; others still do not recognize it to this day. To them, the founders of the RAF were martyrs.

As the mourners and demonstrators left Stuttgart's Waldfriedhof, their personal details were registered. Many of them walked past the police officers lining the path with their hands above their heads. No one had asked them to make that gesture of submission. It was a demonstration.

38
The Time of the Myths

'The urban guerrilla aims to destroy the ruling machinery of state at individual points, to put parts of it out of action, to destroy the myth of the omnipresence of the system and its invulnerability,' the Red Army Faction had written in their *The Urban Guerrilla Concept*.

Seven years after they had gone underground, the 'omnipresence of the system' was no longer a myth, but an everyday reality: investigation by scanning, by surveillance, the PIOS computer system, Nadis, Inpol; more money, more offices, better equipment for the police, for Counter-Intelligence, for the Border Police; new laws, fortified courtrooms, high-security sections in prisons . . .

In the end, they had felt the total 'omnipresence of the system' themselves, while the contact ban was in force. They had nothing but 'the system' around them then, in the form of warders, bars and concrete.

In prison, they experienced the 'pigs' system' as it had previously, while they were at liberty, existed only in their heads.

They compared themselves and their situation with the situation of concentration camp inmates.

'The difference between the dead section and isolation is the difference between Auschwitz and Buchenwald,' wrote Gudrun Ensslin.

They had divided the world in two:

> Either a pig or a human being
> either survival at any price
> or a fight to the death
> either a problem or a solution
> nothing in between.

In this concept of the world, new equations were set up. 'Murder equals suicide equals murder,' members of the Socialist Patients' Collective had sprayed on the walls of buildings in 1971. Sympathizers called out the same slogan after Ulrike Meinhof's death in 1976.

A member of the Bundestag on the Commission of Inquiry set up to investigate the circumstances of the deaths in Stammheim asked the sole survivor, Irmgard Möller, during her interrogation, 'Suppose you are on hunger strike so long that you die, do you call that kind of thing suicide?'

Möller: 'Never.'

Member: 'Why not? What would you call it?'

Möller: 'It's obviously murder.'

Member: 'Well, Frau Möller, suppose you were on hunger strike, and there was no forcible feeding, and you died. Would you describe that as suicide, or would it be murder, according to your terminology?'

Möller: 'What do you mean, according to my terminology? According to the facts.'

Member: 'That would be murder too, according to the facts?'

Möller: 'That's where the responsibility lies.'

Member: 'Frau Möller, if I may ask you a further question, suppose a prisoner who had, perhaps, spent years alone in a cell, suppose he took a pistol and shot himself? Would you call that suicide or murder?'

Möller: 'That's a very provocative and hypothetical question.'

The question of whether it had been murder or suicide became an article of faith. In RAF circles, those who thought it conceivable or probable that the Stammheim prisoners had committed suicide were considered 'counter-RAF swine', or at the very least uncritical, gullible folk.

The same applied the other way around. Anyone who publicly expressed any doubt of the official suicide version was suspected of being an RAF sympathizer.

Even before the police and the Commission of Inquiry began their investigations, most politicians were sure that it was suicide, and that the prisoners' lawyers had smuggled the guns into the high-security section.

'One can take perfidy so far as to make one's own death look like an execution,' said Federal Interior Minister Maihofer, the very day after the night of the Stammheim deaths, thus making it clear that everything which might point to the intervention of any other party really bolstered up the suicide version.

Conversely, in RAF circles – and not only there – everything pointing to suicide was taken as evidence of murder made to look like suicide.

In any complicated investigatory proceedings, there will be incidents susceptible of only partial explanation. There are limits to the reconstruction of the past. The evidence does not always speak for itself, and can be subject to various possible interpretations. Every incomprehensible act of carelessness can be seen as part of a diabolical plan if one wants to see it that way, every piece of stupidity as strategic, every coincidence can become the basis of bold speculation.

Just as the RAF often served in its founders' lifetime for the projection of hopes and wishes, fears and hatreds, so such transferences accumulated in people's assessment of the night of death at Stammheim. Abroad especially, the Germans were considered capable of anything. However carefully the investigation into the deaths had been conducted, it would not have dispelled all speculation and suspicion. Those who believe what they want to believe are not to be convinced by any evidence.

And yet if the investigation had in fact been conducted more thoroughly, and the investigators had shown less bias, much of the speculation about the night of death at Stammheim might never have arisen at all.

The Commission of Inquiry set up by the regional parliament in Stuttgart met nineteen times, with the purpose of shedding light on the darkness of that night in Stammheim prison. Some of the sessions were held in camera – providing food for conjecture. Seventy-nine witnesses and experts were questioned. 'For reasons of security, the public was sometimes excluded from the questioning of a witness,' says the report of the Commission. Witnesses could not be asked anything at all about details of the meetings of the crisis staff in Bonn; the minutes of those meetings are and will remain secret.

All that eventually came of the comprehensive account of those forty-four days in the autumn of 1977, which the authorities had said at the time of the news blackout during the Schleyer kidnapping would be published later, was a meagre 'documentation' of the 'events and the decisions taken in connection with the kidnapping of Hanns Martin Schleyer and the hijacking of the Lufthansa aircraft Landshut', released by the Federal Press Office, and less than a hundred pages long.

The Commission of Inquiry made its report before the last of the technical criminal investigations had been completed. It contradicts itself on several pages in close proximity to each other. For instance, page 88 speaks of 'a nickel-plated Smith & Wesson pistol', found in a hiding place in the wall in Cell 723, which on page 90 has become 'a chrome-plated Colt Detective Special revolver'.

No witness was asked the obvious question of whether the monitoring measures taken in Stammheim went on after the spring of 1977, whether the prisoners' cells were bugged during the Schleyer kidnapping, whether there could perhaps be a tape recording of conversations or of sounds made on the night of their deaths. The theme of bugging was taboo to the Commission of Inquiry.

The Public Prosecutor's final report, closing the 'investigatory proceedings concerning the deaths of Baader, Ensslin and Raspe', is all of sixteen pages long. It says not a word about discrepancies in the findings.

For instance, in the official order closing the investigatory proceedings, the wording runs: 'The nature of the mouth of the pistol found lying to the left of Baader's head in his cell was entirely consonant with the appearance of the entry hole of the projectile at the nape of Baader's neck. Technical investigations also showed that the fatal shot, like the other projectiles fired from the gun and found in Baader's cell, had been fired from this pistol.'

But other technical investigations had been made in that connection, investigations which the Public Prosecutor did not think worth mentioning.

Dr Roland Hoffmann, scientific adviser to the Federal Criminal Investigation Office, in his evidence determining the firing range, found clues which could be reconciled only with difficulty with the 'self-infliction' of the fatal shot.

The BKA specialist had been sent a piece of skin from the back of Baader's neck to examine. He wrote, in his report, 'The skin has suffered a canaliform injury which . . . could have been caused by a projectile from a 7.65 calibre pistol. On the upper side of the skin, the injury is surrounded by a pressure mark whose outline corresponds to the shape of the mouth of the pistol previously referred to.' Traces of powder smoke had been found in the smoke cavity. The BKA expert came to the conclusion that 'experience shows that a pressure mark and a smoke cavity are found only when a shot has been fired with the gun placed or pressed against the skin'.

Thus we have a shot fired with the gun against the skin.

Dr Hoffmann also examined the piece of skin with the aid of fluoroscopic analysis, to determine the amount of lead deposited on it. The distance from which a shot has been fired can be deduced from the impulse rate.

On the upper surface of the skin, the scientist found an impulse rate of 14,300 per second.

For purposes of comparison, he fired shots from the gun which had killed Baader at pigskin, which has qualities similar to those of human skin.

He got a result of 74,000 impulses per second with a shot fired from the gun when placed against the skin. To get the impulse rate of 14,300 which he had found on the skin of Baader's neck, he had to step back with the pistol a considerable way. He came to the conclusion that, 'comparatively speaking, the shot must have been fired from a distance of between thirty and forty centimetres'. Thus we have a shot fired with the gun against the skin – and from a distance of thirty to forty centimetres?

The Federal Criminal Investigation Office's scientific adviser explained this obvious contradiction by saying, 'As, however, this can certainly be discounted, on the grounds of the findings above, some dispersion of the traces of powder smoke must have occurred.'

Then someone had been fingering the area around Baader's gunshot wound? Or how else could 'dispersion of the traces of powder smoke' be explained? Or is a comparison of shots fired at pigskin with shots fired at human skin invalid after all? Or did the BKA expert perhaps use Baader's pistol, but different, more powerful ammunition?

No plausible explanation is given of the obvious contradiction: how can someone have fired a gun which was simultaneously against the skin and thirty centimetres away?

An invitation to speculation: given a pistol with a silencer, one could fire a shot with the gun against the skin and leave less of a powder smoke deposit. However, as the pistol found beside Baader had no silencer, it must in that case have been murder.

And one may link that thought up with the next conjecture: if none of the prisoners in the cells below Baader heard a shot that night, the explanation might have been the use of that silencer.

It ought to have been the business of any public prosecutor to pursue such considerations unreservedly, at least in a case like this.

The investigating public prosecutor received Dr Hoffmann's expert opinion on the distance from which the shot had been fired at Baader almost two months before the close of his inquiries – and never said a word about it. It was easier for the Stuttgart Commission of Inquiry: they made their report before Dr Hoffmann's evidence was available at all.

An invitation to speculation.

There are plenty of contradictions, large and small, serious and insignificant. Some, to which fanciful legends have attached themselves, can be explained easily enough.

Take the famous case of the sand on Baader's shoes. When they first examined the cell, the medical experts found traces of light-coloured sand on Baader's shoes. The source of these grains of sand could not be established beyond doubt.

A rumour was soon going around, to the effect that Baader had been flown out to Mogadishu by night as a means of tricking the hijackers of the Lufthansa jet. After the storming of the plane by the GSG 9, said this rumour, he had been shot and taken back to his cell at Stammheim. A whole theory was constructed from the association of sand with deserts. And yet a look at the map of the world would have sufficed to tell anyone that the distance between Stuttgart and Mogadishu is so great, it would have taken a supersonic plane to cover it both ways between 11.00 p.m. and 7.00 a.m.

Irmgard Möller herself, the only survivor of the night of death at Stammheim, said in a pamphlet which was in fact intended to support the murder theory, 'During the conversion of the high-security section [in June 1977], when walls had to be removed, there was cement, sand and other building materials lying about the floor. Andreas often went off to the section where we were put later to see what the builders were doing . . .'

As the prisoners usually went about their cells barefoot, or in stocking feet, the sand could have been clinging to Baader's shoes since the time of the building works.

However, legends are tenacious of life. And no public prosecutor or Commission of Inquiry thought it necessary to make any real response to the demand for 'an investigation above all suspicion'.

39
'Everything That Could Be Done Was Done'

And yet it might have been simple enough to counteract the formation of myths from the outset – albeit at a high price. There are certain indications that, as happened with the cover-up of the disastrous failure to investigate the Erftstadt-Liblar lead, another failure of the security services has been kept strictly secret to this day.

There is much circumstantial evidence to show that the conversations of the Stammheim prisoners were bugged – and if not, one has to wonder, why not? Misgivings about the constitutional legality of such a procedure can be ruled out.

When it became known in the spring of 1977 that discussions at Stammheim between the prisoners and their lawyers had been bugged, Interior Minister Schiess of Baden-Württemberg, the man responsible, gave the reasons as the Lorenz kidnapping and the attack on the German Embassy in Stockholm. He would, he said, 'be obliged to act in the same way in any comparable situation'. The bugging system, he added, had been intended to forestall any other potential kidnapping by listening in to the prisoners' conversations with each other before any question of exchanging hostages arose.

If there had ever been an occasion to make practical use of the technical devices available and put the declared purpose of their installation into practice, then surely it would have been the Schleyer kidnapping – particularly as there was never any official indication that the Stammheim devices had in fact been dismantled after that first bugging scandal.

All the laws of probability suggest that, throughout the Schleyer kidnapping and the hijacking of the Landshut, there were also recordings of conversations between the prisoners over their own communications system on the seventh floor – which could hardly have escaped the attention of the prison officers. In which case there ought to be a tape of the night of the deaths in Stammheim. That, however, was vigorously denied by the authorities and by individuals concerned on both sides.

Irmgard Möller, the only survivor of the night of death in the prison, must have known what Baader, Ensslin and Raspe – and perhaps she too – were discussing before the suicides. But she not only claims that she did not inflict the stab wounds to her chest herself, she also denies any knowledge of discussions over the communications system. In a long interview with the journalist Oliver Tolmein, which appeared in book form in 2002, Irmgard Möller said: 'I've already mentioned that from time to time we had a communications system using the wiring of the prison radio. And it's correct that the Federal Intelligence Agency tapped into our conversations over it . . . But when we were banned from contact with each other we hadn't used our system for months. What's the point of going to all that trouble, we thought, if they're going to bug us anyway?'

When the interviewer mentioned the communications technology found in the cells, Irmgard Möller replied: 'That's all very ingenious, but it makes no sense. For instance, I had no amplifier at all in my cell.'

In fact that was not the case. The technology expert Otto Bohner, a qualified engineer, investigating Irmgard Möller's cell, No. 725, on the day after the suicides, found everything that would have enabled her to use the prisoners' communications system: headphones, several cables, two loudspeaker boxes, and a Philips record player with a 22 GF 351/04 amplifier – the same type as those found in Cells 716 (Raspe) and 720 (Ensslin).

To this day, the heads of the authorities responsible both at the time and today do not see their way to answering many puzzling questions that are still outstanding. They stonewall and deny everything. Yet the question, in particular, of whether or not conversations were still being recorded in Stuttgart-Stammheim jail at the time of Schleyer's kidnapping is still of considerable importance.

There is much to suggest that the night of death at Stammheim was, so to speak, under state supervision. A leading investigator from Department 8, the state security section of the Baden-Württemberg Criminal Investigation Office, who was directly involved with Stammheim at the time and wishes to remain anonymous, said in 2007: 'This is a hot potato, a very ticklish subject. The problems and difficulties at that time, on the night in question, there were some oddities about them. I've never really read all about it anywhere. And I've always thought, some time or other someone will get to the bottom of it.'

On the second day of the Stammheim trial, 5 June 1975, Andreas Baader had complained to the presiding judge that conversations between the defendants and their lawyers had been monitored 'by planting bugs in the cells used for our lawyers' visits; we've known about those since the summer of '73.' Baader's remarks led, as we have seen, to much public head-shaking. Who could imagine the authorities of the Federal Republic of Germany intervening in the sacrosanct confidential relationship between lawyers and defendants with the aid of bugs and tape recorders? The accusation was considered more likely to be a manifestation of the paranoid delusions of the Baader–Meinhof group. In fact Baader was not so very wrong after all.

The prison officers and the criminal investigation officers who had often searched the cells knew that Raspe in particular had a large quantity of electrical components, cables and plugs. Even a microphone had been found in his cell. He was allowed to keep it. Apparently the officers had no idea what the prisoners used these things for.

Only after the deaths did criminal investigators and an engineer from the Federal Mail reconstruct what the prisoners had done with all this equipment. Yet some warning should have been issued in the jail, for three years earlier the ingenious prisoners in Stammheim had developed their own cell-to-cell communications system.

During the Schleyer kidnapping, the prisoners Raspe and Baader had been moved twice: Baader from his usual Cell 719 to Cell 715, and then back to Cell 719. While Baader was in Cell 715, Raspe was left in Cell 718. The two wiring systems, the cable for the prison's own radio network, and the wiring of the low-voltage electric shaver circuit could all be connected up. The connecting cable was found in Raspe's cell later.

When, at the end of September, Raspe was moved from Cell 718 to Cell 716, Baader was moved back at the same time to his old cell, 719. A cable which could be used to link the two parts of the communications system was also found in that cell later.

Throughout the duration of the Schleyer kidnapping, the prisoners were able to speak to each other in that way.

The claim that no one in the jail suspected anything is barely credible. Otto Bohner, the engineer who reported to the Stammheim Commission of Inquiry on the communications system, conjectured later: 'There must have been some reason why those prisoners were allowed to have so much technical stuff in their cells.'

A consignment of books ought to have given some cause for concern too. On 12 May 1977 four books were sent to Gudrun Ensslin at the jail: 1. 'Transmitter Tables'; 2. 'Practical Aerial Construction'; 3. 'Short-Wave Transmitter Construction Manual for Amateurs'; 4. 'Short-Wave and Ultra Short-Wave Aerials for Amateur Radio'. When the prison staff supervising visits prevented the books from getting through to Ensslin, she simply said she had never ordered them.

When the radios that had been in the possession of the prisoners were investigated, it was done by a department that could hardly have missed noticing any manipulations: the telecommunications group, Group F for short, of the Federal Border Police. At the time this was a department unknown to the public, used principally for radio surveillance within Germany. Group F was a secret organization much like the American surveillance service, the National Security Agency (NSA). Only in 1994 was this undercover branch of the secret service legalized; it was under no kind of parliamentary control, and had a staff 500 strong. The group was also involved in the field of anti-terrorism.

Since 1977 the authorities and ministries concerned have answered the obvious question of whether the prisoners were also bugged during the Schleyer kidnapping by claiming to know nothing about it. Yet it would have been easy to tap into the prisoners' own communications system. The technology was in place. Schreitmüller, deputy prison governor of Stammheim at the time, said later that he had heard 'almost nothing' about the bugging measures. He thought the *Land* Criminal Investigation office 'had its room in the multi-purpose hall, not with us'.

In the first bugging phase, in 1975, the agents listening in on the seventh floor had been sitting in the visiting cells running their tape recorders there. After that they obviously moved to the building where the trial was held, known as the multi-purpose hall. It contained a technology room with monitors and tape recorders. Several official departments worked there, as an application in 1975 for an extension shows: the *Land* Criminal Investigation Office, the Protection of the Constitution Agency and the BKA.

After the end of the Stammheim trial in April 1977, this control centre must have been used for acoustic surveillance of the cells. There are definite hints from people concerned who wish to remain anonymous that during the Schleyer kidnapping the cells on the seventh floor were monitored from here. To date questions on the subject put to authorities and ministries have always been answered evasively: no files, the questioners were told, could now be found.

Even high-ranking officers of the security services take refuge in silence when asked whether the prisoners in Stammheim were bugged in the autumn of 1977. An officer from the Terrorism Department of the BKA (the department known as TE for short), said in 2007, just before he retired: 'It wasn't known at TE, either before or afterwards, and there are no records on the subject.' He knew Gerhard Boeden, then head of TE, very well, and added: 'Assessing who could have been responsible must be along the lines we briefly considered: it can only have been the BND (the Federal Intelligence Agency), because from what we now know and the way we saw it then, the Office for the Protection of the Constitution wasn't in a position to do the job. Our assessment is that at the time it was done with the knowledge or on the orders of Federal Prosecutor General Rebmann, and that activities, in so far as any auxiliary functions or political activities were required, were then carried out by the *Land* Criminal Investigation Office.'

The whole operation, then, probably went on under the roof of prison security, which was within the competence of the judiciary of the *Land* of Baden-Württemberg. The officer says: 'I should think that some federal prosecutor or other was involved in giving the go-ahead, and then it duly went ahead. That's all. There wouldn't have been anyone from the BND department concerned in charge, there wouldn't have been anything on record, unless there was just one small, personal file, and then they would have gone ahead on the principle that when they'd left it would be as if nothing had ever happened.' He added: 'It was a different world back then; basically, you could do anything.'

The head of Department 8, State Security, in the Baden-Württemberg *Land* Criminal Investigation Office at the time, Hans Kollischon, said in 2007: 'The aim of the bugging was to prevent operations intended to free the prisoners in Stammheim through blackmail. That problem had solved itself when they died. So all the documents were destroyed.'

Kollischon added: 'None of it is yet in the public domain.' When asked if there was bugging during the Schleyer kidnapping, he said 'It would have been idiotic not to use such equipment to save Schleyer's life. Everything that could be done was done.'

In fact there was a department for telephone surveillance, part of the *Land* Criminal Investigation Office, the LKA, in Johannisstrasse in Stuttgart. Measures required by the examining judge of the Federal Supreme Court were carried out there. Inhouse, the department was known to the LKA as 'Special Measure'. And sure enough, this term is found in a record of activities on the day of the Stammheim suicides. For the time 10.21, Criminal Investigation officer Dieter Löw noted: 'Special Measure officers told of the incident in Stammheim, and instructed to pass on any findings in their own field connected with the Stammheim incident to Department 8 at once.'

Obviously surveillance of the Stammheim prisoners was also co-ordinated under the cover name of 'Special Measure'. How else could the Special Measure officers have known what happened on the night of the prisoners' death?

Directly after their suicide, the LKA knew exactly how the prisoners were able to communicate with each other. Things that had allegedly been overlooked for months were suddenly known in every detail, as an LKA document of 21 October 1977 proves. This was before the expert from Federal Mail had begun his work. The document says: 'Communications were unusually good.' That couldn't really have been known yet, since the amplifiers, loudspeakers, headphones and cables were not connected up when the bodies were found.

There can be hardly any doubt that the communications system on the seventh floor must have been discovered long before the death of the prisoners, and the officers monitoring them tapped into it. The inescapable question arises: were the Stammheim prisoners being bugged on the night of their death, were there or are there any recordings on tape, what was or is to be heard on them? Were the tapes running automatically, or were there officers listening in at the time? If so, what did they do as they heard the prisoners arrange to commit suicide?

These are questions which have been put to the Federal Ministry of the Interior, Federal Intelligence, the BKA, and above all the authorities of Baden-Württemberg. Their answer was always the same: there are no records extant of any monitoring measures in Stammheim. Only the Baden-Württemberg Interior Ministry, during a search of its own premises, came upon four and a half metres of secret files dealing with the RAF and Stammheim. The Interior Ministry said that 'investigating the possible release of confidential information' was 'a complex and involved process'. No final decision, it said, was yet possible, adding that examination of these records had not at the time come up with anything new.

Former State Security officer Dieter Löw, who drew up the record of the day's activities that mentions 'Special Measure', has said he was 'not prepared to give an interview'.

Permission for named officers to make statements has been given only within strict limits or not at all. In fact it was given by the Baden-Württemberg Interior Ministry with so many restrictions that an interview was hardly worthwhile. Nothing could be said about any process tagged as ranging from 'For official use only' to 'Secret'. A threat of legal penalties has accompanied any transgression of these guidelines on secrecy. Even a legal report in which the Stuttgart Ministry of Justice considers the question of which procedures could be still classified as secret or should be released has itself been kept secret. No doubt about it, there is something here which is still supposed to stay outside the public domain, for whatever reasons.

Weeks after the suicide of the prisoners, when the plaster was removed from the walls of their cells so that they could be renovated, it was done under the supervision of the telecommunications experts of Group F, as a document of 22 November 1977 addressed to the Baden-Württemberg Interior Ministry shows.

The job of the experts was defined thus: 'All high-voltage and low-voltage connections as well as the wiring to be checked by expert officers of the BGS [the Federal Border Police]. Removal of plaster in the cells and the surrounding area to be done by a private firm to be chosen by the Construction Office, with the BGS officers to be available to that firm as expert advisers for the entire duration of the work.'

Bugging devices and low-voltage circuits: it suggests that those who supervised their dismantling had also been responsible for installing them.

There are many indications that the prisoners in Stammheim were bugged during the Schleyer kidnapping, through either the communications systems made by the prisoners themselves or the bugs installed in the cells – or both. Legally, it would have been perfectly justifiable to tap into a communications system built by the prisoners at the time. The only question is what the agents listening in heard, and what conclusions they drew from it.

40
Aftermath

The Red Army Faction was now a dead army. The group in Baghdad was bereft. Their aim of freeing the prisoners from Stammheim had failed three times over. The Federal Government had not succumbed to blackmail exerted through the kidnapping of that quintessential capitalist Hanns Martin Schleyer, the president of the Employers' Association. The passengers on the Landshut had been freed in Mogadishu by the crack GSG 9 anti-terrorist unit. The prisoners on the seventh floor of Stuttgart-Stammheim jail had released themselves from the high-security wing by their suicide. No blackmail could get them out of prison now. The RAF had lost its aim in life.

Years later, several RAF members who had served their prison sentences met for group therapy to come to terms with the terrorist past that they all shared. One of the perpetrators of the Stockholm attack, Karl-Heinz Dellwo, came to this conclusion:

'Oddly enough, their death reconciled me to them later. My surge of feelings when the news came had in it some anger that they had cut and run, leaving us to clear up the mess after them. Today I tell myself: they set up political criteria for themselves, or returned to them. The lack of proportion is barbarism. For years, everything revolved around the release of the prisoners. Some of us had died for that, others ended up in jail, or there were other consequences. We had to answer for a number of victims, finally the entire morality of the RAF was overturned – and all the time their release was at the centre of everything. But they also set bounds to everything with their deaths.

'The message they sent was: don't do any more now on our account. End it or find a meaning in it for yourselves! The staging of their death was a number of things: a last blow struck against the power from which they saw themselves escaping entirely. A glimpse of the old morality – "we are the missile". But also the assumption of responsibility, perhaps even something like atonement, and the recognition that none of it was in proportion for them any more.'

The remaining members of the RAF spent weeks in their Iraqi exile, tolerated by Saddam Hussein's secret service, provided for, financed, and made use of by various Palestinian terrorist groups, in particular the Popular Front for the Liberation of Palestine, the PFLP, of Wadi Haddad.

The shock of Stammheim went deep. Peter Jürgen Boock claimed to be suffering from cancer and to need medication which was available only in Europe. In fact he was severely addicted to drugs, and couriers were repeatedly sent to the Netherlands to get him the substances he needed. Brigitte Mohnhaupt, who was still in a relationship with Boock, gave the orders, and the drug-runners obeyed. Some of them were arrested while obtaining supplies.

By the 'German Autumn' of the year 1977, twenty-eight people had lost their lives in assaults mounted by the RAF or had died in exchanges of gunfire. Seventeen 'urban guerrillas' died. Two entirely innocent people were accidentally shot by the police during their investigatory operations.

Forty-seven dead is the balance sheet of seven years of 'underground conflict' in the Federal Republic of Germany. They were seven years that changed the country.

It had rearmed, both in terms of the legal system and the powers given to the police, and in the perception of the population as a whole. The country had lost some of its liberalism. But even the finely tuned engine of the police forces proved unable to stop the war waged by the next generation of the RAF.

The bloody end of the 'German Autumn' was not the end of terrorism in Germany. The new RAF had in fact learnt from it: they now murdered without warning.

In June 1979 Rolf Clemens Wagner ignited an explosive charge by remote control in a tunnel under a road when NATO General Alexander

Haig was driving along it on his way to headquarters. The detonation came just a fraction of a second too late, so the damage was limited to slight injuries to three of the general's accompanying bodyguards in an escort vehicle. The statement claiming responsibility by the 'Commando Andreas Baader' concluded with the words: 'The battle will never end.'

Meanwhile Peter Jürgen Boock had left the group, and Christian Klar was now the male part of the double leadership, heading the RAF together with Brigitte Mohnhaupt.

At the end of 1979, eight group members wanted to withdraw from armed conflict. They had to hand in their guns and wait in a holiday house in Brittany for a safe place of exile to be found for them. It was to be in a Third World socialist country.

Inge Viett, a veteran of the armed conflict in the Federal Republic, pulled the strings. In the spring of 1978, more by chance than anything, she had met a Stasi major at East Berlin's Schönefeld airport, and fell into conversation with him. In June she and two other women were arrested while they were travelling through Czechoslovakia. The comrade from East Berlin hurried to her aid and got her released. At the end of 1980 Inge Viett had a discussion with the Stasi officer and one of his colleagues from Central Department XXII of the Ministry of State Security about the plans of several members of the RAF to withdraw from armed conflict and go to Africa.

The secret service men advised against it. A group of whites would attract notice in Africa, and anyway the situation in most of the likely countries was too insecure. The head of Central Department XXII informed the head of the Stasi, Erich Mielke, who decided: they'd better just come to us, then.

Everyone leaving the RAF was given 3,000 Deutschmarks from RAF funds, as starting capital for their integration into the Workers' and Farmers' State of East Germany. There was plenty of money available: the kidnapping of Austrian underwear magnate Walter Palmer in 1977 had brought the 2 June Movement 4.5 million marks alone in various currencies, and the 2 June Movement had contributed what remained of this 'war chest' to the RAF.

Those leaving the RAF were first accommodated in a Stasi safe house near Frankfurt an der Oder. They had to devise new life stories for themselves, with the backing of forged documents.

Susanne Albrecht now became Ingrid Jäger and began a correspondence course, studying at Karl-Marx University in Leipzig. The woman who a few years earlier had delivered up a family friend, the banker Jürgen Ponto, to his murderers now wanted to teach English.

Silke Maier-Witt was now Angelika Gerlach, and registered for training as a nursing auxiliary in Erfurt.

Werner Lotze and Christine Dümlein became Manfred and Katharina Janssen. She went to work as a secretary in the works training school of the state-owned synthetics factory at Schwarzheide, where he even made it to foreman.

The Stasi gave the former RAF members more than just a safe refuge. It also stayed in touch with the RAF leaders still active in the West, and offered them a place where they could recover from the strain of the underground conflict. Stasi officers even arranged for Christian Klar and another six RAF members to get some target practice on military training areas, also instructing them in explosives techniques and the operation of the RPG-7 anti-tank rocket launcher, a Soviet model.

On 15 September 1981, Christian Klar and three other RAF leaders decided to attack US General Kroesen's Mercedes limousine with one of these bazookas.

After 1989 and the reunification of Germany, when the RAF members who had gone underground in the GDR were arrested and Stasi documents concerning them were analysed, the Federal Supreme Court prosecutors brought proceedings against some of the former Stasi officers. However, it turned out impossible to prove that the target practice with the bazooka had taken place *before* the attack on Kroesen and not after it, as the defendants claimed. The target practice, they said, had been carried out at the request of the personal protection department of the Stasi. They had only wanted to reconstruct the course of the attack.

For purposes of the test firing, a German shepherd dog had been put on the back seat of the vehicle, standing in for the US general. When the bazooka was fired, the dog was injured and was put out of its misery with a pistol shot. The Stasi officers were acquitted of aiding and abetting attempted murder.

While the former RAF members now in East Germany were accustoming themselves to the realities of life in a socialist country, in May 1982 the RAF released a strategy paper for the first time since Ulrike Meinhof's *The Urban Guerrilla Concept* of 1972. Its title was *Guerrilla Warfare, Resistance, and an Anti-imperialist Front*. It said: 'In 1977 we made mistakes, and the offensive became our worst defeat.' The paper criticized the hijacking of the Lufthansa plane Landshut by Palestinians allied to the group, but said the RAF had emerged from the autumn of 1977 'stronger than ever'. Now it was up to them to 'open a new chapter in revolutionary strategy in the centre of imperialism'.

It soon became clear what they meant by that – downright murder.

February 1985: bomb attack on Ernst Zimmermann, boss of the MTU company (Engines and Turbines Union). Zimmermann suffered fatal injuries.

August 1985: murder of US soldier Edward Pimental in order to get his admission pass to the US base in Frankfurt. Two died in the bomb attack that ensued.

July 1986: bomb attack on Siemens manager Kurt Beckurts. Beckurts and his driver Groppler died.

October 1986: murder of Gerold von Braunmühl, head of department in the Foreign Ministry.

November 1989: bomb attack on the head of Deutsche Bank Alfred Herrhausen, who was killed. His driver was injured.

April 1991: murder of Detlev Karsten Rohwedder, the head of the Treuhand, the agency in charge of the privatisation of state-owned assets in the former GDR. His wife was injured. In all probability this was an RAF operation, although there is still no conclusive proof.

Finally, in June 1993 the Protection of the Constitution Office succeeded in infiltrating an informer into the new RAF leadership. At this time the two leaders were Birgit Hogefeld and Wolfgang Grams. The couple were to be arrested by a GSG 9 unit in Bad Kleinem. The operation failed, and GSG 9 officer Michael Newrzella was fatally injured. Wolfgang Grams shot himself. Birgit Hogefeld was arrested.

Although without Grams and Hogefeld the RAF was now hardly able to operate, it took the organization another five years to take final leave of its madness.

On 20 April 1998 an eight-page letter sent from Chemnitz arrived at the Cologne office of the Reuters news agency. Using the absence of initial capitals typical of the RAF (conspicuous in German, where all nouns are capitalized), it said that 'the urban guerrilla in the form of the raf is now history, the end of this project shows that we cannot succeed that way.' No regret is expressed for the victims of the urban guerrilla warfare, no self-criticism, no sense of guilt.

After enumerating all the members of the RAF who had died since it was founded in 1970, the document dissolving it quoted the words of Rosa Luxemburg: 'The revolution says: I was, I am, I will be.'

The horrors that had begun with the springing of Andreas Baader from jail on 14 May 1970 had come to an end twenty-eight years later.

Illustrations

Mourners and demonstrators leaving the funeral of Baader, Ensslin and Raspe, 27 October 1977 (*Keystone*).

Chancellor Helmut Schmidt with the widow of Hanns Martin Schleyer, 25 October 1977 (*Sven Simon*).

Index